Labor Law in America

THE JOHNS HOPKINS SYMPOSIA IN COMPARATIVE HISTORY

The Johns Hopkins Symposia in Comparative History are occasional volumes sponsored by the Department of History at the Johns Hopkins University and the Johns Hopkins University Press comprising original essays by leading scholars in the United States and other countries. Each volume considers, from a comparative perspective, an important topic of current historical interest. The present volume is the twentieth. Its preparation has been assisted by the James S. Schouler Lecture Fund and the University of Maryland Law School Fund. The editors also gratefully acknowledge the assistance of the School of Social Sciences, La Trobe University, Melbourne, and of the American Bar Foundation, Chicago, in expediting their work.

Labor Law in America

HISTORICAL AND CRITICAL ESSAYS

Edited by Christopher L. Tomlins and Andrew J. King

The Johns Hopkins University Press   Baltimore and London

The Johns Hopkins University Press
701 West 40th Street
Baltimore, Maryland 21211-2190
The Johns Hopkins Press Ltd., London

Library of Congress Cataloging-in-Publication Data

Labor law in America : historical and critical essays / edited by Christopher L.
  Tomlins and Andrew J. King.
     p.   cm.—(The Johns Hopkins symposia in comparative history; 20th)
   Revised versions of papers presented at a conference held Mar. 20–21, 1990,
jointly hosted by the University of Maryland School of Law and the Johns
Hopkins University History Dept.
   Includes bibliographical references (p.   ) and index.
   ISBN 0-8018-4362-6
   1. Labor laws and legislation—United States—History. 2. Labor—United
States—History. I. Tomlins, Christopher L., 1951–   . II. King, Andrew J.,
1941–   . III. Series.
   KF3319.L274   1992
   344.73'01—dc20
   [347.3041]   92-3996

Contents

Labor Law in America

Introduction: Labor, Law, and History

Christopher L. Tomlins and Andrew J. King

On March 20–21, 1990, the University of Maryland School of Law and the Johns Hopkins University Department of History jointly hosted a conference to discuss the burgeoning history of American labor law. Entitled "Labor Law in America: Historical and Critical Perspectives," the conference—held under the auspices of the James S. Schouler lecture series—brought to Baltimore an audience of some forty-five people, composed in roughly equal parts of historians, law academics, and political scientists. This audience heard eleven papers commissioned by the organizers to reflect the broad range of current scholarship in American labor law history. Papers were distributed to attendees beforehand to encourage discussion and commentary. Throughout seven sessions spread over a day and a half, exchanges were keenly informed, lively, and on occasion, passionate. Fully revised, the papers now appear as a collection of essays.

The objectives of this enterprise are quite straightforward. Labor law history—a disciplinary intersection in the study of workers, unions, state, and society in America—promises much as a field of study. At this intersection one may reasonably expect to encounter a productive reconciliation of labor history (the study of organized labor and of working-class culture) with scholarship examining labor and employment in law, legal history, political science, and eventually, industrial relations, industrial anthropology, and industrial sociology. As conference organizers and now as editors our aim has been to advertise the field's possibilities. We believe these essays suggest the potential of labor law history as an area for interdisciplinary inquiry and also mark the arrival of substantively new research and interpretation.

Only recently has interest and activity in labor law history surged. Before the 1980s, notwithstanding some highly suggestive forays on the part of John R. Commons and the voluminous empirical research of Richard B. Morris,[1] the history of American labor law was rarely thought worth pursuing in its own right. Legal and industrial relations scholars more commonly wrote such history to support positions taken in contemporary debates over labor policy or jurisprudence.[2] They invoked history as an important but quasi-evolutionary "background" to the real stuff of scholarship—engagement with the practices of the present.[3] Thus, in law and in industrial relations, as in other "applied" social sciences,[4] scholars used historical studies primarily to set the stage for what they considered their most important tasks. At its worst, this work could degenerate into the simple celebration of the way we are.[5]

Historians' professional commitment to the recovery of the past on its own terms supposedly sets them apart from the presentism of law and the social sciences. In practice, however, they tend to be no more immune to the concerns of the moment than scholars in other disciplines. In any case, historians until recently have not been much in evidence in the field.[6] We may attribute this relative lack of interest partly to labor history's original role as a subordinate element of labor economics. As such, for most of the twentieth century, labor history has taken from labor economics a functionalist view of law.[7] Even after the "new" labor history began its disengagement from labor economics/industrial relations in the early 1960s, most labor historians continued to ignore the legal order prevailing in past societies. Instead of launching a critical institutional history to replace the conventional wisdom, they largely disavowed institutional study altogether, choosing instead to follow the path of social history and the history of working-class culture. Those few labor historians who paid attention to law focused on union activity rather than the wider realm of employment itself and limited their theoretical engagement largely to acceptance of the legal-political order or to its condemnation.[8] Rarely have labor historians found the substance of labor law—its doctrines, ideologies, procedures, cultures—worth investigating. They have preferred to treat these topics, implicitly or explicitly, as epiphenomenal expressions of more fundamental economic or political forces.[9]

Scholarly engagement in labor law history has grown quite dramatically over the last eight years or so, predictably involving scholars who have come mostly from outside the mainstream of the new labor history. Influenced by the diverse methodologies of legal scholarship, political science, history, and social theory, these scholars are developing a welcome and fruitful interdisciplinary perspective. They are bringing about fundamental change in the research undertaken and conclusions reached. No longer evolutionary in perspective, research in labor law history has become far more historicist. Less policy minded, it is proving predominantly critical. Otherwise, however, no new orthodoxy has emerged. The contemporary voice of labor law history is plural, not singular; its project, at least for the present, is one of exploration, not synthesis.

The upsurge of interest in labor law history follows from a conjunction of influences, some scholarly, some societal. Inside the academy one may point to three developments: first, the renewal in the 1980s of interest in institutions on the part of historians reacting to the limitations of a purely sociocultural approach to labor history;[10] second, the critiques of determinism, functionalism, and positivism in the social sciences and the accompanying rediscovery of ideology, discourse, and hermeneutics;[11] and third, in the law schools, the crucial stimulus given legal history and the critical investigation of legal phenomena by the Critical Legal Studies movement.[12] Looming over the academy's scholarly debates one finds the contemporary plight of the organized labor movement in the United States and the movement's own admission that legal institutions and doctrines have contributed to labor's weaknesses.[13] Evidence of labor law history's fecundity appears in the programs of legal and historical professional association meetings, which have featured papers and discussion sessions devoted to labor law historical research;[14] in specialist colloquia, notably the one held at the Georgetown Law Center in 1987;[15] and in legal and historical journals, where articles, arguments, even whole issues devoted to research in the field may be found.[16] Monographic literature has begun to appear and is destined to grow rapidly.[17]

The goal of the Baltimore conference was to tap into this dynamism and forge the organizational and personal ties that would help sustain it. Consequently, the program featured both those scholars who have already made important contributions to the field and younger persons whose work over the next few years should maintain the discipline's air of excitement and diversity. In particular, we sought out papers reflecting substantive work in progress rather than mere summary or historiographical reflections.

THE STATE OF THE ART

Chronologically, the essays presented in this volume cover the whole range of American history, from the 1600s to the 1980s. In substance, they represent a broadening beyond the traditional identification of labor law scholarship with modern labor organization and collective bargaining and their institutional precursors. To be sure, readers will continue to encounter here essays discussing organizational action and its legality in different contexts. But they will also begin to encounter the social and legal relations of master and servant, employer and employee. They will find discussions of the statutory, common law, and equity underpinnings of the colonial and nineteenth-century employment contract. And they will find investigations of the politics and ideology of the key statutory expressions of the twentieth-century welfare state—unemployment insurance and fair labor standards.

As befits the field's eclecticism, readers will also discover here considerable methodological diversity, with authors employing a variety of analytic techniques from doctrinal analysis to political and social theory, from the history of ideas to feminist and class analysis. Readers will be able to assess the challenges issuing from these methodologies—VanderVelde's and Boris's analyses of the salience of gender as a catalyst in the construction and transmission of legal rules, Stanley's meticulous depiction of the dialectic of coercion and freedom at the heart of northern conceptions of free labor, Ernst's call for an understanding of Progressive Era labor law as at least as much a realm of cultural as of class conflict. They will be asked to reconsider and reevaluate conventional wisdom—by Steinfeld and Hattam in their accounts of the proper significance to be accorded the law of conspiracy in nineteenth-century conflicts between workers and their employers; by Tomlins and Orren, from very different perspectives, on the long-term continuities, or lack of them, in the law of the employment relationship; and by Forbath, Casebeer, and Rogers—again from different perspectives—on the proper historical and theoretical formulation of that hardy perennial, American exceptionalism. Throughout, however, readers will note an underlying unity in this collection of essays—a willingness to explore the interrelationship of law and power wherever in the world of labor they are found: in institutions; in ideology and discourse; in gender, class, and race relations; and in culture.

The essays by Robert Steinfeld and Victoria Hattam address the role of law and the courts in the political economy of postrevolutionary America. They revisit a relatively traditional topic in labor law history: workers' combinations and the legal doctrine of criminal conspiracy in the nineteenth century. Steinfeld offers a case study of the first known American labor conspiracy prosecution, *Commonwealth v. Pullis* (better known as the *Philadelphia Cordwainers'* case). Stressing the essential role of legal artifice in the construction of economic institutions and the contingency of the institutions so constructed, Steinfeld treats the case as an emblematic instance of conflict between masters and journeymen over the forms of market action to be privileged by law. Eighteenth-century journeymen, he argues, had customarily deferred to their masters' asserted right to "govern" the artisan trades, in particular to set prices and wages. The Revolution accustomed journeymen to self-organization and self-government and aroused their antagonism to the unilateral regulation of masters. In this setting, the *Cordwainers'* case may be seen as exemplary of a larger process in which the two sides continually counterposed contrasting definitions of power, government, and freedom—contrasting systems of rules constituting different kinds of "free" market in labor and governing market transactions in very different ways.

In contrast to Steinfeld's detailed focus on the *Cordwainers'* case, Hattam presents a broad analysis of nineteenth-century conspiracy prosecutions, both before and after the Civil War, one that seeks to correct what she sees as a prevailing scholarly tendency to resort indiscriminately to class explanations. Critical of existing interpretations for their tendency to deal with the issue of labor conspiracy in isolation, Hattam argues that in fact little distinguishes judicial attitudes toward pre–Civil War *labor* conspiracy prosecutions from judicial attitudes toward *nonlabor* conspiracy prosecutions—that is, conspiracies to cheat and defraud, against public policy, against the government, against individual rights, and so forth. The courts' treatment of workers in the antebellum cases was mild, and workers responded by generally ignoring convictions. The courts during the second half of the century took a far more coercive (and far more contested) approach. In this light, "class bias" becomes an inadequate explanation of judicial behavior during the early period. Seeing, like Steinfeld, the conspiracy cases as arguments over the terms on which economic growth was to proceed, Hattam proposes that the view of the courts throughout the first half of the nineteenth century was shaped primarily by the continuing influence of an eighteenth-century republican world view, which highlighted the role of the courts in policing threats to communal welfare, rather than by more modern considerations of class. In line with recent work on class formation,[18] Hattam sees the labor movement of the second half of the nineteenth century as quite distinct from that of the first half and emphasizes its more emphatic record of political protest against the courts' renewed and more ruthless resort to conspiracy doctrine to punish strikers. On both sides, according to Hattam, class becomes a significant explanatory factor in the second half of the century.

The third essay published here, by Christopher Tomlins, draws attention to the power asymmetries immanent in legal descriptions of the roles of the parties to the nineteenth-century employment relationship and traces the origins of those descriptions in American law. Nineteenth-century legal discourse, Tomlins argues, cast the subjects of wage labor relationships in roles quite distinct from those prevailing during the colonial era, attributing to them legal statuses of master and servant, which had previously been applied to a more limited category of relationships. Tomlins attributes this change to a postrevolutionary reception of a "generic" English law of master and servant. According to Tomlins, relatively few indications can be found in eighteenth-century legal records that the colonies had developed an all-encompassing law of the employment relationship. In America such a conception only appears during the first half of the nineteenth century, when treatise writers and courts begin to apply important disciplinary incidents of the common law of master and servant to the generality of employees. Tracing the application of these disciplines in juridical practice, Tomlins also underscores the contradiction between the doctrinal representation of employment as a relationship of hierarchy and subordination and the courts' simultaneous commitment to an ideology of free contract. While the former stressed the controlling power of the employer as a sufficient test of the existence of a relationship of employment, the latter represented employment as a relationship free of power disparities, such that the employee might reasonably be held willingly to have assumed all the risks of entry, even the risk of accidental injury or death resulting from the actions of another employee following the orders of a superior.

The asymmetries and contradictions characteristic of the law of the nineteenth-century employment relationship are also canvassed suggestively in the next two essays. In the first of these, Lea VanderVelde seeks to analyze the influence of free labor ideology on courts dealing with employer attempts to invoke the equitable doctrine of specific performance in the case of contracts for personal services and to enforce covenants not to work for competitors. She finds that the courts' concern in the immediate aftermath of the Civil War to follow a substantive "free labor" principle protective of the substance of an individual employee's freedom from infringement by deleterious contractual terms had by the 1880s been displaced by a far more restrictive attitude. Dealing here with issues first raised in the important English cases *Lumley v. Wagner* (1852) and *Lumley v. Gye* (1853), both stemming from the decision of the opera singer Johanna Wagner to refuse to perform her contract with Her Majesty's Theatre and instead to sing for a rival theater, VanderVelde's argument focuses on a group of American cases similarly involving suits by theater owners or managers against actresses. These, she shows, were pivotal in American courts' adoption of the *Lumley* rule and of its restraints on the freedom of movement of professional employees. Particularly important, VanderVelde argues persuasively that the gender of this group of defendants was central to American courts' decision to "receive" the *Lumley* restraint. Courts, she finds, were initially willing to apply the rule only in cases involving a segment of the population whom they were culturally conditioned to regard as subordinable. VanderVelde also demonstrates how the processes of common law adjudication both concealed the gender specificity of the restraint and then, subsequently, facilitated its application to professional employees as a class. Gender, in short, was the decisive factor in the transmission and adoption of a legal rule deleterious to the free labor principle.

Dealing, like VanderVelde, with the ideological consequences of emancipation, Amy Stanley's essay presents an equally powerful analysis of another dimension of the relationship between freedom and restraint: the criminalization of vagrancy in the post–Civil War North. Stanley's point of departure is the hegemony of marketplace contractual ideology in postbellum America, a hegemony suffusing contemporary debate both on the meaning of free labor and unemployment and on the function of charity. Tellingly, Stanley stresses that the creation of market relations in no sense implies the withering away of coercive labor laws; rather (stressing here a theme to be found in many of the papers presented) rules of contract mask legal compulsions that underlie free labor and imprint on freedom a definition couched exclusively in market terms. Here, vagrancy laws criminalizing begging in the name of weaning the poor from "dependence" enforced participation in the labor market and thus made it effectively impossible for the unemployed laborer to escape from the market whose operation had brought about the condition of unemployed poverty in the first place. So complete was the vagrant's "capture" by the market that charity itself—the giving of relief—came to be justifiable in the eyes of the charity reformer only as a market transaction—a quid pro quo. In all cases "a return in work" was to be "extracted in proportion to the relief thus given."

Both VanderVelde's and Stanley's essays point up the decidedly equivocal quality—legally, culturally, racially—of "free" in the nineteenth century's "free labor" ideology. Particularly fascinating in this regard is Stanley's convincing demonstration of the close relationships (obscured in contemporary political debates) among the Black Codes enacted in former Confederate states, the Freedman Bureau's own rules against idleness and vagrancy, and northern vagrancy statutes.

The same message is delivered, more starkly, in Karen Orren's essay, which both reinforces and contradicts aspects of the arguments advanced in preceding essays. Like Tomlins, for example, Orren sees American labor law in the second half of the nineteenth century very much as an echo of English master and servant concepts. Unlike him, however, she regards this conceptual unity as in all essential respects an expression of six centuries of institutional and ideational continuity in labor law—a continuity transmitted from premodern England to colonial America through to the post–Revolutionary republic. Thus, where Tomlins, VanderVelde, and Stanley deal with law in terms largely of discourse, ideology, and culture and tend to focus on its contradictions, ruptures, and discontinuities, Orren's is a far more structural argument.[19] Orren's main concern in this essay, however, is less with the origins of American labor law in ancient feudal tradition than with the final loosening of that intellectual structure's stranglehold in the labor struggles of the late nineteenth and early twentieth centuries. Departing from prevailing scholarly assessments of those struggles, Orren characterizes them as a "monumental historic success," in that American unions, through actions that challenged "the categories of the ancient law," helped bring about a transformation of the old labor-legal regime which speeded the more fundamental transformation of American politics and culture as a whole. The political promise of this rebellion was not finally realized until the 1930s, when the New Deal's revolutionary reordering of both the practices of governance and the structure of the state in America finally broke the power of the judiciary, against which labor had struggled so mightily. Its cultural effects, however, were more immediate. Reinforcing her focus on law in the context of the history of ideas, the last part of Orren's essay dwells briefly but suggestively on the important relationships between labor's struggles to create a regime of voluntary action to replace master and servant law's structure of prescriptive legal regulation and what Morton White called "the revolt against formalism"—the rise of philosophical pragmatism in American social and political thought and the creation of a truly liberal culture. Labor, in short, played a vital part in the formation of American liberalism, its late nineteenth-century rebellion being the final and decisive act in a centuries-long developmental process of feudal attrition and liberal emergence.

Cultural change is also the theme of Daniel Ernst's essay on the *Danbury Hatters'* case, although the transition he focuses on is not that from feudalism to liberalism but rather from a culture of small proprietors—the up side, as it were, of free labor ideology—to one of large organizations. Critical of those who have presented the *Danbury Hatters'* case (*Loewe v. Lawlor*) simply as one further example of corporate capitalist ascendancy over American labor, Ernst offers an almost poetic reflection on the fate of the individual in the organizational economy. The case, he shows, ruined everyone it touched, employer and employees alike. To explain this he invites us to view the case in the context of a confrontation between the entrepreneurial capitalism of the nineteenth century and the reconstructed corporate economy of large organizations—business *and* labor—which emerged from the depression of the 1890s. According to Ernst, the *Danbury Hatters'* case cannot be understood simply as a class struggle, although that, in part, it surely was, but must also be seen as the struggle of a small proprietor against the logic of corporatism, a logic represented, in this instance, by the United Hatters' determination to organize the industry no matter what the impact on the competitive position of firms like Dietrich Loewe's. Equally, it must be seen from the perspective of the individual workers caught up in the dispute, whose relationship with both employer and union—mediated, Ernst argues, by free labor discourse—was rather more ambiguous than the simpler verities of class analysis would have us believe. Rather than a strategic engagement in a corporate antiunion war, *Loewe v. Lawlor's* poignant outcome expressed the decline of a way of life. The proceedings' incapacity to furnish or even appear to furnish a solution to the problems of either proprietor or workers signified the inapplicability of nineteenth-century ideas to twentieth-century conflicts. Its aftermath in the period's labor law—legal change suggesting the beginnings of an accommodation to the logic of corporatism—is, Ernst suggests, confirmation of its status as the marker of the end of an era.

Like Orren and Ernst, William Forbath focuses on the last decades of the nineteenth century and the first of the twentieth, which have long been recognized as pivotal in the formation of the modern labor movement. In contrast to Ernst's tight microcosm, Forbath offers a broad reinterpretation, based upon a comparative analysis of the differing roles of legal and political institutions in the polities of America and England, of the impact of those institutions upon the formation of the modern labor movement. Reflecting on themes developed in both traditional and more recent accounts of labor's social and political history in the two countries, Forbath seeks to supply the missing link in the American story—the unique role of the judiciary in America's institutionally fragmented federative state and hence the disproportionate power of courts vis-à-vis labor when compared with the unitary sovereignty of the British parliamentary state. These profoundly different institutional environments, he argues, account for the profoundly different paths followed by English and American labor movements, which were otherwise essentially similar both in themselves and in the situations faced at the turn of the century. Both movements confronted hostile employers, a hostile judiciary, and a hostile legal environment, but while English unions could and did seek redress through political activity intended directly to alter in their favor the composition and output of a constitutionally sovereign legislature, American labor had no such option. Its political potential always ultimately subject to the judiciary's constitutional trumps, American labor retreated into a voluntarist shell. Adding to this institutional twist on American exceptionalism, Forbath stresses the absence from the U.S. scene of an influential "administrative state elite" equivalent to England's professional civil service—that is, an alternative locus of administrative power comparable to that represented in the judiciary. In England, Forbath claims, the civil service elite could be found in alliance with English unionists behind a collectivist program of social legislation. In the United States no such alliance was available. Much as one might deprecate outcomes, one begins to appreciate the institutional logic of American labor's largely nonstatist strategy.

The thorny issue of exceptionalism is also an acknowledged subtext of Kenneth Casebeer's richly detailed essay on the struggle for a radical alternative to the Wagner-Lewis Social Security Act of 1935. Casebeer's subject is the progress of Ernest Lundeen's revolutionary Workers' Unemployment and Social Insurance Bill, introduced in the House of Representatives in February 1934. Casebeer does not limit himself to detailing the bill's proposals—essentially an assault on unemployment through the creation of wage floors funded by redistributive taxation and administered through workers' councils—or to recounting its legislative history. Rather, he seeks to explain its extraordinary rank-and-file popularity; the increasingly frenetic resistance of the AFL to the bill, and the relationship between that resistance and the AFL's organizational ideology; and the crucial role of the conflict over the Workers' Bill within the AFL in generating the split between the AFL and the CIO. The latter is a particularly important point, given historians' tendency to see the split almost entirely in terms of organizational rather than social policy. Casebeer also uses the story of the Workers' Bill to throw into sharp relief the very structure and logic of American labor relations law. American labor law, he says, is a regime of rules facilitating the imposition of economic risk directly upon the work force through managerial decision making, mediated, if at all, only by limited commitments to bilateral bargaining in some restricted areas. Certainly this regime is quite free of any form of social wage guarantee. At the same time Casebeer shows that it is in no sense immutable, but rather clearly contingent. As the "near miss" of the Workers' Bill shows, a very different structure of social security legislation could have appeared during the 1930s. Interested like Forbath, and like Joel Rogers, in the relationship between institutional structures and political action, Casebeer is less committed than either to the idea of America's exceptionalism. The Workers' Bill episode, he argues, demonstrates the capacities of an American labor politics; if that politics appears in a vernacular form unfamiliar to those used to the European example, that is a sign of its particularity (and, one might add, of theirs), not of its exceptionalism.

The institutional innovations of the 1930s and their legacies also provide the subjects of the final two essays in this collection, by Eileen Boris and Joel Rogers. Each deals with a central aspect of the institutional matrix bequeathed by the New Deal and its eventual decomposition. Boris's essay on labor standards employs feminist theory to explicate the profoundly gendered implications of the regulatory dichotomy between home and workplace manifested in the prohibition of industrial homework in seven garment-related industries under the Fair Labor Standards Act (FLSA). According to Boris, the labor liberals who drafted the FLSA created the legislation in the service of maintaining the home as a private family realm protected from the intrusions of the market and distinct and separate from the workplace. Thus the home/work regulatory dichotomy the act embodied was founded upon a conception of the normal relationship of workplace to home that was completely insensitive to the diversity of factors influencing the division and location of labor in working class families—sex, race/ ethnicity, age, kinship, cultural values—and that in any case rendered invisible the unwaged labor of women in the household by treating it as not-work. Boris's essay offers an account of the postwar history of this labor standards regime, explains the sources of continuous pressure for homework throughout the postwar period, and develops an extended critique of the dichotomy (regulatory *and* conceptual) the FLSA was based on for its failure, which became particularly apparent during the 1980s, to provide a sufficient basis for resisting the spreading rightist assault on labor standards, whether in homework or factory work. Through this critique, Boris hopes to move the conceptualization of labor standards beyond the simple, and crippling, dichotomy she describes.

Joel Rogers's essay, like Forbath's a wide-ranging overview, addresses and explains the institutional dynamics of postwar union decline. Rogers argues that the hostility of the postwar legal environment toward organized labor resulted in the confinement of the labor movement to sectors of the economy it had organized by the end of World War II. Legal barriers subsidized employer resistance, keeping the costs of new organizing high and encouraging unions to concentrate on the pursuit of particularistic strategies tailored to maintaining their influence in those areas of the economy where they had already achieved enough strength to take wages and benefits out of competition. The result was a reasonably well organized union "core" that was, however, always a vulnerable island in a sea in which organized labor was otherwise weak or nonexistent. Within the core, unions were divided from one another by their studious pursuit of self-interest. The result was the further weakening of labor as a national political force and thus, ironically, reinforcement of each union's tendency to go it alone. Notwithstanding a continual downward trend overall, however, union strength in the organized core remained sufficient to maintain the postwar "truce" with employers until the 1970s. Then recession and trade shocks—the impact of a rapid internationalization of competitive pressures on the U.S. economy—brought a rapid escalation in corporate assaults on these labor movement strongholds and the beginnings of the catastrophic slide in membership and influence which continued throughout the 1980s. In a way implied but not particularly dwelt upon by Forbath in his analysis of the labor movement's encounter with a hostile institutional environment, Rogers emphasizes the rationality of union behavior: given the highly centrifugal structural dynamics of the U.S. political economy, particularistic pursuit of self-interest made sense. But institutional determinism is not the whole story. Because his analysis is predicated to such an important extent on the premise of legal hostility, Rogers implies that had it not been for the legal constraints imposed on it by the Labor Management Relations Act, the labor movement might well have behaved differently.

NEXT STEPS

We have indicated that the overall project of this collection is not interpretive synthesis. Nor have these essays been brought together to advertise the advantages of one methodology or mode of analysis over another. They are intended, rather, as a demonstration of fruitful diversity and, in particular, of scholarly vitality in an area of study overlapping several disciplines and many different analytic approaches, an area brimming with opportunity. There is, nevertheless, much shared ground here, and it is worth reflecting briefly on that ground for what it tells us about the generality of contemporary scholarship on the history of American labor law.

Most basic is the authors' definition of their field. Labor law history apprehends law and labor socially, culturally, institutionally, ideologically, discursively. Its object is not an anatomy of labor law—a dissection of cases and statutes—nor is it the diagnosis of ills, the prescription of institutional cures, the "reform" of the law. Its object rather is to investigate law in terms of the social relations and, therefore, the power relations persisting among humans. These are relations constituted in cases and statutes, institutions and procedures, the behavior and ideas of officials and reformers. In other words, they are relations in which law is actively implicated, both practically and conceptually.[20]

With this common purpose established, the scholars represented here employ multiple techniques and trajectories of analysis in pursuit of those relations. Doctrinal analysis, for example, makes appearances here, although its purpose is not the exegesis of rules familiar to generations of law students but rather the elucidation of the "subjects" of legal discourse and the processes of their creation.[21] Legal doctrine is also recapitulated in the context of histories of ideas and institutional formations,[22] and of ideologies.[23] For many of this subset of contributions the particular issue is the imbrication of law and politics, exemplified in the organization of social relations around concepts—notably contractualism—open to multiple avenues of realization but in practice conventionally realized in official discourse in ways that most accord with, or least depart from, prevailing structures of power.[24] Other essays recommend a more complete departure from official texts in order to draw our attention to culture and cultural conflicts as powerful mediators of the social and legal relations under observation,[25] to accord a more determinative role to institutional structures,[26] or to underline the contingency of those relations, whether according to time and place or simply to the power of human agency to work change.[27] In short, there is no particular consensus here on the processes by which legal relations are brought into existence. All contributors, however, see the relationship between legal knowledge and social/power relations, and the dialectical role of each as a condition of the existence of the other, as the fundamental issue to be addressed.

In investigating that relationship, this collection quite crucially underscores the multidimensionality of social relations and thus the multiplicity of points of nexus between law and power. The salience of class to explanations of the distribution of power in society clearly remains a basic assumption for many, though not necessarily all, these authors. What emerges with great clarity however, particularly in the work of VanderVelde and Boris, is the fundamental salience of gender as an equally irreducible social relationship. These authors make clear that to apprehend law and labor from a feminist standpoint yields knowledge that simply cannot be gained from the standpoint of class.[28]

From our point of view as editors, it is a matter of as yet comparatively little regret that work in this field is being undertaken from the standpoint of race, a third such irreducible social relationship. The evidence of those essays in this collection that do touch, even fleetingly, on race—VanderVelde's, Casebeer's, Boris's, and particularly Stanley's—suggests that the specific knowledge and interpretive insights to be gained from specialized research undertaken from that standpoint is enormous.[29]

This proffered multidimensionality of legal and social, and hence power, relations tells us much about where this field of study should go next. One can divide new directions into empirical and methodological components. So far as the former is concerned, we have already drawn attention to one major empirical silence—the salience of race in the history of labor law, whether as a legal category, as a mode of rule transmission, or as a social relationship—that obviously needs addressing. Another, clearly related and already canvassed here to an extent sufficient to reveal its rich potential,[30] is American labor's legal consciousness. Investigations are needed of both the legal consciousness manifested in the ideologies and programs of labor organizations, and also the popular consciousness of law in the United States. We already have some examples of each kind of study.[31]

Each of these dimensions of legal consciousness is integral to what one might term the legal culture of American workers, itself a contributing voice in the cacophony of legal cultures that collectively constitute the range of possibility, though only rarely the official actuality, of law's American empire. The components of American workers' legal culture, that culture's influence on official legal ideology and practices, and the reverse, are crucial areas that have yet to be systematically investigated and thoroughly understood by scholars.[32]

Methodologically, the most important single lesson to be learned from this collection is that standpoints in addition to class will now play a key role in the field's development. The insights of the essays adopting a feminist perspective provide an especially notable example, and their success is to be welcomed as a matter of fundamental *theoretical* importance. First, as Maureen Cain has put it, research undertaken from any standpoint that treats gender relations as irrelevant "quite simply, is bad research," bad because it denies one of the fundamental relationships in social life. Like class, she goes on, "gender is something that is never absent just because the other is not empirically observable or in the same situation."[33] Second, it is clear here that the essays manifesting the greatest sensitivity to the diversity of social and legal and power relations which the collection as a whole so powerfully underscores, and most explicitly seeking its methodological accommodation as part of the field's theoretical project, are those written from a feminist standpoint.[34] In contemplating the long-term future of labor law history, one looks for additional means of reinforcing a multidimensional approach in theory and research.

Because the basic message of these essays is that of the multiplicity of social and power relations mediated by and constituted in law, our other methodological advisory must of necessity be that the subject makes considerable demands for interpretive sophistication upon the researcher. We must be sensitive to the distinctions between official and unofficial legal discourses, between texts and meanings, among the differing meanings ascribable to texts existing simultaneously in multiple social contexts, among differing modes of construction of legal relations—cultural, ideological, institutional, material. We must understand, further, how law is, and simultaneously is much more than, *the* law; that is, how law is both an official legal culture *and* a plurality of unofficial legal cultures existing in political contest, and hence how descriptions of *the* law unacceptably elide examination of the particular modalities of law which emerge from those contests as the chosen agencies of rule.[35] We must in short avoid treating law as if it were some kind of ontological singularity or metanarrative. This was the trap on the edge of which E. P. Thompson, to use one famous example, teetered in the course of an otherwise insightful critique of instrumentalism when he wrote of the law as "a genuine forum" within which "certain kinds of class conflict" could take place and which, because it elaborated rules and procedures and an ideology ("the rule of law") that regulated and reconciled those conflicts, therefore could, and should, be seen as "an unqualified human good."[36] Law, we may agree, determines that a site (a playing field, in current parlance) will be provided where procedures and modes of conflict determine a victor. But parties do not necessarily arrive on the field with the same understanding of what is to transpire. Law, in other words, is not a unity. Law is rather an array of alternative possibilities for social knowledge, alternative ways of describing "the facts of life," some admitted to rule as legal truths, some not.[37] Rather than an unqualified human good, *the rule of law* best signifies that regime of legal truths which sustains the form of fighting currently in favor, a regime that is nevertheless still social warfare by other means.

In the past, American labor historians confronted by the demanding task of theorizing law have tended to resort too uncritically to invocations of Thompson's formula without pausing also to consider its limitations.[38] Among these essays, we find suggestions of alternative formulations which step around those limitations. They lead us into a more sceptical, but also a more multifaceted, legal world.

Also among these essays, we encounter a new genre for labor law history, supplementing the "moral passion" that has been identified by some as the characteristic voice to date of those writing in this field. Described as emblematic of a tradition of radical historiography deriving from Engels, Tawney, and Thompson, this has been a voice "suffused with sympathy for the poor and laboring classes and admiration of their heroic qualities, and with indignation at propertied or governing classes who exploit their misery or are indifferent to it."[39] Such moral passion remains an easily detectable subtext in most, perhaps all, the essays presented here. But moral passion of itself provides no standpoint, no starting place, for knowledge. It is motivation but not explanation; it cannot substitute for theory, nor, indeed, for data. These essays do not eschew passion (nor, for that matter, do they eschew E. P. Thompson), but they do seek to ground it, theoretically and empirically, and thus to justify it.

Obviously, given the scholarly agendas of most of its contributors, this collection will not supply the last word (nor the only one)[40] in the field. Nevertheless, this collection represents the preponderance of the work now being done in labor law history. As such it provides an opportunity to judge the field's merits and consider its further development. We hope here to provide enlightenment—but also an occasion for discussion and argument. In this way, we can continue the dialogue that we began among ourselves and with our audience in Baltimore.

NOTES

1. Commons 1921; Commons 1924: 283–312, and R. B. Morris 1937; 1981 [1946].

2. See, for example, Frankfurter and Greene 1930; Laube 1935. The flurry of law review articles on labor conspiracies and the labor injunction written in the 1920s and early 1930s also generally fit this mold. See W. W. Cook 1918; Nelles 1931a; 1931b; 1932; Sayre 1922; 1923; 1930; Witte 1926. Some historians have argued that this continues to be a characteristic of contemporary labor law history scholarship. See, for example, Salvatore 1986.

3. Landis 1934; Gregory and Katz 1979; Kochan 1980.

4. Tomlins 1988b: 443–44. Brody 1989a: 8–9.

5. On this see the somewhat alienated commentaries of Neufeld 1962 and Brooks 1962. Appropriately symbolic, for our purposes here, is the title chosen for a major collection of labor/industrial relations "classics" republished in 1969 under the editorship of Stein and Taft: *American Labor: From Conspiracy to Collective Bargaining*. See also Zieger 1983: 59.

6. Professional historians who did attempt to engage with the history of labor law were usually roundly criticized, by lawyers, for their lack of legal

sophistication. See, for example, J. H. Smith 1946 (review of Morris, *Government and Labor in Early America*).

7. Tomlins 1988b: 428–29; Brody 1989a.

8. As exemplified, for example, even in works in other respects deeply influential and impressive such as Bernstein 1960, 1969, 1985, and D. Montgomery 1987. See also Tomlins 1988b: 428–29, 440–42.

9. According to one labor historian who has for some years offered friendly criticism of trends in labor law history, for example, such history is only really worth anything when situated in relation "to shifts in the balance of power between labor and capital and to the political forces contending for power within the state." See Dubofsky 1981: 501.

10. See, for example, Evans, Rueschemeyer, and Skocpol 1985; Fox-Genovese and Genovese 1976; Judt 1979; Henretta 1979; Brody 1989a: 16.

11. See, generally, A. D. Smith 1973; Giddens 1982; 1987; J. B. Thompson 1984; Unger 1987; Calhoun 1988. See also Haskell 1977a. During the 1970s and 1980s, scholars in many disciplines criticized post–World War II social science for adopting a model of inquiry based on the natural sciences (positivism). In their effort to produce a science of human behavior, the postwar functionalists had stressed the need for empirical theories that would predict behavior (determinism). The critics of the positivist model, on the other hand, sought to recapture the role of historical actors and their ideas in the production of both knowledge and social relations. A hermeneutic explanation of human action, they said, must always include "an attempt to recover and interpret the meanings of social actions from the point of view of the agents performing them" (Skinner 1985: 6). This has led these scholars into an exploration of ideology, beliefs, and the rules that permit the creation of knowledge (discourse).

12. R. W. Gordon 1981; 1984. See also, generally, Kairys 1982. Within this genre it is important to single out Klare 1978 as a foundation work in the particular area of labor law history. See also Klare 1981; Stone 1981; Atleson 1983; W. Holt 1986. The Critical Legal Studies movement began in the mid-1970s among a group of young law school scholars who had become disenchanted with mainstream legal thought. Using techniques borrowed from neo-Marxist thought and from contemporary developments in literary and social theory, these scholars have developed a methodology of critiquing contemporary jurisprudence. While the impact of critical legal studies has been felt mostly in law schools, its methods of analysis have proven useful to the generality of scholars doing law-related research.

13. Tomlins 1985; Schatz 1989.

14. To offer just a few examples: American Society for Legal History 1980 (papers by Klare and Lynd); American Historical Association 1985 (roundtable on history and industrial relations); American Society for Legal History 1986 (roundtable on Tomlins's *The State and the Unions*); Organization of American Historians 1987 (papers by Forbath and Tomlins); Law and Society Association 1987 (papers by Ernst and Orren); Law and Society Association 1989 (paper by VanderVelde); Law and Society Association 1990 (papers by Steinfeld and Forbath); American Society for Legal History 1990 (papers by Steinfeld, Stanley, Forbath, and Ernst).

15. "Critical Perspectives on the History of American Labor Law," 10 June 1987 (featuring papers by Forbath, Lynd, and Rogers).

16. To offer only two examples, see (1) the wide-ranging argument over critical perspectives on modern labor law history in the *Maryland Law Review* (1984–86), conducted largely between Finkin 1984, 1985 and Klare 1985a, 1985b, but also benefiting from a contribution from Stone 1986; (2) the spring 1989 issue of *Labor History* devoted in its entirety to the history of labor law (featuring articles by Hogler, Erickson, Holt, Tomlins, and Ernst).

17. See, for example, Atleson 1983; Tomlins 1985. At least nine of the participants in this collection (Steinfeld, Hattam, Tomlins, Stanley, Orren, Ernst, Forbath, Boris, Rogers) have either recently published books or plan to publish books within the next two or three years.

18. For example, Bridges 1986.

19. This is a trait she shares with Hattam and Rogers (suggesting—a point raised during the conference—that even as we pursue methodological catholicity we do so continuing to wear disciplinary spectacles), and also to some extent with Forbath.

20. For a brief but suggestive comment on the formulation of a "relational" theory of law, see A. Hunt 1987: 16–18.

21. As in, for example, the essays by Steinfeld, Tomlins, and VanderVelde.

22. As in Hattam's and Orren's essays.

23. As in Stanley's essay.

24. In addition to Stanley's essay, that of Boris is particularly suggestive on this point.

25. As in the essay by Ernst.

26. As in the essays by Hattam, Forbath, and Rogers.

27. As in Casebeer's essay.

28. In addition to the essays by VanderVelde and Boris, see also Stanley 1988, Erickson 1989. On the concept of standpoint in the sociology of knowledge, see Cain 1986.

29. For some discussion of the irreducibility of race and the law of slavery, see Tushnet 1981: 139–56. Grossberg 1988: 378–79 is also suggestive.

30. The essays by Forbath, Ernst, and Casebeer are perhaps the clearest examples, but see also those by Steinfeld, Hattam, and Orren.

31. In addition to the essays in this collection see, for examples of the former, Tomlins 1985; Forbath 1985; 1989. For examples and discussion of the latter, see Hartog 1985; Merry 1985; 1986. See also Pollack 1987; Wallace 1987: 314–66; Thelen 1986: particularly 59–85.

32. For a critique of prevailing uses of the concept of legal culture in legal history, see Tomlins 1991.

33. Cain 1986: 258.

34. See, for example, the essay by VanderVelde.

35. Tomlins 1991: 363–65.

36. E. P. Thompson 1977: 264–67. See also Horwitz 1977a: 565–66; Klare 1979: 133–34.

37. Wickham 1989.

38. See, for example, Dubofsky 1981: 501; Fink 1987: 905–6.

39. R. W. Gordon 1988: 144.

40. In addition to works already cited see, for example, Feinman 1976; Jacoby 1982; Kelman 1983; W. Holt 1984, 1986, 1989; Minda 1985; Hurvitz 1986; Hogler 1987a, 1987b, 1988, 1989; Hovenkamp 1988; Woodiwiss 1990. For different perspectives, see, for example, Petro 1978; 1980–82; Dickman 1987.

1 The *Philadelphia Cordwainers'* Case of 1806: The Struggle over Alternative Legal Constructions of a Free Market in Labor

Robert J. Steinfeld

The distribution of income . . . [in free markets] depends on the relative power of coercion which the different members of the community can exert against one another. Income is the price paid for not using one's coercive weapons. One of these weapons consists of the power to withhold one's labor. . . . Another is the power to call on the government to lock up certain pieces of land or productive equipment. . . . By threatening to use these various weapons, one gets . . . an income in the form of wages, interest, rent or profits.
—Robert Hale

Most accounts of the emergence of free markets in the United States portray that development as a simple matter of the liberation of acquisitive individuals from traditional communal constraints. This process is supposed merely to have involved barrier removal, the elimination of traditional obligations, which left people free to pursue their natural selfish inclinations. Free markets came into being, in this view, as nature was finally allowed to take its course. One consequence of telling the story this way has been to divert attention from the deliberate legal choices that were an inevitable part of the process of free market formation. Another has been to obscure the political changes that were responsible for bringing into being in the first place a world in which independent, self-governing actors would confront one another in the marketplace. The traditional account operates from the implicit assumptions that free markets take only a single legal form and that economic man is not a product of history and culture.

A reading of the early labor conspiracy cases yields a different, more complicated story about the emergence of "free" markets toward the end of the eighteenth and beginning of the nineteenth centuries—at least "free" markets in skilled urban wage labor. Part of this story certainly continues to be that a "free" market in skilled urban wage labor developed as wage workers and employers began to turn their backs on their traditional obligations to one another in order to pursue their interests. The very existence of these cases is testimony to the facts that, by the early decades of the nineteenth century, journeymen in the skilled crafts were considerably less willing to defer to their traditional "superiors" and that employers were no longer prepared, in many cases, even to pay lip service to their traditional obligations to journeymen. Unquestionably, these developments marked a liberation from the constraints of traditional social and moral order, from the norms of deference on one side and responsibility on the other. But much more than simple liberation was involved; ordinary people were remaking themselves. The profound political changes ushered in by the American Revolution contributed to reshaping artisan communities, bringing into being the cultural and political preconditions for free markets. In the years following the Revolution, journeymen redefined themselves. They began to assert that they were the equals of master artisans. They contended that they alone owned their labor and, as separate and independent property owners, were alone entitled to place a price upon it. We might almost say that a free market in urban wage labor was brought into being as these newly independent, property-owning journeymen and masters confronted one another in economic life. This is an important part of the story the conspiracy cases tell.

Much of the rest of that story is of the contested process by which decisions were made to give this "free" market in labor one legal construction rather than another as states were forced to choose between the conflicting new freedoms of journeymen and masters. Such legal choices are an integral aspect of the construction and operation of free markets. Too often we imagine that the "free" market is an institution with only a single, unproblematic legal form. We think of it as a set of economic practices conducted under an unvarying legal regime of private property and free contract. The differences among "free" markets, we suppose, are not legal-structural but factual, deriving from the accidents of the particular distribution of resources and the supply and demand curves in each market. Law in this familiar image is not substantively constitutive of "free" markets; it merely provides a set of neutral background rules under which market actors are free to shape their relationships with one another (under these particular factual circumstances) through bargaining.

This image, the conspiracy cases should make clear, is largely illusory. As one eminent legal scholar has put it, "the freedom of the 'market' [is] essentially a *freedom* of individuals and groups to coerce one another, with the power to coerce reinforced by agencies of the state itself."[1] As such, the process of "free" market formation inevitably made necessary collective choices about whose and what kinds of freedom would be legally privileged and whose and what kinds of freedom would be legally restricted.

In the *Philadelphia Cordwainers'* case of 1806 and in the other early labor conspiracy cases, the choices presented among the conflicting freedoms of market actors were simple enough. On the one hand, the law might privilege journeymen to form associations and through these associations to withhold as a body their labor from employers whenever they thought that would be a useful weapon. If journeymen were legally so privileged, however, the real freedom of other market actors might well, as a practical matter, be reduced. Organized journeymen had used the power that association gave them to pressure employers into hiring only journeymen who were members of their societies. If journeymen were legally entitled to exercise their freedom of association in this way, the real freedom of both masters and journeymen *as individuals* to choose their own employers and employees might well be sacrificed. According to prosecutors, journeymen had also used the power that association gave them to try to impose other regulations for the government of the trade on both masters and journeymen. As a practical matter, if journeymen continued to enjoy this freedom, the freedom of masters to govern their own business affairs as they alone saw fit might well be reduced. And if journeymen were legally privileged to associate for these purposes, they would almost certainly command more effective power to pressure masters to pay wages they might not otherwise have freely chosen to pay.

On the other hand, the law might prohibit journeymen from associating or might restrict the things they would be permitted to do when associated. But if this were the legal course chosen, journeymen, as isolated and economically vulnerable individuals, might well enjoy considerably less real freedom. Masters might then be in a position to place employment on a "take it or leave it" basis, exercising more power both to fix journeymen's wages unilaterally and to demand obedience to their commands. "The body-men have a right to say" with one voice, Caesar Rodney argued for the journeymen in the *Philadelphia Cordwainers'* case, "we will work only where we please, and at what price we please; and we know that no earthly power can in this free country compel us. But give a verdict against [the journeymen], and farewell to the dearest privilege which they enjoy! The masters may then dictate where they shall work, with whom, and at what prices."[2] All alternatives involved a deliberate legal choice between one kind of freedom and another, between someone's power of self-government and someone else's. No set of natural, neutral background rules existed to make these choices unnecessary. Inevitable legal decisions like these about the legitimate scope of the freedom to coerce in markets may radically alter the relative power of different actors in a particular market. In this way, the choice of legal rules can contribute to structuring any particular free market in quite different ways, leading to quite different relationships between the actors in that market.

It is important to recognize that law plays this basic structuring role in free markets generally, not merely in those marked by overt conflict. All "free" markets are characterized by the play of coercive power and all are "regulated" by law. And these two features are intimately related. It is the law of private property, after all, that gives owners the broad authority to say, "Do what I wish and I will make the resources you need available to you. If you do not, I am authorized to call on the force of the state to assist me in keeping what you need out of your hands." Depending upon how unpleasant a market actor's other options are, the law of property has given the property owner greater or lesser power over him. The ground rules for the use of this law-based power are always a legal issue in "free" markets. Sometimes this issue arises in the process of defining the detailed legal incidents of "private property," sometimes in the process of defining the legal incidents of "free contract." Sometimes, as in the conspiracy cases, the issue arises in defining criminal behavior. On the disposition of such legal issues may well turn the shape of particular "free" markets.

For many journeymen in the early nineteenth century, the choice of one set of legal rules rather than another to govern their market relations with master artisans represented a political as well as an economic choice.[3] One legal version of the "free" market in labor, the version they contended for, would have made it possible, many of them thought, to achieve a form of genuine republican liberty by giving them effective power to participate in the government of their trades, and hence in the government of their daily working lives. It would also have increased their power to secure adequate material rewards for their labor and to enjoy the kind of freedom that material sufficiency brings. If the other legal version of the "free" market—we might call it the individualist version—were adopted, many of them correctly feared that they were more likely to be left as isolated individuals subject to the wills of their employers. In their view, this state of affairs would leave intact the traditional hierarchical authority structure of the trades which they had been struggling to overturn. They would then continue to be subject to the government of their traditional "superiors," the masters in the trade.

To understand fully why these legal disputes over labor organization represented a crucial political as well as economic issue for journeymen at the beginning of the nineteenth century—to understand why the question of "government" in general loomed so large for both sides in the early conspiracy cases—it is necessary to try to reconstruct their common frame of reference. Both sides were still largely working out of a tradition in which issues of polity and economy did not occupy clearly separate realms. The next section examines the eighteenth-century background against which the early conspiracy cases were fought out.

GOVERNING THE TRADE: WAGE AND PRICE SETTING BY MASTER ARTISANS IN THE EIGHTEENTH CENTURY

In *The Ideological Origins of the American Revolution*, Bernard Bailyn wrote that

> Americans of 1760 continued to assume, as had their predecessors for generations before, that a healthy society was a hierarchical society, in which it was natural for some to be rich and some poor, some honored some obscure, some powerful and some weak. And it was believed that superiority was unitary, that the attributes of the favored—wealth, wisdom, power—had a natural affinity to each other. . . . Manifest, external differences among men, reflecting the principle of hierarchical order, were necessary and proper, and would remain; they were intrinsic to the nature of things.[4]

In this kind of universe, "government" was not strictly confined to governments. Persons up and down the social hierarchy owed respect to "superiors" and exercised authority over "inferiors." To an extent we now have difficulty comprehending, the power men disposed of over women, children, and other men in what we would consider their purely private relations was commonly viewed as a form of government. But as a form of government, the exercise of this power also entailed responsibilities toward the community and toward those over whom authority had been assumed.

Master artisans exercised two distinct levels of hierarchical authority over journeymen, apprentices, and other skilled workmen in the eighteenth-century colonial crafts. In their individual shops, the traditional master-servant relationship gave masters varying degrees of authority over their workmen. Within the wider eighteenth-century urban craft community, master artisans commonly assumed responsibility for placing their *"Trade* under proper Regulations"[5] by combining to set standard prices for their work and wage or piece rates for the work of journeymen.

Most eighteenth-century colonial craft production took place in the household. The image of a small shop beneath living quarters in which a master worked alongside a few journeymen and apprentices, though it fails to convey the diversity of forms in which craft production took place in the colonies, probably paints a roughly accurate picture of the urban craft economy in the eighteenth-century colonies.[6] In the seventeenth-century colonies, this household economy had been subject to the strict authority of the head of household.[7] By the eighteenth century the traditional authority of heads of household had probably weakened somewhat. But for those workers such as apprentices, indentured servants, and many journeymen, who still lived with and were fed at the table of a master artisan, his status as head of household continued to play an important role in setting the tone of the relationship between them.[8] As late as 1773, for example, the Reverend Ebenezer Parkman of Westborough, Massachusetts, can be found chastising one of his resident farm workers for failing to "observe the order of my House.'"[9]

Many of the harshest provisions of traditional English master-servant law continued to apply in the eighteenth-century colonies to two kinds of workers who were commonly found in urban workshops: apprentices and skilled immigrant indentured servants. Because of the limited availability of journeymen in the American colonies throughout the first half of the eighteenth century, many master artisans relied heavily on apprenticed labor and, in places like Philadelphia, on indentured servants to supply their labor needs.[10] In mideighteenth-century Philadelphia, in fact, the majority of male indentured servants were owned by master artisans.[11]

Both apprentices and servants were bound by indenture for multiyear terms of service and were legally obligated to obey the commands of their masters. Both could be lawfully "corrected" by their masters for disobedience or other infraction. And both were subject to recapture if they left their masters before they had served out their terms. Following the traditional paternalistic pattern, in both forms of labor legal responsibility was joined to legal authority. Masters were obligated to provide room and board for their apprentices and for their indentured servants throughout their terms of service in the same way that they were obligated to support their other household dependents, their wives and children. The presence of these kinds of bound workers in the eighteenth-century craft workshop must have contributed to the establishment of a thoroughly hierarchical atmosphere in many workshops.

The master artisan's relationship to his ordinary journeymen is harder to pin down. We know that many journeymen in the mideighteenth century also lived with their masters and ate at their tables.[12] Some contracted to serve for as much as a year at a time. In England, and during the previous century in many of the American colonies as well, such a resident workman by the year would have been subject to the full authority of the head of household. He would also have been liable to imprisonment for leaving his master before fulfilling his contractual term.[13] In a number of colonies by this time, it seems pretty clear that such workers were no longer subject to imprisonment for premature departure,[14] but other paternalistic features of the traditional English service relationship may well have survived.

In England, the rule had been that "if a servant retained for a year, happen within the time of his service to fall sick, or to be hurt or lamed . . . by the Act of God, or in doing his Masters business; yet it seemeth the Master must not therefore put such Servant away, nor abate any part of his Wages for such time."[15] The same protections were not extended to casual workers by the day or task. Gary Nash has found roughly similar practices in effect in certain crafts in mid-eighteenth-century Philadelphia. Nash notes that carpenters hired on a casual basis normally had their pay docked when they missed days of work because of injury or sickness. Carpenters hired for more extended periods who took their wages on their master's diet, however, were paid when injury or illness caused them to miss days.[16] Other features of the traditional paternalistic relationship may also have survived into this period to shape the relationship of master artisans to their resident contract journeymen.

Many journeymen hired to work even on a casual basis also boarded with their masters. Of these we can only follow Gary Nash and E. P. Thompson in saying that "to eat at one's employer's board, to lodge in his barn or above his workshop, was to submit to his supervision."[17] While, by the eighteenth century, the limited availability of American journeymen and their greater rights of mobility seem to have contributed to a significant relaxation of traditional obligations, within the eighteenth-century colonial craft workshop the norms of authority and responsibility on one side and of deference and respect on the other continued to play important roles in shaping labor relationships.

These traditional attitudes of deference and authority may help to explain the role master artisans assumed for themselves within many of the eighteenth-century colonial craft communities. By and large, the colonial crafts operated without formal guild organization. Early attempts to establish guilds on the English model came to very little.[18] The impulse to limit competition and to give order to the trade, however, did not disappear among colonial master artisans. This impulse, moreover, was reinforced by the persistence in the colonies of powerful "corporatist" strains that continued to influence the behavior of colonists even as colonists simultaneously began to embrace a newer competitive commercial spirit.[19] In the early eighteenth century, Gary Nash explains, "unrestrained competition, with each artisan or merchant playing for advantage to the limit of his ability, was an alien notion. It was thought of as a prescription for chaos and corruption rather than for material blessings and harmonious social relations. Commercial transactions were more than mere exchanges of goods or money; they composed 'part of a network of human intercourse that held society together.' "[20]

In various crafts in the larger towns, master artisans joined together on an ad hoc basis throughout the eighteenth century to try to impose some order on their trades, normally by establishing a schedule of standard rates for their work and standard wage or piece rates for journeymen. The most successful of these efforts was undoubtedly the Philadelphia Carpenters' Company established by master carpenters in the mid-1720s. This organization incorporated many features of the formal craft guild and continued to operate throughout the rest of the colonial period. One of its principal purposes was to establish a schedule of standard rates for carpenter work and standard wages for journeymen.[21] Around 1750, the carpenters of Providence, Rhode Island, similarly joined together to issue *Rules for House Carpenters' Work in the Town of Providence* and to establish a uniform schedule of rates for their work.[22] In 1756, they were joined by a group of Providence cabinetmakers who subscribed to an agreement to abide by a uniform schedule of prices for thirty-five items of furniture. Piece rates for "Journeymen's Work for making" were part of this price list.[23] The overwhelming majority of cabinetmakers' price books that survive from this period include such schedules of "wages to be paid the workman on a piecework basis."[24]

Though master carpenters and cabinetmakers organized to establish uniform rates more frequently, masters in other crafts also joined together from time to time for similar purposes. The *New England Courant* for December 7, 1724, for example, carried the following announcement:

On Tuesday the first of this Instant in the Evening, Thirty Two Principal Barbers of this Place, assembled at the Golden Ball, with a Trumpeter attending them, to debate some important Articles relating to their occupations; where it was proposed, that they should raise their Shaving from 8 to 10s. per Quarter, and that they should advance 5s. on the Price of making common Wiggs and 10s. on their Tye ones. It was also propos'd, that no one of their Faculty should shave or dress Wiggs on sunday Mornings for the future, on Penalty of forfeiting 10 pounds for every such Offense.[25]

"With less fanfare Bay Town booksellers convened [in the same year] to establish 'a company and raise the Price of their Goods'."[26]

To place in perspective these eighteenth-century efforts by master artisans to establish uniform prices for their work, it is necessary to understand something of the earlier practice of wage and price setting. When the American colonies were settled, the public authorities in England had been setting the price of artisan work on and off for centuries. Two aspects of traditional price setting that have practically always been neglected in modern accounts are crucial for understanding the background against which artisan price setting took place in the eighteenth century. First, price setting was invariably done from the perspective of noncraft employers of craft labor. All artisans were lumped together in wage assessments as members of the common laboring people. The prices of master artisan labor were set in the same assessments that also set the prices of their skilled and unskilled helpers. One rate was to be paid to workers at a high skill or responsibility level and, derivatively, something proportionately less to those at lower skill levels. Almost formulaically, a standard scale of wages emerged in which the wage at each skill level was pegged lower than the wage at the next higher skill level. Thus, for example, in 1560 the Worcester Wage Assessment mandated:

> *All head artificers*, as master carpenter, free masons, rough masons, bricklayers, master tilers, plumbers, glaziers, carvers and joiners to have from Easter to Michaelmas *8d. the day without meat and drink, and 5d. the day with meat and drink;* and from Michaelmas to Easter but *6d. the day without meat and drink and 4d. the day with meat and drink.*
>
> *All other artificers* or *day labourers* to have from Easter to All Saints' Day *6d. the day without meat and drink, and 3d. the day with meat and drink;* and from All Saints' Day to

Easter *5d. the day without meat and drink and 2d. the day with meat and drink.*[27]

The second noteworthy feature of this traditional English system was that the distinctions among work taken for wages by the day, work taken on a piece rate or task basis, and work taken for a total bid (workman supplying the materials), which seem so significant to us, were not particularly significant then. For those who were setting the price of artisan work in earlier centuries, the objective was simply to regulate the price at which the skilled labor of common people was offered, whatever form that labor took. Hence the price of task and piecework, the price of total bid work, and the price of daywork were all normally set in the same assessments. Frequently, task work and work taken by the great (total bid) were performed by master artisans. From the perspective of the persons who were regulating artisan labor, however, it was not critical to make a sharp distinction between self-employed masters and those who worked for them. Their objective was simply to set the prices for artisan labor performed in different ways—by the day, by the task, or by the great, and at different skill levels—whether by self-employed master artisans or by their less skilled helpers.

In the seventeenth century, this English tradition had not completely died out in the American colonies, especially in New England. By taking a closer look at the terms of a Massachusetts wage-setting bill introduced into the General Court in 1670, but never enacted, we can get a better understanding of this traditional way of approaching the question of the prices of artisan labor.

		s.	d.
3.	*Carpenters and Masons and Stonelayers,* from 1 March to 10 of October	2—0 *per day*	
	and all worke taken by the great or peice by Carpenters, masons, joyners, or shinglers, is to be apportioned according to the equitie of the value of Daye's worke as above they dyeting themselves.		
4.	*Master Taylors,* and Such as are fully workmen of that Trade for *one daye's worke* of 12 hours.	1—8	
	Apprentices to that trade the first 4 yeares, *the like daye*	1—0	

> And all weavers for thier worke at 12
> hours per day, are to have the like
> wages as Taylors. . . .
> 7. No person shall pay, neither shall any
>   *Shoemaker receave, more than 5s. for*
>   *men's Shoes of elevens or twelves, nor*
>   *for women's Shoes of Seavens or Eights*
>   *more than 3s.-8d.*
>   And all bootes and shoes of other Sizes
>   proportionable to the rates
>   abovesaide . . . . [28]

By the eighteenth century, this kind of comprehensive price and wage setting was no longer being done for the most part in the colonies. Aside from a few necessaries such as bread, and outside of the licensed trades, prices and wages were no longer being set by the public authorities. As the constraints of traditional economy and society were relaxed in the eighteenth century, and as commercial activity increased, a new world was being brought into being. This new world, however, was shaped by tradition as much as by innovation.

Let us return, in light of this background, to the efforts of master artisans in the eighteenth century to set uniform prices for their work within various crafts. When the Boston barber/wigmakers publicly announced in 1724 that they were raising the prices for their work (see above), their implicit perspective was the mirror image of the one that had traditionally guided the public authorities in setting the price of artisan work. The barber/wigmakers adopted a posture in which they, as a body, were addressing the noncraft employers of craft labor. Their object was to set the prices customers would have to pay for artisan work in the craft whether that work involved producing a product (wig making) or performing a service (giving a shave). The powerful master carpenters of Philadelphia adopted a similar posture in their 1786 price book. The introduction to the price book was formulated as a statement by the carpenters addressed to noncraft employers, the "gentlemen" having houses built for them. The 1786 price book announced a new schedule of prices to be paid by these gentlemen for carpenter work.[29] It is indicative of the traditional position that self-employed master artisans continued to occupy in the eighteenth century that they frequently referred to their "customers" as "employers."[30]

In their attempts to establish uniform prices for artisan work, master artisans were in effect substituting themselves for the public authorities,[31] legislating the prices of artisan labor to be paid by non-craft employers. In that posture, master artisans spoke as self-appointed representatives of the craft community as a whole. Their efforts to establish prices for their work necessarily involved setting the entire schedule of prices for artisan work performed at different skill levels within the craft. Traditionally, the different prices for work performed in a particular craft at different skill levels were arrived at derivatively on the basis of the prices master artisans were paid for their work.[32] This kind of customary scale for artisan work differentiated by skill and responsibility level can be seen quite clearly operating among Philadelphia carpenters in the mideighteenth century. Roger Moss notes that

> when Carpenters' Company member William Dilworth was building St. Paul's Church in 1761 he kept detailed work records for each member of his crew and their rates of pay. As the supervising master on the site he credited himself 7s 6d per day. Samuel Rhoads, also a member of The Company and one of the most prominent men of his craft, received 7s, as did Frederick Trussey, Charles Finney and Samuel Hill—all master craftsmen. The Southwark carpenter Thomas Tresse, who was of less than average estate, was paid 5s per day and James Gibson, at this time quite young, 4s 6d. Interestingly, the "Negro Isaac" who, like Gibson, was always listed next to Dilworth's name and worked continuously on the job, was credited for the same 4s 6d. These rare accounts suggest several levels of skill and experience at work: the supervising master who was paid a premium, three other masters, a journeyman, an apprentice (James Gibson), and a Negro slave. The pay of the last two, of course, would have gone to Dilworth.[33]

Because, before the eighteenth century, wage and price setting had been a responsibility of government, part of what it meant to be governed was to have the price of your labor subject to governmental price setting. Government was cast as a kind of caretaker of the common people, responsible in theory for ensuring that labor was offered at a fair price and that the prices paid by laborers for necessaries were also fair. Obviously, when master artisans began to try to establish uniform prices for their work in various crafts, their objective was to keep the prices of artisan labor from being lowered by competition, to keep prices up rather than to keep them down, as government had often tried to do in the past. Obviously too, these artisans were operating in an increasingly freewheeling commercial environment. By substituting themselves for the public authorities and legislating the prices of their own work, however, they were exercising an important form of *self*-government. In these efforts, they had not completely lost sight of the ideals that motivated traditional governmental price setting. Announcing a new schedule of prices for carpenters' work in 1786, for example, Philadelphia master carpenters proclaimed that "the real intent and meaning of what hath been done is, that every gentleman concerned in building may have the value of his money, and that every workman may have the worth of his labour."[34]

If this picture of the eighteenth-century crafts is accurate, it means that journeymen remained in the same position they had traditionally occupied, the price of their labor still subject to regulation, although now by the masters who had assumed the government of the craft rather than by the public authorities. This power, of course, was not formal. Nevertheless, the masters did view their role proprietorially. They were the property owners in the craft, they had the greatest stake in it, and they were responsible for its welfare. They took upon themselves the task of establishing the prices for artisan work to be paid by noncraft employers. As they did so, they continued to treat their journeymen and apprentices as members of the craft who were, in a sense, included in the master artisans who bore responsibility for the craft and for them as subordinate members of the craft.[35] They treated their journeymen as propertyless people who were less than fully responsible persons.[36] By and large through most of the eighteenth century, journeymen had no organized voice in their crafts, no voice in the process of craft self-government. And with few exceptions, they played no organized role in that important aspect of self-government, setting the price of one's own labor.

THE IMPACT OF THE AMERICAN REVOLUTION

The revolutionary movement which began in the American colonies in the mid-1760s transformed the artisan communities of Boston, New York, and Philadelphia. As Bernard Bailyn has observed:

> In no obvious sense was the American Revolution undertaken as a social revolution. No one, that is, deliberately worked for the destruction or even the substantial alteration of the order of society as it had been known. Yet it was transformed as a result of the Revolution. . . .
>
> What did now affect the essentials of social organization— what in time would help permanently to transform them—were changes in the realm of belief and attitude. The views men held toward the relationships that bound them to each other—the discipline and pattern of society—moved in a new direction.[37]

In the wake of the Revolution, the tempo of artisan organizing accelerated sharply. Artisans began to find language to express their deeply felt dissatisfaction with their role as social "inferiors." Within artisan communities, master artisans developed a self-consciousness about their activities which they had not previously shown. For decades, they had acted de facto to try to place their trades under proper regulation. Now their activities began to be undertaken more aggressively. But the deepening feeling that all men were equals and all were entitled to have a say in the government of their world was not confined to master artisans. Journeymen too began to be transformed as a result of the revolutionary experience. Under the pressure of political and economic events, they began to think of themselves and to act as persons who were responsible for themselves and entitled to speak on their own behalf.

Edward Countryman writes that "the artisans present the clearest example of how the Revolution changed ordinary people, not just in Philadelphia, but in New York, Boston, and smaller towns as well." "In all three major cities," he observes, "the end of the 1760s saw independent artisan consciousness on the rise." When New York merchants asserted that they and they alone were entitled to make all decisions with respect to nonimportation, one of the city's mechanics could not contain his rage. Nothing, he said, could be "more flagrantly wrong than the assertion of some of our mercantile dons, that the Mechanics have no right to give their sentiments." In the end, Countryman concludes, "artisans not just in New York but all over the country [had been transformed]. Their experience of Revolution had convinced them that they had as much right as anyone to a voice in the governance of their world. Their experience of dispute with other Americans, of runaway inflation, and, in the war's aftermath, of depression had convinced them that only by asserting themselves could they get what they wanted."[38] By the 1780s, such habits of self-assertion and self-organization had led to a proliferation of voluntary societies in places like New York and Philadelphia which embodied practically every conceivable interest. Among these, organizations centered on occupational interests were not the least important.[39]

In the late 1780s and early 1790s, these habits of self-assertion and self-organization, which by this time journeymen as well as masters were cultivating, began to produce a level of conflict in the crafts that had not previously been seen. More frequently now, masters were forming semipermanent organizations by means of which they hoped to regulate their crafts. Among the important items on the agenda for this craft government were setting the prices customers were to pay for craft work and setting the wages to be paid to journeymen. Journeymen in turn began to form their own organizations by means of which they strove to protect their standard of living and to win a role as participants in the governance of the trade. Among the items on their agenda was legislating the prices of their own labor.

These journeyman and master organizations were commonly cast in a corporate form, even where they were not formally incorporated. The corporate form is well suited to the purposes of government. Typically in these organizations, the members at large were responsible for electing a chief officer and subordinate officers who conducted the affairs of the organization. The members were all bound to observe a set of articles or bylaws under which the organization operated. The officers of the organization were empowered to adjudicate disputes between members and to fine members who were in violation of any article, bylaw, or other ordinance. Article VII of the Carpenters' Company of Philadelphia, for example, published as part of the introduction to the company's 1786 price book, spelled out some of the details of this craft government:

> Article VII. Every member of this Company hereby engages, that he will not enter into or undertake work begun by any other member, until the first undertaker is satisfied for the work done, unless by his or their consent. Any member transgressing this article, and it being duly proved before the President and one or more of the Assistants and any five members, shall pay to the first undertaker such sum as they shall judge reasonable.[40]

When the master printers of Philadelphia formally organized in 1794, among the articles adopted was one authorizing the society "to regulate the prices [at] which its members shall execute printing work; to determine the terms of employing journeymen; to fix penalties for the violation of their regulations; and, in general, to adopt such rules as may be considered conducive to the prosperity of the printing business."[41]

Journeymen in many trades, however, were no longer willing to remain silent in the face of efforts by master artisans to regulate the crafts unilaterally. In many cases, journeymen were aware that their efforts to organize represented a novel departure. In an early clash between journeymen and masters in New York, for example, the journeymen modeled their statement of grievances on the Declaration of Independence. In Philadelphia in 1794, when journeymen and master cabinet- and chairmakers clashed, one of the first acts of the journeymen was to legislate the prices of their own work. In that year, they copyrighted and issued their own book of prices for journeyman work. The clerk of the district of Pennsylvania recorded that on "the thirteenth day of April, 1794, Thomas Timmings, Christopher Appleton, and John Gregory, have deposited in this office the title of a book, the right whereof they claim for themselves, and for and on behalf of the Federal Society of Chair Makers, as authors and proprietors, in the words following to wit, 'The Philadelphia Cabinet and Chair Makers' Book of Prices'." A two-year struggle ensued between journeymen and masters over government and self-government in the craft. In 1795, the journeymen issued a second edition of their price book, "corrected and enlarged." A month after issuing yet another book of prices in March 1796, the journeymen in an "Appeal to the Public" wrote that "in consequence of the rapid advance of price in every article of life, we found it necessary to our receiving even a bare support, *to raise the price of our work. Accordingly, with all that respect which is due from man to man, we submitted our New Book of Rates to our Employers for their perusal and approbation."*[42]

Eventually, the journeymen and master Philadelphia cabinet- and chairmakers reached an agreement. Apparently they arrived at terms close to those the journeymen had been demanding all along. And then they proceeded jointly to issue new legislation for the craft, a new book in which "the prices of Chairs, &c. &c. *have been fixed by us, mutually."* Three masters and three journeymen jointly signed the introductory statement. "This book," they agreed, "shall be the standard . . . by which *we will regulate the prices of our work."*[43]

In these ongoing conflicts over craft government, as each side acted to protect and advance its interests, the results jointly arrived at were determined less and less by traditional considerations of deference and obligation, and more and more by the relative power each could bring to bear against the other. As Americans turned their backs on the hierarchical order of traditional society, they created for themselves difficult choices among freedoms. As more and more people strove to assert rights of self-government in the economic realm as well as in the political, the inevitable clash of freedoms that ensued made choices necessary about whose freedom and whose self-government was to be chosen and whose sacrificed. These were precisely the choices presented in the early labor conspiracy cases as master artisans and journeymen struggled over alternative sets of legal rules for governing the terms on which they would be privileged to inflict injury on one another, terms that would affect each one's relative power of government and self-government in the market.

CHOOSING RULES FOR THE EXERCISE OF FREEDOM AND POWER

Both sides in the labor conspiracy cases were working out of a tradition in which the spheres of polity and economy were as yet not sharply distinguished. Both understood that the operation of markets posed questions of power and government as well as freedom. Both understood that the precepts of natural liberty provided no determinate resolution for their controversy, because what was involved was precisely a clash of liberties. Both understood that deliberate choices had to be made among different possible legal rules for governing their market transactions. And both understood that on this choice of one set of rules rather than another might well ride their effective ability to govern their own affairs.

In the *Philadelphia Cordwainers'* case of 1806, these understandings are laid out quite clearly. On the one hand, prosecutors argued, the journeymen were trying to establish what amounted to "private" government. They sought power not only to legislate rules for the trade, but to govern the people who worked in the trade, journeymen as well as masters. Count 3 of the indictment accused the journeymen of "deceitfully designing and intending to form and unite themselves into a club and combination, *and to make and ordain unlawful and arbitrary bye laws, rules and orders amongst themselves, and thereby to govern themselves and other artificers*, workmen and journeymen in the art and occupation of a cordwainer." In his opening statement for the prosecution Joseph Hopkinson went further. The journeyman society, he said, was

> merely a society for compelling by the most arbitrary and malignant means, the whole body of the journeymen to submit to their rules and regulations; it is not confined even to the members of the society, it reaches every individual of the trade, whether journeymen or master. . . . You will find that they not only determine the price of labour for themselves, but compel every one to demand that price and receive no other, they refuse to hold communion with any person who shall disobey there [sic] mandates, *in fine, they regulate the whole trade* under the most dreadful pains and penalties.

At a later stage of the argument, Hopkinson offered this summary of his position:

> Why a combination in such case is criminal, will not be difficult to explain: we live under a government composed of a con-

stitution and laws, . . . and every man is obliged to obey the constitution, and the laws made under it. . . . Do you feel your-selves bound to obey any other laws, enacted by any other legis-lature, than that of your own choice? Shall these, or any other body of men, associate for the purpose of making new laws, laws not made under the constitutional authority, and compel their fellow citizens to obey them, under the penalty of their existence?[44]

The lawyers for the journeymen also saw the issues presented by these cases in terms of power, government, and self-government, but they saw them in the opposite way. The thrust of their arguments was that if journeymen were prohibited from organizing, masters would be in a position unilaterally to set the price of their labor; to govern them. In his opening statement Walter Franklin developed this theme, defending the journeymen's association as a body that gave journey-men the power to set the price of their own labor. The journeymen, he argued,

thought they had a right to determine for themselves the value of their own labour! *and among other acts of their association, committed the unpardonable sin of settling and ascertaining the price of their own work!!!*

If this offence, against the master workmen were really an off-ence against the laws of their country, how were these journey-men to know it? they know, that their would-be-masters had united against them; they had set the example of combining, and confederating together. They had their meetings, and passed their resolutions; they had joined all their forces: *not for the purpose only of establishing the prices of their own goods; but also, for the purpose of determining the rate, at which the jour-neymen should work. They assumed the right of limiting those whom they employed, at all times, and under all circum-stances . . . without consulting the interests, or wishes of the workmen, or permitting them to have a voice upon the ques-tion.*

To this state of slavish subordination, the journeymen re-fused to submit. They conceived that every man being the sole owner, and master of his own goods and labour, had a right to affix the price of them; leaving to those who were to employ or purchase, the right to accept or reject as they might think proper.[45]

The lawyers for the journeymen stressed that adoption of a legal rule that prohibited journeymen from organizing would be tantamount to giving masters the legal authority to set the price of journeyman labor: "Neither custom nor law, has fixed the price of this or any other kind of work. Has the master then the sole right of determining the wages which are to be given for the labour of his journeymen? This would be too arbitrary a power for any man to contend for." Speaking for the journeymen, Caesar Rodney felt certain that in choosing between one legal rule and another, the law was making a choice between authorizing masters and authorizing journeymen themselves to legislate the price of journeyman labor. When the prosecutors ask you to convict the journeymen in this case, he argued to the jury,

> ought they not to produce some new act of the legislature regulating the wages of labourers, and fixing the maximum and minimum. . . . This is out of their power, and they now press you to usurp legislative authority and to enact the law yourselves. . . .
>
> I must confess, if prices are to be regulated, the legislative body should perform the task, and let us see what political doctors will undertake it. I hope, if they fix the wages of journeymen, they will settle the rent of every house in town, and every farm in the country; that they will establish permanently, the price of coffee, tea, sugars and salt; set a value on all dry goods, particularly boots and shoes which will bear a reduction, and then enter the market to reduce, beef, eggs, and butter, &c. to a proper standard![46]

On these things the journeymen cordwainers and their lawyers agreed. The journeymen's attitudes reflected a traditional perspective in which the central issue was: Where would the authority lie to set the price of journeyman labor? Would social "superiors" be authorized by law to continue to govern as before, among other ways by unilaterally setting the price of labor? Or would the Revolution's promise that all men were equal and entitled to govern themselves be translated into legal rules that authorized journeymen to form their own societies to participate in the government of their trades, including that supremely important aspect of self-government, setting the price of their own labor? In an "Address of the Working Shoemakers of the City of Philadelphia, to the Public," published shortly before the conspiracy prosecution began, the journeymen cordwainers made their position clear:

> In the constitution of this state, it is declared . . . "that citizens have a right in a peaceable manner to assemble together for the

common good." For fifteen years and upwards we have assembled together in a peaceable manner and for our common good . . . to promote the happiness of the individuals of which our little community is composed. . . .

It is notorious that for many years back the working shoemakers have been associated and peaceably assembled together, and . . . have regulated the wages which they ought to accept for their labor. It is notorious that the retailing or shopkeeping shoemakers have also had and now have a similar association in which they have regulated the prices for which they sell goods to the public.

In both these cases we think the parties are justified and correct; because every man being the sole owner and master of his labor and of his property, has the right to affix the price of his own labor or his own property. . . . it is not to us a matter to be submitted to, that because we are working men, that our labor is to be paid for not as we estimate it, but at the will of another person.[47]

In many respects, however, their position was not traditional but represented a radical reshaping of tradition. Journeymen aimed to democratize price setting. All men now were to have principal authority for placing prices on their own property. That authority was no longer to reside in government, either public or private, but in self-governing property owners themselves. The labor of journeymen was their property, and as independent property owners, they were the ones who were entitled to set a price for it. The aims of this democratic price setting, moreover, were subtly different. Prices were no longer primarily to be established with an eye toward providing quality goods at fair prices to the larger community. Instead, journeymen assembled together in a peaceable manner, they announced, "for *our* common good [and] to promote the happiness of the individuals of which *our* little community is composed." And they expected that other individuals such as the master shoemakers would do the same—work to promote the happiness of the individuals of *their* little communities by establishing the prices of *their* property. Journeymen understood that if price setting was to be democratized, power would have to be more widely distributed. A legal rule that prohibited or restricted their associations would cut off any hope they might have of exercising such power. They viewed this version of the market as an advance over traditional hierarchical arrangements and feared the competing version as little more than a reimposition of those arrangements.

These journeymen, however, continued to operate from a traditional perspective in the sense that they did not distinguish very clearly between legal authority and economic power. At least in part, they viewed the adoption of a rule giving them the legal privilege to form journeyman societies in traditional terms, as a kind of official recognition of corporate privileges. They saw the power such a rule would give them as a direct legal grant, authorizing them to establish societies to set the prices of their labor. And they imagined that implementing this rule would produce markets in skilled urban labor with a distinctly corporatist tone—master and journeyman societies each setting the prices of their own property. Journeymen understood that the legal rule they were contending for would give them economic leverage. But they did not view the formal legal privilege to establish societies, on the one hand, and the economic power that might flow from this legal privilege under certain market conditions, on the other, as partially distinct phenomena. Legal privilege and economic power, in their minds, were largely identical.

The lawyers who represented them, however, held somewhat different views. Throughout their arguments, these lawyers drew on traditional ideas that emphasized the organic connections between law, polity, and economy. They also made use, however, of a newer strain of discourse to which the journeymen themselves may not have subscribed.[48] At times, these lawyers invoked laissez-faire arguments that portrayed the market as a sphere of natural exchange unconnected to law and politics.

The laissez-faire perspective of lawyers for the journeymen may have helped them to see more clearly than the journeymen themselves that what was at stake in the choice of legal rules in these cases was relative market power, not the absolute power of self-government. The power that market actors can bring to bear in any situation depends upon a multitude of circumstances, not upon the choice of a single legal rule. Market power depends not only upon the numerous legal rules that create the framework for market transactions, but upon innumerable other circumstances as well: the supply and demand of labor, the availability of unsettled land, and so forth. The lawyers for the journeymen seem to have had a clearer sense of these things. Walter Franklin noted that "the real value of labour, in a country, must depend upon a variety of circumstances, which neither the master or his journeymen can in any way controul." Caesar Rodney put the matter more directly. "Let [the journeymen] ask as freely as they breathe the air, wages for their services. No person is compelled to give them more than their work is worth, the market will sufficiently and correctly regulate these matters."[49] What these lawyers missed when they made their laissez-faire arguments, nevertheless, was what they correctly asserted when they made their more traditional arguments. The "market" is not governed by circumstance alone but in critical ways is a creature of the legal rules that together give it one form rather than another. And certain of these rules play especially strategic roles in the distribution of power in markets. Legal rules allowing or disallowing labor organization fall squarely into this category.

CONCLUSION

Many of the early labor conspiracy cases went against the journeymen.[50] Those outcomes represented decisions to increase the relative power masters could legally exercise in the "free" market for artisanal wage labor. They represented decisions to give masters greater powers of government and self-government at the expense of journeymen. Those decisions left journeymen free only to withhold their labor as individuals and prohibited their efforts to establish their own associations for self-government. They represented decisions to sanction one legal form of a "free" market in labor, an individualist one, and to reject another possible legal form, one that embodied a more corporatist cast.

That it is necessary to work so hard to recover the sense contemporaries had that these cases posed complex questions of government, that economic questions may also be questions of government, is testimony to the power laissez-faire conceptions have silently exerted on our way of seeing markets. A reading of the labor conspiracy cases provides a useful corrective, showing "free" markets to be the product in part of deliberate legal choices and to pose crucial questions about the exercise of power by some persons over other persons. At bottom, a reading of these cases brings into focus again the fundamental political question that has been almost completely obscured in recent times in the rush to celebrate the freedom of "free" markets: what kinds of legal arrangements are necessary if the propertyless are to have real hope of enjoying the promise of our system that all persons shall be free and self-governing?

NOTES

Epigraph: Robert Hale, "Coercion and Distribution in a Supposedly Noncoercive State," *Political Science Quarterly* 38 (1923): 478.

1. Dawson 1947: 266. More recently, Duncan Kennedy has pushed this analysis further. See, for example, Kennedy 1985 and 1989.

2. Commons 1910–11, 3: 178.

3. Tomlins 1985: 35–43; Rock 1979: 279–84; Wilentz 1984b: 61–103.

4. Bailyn 1967: 302–3.

5. Crowley 1974: 111 (quoting from the *Virginia Gazette*, 2 March 1739).

6. Brody 1989b: 16–17; Bridenbaugh 1950: 125–29. Rural craftsmen were common and frequently plied their trades part time while they also farmed. Itinerant craftsmen who traveled through the countryside offering their services to inhabitants were also common. Construction craftsmen frequently worked on site, etc.

7. See, for example, Morgan 1966: 142–50; Fischer 1989: 279–80.

8. Nash 1979: 258–59.

9. Beales 1989: 132.

10. Salinger 1987: 65–66; Bridenbaugh 1950: 129. The line between small master and journeyman in the colonies was often indistinct. Nevertheless, a number of scholars have recently concluded that journeymen were not as rare in the eighteenth century, particularly in the large towns, as had once been supposed. Barbara Ward, for example, reports that there is solid "evidence that journeymen goldsmiths existed in considerable numbers in Boston between 1690 and 1730." See Ward 1984: 142. Billy G. Smith has found that during the two decades before the Revolution journeymen made up between 30 and 40 percent of cordwainers and tailors in Philadelphia. See B. G. Smith 1981: 197, 200; 1990: 139–40. Journeymen made up a similar proportion of Philadelphia printers. Brody 1989b: 13. By the 1760s, journeymen possibly constituted as many as 55 percent of all Philadelphia carpenters. Moss 1972: 135–40.

11. Salinger 1987: 67. See also 65–69.

12. Dawley 1976: 18–19, 61; Brody 1989b: 17.

13. Steinfeld 1991: chap. 2.

14. Moss 1972: 144; Benson 1937, 1: 204.

15. Dalton 1682: 129; Burn 1785, 4: 128; see also Kussmaul 1981: 32.

16. Nash 1979: 258–59. See also Moss 1972: 144–46.

17. Nash 1979: 258–59.

18. R. B. Morris 1981: 139–41.

19. On the persistence of a moral economy through the eighteenth century, see Countryman 1985: 29, 78; 1981: 56–57, 182.

20. Nash 1979: 32.

21. Moss 1972: 90, 185; R. B. Morris 1981: 142.

22. R. B. Morris 1981: 143–44.

23. C. F. Montgomery 1966: 20.

24. Ibid., 19.

25. Quoted in R. B. Morris 1981: 195.

26. Bridenbaugh 1950: 145.

27. Reproduced as Appendix I in Woodward 1980: 43 [emphasis added].

28. Reproduced in R. B. Morris 1981: 65–66 [emphasis added].

29. Peterson 1971: vi.

30. Hall 1954: 47 n. 89.

31. Wage rates had traditionally been set in England in two basic ways. In certain periods, they were established by statute or ordinance. At other times, they were assessed by justices of the peace in the counties or by local magistrates in towns on an annual basis. Not infrequently, these officials con-

sulted with prominent members of the crafts in the process of establishing rates. See, for example, Alford and Barker 1968: 18, 35.

32. Brody 1989b: 40–41.

33. Moss 1972: 152–53.

34. Peterson 1971: vii.

35. Foner 1976: 39; Wilentz 1984b: 41.

36. Brody 1989b: 14–15.

37. Bailyn 1967: 302.

38. Countryman 1985: 219–20, 225.

39. Countryman 1981: 293–94; see also Appleby 1978: 64–78.

40. Peterson 1971: x–xi.

41. Quoted in R. B. Morris 1981: 202 n. 40.

42. C. F. Montgomery 1966: 21–23 [emphasis added].

43. Ibid., 23, 24 [emphasis added].

44. Commons 1910–11, 3: 66, 69–70, 135 [emphasis added].

45. Ibid., 110–11 [emphasis added].

46. Ibid., 144, 201.

47. "Address to the Public," printed in the *Philadelphia Aurora*, 28 November 1805.

48. On the differences in the positions of journeymen and their lawyers, see Twomey 1989: 193–13; Twomey 1984: 290–92.

49. Commons 1910–11, 3:144–45, 180.

50. Journeymen, however, did prevail in a number of the early prosecutions. See Wilentz 1983; and Tomlins 1987.

2 Courts and the Question of Class: Judicial Regulation of Labor under the Common Law Doctrine of Criminal Conspiracy

Victoria C. Hattam

Surveying the broad panorama of nineteenth-century labor history, we find that one of the most striking features of the American case is the dominance of the judiciary in regulating industrial conflict. Governments in almost all advanced industrial societies sought to contain workers' collective action during the nineteenth century, but only the United States relied so heavily on the courts to implement its policy.[1] For most of the nineteenth century the principal legal doctrine for regulating strikes was the common law doctrine of criminal conspiracy. In order to explore the impact of the conspiracy prosecutions on working-class formation I have examined state-labor relations in New York and Pennsylvania for almost a century, from 1806 to 1896. The conspiracy cases were by no means limited to these two states; nevertheless, we can begin to decipher the significance of judicial regulation for American labor through a detailed investigation of these early industrializing states.[2] Two arguments are developed here. First, I advance a new interpretation of the conspiracy doctrine in which both the periodization and the nature of the labor cases are reevaluated. Second, I argue that the conspiracy convictions shaped working-class formation in the United States, but only after the Civil War and in ways more subtle and indirect than previous scholars have allowed. Before exploring the impact of judicial regulation on American labor, however, I must first lay out the basic elements of the doctrine and clear up some common misperceptions in existing accounts of labor conspiracy.

THE CONSPIRACY DOCTRINE AND AMERICAN LABOR

Throughout most of the nineteenth century the conspiracy doctrine set the terms of negotiation between labor and capital by determining whether or not workers would be permitted to organize and by establishing which tactics were legitimate weapons for workers to use during industrial disputes. Definitions of the conspiracy doctrine were notoriously vague and were the subject of much debate among legal scholars during the eighteenth and nineteenth centuries. Despite this uncertainty, some central elements of the doctrine can be identified. In essence, the conspiracy doctrine considered almost all collective action so dangerous that combination alone transformed otherwise unlawful or even immoral actions into criminal offenses. Serjeant Hawkins captured the expansive aspects of the doctrine nicely in his *Pleas of the Crown* (1716): "There can be no doubt, but that all confederacies, whatsoever, wrongfully to prejudice a third person are highly criminal at common law."[3] Unlike most crimes, execution of the deed was not required to sustain the charge: combination in itself was considered "the gist of the offence, though nothing be done in pursuance of it."[4] Enacting the plan devised by the confederacy aggravated the crime but was not necessary for conviction.

Conspiracy charges did not originate with workers' combinations but rather were used first in England during the fifteenth century in cases involving the obstruction of justice. The doctrine was extended in the seventeenth century to cover conspiracies to cheat and defraud and conspiracies in restraint of trade. It was not until the eighteenth century that workers were brought before the courts for acting collectively. Similarly in the United States, conspiracy was never limited to labor cases but was applied to a wide range of offenses including conspiracies to cheat and defraud, conspiracies against public policy, conspiracies against the government, and conspiracies against individual rights and property. Thus, workingmen's assemblies in both England and the United States were only one instance of a much larger group of collectivities that were subject to criminal prosecution under the common law.[5]

Standard accounts of the labor conspiracy cases have been dominated by two characteristics. First, most accounts of American labor law divide the nineteenth century into two periods. The conspiracy doctrine is said to have prevailed in the antebellum decades from 1806 until 1842, when the landmark case of *Commonwealth v. Hunt* is thought to have put an end to the conspiracy convictions. Adoption of the labor injunction in the mid-1880s is supposed to have signaled

the next era of American labor law, which continued through passage
of the Norris-LaGuardia Act in 1932. Thus, traditional accounts of
American labor law limit the conspiracy doctrine to the antebellum
era and generally ignore the middle decades of the nineteenth century
as they jump directly from *Hunt* to the labor injunction.[6]

The second major claim of legal historians has been to stress the
class bias inherent in the conspiracy convictions. For many scholars,
the antebellum conspiracy cases revealed the courts' hostility toward
American workers. By preventing workers from organizing, so the argument runs, the courts sided with capital in the class struggle.[7] One
of the clearest examples of a class analysis has been presented by Wythe
Holt, who concluded his discussion of conspiracy claiming: "It is important to recognize that the law rarely recognizes the point of view
of the worker. Class bias does exist in the law."[8] The class bias of the
courts can be seen, several scholars claim, in three aspects of the
antebellum conspiracy trials. First, several antebellum judges revealed
their class allegiance by adopting the rhetoric and arguments of prosecution attorneys in their charges to the juries. In so doing, judges
identified with and protected the entrepreneurial property rights of
employers over the economic interests of the working class. Second,
several scholars look to workingmen's protest against the antebellum
convictions as further evidence that participants themselves believed
the convictions to be inequitable and unjust. The New York protest
against decisions in *People v. Fisher* and *People v. Faulkner* figures
prominently in these interpretations. At the height of the workingmen's protest in 1836, a crowd of twenty-five thousand gathered in
the park, burnt effigies of Judges Savage and Edwards, and called for
creation of their own political party. Workers, so it is argued, understood all too well the class bias of the courts. Finally, some scholars
have claimed that judicial bias can be seen most easily when we compare nineteenth-century corporation and labor law. The courts did not
oppose all forms of collective action but were concerned only with
preventing workers from organizing. They allowed employers to act
collectively under nineteenth-century corporation law.[9]

Although existing accounts of the conspiracy cases have enabled
us to see how the antebellum trials grew out of the increased class
conflict that accompanied the early stages of industrialization, I believe
these interpretations have presented too narrow a view of the cases
and have obscured other issues that were being negotiated in the conspiracy trials. Increased tension between master craftsmen and their
journeymen certainly played a role in bringing these disputes before
the state courts.[10] However, it is a mistake to assume that containing
class conflict was the only, or even the principal, issue motivating

judicial decisions in the conspiracy trials. By relegating conspiracy to the antebellum era and by focusing almost exclusively on questions of class, traditional accounts have misconstrued the conspiracy doctrine and have misunderstood its significance for American labor. In order to develop a more complete account of conspiracy we must look anew at judicial regulation in the years between *Hunt* and the labor injunction, as well as examine the class analysis more carefully by considering alternative explanations of judicial behavior.

A note of clarification is required before I begin my interpretation in detail. I use the term "class analysis" throughout this essay to refer to the prevailing view of nineteenth-century labor law, the defining characteristics of which are twofold. First, these accounts consider the principal social conflict, even in the very early decades of the nineteenth century, to have centered around division between labor and capital, or workers and employers. Second, the principal focus of the class analysis generally has been to identify both the extent to which and the means by which courts structured the struggle between these contending forces. By referring to class analysis in this way I by no means wish to imply that alternative explanations have abandoned social relations altogether; indeed, the explanation developed in the remainder of the essay also considers the social context of legal doctrine and decisions to be critical, but finds the relevant social relations in the early nineteenth century to lie elsewhere than in conflicts between labor and capital. Instead, I will contend that judicial regulation of labor in the antebellum decades was influenced primarily by the preceding economic and political concerns of how to maintain a healthy republic in the aftermath of the Revolution and political independence.

RETHINKING THE ANTEBELLUM CONSPIRACY CASES

When we turn to the neglected middle decades of the nineteenth century it becomes clear that the conspiracy convictions did not cease with the landmark case of *Commonwealth v. Hunt* but were revived with a vengeance after the Civil War. From 1865 through the 1890s, district attorneys in New York and Pennsylvania continued to charge striking workers with conspiracy. Unfortunately, it is difficult to gauge the full extent of postwar cases as many trials were not included in the official law reports. Nevertheless, the major New York and Pennsylvania cases can be identified through newspapers and state bureaus of industrial statistics. Clearly, the earlier *Hunt* victory by no means put an end to the labor conspiracies: state courts continued to convict workers in the postbellum trials and, if anything, imposed harsher sentences than had been handed down in the antebellum decades. Workers were fined more heavily and were frequently sentenced to jail for several months and in a few cases years of hard labor.[11]

The postwar conspiracy convictions suggest that the periodization of nineteenth-century labor law needs to be redrawn. Rather than skipping directly from *Hunt* to the labor injunction, we must distinguish *two waves* of conspiracy convictions and three eras of nineteenth-century labor law. The first era continues to encompass the early conspiracy trials, which lasted from 1806 through 1842. A new second era of conspiracy convictions now must be recognized on the basis of the resurgence of conspiracy prosecutions in the three decades following the Civil War. The shift in legal remedy from conspiracy to the labor injunction in the 1880s marks the beginning of the third era of nineteenth-century labor law, which continues through to passage of the Norris-LaGuardia Act in 1932. The second wave of convictions, we will see at the end of the paper, played an important role in shaping labor strategy in the United States. However, before turning to the late nineteenth-century cases, we must first reconsider the initial wave of conspiracy trials before the Civil War.[12]

Although it is tempting to link workingmen's protest of the 1820s and 1830s with judicial regulation of labor and to assert an antagonistic relationship between labor and the courts, I have found the prevailing class analysis to be inadequate and in need of review. Moreover, several aspects of the early conspiracy trials have not been adequately addressed to date. Elaborating criticisms of all three claims concerning judicial rhetoric, workingmen's protest, and corporate regulation helps clear the ground for a new interpretation of the antebellum conspiracy trials.

When charging juries in the antebellum trials, several judges indeed noted that striking journeymen were disrupting trade and manufacturing of their cities and as a consequence ought to be convicted of conspiracy.[13] The judges' progrowth language, however, tells us little or nothing about the class allegiance of the courts. Workingmen, after all, had no desire to ruin trade or to turn back the clock to some preindustrial age. On the contrary, they too hoped to benefit from the increased production that accompanied industrialization. The matter before the courts was not whether to promote or halt growth, but rather to establish on whose terms economic change was to proceed. The judges' language in the early trials, I will argue, was not simply the language of employers, but rather was shaped primarily by longstanding eighteenth-century conceptions of political and economic relations. When analyzed in light of this republican world view, we will see, the judges' remarks take on quite a different significance than as a signal of the courts' class bias.

Even though workers protested conviction of the twenty journeymen tailors in the case of *People v. Faulkner* in 1836 and identified both Judges Savage and Edwards as hostile to their interests, this particular protest against the courts was more an aberration than the general rule. In fact, there is little evidence that workers contested the earlier convictions. To be sure, periodic complaints were voiced against the conspiracy trials, but generally workers did not challenge the conspiracy convictions before 1835 and showed little interest in the major antebellum movement for legal reform, namely the codification movement of the 1820s to the 1840s.[14] Moreover, when workingmen organized labor unions and political parties in the 1820s and 1830s they rarely mentioned the conspiracy convictions and did not make repeal of the doctrine a high priority. In fact, one gets very little sense from reading the platforms and proceedings of their organizations that the conspiracy trials had taken place at all. Instead of remonstrating against judges and the courts, antebellum Working Men's parties and General Trades Unions called for education and financial reform, strongly opposed rechartering the national bank, and demanded a reduction in hours of labor and abolition of imprisonment for debt and convict labor. Protesting the conspiracy convictions and demanding repeal of the doctrine simply were not major preoccupations of most workingmen's associations before the Civil War.[15]

The claim that the courts treated labor combinations more harshly than corporations also needs to be reevaluated. To be sure, employers' combinations rarely were subject to prosecution for conspiracy and thus generally escaped the criminal arm of the law.[16] Nevertheless, it is a mistake to jump to claims of judicial bias on the basis of unequal application of the conspiracy doctrine alone. After all, employers' combinations were by no means exempt from government regulation altogether; legislative charters and the doctrine of *ultra vires* rather than conspiracy were the principal legal remedies used to contain combinations of capital before the Civil War. In the late nineteenth century, after the *Santa Clara* decision in 1886, in which the Supreme Court recognized the corporation as a person, claims of unequal treatment of labor and capital have more force. In the first half of the century, however, both workingmen's and employers' combinations were considered to be unhealthy developments that endangered the republic and as such required special regulation by the state.[17]

Claims about the especially harsh treatment of labor unions by the courts are undermined further when we look beyond the labor cases to nonlabor conspiracy trials. If we are to determine whether labor was treated unfairly by the courts, it is useful to see how other combinations fared in the hands of state courts. What we find is that all kinds of combinations, including combinations to slander, to cheat and defraud, and to restrain trade, also were subject to prosecution under the conspiracy doctrine. The doctrine was by no means reserved exclusively for workingmen's associations but rather was applied to a number of quite different combinations, all of which were treated similarly by the courts. Interestingly, several late nineteenth-century legal commentators also bemoaned the unequal treatment of workers and employers under the conspiracy law, but from their perspective it was the unusually *favorable* treatment of labor combinations that needed to be explained and reformed.[18]

Finally, a class analysis of antebellum conspiracy cases does not capture several important aspects of the antebellum conspiracy trials. The imposition of light penalties in the early labor cases, for example, does not fit easily into a class analysis of the courts. Even though most conspiracy cases ended in conviction, no antebellum workers were sentenced to jail and fines generally ranged from $1 to $10 plus costs of the suit. An important exception again was the case of *People v. Faulkner*, in which Judge Edwards fined the New York tailors $1,150. In all other antebellum conspiracy convictions identified to date, however, fines remained less than $10. To be sure, in real terms these penalties were equivalent to approximately one to seven days' wages for many skilled workers and thus should not be dismissed as trivial.[19] Nevertheless, workers were not deterred from organizing by the antebellum convictions and often resumed their collective protests quite quickly. Why did judges hand down such light penalties in these early trials? If the courts' main objective had been to contain working-class organization, a more effective strategy would have been to impose heavier fines and jail terms on convicted workers, yet neither the New York or Pennsylvania courts adopted this strategy. We will see that an alternative analysis of the antebellum conspiracy cases which places less emphasis on working-class protest enables us to make better sense of the light penalties imposed by the courts in the antebellum era.

When reading the antebellum trials I was struck by the recurrence of a number of different themes that have been largely ignored by previous scholars. I did not find judges and attorneys trying to contain class conflict by convicting workers of conspiracy. Rather, they were preoccupied with two very different issues: how to maintain judicial authority in the wake of the Revolution, and how to sustain economic growth in line with republican precepts. By attending more closely to these neglected aspects of the conspiracy cases, I have constructed an alternative interpretation of these early prosecutions and their significance for American labor.

AN ALTERNATIVE EXPLANATION: JUDICIAL AUTHORITY AND REPUBLICAN GROWTH

In the very early cases decided in the first two decades of the nineteenth century, judges and attorneys alike made frequent reference to the American Revolution and its impact on the continuity of common law.[20] Political independence had raised a number of awkward questions about the nature and extent of judicial power in the new republic: Should American courts continue to rely on English precedents or develop instead their own tradition of American law? If legal doctrine was no longer to be founded on natural law, what was to be the basis of judicial authority in the new republic? In short, how were state courts to reconcile the Revolution and the common law?

Conspiracy cases, in particular, brought questions of judicial authority to a head because of their status as common law crimes. It was not necessary, many treatise writers and practitioners agreed, for defendants in conspiracy cases to have violated statute law; conviction could be sustained at common law.[21] Thus, conspiracy cases provided an excellent opportunity for critics of the common law to question the natural law foundations of judicial authority and to argue that a democratic republic ought to make the courts more accountable to the polis. By convicting striking workers of conspiracy, state courts followed English precedent and sent a clear signal of legal continuity despite political independence. Acquittal, on the other hand, opened up a Pandora's box of questions of judicial accountability that many lawyers were anxious to keep tightly closed.[22]

One of the first labor conspiracy cases in the United States, *Commonwealth v. Pullis* (1806), provides an excellent place to begin a reevaluation of the antebellum trials; many themes in addition to class conflict can be seen in this well-recorded trial.[23] George Pullis and seven other cordwainers (shoemakers) appeared before the Philadelphia Mayor's Court under indictment for combining and conspiring to raise their wages. Recorder Moses Levy presided at the trial and early in his charge to the jury raised the question of how to sustain the common law in the wake of the Revolution. Levy put the issue in the following terms:

> An attempt has been made to shew that the spirit of the revolution and the principle of the common law, are opposite in this case. That the common law if applied in this case, would oper-

ate an attack upon the rights of man. The enquiry on that
point, was unnecessary and improper. Nothing more was required than to ascertain what the law is. The law is the permanent rule, it is the will of the whole community. After that is
discovered, whatever may be its spirit or tendency, it must be
executed, and the most imperious duty demands our submission to it.[24]

Despite Levy's protestations, whether or not the common law
remained the "will of the whole community," or what the relevant
community boundaries were, was not at all clear in the postrevolutionary era. The difficult question raised by the Philadelphia Cordwainers' trial was whether the new political community in fact could
be reconciled with the older unity of the common law.

When discussing the conspiracy doctrine directly, Levy again
stressed the continuing authority of the common law, saying, "If the
rule [of law] be clear, we are bound to conform to it even though we
do not comprehend the principle upon which it is founded. We are not
to reject it because we do not see the reason of it. . . . But the rule in
this case is pregnant with sound sense and all the authorities are clear
upon the subject."[25] By asserting the continuity of common law, Levy
was able to claim that the American courts ought to follow the English
precedents. However, his inability to articulate "the reason" behind
the doctrine left the Cordwainers' conviction on precarious ground.
Without a clear definition of the offense, it was impossible to distinguish lawful and criminal combinations with any consistency. The
courts were left open to charges of judicial arbitrariness and mind-
less adherence to English law—a dubious honor in the postrevolutionary era.

The courts' concern with maintaining the common law in the
aftermath of the Revolution was raised explicitly in the nonlabor conspiracy cases as well. For example, in one of the leading cases of conspiracy to cheat and defraud, *State v. Buchanan*, the Maryland judge
declared, "If the political connection between this and the mother
country had never been dissolved, the expression of a doubt would not
now be hazarded on the question, whether the same law was in force
here."[26] But the political connection with England had been severed,
and the question of whether or not English law was in force in Maryland had been raised. As in the labor cases, the Maryland Court of
Appeals upheld the common law, reversed the lower court dismissal,
and ordered a new trial.

Although many of the antebellum conspiracy cases refer directly
to the Revolution and independence, the pervasiveness of questions

of judicial authority is not captured in these remarks alone. On the contrary, it is important to recognize that the entire debate that dominated the antebellum conspiracy trials over the origins of the English convictions was at bottom a debate over how best to ground American law. Each of the antebellum conspiracy trials rehearsed similar legal arguments over whether the English cases had been statutory or common law crimes. Defense attorneys generally claimed that American workers should not be subject to conspiracy prosecutions because the English precedents had rested on specific English statutes that were not in force in the United States. Given the defense counsels' emphasis on the importance of acknowledging the statutory origins of the English precedents, it is not surprising to find that two leading codification reformers, William Sampson and Robert Rantoul, Jr., acted as defense counsel in subsequent conspiracy trials.[27] In contrast, prosecution attorneys such as Jared Ingersoll and Joseph Hopkinson disagreed and claimed that English convictions had been sustained at common law. As a consequence, if the common law was to remain in force in the new republic, then English precedents must be followed and the defendants convicted of criminal conspiracy.[28]

Placing the question of judicial authority center stage provides a new perspective on the light penalties handed down by the courts in the antebellum labor trials. If the courts had been primarily concerned with working-class organization, then conviction *plus* heavy fines would have been the most effective strategy for deterring subsequent working-class organization. However, conviction alone was sufficient to ensure the continuity of the common law. Whatever the penalty, conviction itself confirmed English precedent as viable authority within the American legal system and thereby maintained the natural law foundation of American law. Heavy fines were not needed to solve the legal problem raised by the conspiracy trials before the Civil War and, indeed, might have provoked greater opposition to the courts' rulings. Thus, the light penalties signal the greater weight accorded to questions of judicial authority over questions of class in the antebellum decades.

Although many judges and attorneys clearly wanted to maintain the continuity of common law, state courts were by no means isolated from the pressing economic issues of the day. In fact, judges and attorneys often referred to the economic changes taking place and stressed the importance of maintaining a flourishing trade in their cities. In addition, when charging juries in the early trials, several judges pointed explicitly to the destructive impact of workingmen's combinations on manufacturing and trade as grounds for convicting the defendants of criminal conspiracy.[29] Previous scholars, we have seen, argued that by promoting economic growth the courts protected employers' economic interests while denying workingmen an effective voice in the future course of industrialization.[30] If we look more closely at the discussions of economic issues in these early trials, paying particular attention to the language and categories used to understand the changes underway, we see the antebellum judges' views in a new light.

When discussing questions of economic growth, judges generally did not present these issues in terms of market competition, individual interest, and private gain. Instead, economic growth was viewed as a public good and an integral component of "public welfare." In order to protect the interests of the community at large the courts had to halt unhealthy accumulations of economic and political power and maintain a well-balanced pattern of economic growth. In *Commonwealth v. Morrow*, for example, Judge Roberts claimed that workingmen's combinations ought to be considered indictable offenses because they restrained trade, created unhealthy monopolies, and as a consequence were "prejudicial to the public."[31] Interestingly, Judge Roberts explicitly instructed the jury not to view this case simply as a struggle between employers and their journeymen, but rather to consider it in broader terms. Roberts cautioned the jury as follows:

> In the investigation of subjects like that now presented to the court and jury, the mind is easily misled. We naturally look at the contending parties—here we see on the one hand, a number of journeymen, whom we are led to regard as poor men, opposed to their employers, some of whom are represented as wealthy. The human mind spontaneously revolts at the idea of oppression; and the attention of the jury is invariably drawn to this point; as if the true question were, whether the journeymen were the oppressed, and the masters the oppressors— whether the profits of the one class be not too great, and the remuneration of the other inadequate.
>
> But it would be taking a very contracted, and by no means a just view of this case, to consider it as a controversy between the employers and the journeymen. And your time would be very unprofitably employed, in calculating the respective profits of one or the other. With the regulations of wages, or the profit of one or the other, you have nothing to do.[32]

Instead of being "misled" by the immediate conflict between employers and their journeymen, Roberts recommended that the jury look beyond the contending parties to the larger interests of the Pittsburgh community. Roberts continued: "It is not for demanding high prices that these men are indicted, but for employing unlawful means to extort those prices. For using means prejudicial to the community. Confederacies of this kind have a most pernicious effect, as respects the community at large."[33]

Even in *People v. Fisher* and the twenty journeymen tailors' case, both of which have been viewed by previous scholars as prime examples of judicial bias, there is considerable evidence that Judges Savage and Edwards continued to stress the public dimension of the conflicts at hand. Chief Justice Savage, for example, described the New York cordwainers' combination as "a monopoly of the most odious kind" which interfered with trade and commerce by "artificial means" and as such was injurious "not only to the individual particularly oppressed, but to the public at large."[34] Similarly, when charging the jury for the twenty journeymen tailors, Judge Edwards, like Roberts before him, urged them to view the dispute as more than a struggle between masters and journeymen: "The Court would again impress upon the minds of the jury that the present question was not to be considered a mere struggle between the masters and journeymen. It was one upon which the harmony of the whole community depended."[35]

To be sure, Judge Edwards's adherence to the collectivist vision was more ambivalent than that of his colleagues in earlier trials. Indeed, several of his remarks indicate greater awareness of the increased "excitement" that accompanied workingmen's combinations in 1835 and 1836.[36] However, references to the danger of workers' increased power did not yet dominate the judges' remarks, but rather remained a minor refrain in a discourse that continued to judge economic behavior by a set of community standards and moral norms that was quite different from notions of self-interest and market competition that came to dominate views of economic relations after the Civil War.[37]

THE POST–CIVIL WAR CASES: A TELLING COMPARISON

For many readers, the language of "community" and "public welfare" does not in itself demonstrate that an alternative view of economic growth informed judges' progrowth position in these early trials. After all, private interests are often dressed up in public rhetoric in order to make them more palatable to the common man. Words alone do not dispel suspicions that the judges' remarks were simply rhetorical devices masking the class bias of the courts. Additional sources of evidence are needed to sustain my claim that an alternative, more collectivist, view of economic relations informed many antebellum judges' views.

It is best to begin by contrasting the first and second wave of conspiracy trials. The increased class conflict of the postwar decades was manifest in several aspects of the second wave of conspiracy trials: the language used during the proceedings, workers' response to the trials, and the penalties imposed by the courts all changed markedly after the Civil War. In all three areas we see that laymen and lawyers alike readily acknowledged class conflict to be a central component of the postbellum conspiracy trials.

By the end of the Civil War, the language and categories used to describe economic relations had changed dramatically. Judges and attorneys no longer stressed the public dimensions of economic prosperity by drawing attention to the negative effects of combination on the health and trade of the community. References to the "public good" and the importance of maintaining a "flourishing trade" had all but disappeared. Instead, the economic injuries identified in the second wave of conspiracy trials were described in individual terms, as losses or harms suffered by specific businessmen and their firms.[38] The decreased trade in Mrs. Landgraff's bakery and in George Theiss's musical club, for example, were accepted by the postbellum courts as legitimate injuries that could be appropriately redressed by convicting protesting workingmen of conspiracy. The contrast with the antebellum cases is striking. Before the Civil War, economic injuries to particular employers were rarely mentioned and, if discussed at all, were couched in terms of public interest and community welfare rather than of the self-interest and injury of particular individuals and their business enterprises.

The language used to describe the defendants and their actions changed as well in the postwar trials. The new language of conflict and class antagonism can be seen clearly in the New York case of *People v. Wilzig* in 1886. Judge Barrett began his sentencing with the following remarks:

> The moral guilt attaching to the crime of which you have been convicted is heightened by the fact that you are not American citizens. Such socialistic crimes as these are gross breaches of national hospitality. What would you think of a man who, having sought an asylum from oppression or poverty in a friend's house, then proceeded to violate his friend's domestic rules, to disregard his customs and to disturb the peace, order and well being of his household! Yet that is just what you and others of your union have been doing with regard to the national house-

hold of this country; a country that welcomed you and offered equal opportunity with its own native-born citizens. Common gratitude should have prevented you from outraging public opinion, and using here those methods of a socialistic character which you brought with you from abroad.[39]

Although questions of citizenship had been raised in some of the antebellum trials, the identification of foreigners with "socialistic" views was new.[40] A quite different level of danger and power was attributed to the postwar defendants and to the un-American nature of their actions. Again, Judge Barrett captured the new sense of fear when he continued the sentencing as follows:

All these things, however, while they may have encouraged your disgraceful proceedings at Theiss' establishment, did not suggest the almost unspeakable excesses which attended the finale of your acts, when, having reduced this man to submission, having compelled him to sign the most degrading document which was ever presented to an American citizen, you completed your outrage by forcing him, still with your boycott pistol at his head, to pay, so to speak, for the powder and ball with which it was loaded, and which had been the threat of his business ruin.[41]

Something had indeed changed since the antebellum trials; the New York and Pennsylvania state courts now viewed the conspiracy cases as dangerous conflicts between workers and employers and were willing to go to considerable lengths to contain the heightened class struggle.

Language and categories were not the only things to change between the first and second wave of conspiracies; workers also responded quite differently to the postwar trials. Unlike their antebellum counterparts, postwar labor unions paid considerable attention to the second wave of conspiracy convictions and embarked on an extensive campaign to repeal the conspiracy law. Between 1865 and 1891, the New York Workingmens' Assembly, the Pennsylvania miners' unions, and later the Federation of Organized Trades and Labor Unions all made repeal of the doctrine one of their highest priorities and tried repeatedly to check the power of the courts and limit application of the conspiracy doctrine to American labor. Thus, after the Civil War several key labor organizations were no longer willing to accept the conspiracy convictions as part and parcel of a larger program of antimonopoly reform. Instead, the conspiracy convictions became highly politicized and were the object of a sustained campaign for legal change, the outcome of which, we will see, had a considerable impact on the future course of labor movement development in the United States.[42]

Finally, the changing significance of the conspiracy trials can be seen in the heavier penalties imposed by the postwar courts. Where antebellum courts imposed quite small fines of one to ten dollars, their postbellum counterparts actually sentenced workers to jail for terms up to three years and eight months and often imposed fines as high as one hundred dollars.[43] The increased penalties awarded by the courts provide a useful marker of shifts in the relative weight accorded to questions of judicial authority versus questions of class conflict. The heavier fines and jail terms signaled, I believe, many judges' increased desire to contain working-class protest after the Civil War. The antebellum problems of judicial authority had been addressed by following English precedents and convicting workers of conspiracy. The recent outbursts of working-class unrest, however, required a different approach; substantial punishments as well as convictions were needed to prevent workers from organizing on a massive scale.

Explaining how and why the conspiracy doctrine was politicized in the middle decades of the nineteenth century takes us beyond the bounds of this article into the transformation of economic and social relations during the nineteenth century.[44] What is important here is to note the ways in which the political significance of the conspiracy trials changed over the course of the century. Judicial policy certainly was influenced by the larger social context, but the particular issues and social relations that provided the relevant reference point for understanding the conspiracy trials changed during the middle decades of the nineteenth century. Initially, state courts were concerned primarily with maintaining the continuity of common law and of ensuring a healthy pattern of economic growth in the new republic. It was not until after the Civil War that the New York and Pennsylvania courts were preoccupied with containing the dramatic displays of working-class power.

Even though issues of class conflict were more salient in the postwar trials, the impact of the second wave of conspiracy prosecutions on American labor still did not lie in the level of judicial hostility or state repression alone. Instead, I have found that judicial regulation played a more subtle and indirect role in shaping working-class consciousness and strategy after the Civil War. To discern the interplay of state-labor relations, we must look more closely at the second wave of conspiracy trials, paying particular attention to workers' campaigns to repeal the conspiracy doctrine in the postwar decades. The outcome of this three-cornered struggle among labor, state legislatures, and the courts, we will see, had a decisive impact on the AFL's turn to business unionism at the end of the century.

STATE STRUCTURE AND LABOR STRATEGY: THE
CAMPAIGN TO REPEAL THE CONSPIRACY DOCTRINE

After the Civil War, labor organizations in both New York and Pennsylvania began to call for repeal of the conspiracy doctrine and to demand state protection of workers' rights to organize and to strike. The basic strategy they adopted was political: workers were to pressure state legislatures into passing anticonspiracy statutes that would exempt workers from prosecution for criminal conspiracy.[45] During their campaign for legal reform, both the New York and Pennsylvania labor unions showed quite detailed knowledge of their respective legislatures. To pave the way for new legislation unions screened prospective legislative candidates, established their own committees to draft potential labor bills, and even hired their own lawyers to review their alternative legislation so as to enhance its chances of passage. Once a labor bill had been introduced into the legislature, the New York and Pennsylvania unions made every effort to ensure its safe passage by mobilizing voters, petitioning representatives, and testifying at all the relevant committee hearings, at times on a daily basis.[46]

In the 1860s through the early 1890s, then, New York and Pennsylvania trade unions committed considerable time, energy, and resources to securing political change. Labor movements in both states clearly believed that workers' interests could be effectively pursued through legislative channels. To be sure, neither the New York nor the Pennsylvania union advocated a revolutionary or socialist ideology demanding sweeping social change. Nevertheless, these postwar campaigns to repeal the conspiracy doctrine brought organized labor into electoral and party politics in an extensive and sustained fashion. Throughout the postbellum decades, New York and Pennsylvania workers continued to look to the state to redress the balance of power between labor and capital and to alleviate the hardships that followed industrialization.

The outcome of labor's struggle to repeal the conspiracy doctrine, at least initially, was encouraging. Between 1869 and 1891, the New York and Pennsylvania legislatures passed a total of eight anticonspiracy laws, four in each state.[47] Each of the laws stipulated that workers' peaceful collective action should not be subject to criminal prosecution under the conspiracy doctrine. Workers had the right under the new laws to act collectively to advance their interests. Legislation in both states stopped short of protecting working-class organization unconditionally by including provisions against the use of force, threats, and intimidation during industrial disputes. The qualifying provisions notwithstanding, the anticonspiracy laws contained the first clear legislative protection of working-class organization in the United States.

Enforcing the legislative protections, however, was no easy matter. Much to the workers' dismay, their political victories were short lived. Neither the New York nor the Pennsylvania statute was able to stem the tide of postwar conspiracy convictions. After each of the anticonspiracy laws was passed, New York and Pennsylvania district attorneys continued to charge striking workers with conspiracy by claiming that they had intimidated fellow workers and employers during the dispute and thus violated the qualifying provisions of the new labor laws. A series of postwar conspiracy cases ensued in which state courts had to determine whether particular actions qualified as intimidation under the new labor statutes.[48]

The New York and Pennsylvania courts consistently ruled for the prosecution in the postwar cases and convicted workers of criminal conspiracy. Judges were well aware of the new labor statutes and often referred explicitly to the new laws in their charges to the juries. While formally acknowledging workers' newly established right to peaceful collective action, however, judges' instructions almost always made clear that the particular activities before the court fell within the intimidation provisions. Reviewing the postbellum labor conspiracies as a whole, we see that almost any form of collective action was defined as intimidation by the courts. New York and Pennsylvania judges stated that no physical force or violence need be used nor overt threats uttered during a dispute for workers to be guilty of intimidation. Instead, the mere number of workers present on a picket line, the distribution of circulars during a dispute, or an "attitude of menace" on the part of striking workers was sufficient grounds for convicting workers of criminal conspiracy.

The New York case of *People v. Kostka* provides a useful illustration of the courts' power in the postwar decades. The case was heard before the court of oyer and terminer in 1886 with Judge Barrett presiding.[49] Paul Kostka and sixteen fellow workers were charged with criminal conspiracy for boycotting a small bakery owned by Mrs. Josephine Landgraff. The boycott was initiated as a response to Landgraff's hiring nonunion workers at reduced wages. Two events were identified as possible acts of intimidation at the trial. First, several workers went to the bakery at night, and a defendant named Linhard allegedly spat in the face of and threatened to kill one of the bakers. Second, for the next three days several defendants returned to distribute circulars outside the bakery. Defense attorneys denied the overt threats of violence on the first night of the dispute. Most of the trial, it seems, hinged on whether the distribution of circulars led the defendants to "overstep the just and lawful line" between peaceful and coercive action as defined in section 168 of the revised New York penal code.[50]

Judge Barrett offered the following guidelines to the jury for their deliberations on the "question of intimidation." First, Barrett noted that the distribution of circulars "was not an isolated act, but was repeated three days in succession, each day with an increased staff of distributors, until upon the last day the number had increased to fifteen persons." Second, Barrett suggested that the jury also consider the "character" and "language" used in the circulars. "You will notice," Barrett continued, "that they commence quite gently, invoking the moral support of their fellow-citizens. In later paragraphs, however, they speak of having been subjected to violence and insult. You may look through the circulars and see whether they contain appeals to passion or are otherwise inflammatory in their character." Finally, Judge Barrett outlined the minimal criteria needed to establish intimidation by instructing the jury as follows:

> The mere fact that no violence was actually used in the street is not conclusive. It is for you to say whether the attitude of these men was threatening. Nor is it necessary that there should have been a direct threat. If you believe that the attitude actually presented by the distributors of those circulars was an attitude of intimidation, either to the passers-by, or to the woman inside (Mrs. Landgraff), considering all the circumstances, then all who participated in it, directly or indirectly, are within the meaning of that word intimidation, as used in the conspiracy act.

The jury returned a verdict of guilty for six of the defendants. The remaining workers were discharged due to insufficient proof of identity. The jury called for leniency in sentencing the defendants; Barrett agreed and sentenced them to jail for ten to thirty days. He warned that in future cases of this sort he would not be so lenient and would punish subsequent offenders to the "full extent of the law."[51]

By interpreting the intimidation provisions very broadly, New York and Pennsylvania courts were able to convict workers of criminal conspiracy throughout the postwar decades. In fact, it is difficult to imagine any collective action that would be exempt from criminal prosecution given Barrett's very broad and nebulous definition of intimidation. *Kostka* was by no means exceptional; most of the New

York and Pennsylvania convictions rested on equally broad interpretations of the late nineteenth-century anticonspiracy laws. Thus, American workers found their efforts to repeal the conspiracy doctrine through legislative channels repeatedly undermined by the courts. Rather than witness the rewards of successful political mobilization, New York and Pennsylvania workers saw firsthand the ineffectiveness of legislative reform for changing government policy toward labor. The repeated conviction of New York and Pennsylvania workers after the Civil War did not prevent workers from organizing collectively to contest employers' power. What the courts' capacity to block political reform did do, however, was lead workers to reassess their strategic options.

WORKERS' RESPONSE: JUDICIAL OBSTRUCTION AND BUSINESS UNIONISM

Workers did not abandon their "political work" lightly and initially responded to their judicial defeats by returning to their respective legislatures with renewed vigor. Unions in both New York and Pennsylvania continued to believe that they could change the courts' behavior by securing new, more carefully drafted anticonspiracy laws. Passage of four successive anticonspiracy statutes in each state reflected this extended campaign for effective political reform. Despite their persistence, the legislative solution failed; no matter how carefully the laws were constructed, they did not protect workers' peaceful collective action from criminal prosecution. By the end of their twenty-five year long struggle to repeal the conspiracy doctrine, labor leaders became disillusioned with electoral politics and began to advocate different strategies for workers to pursue.

The first signs of dissatisfaction with legislative reform can be seen as early as 1884 in Frank Foster's attacks on the eight-hour laws. As secretary of the Federation of Organized Trades and Labor Unions, Foster delivered a scathing report on the legislative campaign in which he declared: "This much has been determined by the history of the national eight-hour law—it is useless to wait for legislation in this matter. In the world of economic reform the working classes must depend upon themselves for the enforcement of measures as well as for their conception."[52] Similarly, in 1886 John Franey, the chairman of the Executive Committee in the New York Workingmen's Assembly's political branch complained that "the judiciary is already too much divorced from politics. Divorce from politics means divorce from the people and concubinage with capital."[53] By the end of the century many labor reformers were frustrated with the American political system and began to doubt whether meaningful change could be secured through political channels.[54]

Samuel Gompers summed up the lessons for labor most succinctly in his autobiography in a reflection on his own efforts to secure legislative reform. As president of the New York Cigar Makers' Union Number 144, Gompers had led an extensive campaign to improve the working conditions in tenement workshops through legislation. The campaign succeeded when Governor Cleveland signed a new tenement law in 1883. As with the anticonspiracy statutes, however, the victory was short lived as employers successfully challenged the new laws in the courts. The Cigar Makers returned to the legislature to obtain a more carefully written law only to have the new statute again overruled by the state Supreme Court and federal Circuit Court of Appeals.[55]

Gompers clearly understood that the power of the courts made political reform difficult. He outlined the lesson he learned from his "political work" in no uncertain terms: "Securing the enactment of a law does not mean the solution of the problem as I learned in my legislative experience. The power of the courts to pass upon constitutionality of a law so complicates reform by legislation as to seriously restrict the effectiveness of that method."[56] As long as the courts could overrule or erode legislation there seemed to be little incentive for workers to mobilize politically to advance their concerns.

As legislative reform proved ineffective, labor began to devise new strategies for protecting workers' interests. The Cigar Makers' response to their failed legislation might well have served as a blueprint for the change in labor strategy more generally. Gompers described the change as follows:

> After the Appeal Court declared against the principle of the law, we talked over the possibilities of further legislative action and decided to concentrate on organization work. Through our trade unions we harassed the manufacturers by strikes and agitation until they were convinced that we did not intend to stop until we gained our point and that it would be less costly for them to abandon the tenement manufacturing system and carry on the industry in factories under decent conditions. Thus we accomplished through economic power what we had failed to achieve through legislation.[57]

The AFL turned to voluntarism, according to Gompers, precisely because of the obstacles it encountered when trying to change government policy toward labor. By negotiating and protesting directly with employers, workers could advance their interests without having to obtain the blessing of the courts.[58]

Business unionism was by no means the only viable response to judicial recalcitrance. In fact, both the socialists and the Wobblies advocated very different strategies for American labor, each of which provided solutions to workers' postwar dilemma. From the socialists' perspective, there was no need to change labor's strategy and turn to business unionism. Instead, workers should mobilize around a more radical platform to transform the state. If the courts were obstructing working-class demands, then the best response, from the socialists' point of view, was to take control of the institutions and make them more responsive to workers' demands. The Wobblies, too, represented an alternative to business unionism because their syndicalist program also contained a strong antistatist element that would have enabled workers to bypass the courts. In many ways, business unionism and syndicalism were two sides of the same coin; both strategies offered ways of avoiding the frustrations of political reform by focusing labor's energies and resources, albeit in very different ways, on the shop floor.[59]

The failure of New York and Pennsylvania workers to repeal the conspiracy doctrine tells us little or nothing about why business unionism triumphed over these other alternatives. All three strategies offered ways of negotiating the peculiarities of the American state. What my research does explain, however, is why after 1900 American workers did not pursue their interests through mainstream political channels and adopted instead their distinctive strategy of AFL voluntarism. The late nineteenth-century struggle to repeal the conspiracy doctrine laid bare the limits of electoral and party politics as effective mechanisms for changing government policy toward labor in the United States.

CONCLUSION: THE CHANGING SIGNIFICANCE OF THE COURTS FOR AMERICAN LABOR

Comparing judicial regulation of labor under the two waves of conspiracy prosecutions bears witness to the changing role of the courts in shaping working-class formation in the United States. During the second wave of conspiracy cases, the division of power within the American state and the dominance of the courts over other branches of government provided an unusual set of incentives and constraints that made political mobilization difficult after the Civil War. At the end of a prolonged and ultimately unsuccessful struggle to check the power of the courts, New York and Pennsylvania labor unions turned away from the state and pursued instead a strategy of business unionism. The courts' persistent obstruction of legislative reform lent business unionism a particular appeal for American workers in the last decade of the nineteenth century.

It is a mistake, however, to assume that state-labor relations remained unchanged throughout the nineteenth century. The antebellum convictions, I have argued, were not simply a means of containing workers' protests and promoting instead the employers' economic interests. Rather, I have shown how maintenance of judicial authority and eighteenth-century conceptions of economic growth provided the relevant social context for the early trials. As a consequence, the early conspiracy cases should not be analyzed in terms of judicial hostility and class bias, but rather are best understood in light of the preceding political struggles. It was only after the Civil War that increased class conflict and rapid working-class mobilization became the focal point of the conspiracy trials.

Thus, tracing the conspiracy prosecutions over the course of the nineteenth century shows how the meaning and significance of judicial regulation shifted as judges and workers alike viewed the pre- and postwar cases in a very different light. Ignoring the changing context of the conspiracy trials leads, I believe, to too static and deterministic a view of the courts' influence over American labor. Judicial regulation was important, but in more varied and indeterminate ways than previous scholars have claimed. Only by attending to differences between the first and second wave of convictions can we begin to decipher the changing significance of judicial regulation for American labor.

NOTES

I would like to thank the following people for helpful comments on earlier drafts of the article: Daniel Ernst, Morton Horwitz, Karen Orren, Joel Rogers, Deborah Stone, Katherine Van Wezel Stone, and the editors of this volume.

1. For comparison of government regulation of labor in England, Germany, France, and the United States, see Valenzuela 1979; Orth 1977; Hattam 1987; Marks 1989.

2. Labor conspiracy cases have been identified in several other states, including Massachusetts, Maryland, Connecticut, New Jersey, Illinois, Ohio, and Virginia.

3. Hawkins is quoted in a number of the antebellum labor conspiracy trials. See, for example *Commonwealth v. Pullis*, 3 Documentary History of American Industrial Society (Commons 1910–11) (hereinafter Doc. Hist.) 196 (Pa. 1806); *People v. Melvin*, 3 Doc. Hist. 280 (N.Y. 1809).

4. Quoted in Carson 1887: 92. For useful discussions of the conspiracy doctrine, see Sayre 1922; Mason 1925; Hattam 1992; Tomlins forthcoming.

5. Carson 1887: chap. 3.

6. For example, see Sayre 1922; Nelles 1932; R. B. Morris 1937; Levy 1967; Quimby 1967; Turner 1967; W. Holt 1984. Important exceptions have been Witte 1926; Kuritz 1950; Hovenkamp 1988.

7. See Turner 1967: 31–57; W. Holt 1984: 619–53; Sayre 1922: 393, 412, 414–16, 420, 427; Sayre 1930: 690, 703–4; Nelles 1932: 1151–62.

8. W. Holt 1984: 656.

9. For judicial rhetoric and class bias, see W. Holt 1984: 619–25; Turner 1967: 31–57. For workingmen's protest and class bias, see W. Holt 1984: 634–36, and Tomlins forthcoming: chap. 5. For the unequal treatment of workingmen's and employers' combinations, see discussion of *Commonwealth v. Carlisle*, Brightly NP 36 (1821) in Sayre 1922: 414–16, 420; W. Holt 1984: 627–29. For a less explicit comparison of judicial regulation of labor and capital which nevertheless implies that workers' combinations were treated more harshly by the courts, see Tomlins 1985: 30–31, 33, 43.

10. For an interesting discussion linking changes in the organization of work to the conspiracy trials, see Quimby 1967.

11. The following are the major postbellum conspiracy cases in New York and Pennsylvania identified to date: *People v. Van Nostrand* (N.Y. 1868), Workingmen's Assembly Proceedings, 1869: 19; *Cigar-makers' Union No. 66, Kingston* (N.Y. 1868), NLU Proceedings, Second Session, 1868: 12; *Raybold and Frostevant v. Samuel R. Gaul of Bricklayers' Union No. 2, New York City*, NLU Proceedings, Second Session, 1868: 12; *Iron Moulders' Union No. 203, Harlem, N.Y. v. United States Iron Works* (1869) Workingmen's Assembly Proceedings, 1870: 23; *Commonwealth v. Curren*, 3 Pitts. 143 (Pa. 1869); *Commonwealth v. Berry et al.*, 1 Scranton Law Times 217 (Pa. 1874); *Xingo Parks and John Siney*, trials, Clearfield County, Pa. (1875), Pennsylvania Bureau of Industrial Statistics 9: 313–15; *Commonwealth ex rel. E. Vallette et al. v. Sheriff*, 15 Phil. 393 (Pa. 1881); *D. R. Jones*, trial, Westmoreland County, Pa. (1881), Pennsylvania Bureau of Industrial Statistics 9: 378–83; *Miles McPadden and Knights of Labor*, trial, Clearfield County, Pa. (1882), Pennsylvania Bureau of Industrial Statistics 10:161–63; *Newman et al. v. the Commonwealth*, 34 Pittsburgh Law Journal 313 (Pa. 1886); *People v. Wilzig*, 4 N.Y. Cr. 403 (1886); *People v. Kostka*, 4 N.Y. Cr. 429 (1886); *Knights of Labor*, trial, Allegheny County, Pa. (1887), in Kuritz 1953: 154; *People ex rel. Gill v. Smith*, 10 N.Y. St. Reptr. 730 (1887); *People ex rel. Gill v. Walsh*, 110 N.Y. 633 (1888).

12. Interestingly, for two decades following *Hunt*, Witte has identified only three labor conspiracy cases. See Witte 1926: 829. It is a mistake, I believe, to attribute this hiatus in conspiracy cases to the *Hunt* victory alone because the doctrine was revived with a vengeance after the Civil War. Instead, the decline and resurgence of conspiracy cases are best analyzed in relation to the larger political and economic changes that dominated the nineteenth century.

13. See *Commonwealth v. Pullis*, 228–29; *Commonwealth v. Morrow*, 4 Doc. Hist. 15 (Pa. 1815), 77–81, 84–85.

14. For example, Stephen Simpson of the Philadelphia Working Men's party occasionally complained about the unequal treatment of workingmen and capitalists by the courts. See S. Simpson 1831: 86, 138. Several resolutions also were passed by the Philadelphia General Trades Union protesting conviction of the New York tailors in 1836. See Commons 1910–11, 5: 361–68. A sizable parade was held in New York City to protest the shoemakers' conviction in *People v. Fisher*. See Wilentz 1984b: 290. No doubt additional evidence of

discontent will be uncovered with further research. However, it is important to look more closely at these protests and not simply to assume that workingmen were finally speaking as a class. In fact, on those occasions when workers did protest the antebellum convictions, they often voiced their complaints in classic eighteenth-century terms. Monopolies and corruption rather than the class struggle remained the dominant terms of analysis in the antebellum decades. Moreover, these protests did not become central issues for the major workingmen's associations before the Civil War. Neither the platforms nor the proceedings of the principal trades unions or workingmen's political organizations actually devoted much attention to the early conspiracy trials.

15. There were three different platforms within the New York Working Men's party. For Skidmore's platform, see "Report of the Committee of Fifty;" for the Commerford platform, see "Proceedings of a Meeting of Mechanics and Other Working Men;" and for the Owen platform, see the minority report of the subcommittee on education. All three documents have been reprinted in Commons 1910–11, 5: 149–68. For the General Trades Unions' demands, see Laurie 1980: chap. 5; Wilentz 1984b: chap. 6.

16. The only reported case against master craftsmen before the Civil War is *Commonwealth ex rel. Chew v. Carlisle*, Brightly Nisi Prius 36 (Pa. 1821). Since the war three conspiracies against employers have been identified. See *Master Stevedores' Association v. Walsh*, 2 Daly 1 (N.Y. 1867); *Commonwealth v. Tack*, 1 Brewst. 511 (Pa. 1868); *Morris Run Coal Co. v. Barclay Coal Co.*, 68 Pa. St. 173, 187 (1871).

17. For regulation of employers' associations during the nineteenth century, see Thorelli 1954: part 1; Hurst 1970; Horwitz 1976. For interesting discussions of the malleability of corporation law and property rights, see Horwitz 1985 and Hurvitz 1986.

18. See Selfridge 1888: 249; Eddy 1901: conclusion; Cooke 1909: 104. More recently, Petro has also complained about labor's favorable treatment under the conspiracy doctrine. See Petro 1982. Despite the title, Petro's essay is by no means limited to discussion of the southern courts. For an interesting discussion of the turn-of-the-century treatises, see Hovenkamp 1988: 925–32.

19. For discussion of light penalties, see Witte 1926: 828. For estimates of defendants' wages before the Civil War, see testimony in *Commonwealth v. Pullis*, 83, 106, 118, 123–24, 171.

20. See *Commonwealth v. Pullis*, 158–59, 222, 225; *People v. Melvin*, 261, 275–76, 320–21, 331, 347, 377; and *Commonwealth v. Morrow*, 62, 71.

21. For discussion of conspiracy as a common law crime, see Brigham 1887; Selfridge 1888; Burdick 1907.

22. For interesting discussions of the politically contentious nature of judicial authority in the wake of the Revolution, see Ellis 1971; C. M. Cook 1981.

23. For a full transcript of the court proceedings in the *Pullis* trial, see Commons 1910–11, 3:58–248.

24. *Commonwealth v. Pullis*, 225.

25. Ibid., 233.

26. *State v. Buchanan*, 5 Harris and Johnson 317 (Md. 1821), 358.
27. William Sampson acted as defense counsel for the New York cord-wainers in *People v. Melvin*; Robert Rantoul, Jr., defended the Boston cord-wainers in the historic Massachusetts case of *Commonwealth v. Hunt*, Thacher's Criminal Cases 609 (1840), and 45 Mass. 111 (1842).
28. Ingersoll was the attorney general in Pennsylvania and prosecuted both *Commonwealth v. Pullis* and *Commonwealth v. Morrow*. Hopkinson joined Ingersoll in the Pullis prosecution.
29. Claims about the importance of manufacturing and trade for the antebellum cities can be found in many of the conspiracy trials. For extended arguments along these lines, see *Commonwealth v. Pullis*, 228–30; *Commonwealth v. Morrow*, 81, 84–85; *Commonwealth v. Carlisle*, 41–42; *People v. Fisher*, 14 Wendell 2 (N.Y. 1835), 17–19.
30. See W. Holt 1984; Nelles 1932.
31. Quoted from *Commonwealth v. Morrow*, 84.
32. Ibid., 80–81.
33. *Commonwealth v. Morrow*, 81.
34. *People v. Fisher*, 18–19.
35. *People v. Faulkner*, 4 Doc. Hist. 315 (N.Y. 1836) 324. For similar remarks urging the jury to consider the conflict more broadly than as a struggle between masters and journeymen, see also pp. 323, 325.
36. For example, in his charge to the jury Judge Edwards also claimed, "[It] would be for the jury to say, whether any body of men could raise their crests in this land of law, and control others by self-organized combination." Edwards went on to note how extensive combination had become and how it had "created so great an excitement." See ibid., 323–24. For even more explicit references to increased class conflict in the antebellum trials, see Judge Thacher's remarks in *Commonwealth v. Hunt*, in which he pointed to the danger that the new workingmen's combinations would "tend directly to array them [laborer and employer] against each other, and to convulse the social system to its core." Quoted from *Commonwealth v. Hunt*, 653–54.
37. For elaboration of eighteenth-century views of economic relations, see Thompson 1970; G. S. Jones 1983: 90–178; Smail 1987. In the American context, see Crowley 1974; Hattam 1992: chap. 3.
38. For example, see *People v. Wilzig*, 414–15, 426; *People v. Kostka*, 436; *Newman et al. v. the Commonwealth*, 314.
39. *People v. Wilzig*, 425.
40. For reference to citizenship in the antebellum conspiracy trials, see *People v. Faulkner*, 326, 331.
41. *People v. Wilzig*, 426.
42. I have elaborated the argument concerning workers' quiescent response to the antebellum convictions elsewhere. See Hattam 1992: chap. 3. The basic point here is that, for the most part, workers generally did not contest conspiracy convictions in the early nineteenth century so long as employers also were prevented from organizing collectively. Thus the Working Men's parties' program of antimonopoly reform went hand in hand with the more quiescent response to the antebellum trials.

43. For example, see the heavy fines and jail terms that accompanied the following cases: *People v. Van Nostrand*, in which fines ranged from twenty-five to fifty dollars; *Commonwealth v. Curren*, in which defendants were ordered to pay the costs of the suit, a fine of one hundred dollars, and a five-hundred-dollar security deposit for one year's good behavior and were sentenced to thirty days in jail; the trial of *Miles McPadden and the Knights of Labor*, in which the defendants' bail ranged from five hundred to one thousand dollars (eventually the suit was dropped); the trials of *Xingo Parks* and *John Siney*, in which several miners were ordered to pay costs of the suit and a twenty-five-dollar fine and were sentenced to jail terms ranging from sixty days to one year; the *D. R. Jones* trial, in which penalties included costs of the suit, a one-hundred-dollar fine, and imprisonment for twenty-four hours; *Newman et al. v. the Commonwealth*, in which defendants were ordered to pay costs of the suit and a one-dollar fine and were sentenced to jail terms ranging from three to eight months; *People v. Wilzig*, in which defendants were sentenced to jail terms ranging from one year and six months to three years and eight months; *People v. Kostka*, where defendants were sentenced to ten to thirty days in jail; and finally the *Knights of Labor* trial in Allegheny County, Pennsylvania, in which the defendants were sentenced to four months in jail.

44. For discussion of this shift in workers' ideology and social relations after the Civil War, see Hattam 1990.

45. For the New York campaign to repeal the conspiracy doctrine, see New York State Workingmen's Assembly 1869–1894. For the Pennsylvania campaign, see Kuritz 1953.

46. See New York State Workingmen's Assembly 1885: 16; 1888: 21.

47. In New York, see *Laws of the State of New York* chaps. 18, 19 (1870); *Penal Code* ss. 168, 170 (1881); chap. 384 (1882); chap. 688 (1887). In Pennsylvania, see *Laws of the State of Pennsylvania* P.L. 1242 (1869); P.L. 1105 (1872); P.L. 33 (1876); P.L. 230 (1891).

48. For a list of postbellum labor conspiracy cases in New York and Pennsylvania, see above, n. 11.

49. In some states the higher criminal courts were referred to by the name oyer and terminer during the nineteenth century.

50. *People v. Kostka*, 435.

51. Ibid., 430, 435–36, 440–42.

52. See FOTLU 1884: 11.

53. See New York State Workingmen's Assembly 1886: 4.

54. For a fascinating discussion of the viability of labor's political strategy, see the debate over the AFL's "Political Programme" at the 1894 Denver convention in American Federation of Labor 1895.

55. For an account of the Cigar Makers' efforts at tenement reform, see Gompers 1925, 1: chap. 9.

56. Ibid., 194.

57. Ibid., 197.

58. For an interesting discussion of the continued struggle between labor and the courts over the labor injunction, see Forbath 1989. Although the AFL continued to push for legal reform through its anti-injunction campaign in the

first three decades of the twentieth century, the turn to voluntarism was already well underway by 1900.

59. For Eugene Debs's reaction to judicial obstruction, see his testimony before the Senate investigation into the Pullman strike in *The Report on the Chicago Strike*, 129–80; Salvatore 1982: chap. 5. For the Wobblies, see Rayback 1959: chap. 16.

3 Law and Power in the Employment Relationship

Christopher L. Tomlins

*The capitalist has no interest in us, than to get as much labor out
of us as possible. We are hired men, and hired men, like hired
horses, have no souls.*
—Third Grand Rally of the Workingmen of Charlestown, Mass.,
Held 23 October 1840

During the first half of the nineteenth century the republican identification of work as *production*, the engagement of members of a community in individual or collective creation of useful artefacts to the
general benefit of their society, was increasingly overshadowed among
the employed by a distinctly different identification of work as *exploitation*, the accumulation of capital, and the securing of profit by
employers at the expense of those who worked for them.[1] Accompanying this change, and a key element in it, was the growth of an
awareness that the supposedly freely bargained relationship into which
workers entered with their employers was in its essentials one of
structured inequality. A contemporary vignette—imaginary, meant as
a metaphor—will illustrate. "Here goes a poor operative," wrote Jacob
Frieze in 1844, "to find a situation in which he can obtain more wages.
Let us slip on our magic rings, and, in our shadowy state, follow him
in his rounds, and learn how he succeeds:"

> "Mr. A——," says the applicant, addressing a pampered agent,
> "do you want to hire a good hand in your establishment?"
>   "Yes," is the reply.

Now mark. The agent does not condescend to inquire the poor man's terms. He does not ask, as though he were about to bargain for a barrel of flour, "what price do you ask?" This makes up no part of the bargain-making for labor. No—the question is by the poor operative himself; and until that is put the lips of the agent are sealed—"What wages *do you pay*?" The reply is seventy-five cents a day—and the hours of labor from sunrise in the morning to seven at night with a deduction of thirty minutes for breakfast and forty for supper. The operative finds the wages and the hours the same as at the place at which he now labors. Aware that these are as fixed, and for the time as unalterable, as the laws of the Medes and Persians, you observe the operative says no more. It is now nearly night. We have followed him from place to place through the day. In every counting room we have heard him put the same well conned question, "what *wages do you pay*?" and heard returned the same everlasting reply. . . . This is the system which prevails everywhere, and in almost every branch of labor. This is the manner in which *bargains* are made.[2]

Frieze's apocryphal tale was intended to illustrate the absence of any equality of exchange in the wage bargain. It was a tale of power—the employer's possession of it, the operative's lack of it, consequent upon the different resources the parties were able to bring to bear on their bargaining. This was power emanating from what one scholar has termed "monetary exchange asymmetry," that is, from the discrepancy in material consequences that failure to enter into exchange visits upon the different parties.[3] It is equally important to an understanding of the nineteenth-century employment relationship, however, to realize that in important respects its legal realities no more comported to the "liberal illusion" of formal equality than its economic realities. Like monetary asymmetry, legal asymmetries meant that the parties to an employment relationship coexisted under conditions of structured inequality.[4] This was a condition that courts would on some occasions simply deny, on others represent as natural and necessary—essential, indeed, to the proper functioning of the relation. On a few occasions they can be found attempting to do both simultaneously.[5]

The clearest expression of legal asymmetry may be found in the presumption that a contract to deliver labor for money also delivers the employee's assent that for as long as the relationship continues the employer shall control the disposition of the labor to be delivered. The existence of this presumption is brought out nicely at midcentury in the words of Judge William B. Caldwell of the Supreme Court of Ohio, in *The Little Miami Railroad Company v. John Stevens*: "When a man employs another to do work for him, each incur their obligations. The person hired is bound to perform the labor according to the agreement, and the employer is bound to pay; besides that, neither party has parted with any of his rights. The employer has no more control over the person he has employed, *outside of the service to be rendered*, than he has over the person of any other individual."[6] The employer's right of control over the employee's rendition of service, however, is precisely the issue. As Caldwell's statement confirms, legally the autonomy of the operative (which monetary asymmetry in any case renders materially illusory in most cases) is confined to the points of entry to and exit from the employment relationship. The relationship itself appears as a realm in which inequality of power is a routine incident, consequential upon the additional rights of control imputed in legal descriptions of employment to inhere in the employer. The operative's decision to enter employment is thus also a decision to become subject to the employer's power. Indeed, to many nineteenth-century writers and courts the existence of a condition of subjection to authority was conclusive in determining whether a relationship of employment in fact existed between two parties.[7]

The legal treatment of power disparities as a necessary incident of the employment relationship distinguished it from the formal civic equalities that collectively constituted everyday life.[8] In this realm government was devolved upon the employer, vested in him as a matter of policy,[9] and in some circumstances backed by criminal sanction.[10] How did these asymmetries come about? In America, as in England, the law that constituted the employment relationship was constructed by courts and by treatise writers as an extrapolation upon the preindustrial relationship of master and servant. As the treatise writer Timothy Walker put it in 1837: "The title of master and servant, at the head of a lecture, does not sound very harmoniously to republican ears. . . . But the legal relation of master and servant *must* exist, to a greater or lesser extent, wherever civilization furnishes work to be done." Walker argued that power disparities in this relationship were socially and not legally determined, rooted in the "difference[s] of condition" which made "some persons employers and others labourers."[11] In other words, the law of the employment relationship simply catalogued people as it found them. Yet what Walker implied was nothing more than legal recognition of a socially determined distribution of power might more appropriately be seen as a grant of power, for what is particularly noteworthy about the use by American courts of master-servant discourse to construe the nineteenth-century employment relationship is the extensive doctrinal migration it entailed, one reaching far beyond more specific categories of work relations which the law concerning "masters" and "servants" had previously encompassed in the colonies.[12] In interpreting an ever-widening sphere of employment relations as master-servant relations (rather than, for example, relations of bailment[13]) on the basis of a necessarily contingent analogy between old and new categories of persons—master/employer and servant/employee—American law effectively granted to the modern class of employers a property right (the right to control how one's employee performs his contract) founded upon the preindustrial master's claim to property in his servant's personal services. It was, in other words, not social conditions alone but also law itself which gave the nineteenth-century employer a controlling authority over his employee. This carryover made the modern employment contract an exceptional and asymmetrical device.[14]

MASTER AND SERVANT IN ENGLAND

Even in England, a law of master and servant did not exist as such—a body of doctrine describing a single generic type, or legal relation, of employment—much before the eighteenth century. Certainly historians have been able to point to instances suggesting that in both social and legal usage "servant" has always described the broad range of social relationships in which one person worked in some capacity for another.[15] Others, however, have insisted on a more limited meaning for the term,[16] and when we turn to the bulk of early-modern English law relating to the regulation of labor, notably that growing out of the Statute of Artificers (1563), the existence of a diversity of relations rather than a single relation becomes evident.[17] For example, Michael Dalton's *Countrey Justice*, for a century following its first publication in 1619 the standard work of reference for English justices of the peace, treated servants, laborers, apprentices, workmen, and artificers as distinct subgroups of working people, to each of which distinct legal procedures, conditions, and disciplines applied. "Servants," for example, were distinguished from "artificers" and "labourers" by the prescribed length of their term of hire (one year), by their identification with employment in husbandry, the regulation of which was rather more extensive than other occupations, and by their domicile in the household of their employer.[18] Through such distinctions law incorporated differences in age, marital status, skill, and craft training which characterized the working population, all of which contributed in turn to variations in the mode and term of their employment. The work of English social historians confirms that these distinctions were adhered to both in legal and social usage into the second half of the eighteenth century.[19] As one has recently concluded, working people "may well have been the least homogenous of all the orders in early-modern society."[20] The legal "conditions of their existence" recognized that heterogeneity.

Robert Steinfeld and others have emphasized that from the time of the Edwardian Ordinance (1349) and Statute (1351) of Labourers, and particularly after the passage of the Statute of Artificers, all these varieties of persons were rendered uniformly subject to criminal sanctions penalizing abandonment of employment before the term or task agreed to had been finished.[21] By restraining the person of the employee, such provisions underwrote the employer's claim to property in his employee's services, a claim already recognized in the common law *actio per quod servitium*.[22] Contemporary opinion, however, casts some doubt upon both the scope and the effectiveness of these sanctions.[23] In particular, we cannot assume their applicability, or the applicability of their common law analogues, to the very substantial population of artisans and independent contractors involved in putting-out industries.[24] Moreover, because employment relations were highly diverse, even the existence of a general restraint on departure cannot be assumed to have homogenized the character of the employment relationship. The severity of the restraint, for example, is not the same for both task and time work. Servants, in fact, were the only category of working people whose status committed them to undifferentiated labor over a lengthy period of time, rather than to short-term casual labor or the performance of specific tasks.[25]

During the eighteenth century, the diversity of employment relations in English law underwent a process of reorganization and homogenization as the variety of statuses recognized in law began to crumble toward the single status of wage labor.[26] This change did not occur overnight. "Even when the factory system developed it by no means necessarily followed that the relationship between the factory owner and the work-people was immediately transformed into the modern one of master and servant. The old attitudes died hard: on the one side the factor or merchant, who did not interfere—and did not seek to interfere—in the process of production itself: on the other the domestic worker, choosing his own hours and methods of work, nominally at least his own master."[27] By midcentury, however, we may detect the emergence of "master and servant" for the first time as a generic description of the employment relation.

One of the earliest examples of this usage can be found in Sir Matthew Hale's *Analysis of the Law*, first published in 1713, which refers to "Master and Servant" as one of the "Relations Oeconomical," or domestic relations (the others being "Husband and Wife" and "Parent and Child"). The very lack of substance—"Touching the Third Oeconomical Relation of Master and Servant," Hale commented, "little is to be said,"—suggests at this point little more than an innovative categorization. Hale, however, indicated (without further specifying who they were) that several "kinds of servants" were to be comprehended under this heading,[28] and listed the civil remedies that a master might have against a third party for retaining his servant "before his Time is expir'd" or for rendering him incapable of performing by beating him. On the other hand Hale dealt with "tradesmen," such as "a common taylor," separately and in a manner indicating that he regarded their relationship with employers as one of bailment; that is, a relationship in which their skills might be hired but without entry into service as such, and therefore not as one comprehended under the master-servant title.[29]

Thirty years later Richard Burn's *Justice of the Peace and Parish Officer*, first published in 1743 as a revision and extension of Dalton's *Countrey Justice*, produced a more comprehensive rendering. Burn reorganized Dalton's treatment of employment by including "labourers, journeymen, artificers, and other workmen" all under the title of "servants."[30] Like Dalton, Burn here drew extensively on the Statute of Artificers. For the first time, however, Burn also grouped under this category all the older statutes regulating disputes over putting out between employers and domestic workers in the cloth trade (these dealt mostly with embezzlement of materials and methods of payment) and also the more recent statutes dealing with the urban handicraft trades passed in the wake of the degeneration of the guild controls of trading companies. Subsequent editions of Burn reflected the further expansion of legislation regulating the employment relation both in husbandry and in craft industries, passed to remedy the "insufficient and defective" laws then in being.[31]

Twenty years after Burn's first edition was published, Sir William Blackstone's *Commentaries on the Laws of England* confirmed the emergence of the designation "master and servant" as the operative legal categorization for all relations of employment. Using Hale's general typology, Blackstone described the "kinds of servants" to which Hale had alluded, but which he had not defined, as menial servants, apprentices, and *labourers hired by the day or week*, "concerning whom the statute so often cited [that is, the Statute of Artificers] has made many very good regulations." In effect, Blackstone filled the empty civil category created by Hale by bringing under the single title "servant" the diversity of occupational statuses to which varying sanctions had been applied in the Statute of Artificers.[32]

MASTER AND SERVANT IN COLONIAL AMERICA

In America, too, we find the same process of conflation occurring in the law of employment. In America, however, this development occurred during the first half of the nineteenth century, rather than during the eighteenth century. Moreover, it grew out of a significantly different colonial legal landscape in which both the criminal penalties against departure, which protected the employer's claim to property in service, and also the analogue common law actions themselves were confined in their application largely to formally bound (indented) labor. To the extent that the variety of legal compulsions regulating wage labor represented in English law were comprehensively imported into the mainland colonies during the period of first settlement, therefore, they do not appear to have survived beyond the turn of the eighteenth century except in that specific, and increasingly distinct, instance.[33]

In colonial America, even more than in early-modern England, work and employment were highly diversified social phenomena. Labor practices varied markedly from region to region, running the gamut from extensive reliance on indentured and race servitude common in many parts of the Chesapeake and, during the eighteenth century, in the middle colonies, to the family-centered labor found everywhere but particularly dominant in New England. Clientage—the combination of tenancy and labor obligations—and reciprocation—the transfer of goods and services among neighbors and in transactions between customers and independent artisan and yeoman proprietors—were common among both the urban and rural populations of the middle and northern colonies. Vocational duality was also common, particularly in the case of rural artisans. Wage labor was known in all regions, both in husbandry and in the artisan trades.[34]

By the eighteenth century, if not before, only some of these relations, notably indentured servitude, appear to have been considered liable to criminal sanctioning. In some areas, evidence of either a customary or a legal identification of unindented wage labor with a condition of criminally disciplinable service becomes patchy quite soon after settlement. In seventeenth-century Massachusetts, for example, anecdotal evidence suggests that wage earners were not regarded as "servants" at all; wage labor was colloquially referred to as "help."[35] The General Court early adopted long-standing English compulsory labor regulations directed at the mobilization of all persons for harvest work and also attempted the regulation of wages paid to laborers and prices charged by artificers in the colony. Powers of wage and price regulation were subsequently devolved to towns to use as they saw fit, however, and appear to have been resorted to only spasmodically.[36] Outside the directive (backed by no statutory sanction) "that all workemen shall work the whole day, allowing convenient time for food and rest,"[37] there is no evidence of statutory regulation of the employment relation per se.

The colony's Court of Assistants promulgated numerous orders and decisions in regard to servants during the early years of settlement which, piecemeal, both reproduced salient elements of English labor law and introduced innovations. These included, for example, a requirement of at least a one-year term in hiring unsettled servants[38] and the punishment of enticers and runaways.[39] The latter, however, were normally required to serve an additional period "att the end of their tyme," implying the existence in almost all cases of an indenture specifying a term of service and not merely a parol agreement.[40] Such a requirement of a written indenture as a basis for a claim of property in service and for the invocation of criminal restraints is also implied in early cases; for example, in 1639 Israell Stoughton was fined forty shillings by the Court of Assistants "for releasing his man before the expiration of his time" but had his fine remitted after demonstrating that "hee could not hold his servant haveing no covenant."[41] During the course of the seventeenth century, court records strongly suggest, the distinction between work for wages and service by indenture or by other form of written covenant became legally explicit; "servants" subject to restraint were increasingly identified as one or other form of bound labor—"covenant" servants or debt servants, apprentices, Blacks, or Indians.[42] Persons working for hire, including artisans contracting to perform specific tasks, were not held criminally liable for failure to perform and at common law appear at most to have been held liable to pay damages in lieu.[43]

A second marked trend in colonial era court records in Massachusetts is toward an increasingly clear identification of criminally disciplinable service with youth.[44] This is also a feature of the statutory record. Although indentured servitude was not a significant institution in Massachusetts' social and economic organization, statutes regulating "servants" continued to be passed throughout the colonial period in Massachusetts. With few exceptions, however, these made clear that what was intended was a regulation of adolescents and apprentices which did not extend to the generality of adult labor.[45] Contemporary opinion supports this identification of servitude predominantly with youth. For example, Cotton Mather's late seventeenth-century sermon, "A Good Master Well Served," which addressed "the Necessary Properties and Practices of a Good Servant *in Every Kind of Servitude*," specifically identified its audience as young people. Later eighteenth- and early nineteenth-century legal texts tell the same story.[46]

In the Chesapeake colonies and the Carolinas there is more compelling evidence that, at least during the seventeenth century, indentured servitude and unindented wage labor represented variations on the same criminally disciplinable legal category. As in Massachusetts, indentured servants departing before term were clearly liable to capture and return, but so were employed former indentured servants who had served out their time and obtained a certificate warranting their freedom, for the latter were required to surrender that certificate upon agreeing to a subsequent period of service with a "new master." Other "hired ffreemen" were also subject to restraint. As for any person who "comeing free into the country shalby any contract agree with any person, and before the time agreed for be accomplished shall depart to another, hee shall performe the tenor of his contract first made, and pay the apparent damage that shall arise by his breach of covenants, and shall after that satisfyed, be lyable to the payment of what damages any other contractor with him shall recover of him by law."[47]

Seventeenth-century court records reveal that hired laborers were indeed made subject to court orders to perform agreed terms of service in the face of refusal to enter service subsequent to agreement or early departure, and on the basis of parol as well as written agreements.[48] Artisans contracting to perform specific tasks were also made subject to court orders to perform, though not consistently.[49] During the second half of the seventeenth century, however, there are indications that legally as well as socially indentured servitude and hired labor in the Chesapeake became more distinct conditions.[50] This pattern of differentiation continued during the eighteenth century[51] until by 1774, "it must be understood that servants are here distinguished from slaves, and that they are also different from Hirelings, who engage themselves in the service of another, without being obliged thereto by Transportation, or indenture."[52] As in New England, furthermore, throughout the colonial era one finds in the Chesapeake colonies and the Carolinas a clear identification of conditions of servitude with youth.[53]

Similar patterns hold elsewhere. In Delaware, Kent County court records describe a servant population consisting at the end of the seventeenth century overwhelmingly of orphans and imported juveniles, with a few voluntarily or involuntarily bound adult debtors.[54] All these "servants" were indentured: there was no identification of wage labor, as such, with unfreedom.[55] Delaware statutes regulating servants dealt only with bound labor.[56] In New Jersey, too, local statute law regulating servants was directed exclusively at the institution of indentured servitude, with unindented wage labor thought of socially and legally as a distinct—and unregulated—status.[57] The same appears to be the case in New York[58] and also in Pennsylvania, one of the major recipients of indentured servants in the eighteenth century.[59] In 1756, for example, we find the assembled representatives distinguishing "hired labourers" from "servants" in the course of petitioning the governor for relief from the pressures of enlistment. "We are drained of our hired Labourers; and as this province has but few slaves we are now obliged to depend principally upon our Servants to assist us in tilling our lands. If these are taken from us, we are at a Loss to conceive how the Provisions that may be expected out of this Province another year, for the Support of the King's Armies, are to be raised."[60]

So far as the common law regulation of labor in the middle colonies in general is concerned, published court records are as yet scarce. Some light may be thrown on the day-to-day activities of local courts and justices, however, by reference to the various editions of the *Conductor Generalis*, colonial abridgments of English justice of the peace manuals, published in New York, Pennsylvania, and New Jersey throughout the eighteenth century. What is remarkable about these abridgments is that not one of them reproduced *any* of the sections dealing with "labourers" or "servants" found in their English counterparts.[61] Also worthy of note in this connection is Zephaniah Swift's observation that in late eighteenth-century Connecticut, "labourers, or persons hired by the days work, or any longer time, are not by our law or in common speech considered as servants."[62]

The legal discipline of servitude, then, appears to have been increasingly confined during the colonial period to the case of persons imported as indentured servants, or bound out by local authorities,[63] as governed by local legislation. Colloquially, the description "servant" might also be applied, as in English husbandry, to persons, usually young and single, hiring themselves to others for extended terms[64] (although Zephaniah Swift's comment suggests that this usage varied according to region). Writing of his travels in the late 1740s, for example, the Swedish visitor Peter Kalm reported that "the servants which are employed in the English-American colonies are either free persons or slaves" and that those who were entirely free (that is, not indented) "serve by the year." Crucially, however, Kalm went on to observe that "they are not only allowed to leave their service at the expiration of their year, but may leave it at any time when they do not agree with their masters." In other words, Kalm's contemporary account, like the legal record, evidences no carryover to the colonies of English law disciplining unindented labor.[65] Further support for this conclusion may be found in the preface to Joseph Greenleaf's *Abridgment of Burn's Justice of the Peace and Parish Officer*, published in Boston in 1773, which states explicitly what the several editions of the *Conductor Generalis* had indicated earlier in the century, that English laws regulating labor had not been carried over. "The circle of a justice's business in [England] is vastly extensive, and is founded chiefly on acts of the British Parliament, which can never have any relation to this colony, such parts are therefore not taken into this abridgment. What we have rejected relates to acts made for the regulating their . . . servants . . . and a number of articles under other heads of no possible use or importance to us in *America*."[66]

MASTER AND SERVANT IN NINETEENTH-CENTURY AMERICA

During the first half of the nineteenth century employment became a much less heterogeneous relationship than it had been throughout the colonial era, acquiring a uniform definition and set of characteristics as a single universal and impersonal relation founded on wage labor.[67] This social transformation, which produced an increasingly numerous class of free hireling laborers, was accompanied by major changes in American law propagated by a professional juridical elite through treatise writing and common law judging activities informed by English legal discourse. The effect was twofold: on the one hand the declining social importance of indentured servitude brought a steady erosion of the local statutory disciplines specifically associated with that status. Simultaneously, however, American legal texts followed English texts in advertising the existence of a generic law of master and servant encompassing all employees.

In Virginia, this development can be tracked by comparing successive editions of William Waller Hening's *New Virginia Justice*, a revised and updated sequel to Richard Starke's *Office and Authority of a Justice of the Peace* (published in 1774). Hening's first (1795) edition contained sections on apprentices and servants which described local practice and its local statutory basis. Just as Starke had reported twenty years before, Hening indicated that in local law "servant" and "hireling" were distinct statuses, the former referring to servants imported under indenture and subject to certain statutory restraints. In the second (1810) edition, however, Hening noted that "the relation of master and servant" was "of general concern" and added a completely new section entitled "Master and Servant" dependent for its substance entirely on Blackstone's *Commentaries* and other English sources and reflective of their much wider definition of the ambit of the relation. Hening continued to carry a section on the local law of servants as he had in the 1795 edition, wherein it was stated that in Virginia law servants were "such as were formerly denominated indented servants." Concerning such persons, Hening added, "many laws have been enacted, which have now become obsolete."[68]

The same process of revision and extension may be observed elsewhere. In Pennsylvania, William Graydon adopted the Blackstonian categorization in his *Justice's and Constable's Assistant*, published in 1803.[69] In Connecticut, twenty years after Zephaniah Swift had reported that hired laborers were not considered servants either in speech or in law, Tapping Reeve's *Law of Baron and Femme* (1816) followed Blackstone in stating that they were.[70] In Massachusetts, where Samuel Freeman's *Massachusetts Justice* (1802) had confined its treatment of servants to minors,[71] Nathan Dane's encyclopedic *General Abridgment and Digest of American Law* (1823) introduced the title "Master and Servant" and followed the Blackstonian categorization in describing its contents.[72] So too did New York's Chancellor James Kent in his *Commentaries on American Law* published in 1826. In a subsequent edition Kent underlined that he saw no legal distinction between "hired" and "menial" or "domestic" servants.[73] By Timothy Walker's time employment and the relation of master and servant had become synonymous.

The master-servant relation described by these commentators was very different from the paradigmatic colonial master-servant relation of indentured servitude. The key characteristic of the latter was, after all, that the servant's abandonment of his or her service was criminally sanctioned.[74] I have found no clear indication that the hired American laborer of the early nineteenth century anywhere risked criminal prosecution for breach of contract.[75] But then neither had the hired laborer of the eighteenth. We have already noted Peter Kalm's midcentury observation that in the colonies unindented wage workers were free to depart their employment at any time they chose. Similar evidence is available from later in the century. When Caleb Brinton hired James Greenway and John Cuff to work on his Chester County, Pennsylvania, farm in 1781, for example, their agreement provided that should Greenway and Cuff neglect or refuse to work Brinton would have the right to hire other workers in their place with Greenway and Cuff liable for the cost. The inference is plain that Brinton was not in any position to force his hirelings to perform their agreement and could only seek damages for the breach.[76] William Nelson's work on colonial Massachusetts similarly indicates that employers confronted by quitting employees had no recourse to criminal sanctions but only to the recovery of damages through a civil suit for nonperformance.[77]

Law, then, had not been fundamentally engaged in regulating the hireling relation during the eighteenth century as it had indentured servitude. As the sociolegal landscape changed—as work became predominantly work for hire—a generic law of employment emerged.

What was significant about the generic employment relation, stressed alike by early nineteenth-century commentators such as Reeve and Dane and by those of the late nineteenth and early twentieth centuries such as Schouler, Wood, and Labatt, was its presumption that employment as a social relation was necessarily defined by the exercise of authority by a superior over a subordinate in whatever processes of production the latter was engaged. Thus, to Tapping Reeve, a master was "one who, by law, has a right to a *personal* authority over another; and such person, over whom such authority may be rightfully exercised, is a servant." According to Reeve, this authority originated in the agreement made between the parties and was thus independent of the provisions of local statute dealing with the several relations of servitude known in Connecticut. *Any* agreement to labor for another, that is, was presumed to be agreement to the exercise of authority by that other over one for as long as the agreement continued.[78]

Reeve's formulation of the master's right to authority over the employee shows that it was a *legally implied* term of the contract; that is, it was part of the definition in law of what constituted a contract of employment.[79] The foundations of that implied term lay in the original categorization of master-servant in English law as one of the "oeconomical" or household relations. As I have stressed, these relations cannot be regarded as synonymous with all forms of employment, even in the early-modern epoch. The colonial evidence, as we have seen, shows hired labor largely outside these relations. Yet they became the basis for the law of employment in the modern era.[80] Moreover, as its catchment area expanded master-servant itself migrated from its home among the personal relations, where Reeve had left it, toward what Timothy Walker called the business relations. This relocation made eminently good sense to Walker: master and servant "has in fact very little to do with domestics, or domestic life," he wrote in 1837.[81] It also made sense to American courts, and by midcentury the tendency to remove master and servant from among the personal relations was becoming manifest in judicial opinion.[82] Yet these same opinions continued to affirm the employer's authority as a necessary incident of the employment contract: the implied term, that is, remained, though now as an incident of "business" not "personal" authority.

LEGAL REINFORCEMENT OF THE EMPLOYER'S AUTHORITY

The authority conveyed in the employment contract was reinforced by a variety of sanctions. Most familiar to labor historians are the criminal sanctions, in the form of conspiracy indictments, that protected employers from *collective* interferences in the employment relation by their employees or by others not party to the employment relationship.[83] In the most famous of the antebellum criminal conspiracy cases, *Commonwealth v. Hunt* (1842), the question whether the defendants charged with a collective refusal to work for an employer were "bound by contract for a certain time" or, alternatively, whether they had sought to interfere with the employment of others so bound was for the first time made an explicit feature of the test of these sanctions' applicability by a court of record.[84] Because in that case the Supreme Judicial Court of Massachusetts dismissed the indictment—on the ground that by failing to allege specific unlawful means or ends it had failed to conform to these tests—*Hunt* has traditionally been represented as a significant departure in the criminal law of collective employee activity.[85] In some respects, indeed, this is an appropriate conclusion to draw.[86] Yet it is worth stressing that in Massachusetts, as elsewhere, criminal conspiracy continued to be invoked as a counter to combinations among employees both before and after the Civil War[87] and that in fact *Hunt* implied no limitation on the use of criminal conspiracy against journeymen's combined interferences with subsisting contracts beyond its requirement of conformity with the procedural safeguards described in the court's critique of the indictment. Indeed, on the fundamental issue exciting most debate over the law of criminal conspiracy in both English and American courts at the time—whether merely private injuries were criminally indictable if procured by unlawful means, even if they posed no threat to the general welfare—*Hunt* was at one with the tendency toward permitting prosecutions to proceed.[88]

Protecting the employer against business injuries consequent upon the activities of combinations of employees through conspiracy indictments used criminal law to underwrite the authority of the employer within his own entrepreneurial walls. As an English court sitting *nisi prius* in Lancaster in 1832 observed, it was not to be contemplated that workmen should be "empower[ed] . . . to meet and combine for the purpose of dictating to the master." To recognize such a right in the employees, said the Supreme Court of New Jersey in 1867, would be to allow workmen "to control the business of another."[89] More specifically, however, *Hunt* invoked an employer's right to be protected from the interference of others with his enjoyment of his property in the services of those he employed. Earlier nonconspiracy cases had already confirmed the availability of this sanction. In *Boston Glass Manufactory v. Binney* (1827), for example, the Supreme Judicial Court of Massachusetts had indicated that as long as the action was founded on a current engagement, courts would agree to protect an employer from any interference by a third party (here a rival employer rather than a combination of employees) attempting to entice an employee from the service of the original employer. The novelty here lay not in the action itself but in the circumstances of its application, for these illustrate the carryover into the generic nineteenth-century law of employment of key disciplinary characteristics derived from the narrower sphere of household relations. Every man, said Blackstone, had a property "in the service of his *domestics*, acquired by the contract of hiring, and purchased by giving them wages." Early nineteenth-century American courts had already confirmed the availability of enticement as an action incident to personal relations to protect a master's property in the service of his apprentice or his indented servant, a husband's in the service of his wife, and a parent's in the service of his child. In *Binney*, the Supreme Judicial Court indicated that the expanding bounds of the master-servant relation had now encompassed hired adult artisans and confirmed that satisfactory evidence of a continuing relationship of employment would enable it to extend protection against enticement to an employer's property in their services as well.[90] Subsequently the action was placed more fully on the contract of employment and reconceptualized as a "tort of interference with contractual relations," effectively making every contract of employment an enforceable grant to the employer of property rights in the employee's labor.[91]

Enticement gave the employer a right of action against both the enticer and the departing employee, although "he cannot recover against both for the same loss." Where the employee had departed in breach of an engagement of his or her own accord, nineteenth-century courts would also allow harboring actions against successor employers if the successor continued the engagement despite notice of the previous breach. Courts also continued to treat simple breach of an engagement as an unlawful act in itself, laying a foundation for a civil action for damages against the employee.[92]

A third legal sanction disciplining the generality of employees firmly established in the early nineteenth century was the denial to employees departing their engagements before term any right to recover such wages as they might be owed at the moment of departure.[93] The first reported American instance of this is the New York case *M'Millan et al. v. Vanderlip* (1815) where Vanderlip, having abandoned his engagement with the defendants as a spinner (to spin for ten and a half months at three cents per run) sued for the wages owed him for the 845 runs he had actually spun. A lower court jury granted him $22.35, being the balance less $3.00 already advanced by the employer.

The New York Supreme Court, however, ruled that Vanderlip had no right of recovery. Citing "the good sense of modern times," the court interpreted the parties' agreement as an entire contract upon which Vanderlip could not sue until he had completed his term of service. The court's statement clearly implied innovation. It also expressed a more general concern that its ruling should be understood to apply to all wage labor engagements:

> It appears to me, that the construction I have put on this contract, is not only warranted by the agreement itself, but that it is a very useful and salutary one. The general practice, in hiring laborers or artisans, is, for 6 or 12 months, at so much per month: the farmer hires a man for 6 or 12 months, at monthly wages; and he takes his chance of the good, with the bad months. It is well known, that the labor of a man, during the summer months, is worth double the labor of the same man in winter; but upon the principles contended for by the defendant's counsel, if the farmer hires in the autumn, for twelve months, at monthly wages, the laborer may quit his employ on the first of May, and sue for his wages, and recover them, leaving the farmer the poor resort of a suit to damages. The rule contended for holds out temptations to men to violate their contracts.[94]

A more complete statement of the issue, one directly underscoring both its innovative character and its disciplinary incidents, came from the Massachusetts Supreme Judicial Court in 1824. Here a farm laborer, John Stark, had sued Thomas Parker to recover money owed for labor on the latter's farm. As in New York, the lower court had allowed recovery. And as in New York, the higher court denied it. "The plaintiff was to labor for one year at an agreed price." It would be "repugnant to the general understanding of the nature of such engagements" and "a flagrant violation of the first principles of justice" to permit him to avoid his agreement and simply recover wages owed for time actually spent laboring. The performance of the year's service was "a condition precedent to the obligation of payment" and must be performed in its entirety "before he is entitled to anything."

Although the court made reference to "ancient and well established principles" and "the usages of the country and common opinion" in support of its ruling in *Stark*, both its own comments and local reaction to the decision indicate that the ruling in fact represented a major innovation in local law. "It has been urged that . . . a different rule of construction has been adopted in this commonwealth," the court noted. "And we are bound to believe that such has sometimes been the fact, from the opinion of the learned and respectable judge who tried this cause, and from instances of similar decisions cited at the bar, but not reported." Such had indeed been the fact, as the Boston *Courier*'s report of the case (reprinted from the *Massachusetts Yeoman*) makes clear:

> It is an evil of which almost every farmer has had cause to com-
> plain, that labourers, after being hired for a term of time, for six
> months or a year, frequently leave the service of those with
> whom they have so contracted before the expiration of the
> term, and at a time when their labor is the most valuable; and
> afterwards claim payment for the time they have worked, pre-
> cisely as if there had been no hiring for any specific time. This
> claim, unfair and unreasonable as it seems to be, has been sus-
> tained by Courts, which have allowed the labourer to recover
> "as much as he reasonably deserved to have," taking into con-
> sideration the time he has worked, and the damages, if any,
> which his employer has suffered by his failing to serve out the
> stipulated time. *This has been generally understood to be the
> common law of the State.*

Hailing *Stark* as a decision of great importance to the community in general, and "agriculturists" in particular, the *Courier* informed its readers that the matter had now been decided otherwise. "It is decided that where this is a contract to labour for a certain term, at a stipulated price for the term, and the labourer voluntarily leaves the service of his employer before the expiration of the term, without sufficient cause *and without the consent of the employer*, he cannot recover any part of his wages."[95]

The decision in *Stark* accompanied increasing resort to undiffer-entiated wage labor in New England agriculture[96] and appears to evince a desire to give Massachusetts law a disciplinary capacity in the case of such labor that it had theretofore lacked. Certainly it was very much to the fore in the court's consideration, as indeed it appeared to have been in New York, that "in this commonwealth . . . the important business of husbandry leads to multiplied engagements of precisely this description." There was, of course, no hint here of resort to the criminal restraints on departure which had characterized English ser-vice in husbandry. But as we have seen, there is little evidence that such restraints had ever been applied in America, and certainly not in New England, to other than indentured servants. Particularly in light of what appears to have been previous practice—that the departing worker could recover wages owed at the moment of departure and be held liable to the employer in set-off only for the cost of finding a replacement—the loss of wages owed on an agreement to labor for a specific term (a parol agreement at that) seems a significant move toward enhanced contractual discipline.[97]

FIDELITY, OBEDIENCE, CONTROL

In *Stark*, the court dealt with the relationship of the parties in ways indicating that it conceived of them as necessarily unequal by dint of the kind of relationship in which it found them. The service of the plaintiff for a year was a condition precedent to his recovery of the stipulated compensation, and this was how "employer and employed alike universally so understand it." The laborer was worthy of his hire "only upon the performance of his contract, *and as the reward of fidelity.*"[98] Employment relationships, that is, had a necessary hierarchical component that distinguished them from other kinds of contracts—the employer was entitled not only to receipt of the services contracted for in their entirety before payment but also to the obedience of the employee in the process of rendering them. As the Massachusetts Supreme Judicial Court put it in 1833 in a general statement of the relationship, the relation of employer and employee was a "relation of superior and subordinate, of master and servant," the engagement requiring that those engaged or employed be "subject to [the] order, control and direction" of the employer.[99]

The presumption that the act of entering employment was simultaneously an accession by the employee to the exercise of authority and control by the employer echoes throughout the case law of the first half of the nineteenth century. Conceiving employment as a relation of legal subordination, however, sat oddly with the courts' simultaneous commitment to an ideology of free contract, which represented employment as a relationship whose design was arrived at in a process of mutual bargaining sufficiently free of power disparities that the employee might reasonably be held responsible for the consequences of her own decision to enter.[100] The contradiction was rendered most acutely in the series of employer liability cases beginning with *Farwell v. Boston and Worcester Railroad* (1842),[101] for these necessarily resulted in the appearance of a sharp contrast between two juridical representations of employees as, on the one hand, *servants* who were bound, because of the particular incidents built into the contract of employment, to follow the directions of their employer and, on the other, as *free-willed actors* who in entering employment took upon themselves its "natural and ordinary risks and perils," including the risk of injury at the hands of another employee similarly answerable, by his contract, to the authority of the common employer.

Almost invariably courts refused to find an employer liable for injuries induced by fellow servants, citing both the theory of contractual allocation of risk and also a theory of public benefit accruing from the imposition on employees of a duty to police themselves. Both theories assumed the autonomy of the employee. Neither gave any recognition to the disparity of power between employer and employee within the employment relationship, to the "order, control and subjection" to which the employee was required to submit.

In some instances, however, notably in cases where the injury to the employee was directly the result of negligent acts of those "fellow servants" employed as supervisors, the disparity became too difficult to ignore. This led to two kinds of discussion. A few courts modified the fellow servant rule. "[The defendant] engaged to serve the company in the capacity of brakeman, and to submit in all things to the orders and control of the conductor who might be placed over him by the company, and put in charge of the train," noted the Supreme Court of Ohio in 1854. "He had no power to determine who this conductor should be, and no right to control or participate in the duties which the company had devolved upon the conductor. He had, by his contract, promised obedience; and this the company had a right to require, and they received it." The quid pro quo of the employee's obedience was the employer's liability for the acts of those placed in positions of command, in this case the conductor. "His will alone controls everything, and it is the will of the owner that his intelligence alone should be trusted for this purpose." Employees bound to obey the orders of the superior placed over them, and performing as directed, could not be made to bear losses arising from the superior's carelessness "until we are prepared to say that justice and public policy require the consequences of duty omitted by one party to be visited upon the other, although stripped of all power to prevent such consequences."[102]

Most courts, however, chose instead to assert the necessity that the authority of the employer remain untrammeled by the restraint of legal responsibility for the consequences of its exercise. "If this were the rule, it would embarrass the conduct of all business, where any risk is to be run" said the Supreme Court of Pennsylvania in *Ryan v. the Cumberland Valley Railroad Company.* "How could a sailor be ordered aloft in a storm, without the employers being liable to the charge that the captain had shown want of proper skill and care in giving such an order in the circumstances?"[103] How indeed?

CONCLUSION

The decision of the Supreme Court of Pennsylvania in *Ryan* was made in the name of "a sacrifice of liberty on the part of those intended to be protected." The duty the plaintiff sought to impose "is substantially one of protection, which cannot exist without implying the correlative one of dependence or subjection." In this court, in this case, the relation of master and servant was not a relation of protection and dependence but one of equality before the law.[104] Yet as we have seen, master and servant was, in its most important respects, precisely a legal relation of subjection, one held to entail fidelity, obedience, and sacrifice of control on the part of the employee. Nor were these assumptions that were dying out in the course of the nineteenth century. On the contrary, since the beginning of the century they had undergone expansion beyond their original boundaries until they encompassed the generality of employment relations.

As we saw at the outset, contemporaries were aware that equalitarian contractual rhetoric existed side by side with disparities of power emanating from the asymmetry of monetary exchange, which undermined the possibility of substantive equality in the wage bargain. Similar disparities emanated from the positional asymmetry of the subjects "employer" and "employee" in legal discourse. In legal contemplation employees had the right to enter the employment relationship on the best terms they could negotiate. Their right of exit, however, was encumbered by significant legally imposed costs. Moreover, the essence of the relation itself—the controlling authority of the employer—was legally inscribed on their contract in a manner that left it outside the realm of negotiation altogether. Employees were thereby legally placed in a condition of disadvantage. The apparent symmetry of civic equality outside the nineteenth-century employment relationship always became asymmetry within it.

NOTES

I wish to thank Dan Ernst and Amy Stanley for their detailed comments on an earlier draft of this essay, and Joel Rogers and Robert Steinfeld for helpful suggestions. Much of the research for this essay was undertaken while I was Senior Fellow of the Commonwealth Center for the Study of American Culture and Visiting Professor of Law, College of William and Mary. My thanks to Bob Gross, Chandos Brown, David Rabban, Saul Cornell, and Richard Johns for their stimulating discussion of some initial thoughts.

1. See, for example, Wilentz 1984b; Dawley 1976.
2. Frieze 1844: 64.
3. Reddy 1987: 64–73, and see generally 62–106. As Reddy notes, mon-

etary asymmetry also has a formidable disciplinary effect once employment has commenced, in that the personal consequences of failing to maintain the relationship, like the consequences of failing to enter into it in the first place, are far more serious for the employee than the employer: 94.

4. Schouler 1870: 599.

5. See nn. 100–104 below, and cases cited.

6. 20 Ohio R. 416, 433 (emphasis added).

7. See, for example, *Elder v. Bemis*, 43 Mass. 599 (1841).

8. Schouler 1870: 599.

9. Tomlins 1988a: 413.

10. In *Commonwealth v. Hunt*, 45 Mass. 111 (1842), Chief Justice Lemuel Shaw distinguished collective interferences with an employer's authority once an employment relationship had been entered into from the collective negotiation of terms at the point of entry. Once bound by contract, interference, as in a collective quitting of employment, was criminally sanctionable. See also nn. 84–88 below and accompanying text.

11. T. Walker 1837: 243 (emphasis added).

12. Schouler 1870: 600. See also Wood 1877: 2–4.

13. For an exploration of the employment relationship considered as a species of bailment, see Schouler 1880: 91–128; Story 1832: 275–88.

14. Tomlins 1989: 197–98.

15. See, for example, Steinfeld 1991; E. Clark 1983: 337; E. S. Morgan 1966: 109; Putnam 1908: 79–80, 181–84. See also Pollock and Maitland 1923, 1: 282–90.

16. See, for example, Laslett 1964: 150–54; 1973: ix. See also Kussmaul 1981: 3–10.

17. For an analysis of the making of the Statute of Artificers consonant with this approach, see Bindoff 1961.

18. Dalton 1619: 68–75; Wood 1877: 3; Holdsworth 1936, 2: 461. See also Malcolmson 1981: 35–38, 54, 65–67.

19. See, for example, Kussmaul 1981: 135–42; Snell 1985: 73–84; McIntosh 1984.

20. A. H. Smith 1989: 31. See also Tawney and Tawney 1934.

21. Steinfeld 1991; Linder 1989: 45–55. See also E. Clark 1983: 332–36.

22. G. H. Jones 1958.

23. Defoe 1724.

24. Ibid., 91–94; Linder 1989: 55. See also Tawney and Tawney 1934: 46–49, 54–57; Millward 1981.

25. Tomlins 1989: 200.

26. Haines 1980: 271–73.

27. G. D. Clark 1967: 7. Here "domestic worker" refers to a worker in the putting-out system and not to a domestic servant.

28. M. Hale 1713: 50.

29. Ibid., 117–18, 123.

30. Burn 1757 [1743], 3: 229–65. See also Viner 1742–53, 15: 308–34.

31. Burn 1757, 3: 244–65.

32. Blackstone 1979, 1: 410–20, at 414–15. See also Kahn-Freund 1977: 508–28, particularly 511.

33. Chapin 1983: 136–37. On the relationship between indentured servitude and service in husbandry, see Galenson 1981: 6–8; J. P. Greene 1988: 10; Steinfeld 1991. On the growing distinctiveness of indentured servitude in colonial law in the later seventeenth and eighteenth centuries, see Steinfeld 1991.

34. Innes 1988a: 18–32, 43–44. Innes notes that "the major social divisions in the colonies were not between labor and capital, but between the free and unfree" and that "rather than class, the boundaries to these categories largely were set by age in the northern colonies and race in the plantation South." 18–19. See also Dunn 1984: 157–94; Salinger 1987; Innes 1988b; Russo 1989; Daniels 1989.

35. Matthews 1900: 21–28; Nellis 1977: 528. Vickers 1988: 56–60 notes that in Essex County, Massachusetts, "the limited system of servitude which did exist on county farms before 1675 bore little resemblance to English practice," that "farm service for native New England men and boys . . . was never common," and that labor needs unmet from the resources of the immediate farm family were covered by exchanges of labor services among interdependent households. See also Vickers 1990.

36. R. B. Morris 1981: 55–77. See also Nellis 1977: 535–38.

37. *Records of the Court of Assistants* 1901–28, 2: 37 (hereinafter RCA). It is worth noting that "servants" departing their masters before term were liable to return by force of arms, but not workmen or laborers. *The Book of the General Lawes and Libertyes* 1929 [1648]: 38.

38. RCA 1901–28, 2: 15.

39. Ibid., 27, 43, 51, 57, 59, 86, 97.

40. In England, in contrast, oral retainers were criminally enforceable. See G. H. Jones 1958.

41. RCA 1901–28, 2: 84, 88. Note also *William Deane v. Mr. Jonathan Wade* ("For prosecuting him after the manner of a runaway, the plaintiff being free"), in Records and Files of the Quarterly Courts of Essex County, Massachusetts (RFQE) 1911–21, 2: 62 (1658).

42. The court records thus agree with the conclusions reached by Towner 1954.

43. See, for example, *Waldron agt. Henderson*, Records of the Suffolk County Court (RSCC) 1933, 2: 901, 924, 1038 (1678). See also *Pennell agt. Pendell*, RSCC 1933, 2: 620 (1675); *Yardley agt. Boden*, RSCC 1933, 2: 775 (1677). In *Joyliffe agt. Nick* and again in *Davie agt. Hall*, both RSCC 1933, 2: 825 (1675) and 2: 876 (1678), the action was for nondelivery of goods and the verdict was for delivery or damages in lieu of performance. Cases of courts apparently ordering specific performance with no opportunity to avoid performance by paying damages in lieu do show up in the records earlier in the century—see, for example, *Henry Archer v. John Fullar*, RFQE 1911–21, 1: 147 (1648); J. H. Smith 1961: 236, 246, 247, 252; Innes 1983: 78–80—but these are very rare, and by the 1670s damages in lieu appears to have become established practice. (Richard B. Morris was in fact roundly criticized when *Government*

and Labor in Early America first appeared for claiming as examples of specific performance cases in which courts ordered performance *or* damages. See J. H. Smith 1946.) Thus see J. H. Smith 1961: 279. See also RSCC 1933, 1: liv.

44. This assertion is based on detailed examination of the following published court records: RCA 1901–28; RSCC 1933; RFQE 1911–21; Shurtleff 1855; J. H. Smith 1961; Konig 1978.

45. This point is developed in some detail in Tomlins 1989: 203–8.

46. Mather 1696: 30, 31, 51–55, emphasis added; W. C. White 1809, I: title XII; S. Freeman 1802. The ongoing scholarly investigation of the relationship between service and youth in early modern Europe is ably summarized in Mitterauer 1990. See also Kussmaul 1981: 72; Hajnal 1983: 93–97.

47. Act of 1662, "Hired Servants," in Hening 1823, 2: 115–16. The requirement that a "hired freeman" possess a certificate of freedom from a former master's service first appears in the Act of 1643. See Hening 1823, 1: 253–54. See also *Abridgment of the Laws* 1704: 59–61.

48. See, for example, S. M. Ames 1975 [1954]: 29; 1973: 61–62, 63, 218–19, 285, 289, 326.

49. See, for example, S. M. Ames 1973: 257, 229–41; Dorman 1962: 18; M. E. Parker 1971: 144, 248, 341.

50. In 1688, for example, we find the Charles City County court holding that "it is very dubious whether or not a hired servant shall be equally punishable as an indentured servant if he strikes his master." *Petition of Thomas Reeve*, in Weisiger 1980: 161. See also S. M. Ames 1973: 219, 353. And see E. S. Morgan 1975; Walsh 1977: 118–28; Carr and Menard 1979; Kulikoff 1986: 30–44; Russo 1989: 314; Daniels 1989.

51. Thus in Virginia the Act of 1705 "Concerning Servants and Slaves," which reenacted that of 1662, did not include the latter's provisions concerning specific performance of contracts by those "comeing free into the country." The Act of 1705 continued to require that all freed servants obtain freedom certificates and lodge these with successor employers on the grounds that "poor people may not be destitute of emploiment, under suspicion of their being servants," and appears to have extended at least in some of its elements beyond "imported" servants (whether bound by indenture or according to the custom of the country) to those "become servants of their own accord here" and "hired" servants. The Act of 1748 "Concerning Servants and Slaves," however, dropped all reference to servants other than those imported and bound by indenture or according to custom. The "Act Concerning Servants" of 1785 limited its definition of servants more explicitly to "white persons not being citizens of any of the confederated states of America, who shall come into this commonwealth under contract to serve another in any trade or occupation." Hening 1823, 3: 447–62; 5: 547–58; 8: 190–91.

52. Starke 1774: 318–19. For South Carolina see "An Act for the Better Governing and Regulating White Servants," passed in 1717, particularly at section VII, and compare the Act of 1744 at the same section. (Comparison suggests that by 1744 South Carolina's statutory regulation of servants was one confined to imported indentured servants.) See Cushing 1978c: 380–87; W. Simpson 1761: 227–38.

53. Rutman and Rutman 1984: 71 suggest that preslavery Virginia's indentured servant population was heavily skewed toward adolescents and young adults in the age range of fifteen to twenty-five years. See also Walsh 1977; J. Horn 1979.

54. de Valinger 1959.

55. One may, for example, note that Captain William Darvall's notice of appointment of his friend William Borne as his attorney to manage a Kent County plantation empowered Borne "to take In att his pleasure any freemen or buy any saruant or saruants." Ibid., 61.

56. See 13 Geo. II. c. LXXVII (1739), "An Act for the Better Regulation of Servants and Slaves within This Government," in Cushing 1981, 1, i: 210–16.

57. See the Act of 1713/14, "An Act for Regulating of White Servants," in Bush 1977, 2: 140–43. The preamble of this statute indicates that it was conceived as a regulation of servants imported into the province.

58. See the Act of 1684, "Concerning Masters, Servants, Slaves, Labourers and Apprentices," in *Records of the States of the United States*, Ser. B2, New York, Reel 1, amending The Duke of York's Laws (1665) tit. "Masters, Servants and Labourers," in Cushing 1978a: 151–52. New York's legislation was sparse, the colony passing no omnibus statute concerning servants during the colonial period.

59. See the "Duke of York's Laws" (1664), tit. Masters, Servants and Laborers (nb. American Addendum); "Laws Agreed upon in England" (1682), para. 23 and 29; "Laws Made att an Assembly Held att Philadelphia" (1683), chaps. 139, 153; all in Beckman 1976, 1: 98, 123, 157, 165. See also "An Act for the better Regulation of the Servants in this Province and Territories" (1700), in Cushing 1978b: 15–17, and the "Supplement" of 1771, in *Records of the States of the United States*, Ser. B2, Pennsylvania, Reel 3.

60. In Franklin 1759: 322–23. See also Matthews 1900: 14; Salinger 1987: 80–81. Franklin indicated that indented servants were distinguished from other forms of labor in that their "purchaser, by a positive Law, has a legal Property in them during the Term they are bound for." Franklin 1759: 93.

61. See *Conductor Generalis* 1711, 1722; J. Parker 1749.

62. Swift 1795, 1: 218. R. B. Morris 1981: 446 provides a similar insight on Pennsylvania law.

63. As in service for debt, or on conviction of crime, or in the case of the children of paupers, bound out as apprentices or servants by local authorities.

64. Instances of such voluntary covenants to serve may be found in all the published colonial court records used in this study. For one group of examples, see de Valinger 1959. Such covenants are also noted in Nellis 1979: 120–24.

65. Benson 1987: 204. See also *Tirrel v. Read*, in Konig 1978, 5: 388 (1731). Equally important, my examination of the Plymouth court records—easily the most comprehensive set of eighteenth-century court proceedings available in published form—discloses no instance of resort to the common law actions against enticement, beating, and so forth which protected an employer's property rights in services except in instances of apprentices or indented Indian or Black servants or slaves.

66. Greenleaf 1773. See also the preface to the *Conductor Generalis* 1722. Like the prerevolutionary justice of the peace (JP) books, Ladd 1792 also omitted those sections of Burn dealing with servants.

As the colonial JP guides indicate, there was no general colonial reception of English labor statutes. For Massachusetts, see the opinion of Chief Justice Lemuel Shaw in *Commonwealth v. Hunt* (1842), at 122. For South Carolina and North Carolina see the respective reception statutes of 1712, in Cooper 1837: 401, and 1749, in W. Clark 1904, 23: 317. Both ignored the English labor statutes. For Pennsylvania see the 1808 "Report of the Justices of the Supreme Court," 3 Binney 595, on English statutes theretofore in force, and the opinion of Brackenridge J. in *Ex Parte Meason*, 5 Binney 167, 180 (1812). In Virginia, Act 30 of 1632, in Hening 1823, 1: 167, announced that "the statutes for artificers and workmen are thought fitt to be published in this colony," but this referred to the 1 Jac. c.6 of 1604, establishing procedures for wage regulation, not to the statutes of laborers and artificers which had preceded it. Nor in any case did this "publication" survive the Grand Assembly of March 1661/62 and its wholesale reform of Virginia legislation. Writing in 1803, St. George Tucker noted that "The statute 5 Eliz. c. 4 [The Statute of Artificers] . . . is not in force in Virginia." Tucker 1803, 2: 425. Rhode Island appears to be the only colonial jurisdiction where the Statute of Artificers had lasting force. See Bartlett 1858, 1: 182–84; "An Act for Punishing Criminal Offences," 16 Car. 2 (1676) in Cushing 1977: 140, 146; "An Act for Punishing Criminal Offences" (1728) in *Acts and Laws of His Majesty's Colony of Rhode Island* 1730: 169–75; "An Act for the Punishment of Sundry Crimes," and "An Act to Prevent Masters and Mistresses Putting away Their Hired Servants," both in *The Charter Granted by His Majesty* 1767: 63, 176. Provision for the criminal liability of workers for hire departing before term does not formally disappear from Rhode Island statute law until the passage of an "Act to Reform the Penal Laws" in 1798. See *The Public Laws of the State of Rhode Island* 1798: 584–605. Colonial Rhode Island's singularity in the matter of criminal justice has been noted by John Murrin, who finds that the colony "enacted a highly romanticized version of English criminal justice," intended to advertise, in contrast to its neighbors, "the colony's dedication to English law." Murrin 1984: 168.

67. Keyssar 1986: 16; Innes 1988a: 31–32. See also Jacoby 1982: 91.

68. Hening 1795: 405–7, and compare Hening 1810: 393–95, 527–28. See also Hening 1820: 466–68, 625–66.

69. Graydon 1803: 281.

70. Reeve 1862 [1816]: 482. When Swift came to revise his treatment in the early 1820s he altered his position to reflect the new circumstances. See Swift 1822: 60–61.

71. S. Freeman 1802, 124–27. See also W. C. White 1809: tit. XII.

72. Dane 1823, 2: 312–13.

73. Kent 1826, 2: 201–14; 1832, 2: 261.

74. Although Darrett and Anita Rutman note that while the law "coerced [servants] back to their proper labor," it also became a site of compromise between servants who "used flight as a bargaining chip" and their masters in

need of their labor. Rutman and Rutman 1984: 132–33. See also J. H. Smith and Crowl 1975 [1964]: 490.

75. Although see *Commonwealth v. Isabella,* Boston Police Court (BPC) 689, 1052 (1824); *Commonwealth v. Daily,* BPC 1195 (1824); *Commonwealth v. Cutler,* BPC 578 (1826).

76. Clemens and Simler, 1988: 106–7. This is consistent with my research on seventeenth- and eighteenth-century published court records discussed earlier in this essay.

77. W. E. Nelson 1975: 57–58. As we have seen, where a defendant had breached an obligation to perform work for a plaintiff, seventeenth-century courts would sometimes order performance. See above n. 43. Neither I nor, to my knowledge, anyone else has found examples of courts ordering specific performance after the end of the seventeenth century, however, and the cases cited are generally confined to instances where a specific task had been undertaken. Such orders are more properly perceived in the context of the predominantly rural colonial economy of interdependent reciprocal obligation described in the scholarly literature; as cases, that is, involving the transfer of services rather than ar instances of courts enforcing agreements to perform labor for wages. In the records I have surveyed the only clear-cut examples of colonial courts using specific performance to police commitments to labor by hirelings are confined to the 1640s. See also Orren 1987: 324; Vickers 1990: 8–9.

78. Reeve 1862: 482.

79. And see Kahn-Freund 1977: 510–12, 521–23; Selznick 1969: 122–37.

80. Kahn-Freund 1977: 518–28.

81. T. Walker 1837: 250.

82. See, for example, *Ryan v. Cumberland Valley Railroad Company,* 23 Penn. State R. 384, 387 (1854).

83. Whereas English and colonial statutes concerning servants criminalized instances of individual behavior, conspiracy doctrine criminalized collective behavior. There are no examples of its application to combinations of wage workers during the colonial period. See R. B. Morris 1981: 136–207; 1937.

84. 45 Mass. 111, at 130–31. In his charge to the jury in the original trial hearing, Boston Municipal Court Judge Peter Oxenbridge Thacher argued that indeed the defendants *had* been guilty of "unlawful interference . . . with a subsisting contract between other persons" and thus merited conviction. See Woodman 1845: 609–54, at 644. The point upon which the Supreme Judicial Court and its Municipal Court colleague differed was not whether such behavior merited indictment but whether, in this case, the indictment had successfully alleged such behavior. In contrast to both Massachusetts courts we may note the opinion of Philadelphia Recorder Joseph Reed in an earlier conspiracy case, *Commonwealth v. Moore* (1827), that "a violation of the contract might be the subject of a civil action, but not of a criminal charge." In Gould 1827: 158.

85. See, for example, Levy 1967: 183–206.

86. The departure lay principally in the court's decisive endorsement of the trend in recent cases making the test of criminality the intentions and

behavior of the journeymen involved. This point is developed at some length in Tomlins forthcoming: chap. 6.

87. See, for example, Heard 1853: 388–89; Commons et al. 1966 [1918], 1: 611–13.

88. See Tomlins forthcoming.

89. *Rex v. Bykerdike*, 1 M. & Rob. 179, 180–81 (1832); *State v. Donaldson*, 32 New Jersey R. 151, 156 (1867).

90. 21 Mass. 425; Blackstone 1979, 1: 417. See also W. E. Nelson 1975: 126.

91. Nockleby 1980: 1510–39. See also Orren 1987: 329; R. B. Morris 1981: 433. Like mine, Morris's research also suggests that enticement actions were confined during the colonial period to formally bound (that is, apprenticed or indentured) servants. See 414–34.

92. We have seen that this was standard practice during the colonial period.

93. In England it had long been stated as well-established doctrine that, in the case of service, "if the Servant depart himself before the End of his Time, he loses all his Wages." W. Nelson 1729 [1704]: 44. See also Dalton 1619: 74; Karsten 1990: particularly 220–21. Yet in *Cutter v. Powell*, 6 T.R. 319, 101 E.R. 575 (1795), the bench adverted to a distinction between the circumstances of parties agreeing to an express written contract, which "speaks for itself," and hirings "in the general way," that is oral retainers for the customary annual term. In regard to the latter, "the general understanding upon the subject [is] that the servant shall be entitled to his wages for the time he serves though he do not continue in the service during the whole year." 577. See also *Worth v. Viner*, 3 Vin. Abr. 8–9; *Ex Parte Smyth*, 1 Swans 337, 36 E.R. 412, at 421 n. (1818); Barton 1987: 49, 60–61; Haines 1980: 277–80. Subsequently, in *Huttman v. Boulnois*, 2 Car. and P. 509, 172 E.R. 231 (1826), the relationship between "express contracts" and "the general understanding" was reversed, Abbott C.J. affirming that in the *absence* of an "express" agreement, the law's presumption that general hirings were hirings for a year was sufficient to defeat claims for wages owed litigated by hirelings departing before the expiry of a year's service, *because it was also to be presumed that yearly hirings were entire.* See also *Beeston v. Collyer*, 130 E.R. 786 (1827).

The American evidence is even less conclusive, no eighteenth-century colonial JP manual reproducing the English rule. The Swedish visitor Peter Kalm reported in the mideighteenth century that servants in the colonies departing before term were "in danger of losing their wages." Benson 1987: 204. On the other hand, Massachusetts evidence provides good grounds for believing that recoveries on an implied assumpsit for a *quantum meruit* had been allowed in cases involving work and labor before the early nineteenth century. See n. 95 below and accompanying text.

94. 12 Johnson 165, 166–67.

95. 19 Mass. 267, at 271–75 (emphasis added); Boston *Courier*, 23 July 1824 (emphasis added).

96. See Rothenberg 1988: particularly at 544–55. But see also C. Clark 1990: 59–60, 105–6; Kulikoff 1989.

97. The practice of *quantum meruit* recovery with damages to the employer in set-off was endorsed in the New Hampshire decision, *Britton v. Turner*, 6 N.H. 431 (1834), but the "entirety" construction prevailed everywhere else until the 1850s. See W. Holt 1986: particularly 678–700.

98. 19 Mass. 267, at 275 (emphasis added).

99. *Sproul v. Hemingway*, 31 Mass. 1, 4, 5 (1833).

100. *Rice v. Dwight Manufacturing Company*, 56 Mass. 80 (1848). See also *Mitchell v. Pennsylvania R.R. Company*, 1 American Law Register 717 (1853).

101. 45 Mass. R. 49.

102. *Cleveland, Columbus and Cincinnati Railroad Company v. Anthony Keary*, 3 Ohio St. R. 202, 208, 211, 219 (1854).

103. *Ryan v. Cumberland Valley Railroad Company*, 388.

104. Ibid., 387. See also *Strange v. McCormick*, 3 American Law Journal 398, 401 (Pa. 1851).

4 Hidden Dimensions in Labor Law History: Gender Variations on the Theme of Free Labor

Lea S. VanderVelde

Over the course of the nineteenth century, labor law underwent tremendous change, sometimes as the result of and sometimes in opposition to the emerging principle of free labor. The principle was developed, battled over, and played out in the law and customs governing various labor statuses—master and servant, indentured laborers, slaves, and apprentices—as well as in the legal treatment of labor organizations. The Civil War and Reconstruction era, in particular, saw a sea change in understandings of free labor. During these years, national attention was focused on the conditions of slavery and its abolition with an intensity and seriousness of purpose that had major implications for the law of labor relations in general.

Unfortunately, the significance of Reconstruction for the law of labor relations is still too rarely appreciated. Racial categories customarily compartmentalize our thoughts about the legal statuses of nineteenth-century workers. The fact that southern antebellum slavery was race based and racist has tended to dominate our understandings of American slavery, blocking examination of the similarities and connectedness of slavery to other systems of labor law. Several excellent works have highlighted differential treatment in working conditions based on race.[1] Little work has been done, however, on the connections between slavery and related forms of labor exploitation, or on how slavery legitimated the larger system of work relations law. Most scholarly work to date reproduces the bifurcation of the two labor systems along racial lines.

The effects of such a compartmentalization of scholarly inquiry are threefold. First, by seeing only one significant dichotomy—between free white men and slave black men—we have tended to ignore other statuses within the range. For example, the working conditions of free blacks are too often ignored, as are the conditions of bound European or Chinese immigrants and Native American laborers, and the often distinctly different conditions and status of women workers of each ethnic group.

A second and related consequence of compartmentalization is that the study of mainstream labor and employment law has focused on the study of the law and customs governing the free white working man, usually to the exclusion of other groups. The subject of slavery is rarely mentioned in standard texts on labor law and labor history. When describing the labor relations of the period, we frequently fail to state the important, and implicit, qualification that we are really only describing the labor relations of white working men. The omission of others is perhaps understandable if it is an attempt to limit the scope of study. Further, in the hegemony of nineteenth-century labor relations the status of free white working men *was* the standard; all other labor statuses were defined with reference to this status. Nevertheless, to neglect coverage of the legal treatment of slaves, or free blacks, or women—white or black, free or slave—is subtly to imply that those persons who together constituted the majority of the American work force did not play a role in labor history or in the formation of labor law.

Third and most important, no system of labor law is so self-contained that it exists in isolation. To compartmentalize all labor into two and only two categories is to preclude examination of those attributes that the different systems share and the complexities of their interrelationship. The common law system occasionally borrows legal rules and analogizes across seemingly intact categories. In its struggles to maintain stasis, it endlessly draws similarities and differences among categories. Legal categories are continuously erected, reconciled and demolished. As a result, legal rules that subjugate one subpopulation can and do spread across legally and culturally constructed barriers to subjugate other groups as well, just as legal rules that benefit one group can spill over to benefit those in other legal categories. By compartmentalizing labor systems in two and only two categories, we preclude ourselves from searching for examples that transcend the racial and gender lines drawn between the legal treatment of the several different types of laborers.

As I have elaborated elsewhere, the abolition of slavery was intended to abolish not one but two factors of subjugation.[2] That is, abolition was intended to establish *both* a condition of racial equality *and* a condition of free labor. In order to appreciate fully what nine-teenth-century labor history can teach us about the multifactored nature of subjugation—slavery both as labor and as racial servitude—we must find ways of disconnecting the familiar conjunctions and studying the different factors separately and in different combinations. Only then can we observe the multiple forces of subjugation and their reinforcing effect.

In this essay, to illustrate the advantages of such a multifactored strategy, I wish to highlight a line of cases known best from a dispute that arose from the refusal of an opera singer, Johanna Wagner, to perform her contract to sing at Her Majesty's Theatre in London. That dispute gave rise to the English cases, *Lumley v. Wagner*[3] and *Lumley v. Gye*,[4] decided in 1852 and 1853, respectively. In *Lumley v. Wagner*, the English Court of Chancery held that although Johanna Wagner could not be ordered to perform her contract, she could be enjoined from performing at any competing concert hall for the term of her contract. In turn, *Lumley* influenced American decisions in similar disputes involving performers throughout the nineteenth and into the twentieth century.

As we shall see, these American cases serve as a barometer of how the free labor principle fared in different decades of the nineteenth century. More than that, however, they offer a unique perspective on the free labor principle itself, in that the suits that provided the central contextual focus in which the *Lumley* rule was examined and adopted in America almost invariably involved the services of free white *women* performers.[5] During the period the *Lumley* rule was under consideration, many more women than men were sued under this cause of action. Moreover, the only cases during the entire century that ever permanently enjoined a performer from performing for an employer other than the one to whom she was originally contracted all involved women.[6]

Such a concentration of women litigants is anomalous in the nine-teenth century, an era in which women were unlikely to be parties to any employment litigation. On no other topic of employment litigation, save the tort of seduction, do women figure so prominently in the leading cases. Women were discouraged from engaging in wage-earning labor, and if they were married, the doctrine of coverture submerged their legal identity under their husband's. Thus, it is unusual in a supposedly gender-neutral subject like an employee's attempt to break with an employer, that where women litigants are present, their cases would outnumber men's by such a margin.

By acknowledging the gender factor, we bring different perspectives to bear on the contribution made by this line of cases to the changing concept of free labor. The compartmentalizing nature of the common law sometimes isolates and sometimes joins the subject "employee" together with different groups for distinctive treatment based on work, class, race, or gender. Arguments and acknowledgments of similarity and difference define these categories. Accordingly, in this line of cases, actresses are sometimes singled out for distinctive treatment, different from that of working people in general. In other cases, one of which I will describe in some detail, the substantive rights of the actress in question are treated as universally representative of all employees' rights, the court crossing racial, gender, and class lines to draw an analogy between the situation of a white actress and the abolition of slavery. Thus, I intend to highlight the gender factor as it reflects upon the evolving idea of free labor.

THE SIGNIFICANCE OF THE *LUMLEY* RULE
FOR FREE LABOR

Its use in law school contracts classes has made the case of *Lumley v. Wagner* one of the most familiar of all cases. In those classes, *Lumley* is usually lauded as a just and fair decision, one that illustrates the proper distinction between equitable orders that force performance (generally unworkable, impractical, and unjust) and equitable orders that prevent performance (sometimes workable, usually practical, and not necessarily unjust).

This legitimization of the *Lumley* rule fails to come to terms with its implications for free labor. Contracts classes rarely consider whether equitable intervention on behalf of the employer to prevent an employee from quitting and working elsewhere violates the American tradition of free labor and the right to quit employment. Yet from an employment perspective, the *Lumley* rule was really a regressive development, for it gave employers considerably greater leverage over purportedly free laborers seeking to quit than they had had under the previous American rule. In the wake of *Lumley*, employers were empowered to prevent employees from working anywhere else for the remaining term of the contract, a period that could last several years. Although the rule was supposed to be limited to employees who provided unique services, employers occasionally threatened to bring actions against employees who were not unique, presumably to deter or delay their departure.[7] The threat of injunctions could thus be used to control an employee's freedom to quit. In fact, by the century's end, theater employees were sometimes forced to sign standardized contracts stipulating that they were unique, presumably so that employers could control the disposition of their labor under the *Lumley* rule.[8]

Less well known than *Lumley v. Wagner* is a connected case arising out of the same incident, *Lumley v. Gye*. In this case, Lumley, the
disappointed agent for Her Majesty's Theatre, sued the rival theater
that had hired Ms. Wagner under the partially statutory, partially common law, cause of action for enticement.[9] Enticement actions allowed
individuals with an interest in the services of another to sue anyone
who interfered with the employee's services by enticing the employee
away from his or her contract.[10] Naturally, rival employers who offered
work to the departing employee fell within the scope of potential
defendants to these actions.

Significantly, enticement actions originated in conditions of compulsory labor. One historical antecedent of enticement actions was
the English medieval Statute of Laborers and Artificers, which made
the service of menial laborers compulsory and which was brought to
the American colonies in various forms.[11] The other significant antecedent was the multitude of cases in the United States seeking recovery of runaway slaves, apprentices, and indentured servants.

When the English courts ruled against Johanna Wagner's interests
in both cases, they permitted the application of negative injunctions
and enticement actions to workers of a particular legal status, professional workers under general employment contracts, who had never
before been subject to either type of employer control. Historically,
only menial laborers had been susceptible to these actions. Together
the force and effect of these causes of action imposed legal and equitable constraints on a performer's election to quit employment: the
one by enjoining the performer from performing elsewhere; and the
other by seeking damages and equitable orders against any other employer for whom the performer chose to work. In essence, these sanctions strengthened the employer's leverage over employees contemplating quitting, served to limit employees' mobility, and held
employees to their employer's consent in finding new jobs even when
the relationship between them had deteriorated.

The *Lumley* rule could not have been imported to the United
States at a less auspicious time. Nineteenth-century Americans prided
themselves on their resistance to the sorts of labor-class designations
and controls that were said to abound in Europe.[12] Midcentury American labor interests were struggling to ensure universal recognition of
the dignity of the laboring man and his equality with his employer.[13]
Working people were also seeking to reform some of the inequities of
the colonial master-servant relation inherited from British common
law by arguing against the very terms "master" and "servant" in favor
of the newer, more progressive language, "employer" and "employee."
Thus, rules such as the *Lumley* rule, which extended the scope of

employer control over menial servants to include control over the relatively independent providers of professional services, were an anathema on the American scene in the midnineteenth century. The Civil War and Abolition further strengthened public concern about working people's independence from their masters. The Thirteenth Amendment formalized the end of slavery and other involuntary servitudes and guaranteed the right to quit employment. The sanctions legitimated in the *Lumley* cases presented a particularly significant obstacle because they burdened the exercise of the constitutional guarantee. Thus *Lumley* sought root in American jurisprudence at precisely the same time that the aftermath of the Civil War had brought the issue of slavery and the right to be free from mastery before the American people.[14]

The problematic relationship between the sanctions endorsed in the *Lumley* cases and the abolition of slavery was more than theoretical. Considerable discussion of the right to be free from an employer's control is found in the Reconstruction debates.[15] In the context of considering the rights of the newly emancipated freedmen, the Reconstruction Congress repeatedly expressed the desire to guarantee that working people be able to quit their jobs without their employers' permission. The debates focused specifically on laws that attempted to order specific performance or to deter quitting by sanctioning employers who enticed away another master's former slaves. This national debate created an atmosphere of hostility to all forms of compulsory control of a working man's labor.[16]

In the midnineteenth century then, the two common law causes of action that potentially had the most impact in conditioning the right to quit were those epitomized in *Lumley v. Wagner* and *Lumley v. Gye,* suits brought by employers directly against employees and suits brought against competing employers to whose service departing employees had gone.

The rule of the *Lumley* cases that allowed employers to burden professional employees' rights to quit by barring them from working elsewhere was virtually alien to American courts in the early part of the century;[17] it was expressly rejected or ignored by American courts at its first introduction in the heady post–Civil War, labor emancipatory era. Yet by the 1890s it had quietly become the dominant common law rule in American courts. How this could occur appears to be related to the fact that most of the cases involved the services of women. It appears that women were seen as relationally bound to their male employers. Unlike the earlier cases, the texts of these opinions evince an inability to perceive women performers as fully free and

independent laborers, capable of disposing of their own labor and entitled to break off contracts with liability only for damages.

THE CASE HISTORIES

The nineteenth-century cases can be divided into two periods:
first, from 1800 to 1865, when employers attempted to sue for specific
performance of performers' contracts and equity courts refused to intervene, even to issue negative injunctions; and second, from 1865 to
1900, when *Lumley* was struggling to take root. In 1897, the second
edition of the definitive American treatise on specific performance,
John Norton Pomeroy's *Treatise on Specific Performance of Contracts*,
was published, establishing the canon.[18] Thereafter, cases tended to
cite Pomeroy as the standard, accepting without examination the ordering of policies in the treatise as it restated *Lumley* as the most
significant rule on the issue.

For the purposes of this essay, I will highlight the contrast between
the cases of the early and the later periods as they pertain to the concept
of free labor and sketch some of the patterns of difference that distinguish women's from men's cases as a means of illustrating the advantages of a multifactored approach to labor law history.[19]

The First Period

From 1800 to 1850, eight out of ten reported cases concerned the
professional or theatrical services of white men.[20] In these cases, the
respective employers asked courts to order specific performance of
their employment contracts (a request that employers continued to
make, though always unsuccessfully, throughout the nineteenth century). In only one of these cases did a court of equity actually grant
the plaintiff's request. The feature that distinguished the single case,
Morris v. Colman,[21] where the court granted both an order of specific
performance and an injunctive order barring work elsewhere, was the
nature of the relationship between the defendant and the theater, a
relationship that was characterized as one of partnership. Colman's
creative contribution to the partnership, in writing plays, was considered equally important to Morris's contribution of capital. "In partnership engagements," the court said, "a covenant, that the partners
shall not carry on for their private benefit that particular commercial
concern, in which they are jointly engaged, is not only permitted, but
is the constant course."[22] Apparently the court would equally enjoin
either of the partners from competing with the partnership—Colman
from writing for another theater, Morris from opening another play-

house. Morris, then, could have some recognizable claim on the commitment of Colman's labor, but Colman had mutual reciprocal claims on the commitment of capital controlled by Morris.

In none of the remaining cases did a court enjoin the employee from performing his, or in one case her, unique services for another employer. "Equity will not enforce a hard bargain," was the way one court put it. "Nothing could be more harsh towards a young man dealing with great traders than that he should be allowed to enter into an agreement which placed him so entirely in their power."[23]

The pre-*Lumley* opinions of this period treated the employment contract as a jurisprudential whole. Where entered into, a covenant not to work for another was viewed as one that merely guarded the "active" covenant of promised performance for the employer.[24] The "guarding" covenant could not be enforced if the primary "active" covenant could not be enforced.[25] The courts recognized that these ten cases involved employment contracts whose primary objective was the professional's performance. Pursuant to this rationale, these cases were distinguished from a separate line of cases involving covenants not to do an act standing alone,[26] or covenants not to compete tied to the sale of a business[27] or the communication of a trade secret.[28] In the cases involving employment contracts the primary agreement is to perform the task; the covenant not to work elsewhere is incidental.

Thus, specialized professional "employees" enjoyed a reciprocity with their employers. They could be bound by contract to the venture only when their employers could mutually be bound as their partners. Only in circumstances in which the performer was a co-partner and therefore liable to an order to perform, as in *Morris v. Colman*, could the performer be enjoined from working elsewhere. Once a performer who was not a co-partner repudiated the contract, the only remedy available was damages at law. Characteristic of the courts' rationale during this period was the statement that specific performance could not issue, absent a partnership, and therefore courts would not attempt indirectly to produce a result that they could not order directly.[29]

The Free Labor Concept in Full Bloom

The most significant American case of the first period is *Ford v. Jermon*, a case remarkable for a number of reasons. First, *Ford* is the first American case of this kind decided after the Civil War as well as after the decision in *Lumley v. Wagner*. *Lumley* is cited, but rejected as a case decided upon a misconceived assessment of the relevant underlying policies. Second, *Ford v. Jermon* is the first case of its kind in which an American working woman was sued in her own name.[30] Mrs. Jermon, a widow, had no husband, so the doctrine of coverture was inapplicable in deciding the case. No man stood as a party principal protecting Mrs. Jermon's interests. Perhaps as a result of this, the court went a considerable distance in giving her interests due consideration. But third, and most important, in this case the free labor principle was in full flower. The court's opinion in *Ford v. Jermon* was an unambiguous affirmation of Mrs. Jermon's independence and her right to be free of domination by her employer.

Judge Hare's opinion in the case shows the influence of the national debate on the abolition of slavery. By 1865, when the case went to court, the nation had witnessed the culmination of its prolonged national debate over slavery in the Emancipation Proclamation, the surrender of the Confederacy, and passage of the Thirteenth Amendment through Congress. Moreover, with the war finally ended, the nation was optimistic and somewhat reform minded. These currents reverberate throughout Judge Hare's opinion.

Mrs. Jermon, who had contracted to perform a play, decided not to go through with the performance. Her contract with the theater manager, Mr. Ford,[31]contained clauses providing both that she would perform on his stages and that she would not appear for any competing theater for the season's duration. In his complaint, Ford had requested an order of specific performance, compelling Mrs. Jermon to perform the play; this request was withdrawn before trial. He had also sought to enjoin her from performing for a competitor. The court concluded that it would be completely inequitable to force the actress to perform her labor contract or to prevent her from performing elsewhere.

Judge Hare's brief examination of the reasons why courts did not attempt to force performance generally tracked the policy reasons listed in *Lumley*. On the primary issue of injunctions, however, Judge Hare emphasized that the very policies for not compelling performance equally explained why Actress Jermon should not be enjoined from performing for competing theaters.[32] Judge Hare saw these orders as part of a continuum. It would be harsh to compel obedience by imprisonment, and it would be difficult or impossible to evaluate the quality of obedience when a performer reluctantly consented to appear. "I am unable to see that these difficulties are likely to be less, because the mode of compulsion is the indirect one of obliging the actor to remain idle until necessity forces him to comply."[33]

What began as a relatively narrow consideration of the practical difficulties of compelling an artistic performance then broadened into a discussion of the policy importance for all employees, regardless of trade or profession, of being able to quit and move on. Judge Hare saw in the request for the injunction an attempt to force Mrs. Jermon back to her employer by exploiting her need to earn a living. "We are asked to say that Mrs. Jermon shall not play at all, unless she will consent to play for the complainant; are we also to declare that she shall not sing? shall not earn her bread by writing or by her needle? To debar her from one pursuit would be vain and futile, unless she were also excluded from others, that might, so far as we can tell, be more profitable."

Embedded in this argument was a recognition of freedom to "earn one's bread" by one's chosen trade. Judge Hare questioned why the actress should be indirectly compelled to come to terms with a theater owner for whom she now refused to work. To what lengths should the court go in keeping her to her contract if the alternative was preventing her from earning her daily bread elsewhere? Hare's words were not simply a description of the court's powerlessness to execute affirmative commands successfully; rather, they were dramatic affirmation of the underlying importance of protecting the employee's right to quit and to pursue her trade elsewhere.

Judge Hare then proceeded to articulate the free labor principle: "Is it not obvious that a contract for personal services thus enforced would be *but a mitigated form of slavery*, in which the party would have lost the right to dispose of himself as a free agent, and be, for a greater or less length of time, subject to the control of another?"[34] This statement must be understood in the context of the free labor agenda that had gained political prominence in the Free Soil party and the newly founded Republican party. One of the precepts of this political movement was the right of all working people to dispose of themselves as free agents and not be subject to the control of another.[35] The Republicans, who dominated the political discourse of the day, saw a vital link between the abolition of slavery and greater employment liberties for all workers.[36]

Judge Hare saw the distinction that the English Court of Chancery had erected in *Lumley* between equitable orders that force performance and equitable orders that prevent performance as exalting form over substance. He viewed them as tending to the same purpose or effect, forming a continuum along the spectrum of employment liberty. Similarly, the relevant issue was not the terms of the contract. It would do theater managers no good to draft stronger language in future employment contracts because it was the substance of the provision, the fact that the individual "would have lost the right to dispose of himself as a free agent, and be, for a greater or less length of time, subject to the control of another" that was objectionable.

It is noteworthy that the free labor principle was being used here to shield a professional employee from her employer's attempt to enjoin her from performing at competing theaters. This particular employment context was one in which the defendant presumably had *more* status, freedom, and bargaining power than the average unskilled or semiskilled working person.[37] Despite these differences in status, the court did not resort to the argument that she must be enjoined because she had voluntarily submitted to this result in the language of the contract. Notwithstanding her position of relatively greater status than most employees, like them she still had to work to eat. The free labor principle still came to her aid as a means of analyzing her relative power with respect to Ford. Significantly, the court never asked her to produce or justify her reasons for quitting. It was her right.

Moreover, the court considered the precedential consequences of this case for other employees. If Mrs. Jermon could be enjoined, would other service providers likewise be subordinated to their employers— "lawyers . . . to their clients, mechanics to their employers, and even servants to their masters, by the same process?"[38] Mrs. Jermon was not just a sympathetic widow in Judge Hare's eyes; she was a representative of an entire class of service providers, a class that exactly spanned the constituency of the Republican party, from lawyers to mechanics to servants.[39] Not only were Judge Hare's instincts the instincts of a Republican free labor adherent; he allowed a woman to be a representative of the class interests of service providers and analogized from her situation to theirs. The fact that she was a woman constituted no disability on her free agency to control how she disposed of her labor.

Ford v. Jermon is an interesting and noteworthy case because from a fully compartmentalized perspective, one would not have expected the court to analogize the defendant's circumstances both to the broad constituency of the Republican party and to slavery, taking the analogy across gender lines, across race lines, and across class lines. Judge Hare rejected the limited view of labor statuses as circumscribed by demographic characteristics in favor of a universal view.

Before the 1860s the compartmentalization of separate labor statuses could be considered relatively intact. With the emancipation of the slaves and the national consideration of their new labor status, however, the edges of the compartmentalized labor system were beginning to unravel. The oppression of slaves could have been considered a unique situation, isolated from other labor statuses by region, by legal status, and by race, a situation making the experiences and legal circumstances of those individuals formally and qualitatively distinct from and inapposite to that of a white actress choosing to leave her employer and thereby breaching her contract. But Judge Hare saw the interests of working people as unified in this respect. Mrs. Jermon's right to be free from the mastery of Ford is the predominant theme of the opinion, and the opinion tells us much about the free labor sentiment of the day.

The Second Period

Daly v. Smith, decided in 1874, was the first American case to follow the *Lumley* rule by permanently enjoining a performer from performing for anyone else for the length of the contract term.[40] In contrast to the circumstances prevailing ten years previously, Reconstruction by this time was nearing its end. The national revulsion against mastery had lessened in general, and it no longer applied to men's domination of women in particular.

In the theater women were coming into their own. Broadway was expanding and flourishing. The American theater was becoming big business. As never before, women were performing more openly in public, forming their own theater companies, designing careers, commanding top billing and top dollar, and heading up touring companies to the West.[41] Outside the theater, however, Victorian ideology was prescribing a stricter code of propriety and conduct of middle-class women than had prevailed in earlier decades. The popular notion that a woman's life was properly limited to hearth and home became more generally accepted. When women appeared in public and did not comport themselves according to the strictures of propriety, the standard reproach was to label them prostitutes. Women were denied access to most professions and to many trades, and they customarily earned less than men even in factory work. In short, women who sought to work for wages outside the home met obstacles ranging from legal and economic sanctions to outright social disapproval.[42]

These contrary trends placed the actress in a precarious position. In the words of historian Claudia Johnson, the late nineteenth-century actress "was able to anticipate professional rewards which few other women in the age enjoyed, but only at considerable sacrifice of intangibles precious to nineteenth-century women—personal esteem and social acceptability."[43] Outside the theater community, the acting profession, and most particularly actresses, were viewed with suspicion. By the very act of performing in public actresses defied the social norm that the place for women was in the home. Moreover, actresses were expected to travel with men and to appear in a mode of dress that violated the expectations of piety in the Victorian ideology of "true womanhood." As a result, actresses were especially apt to be characterized as fallen women.

Cases involving women performers dominate the litigation base of professional employment cases decided during this period: Annette Galetti, Auguste Sohlke, Fanny Morant Smith, Loie Fuller.[44] Most important was Lillian Russell, who appeared in three of the major cases of the period and whose memoirs disclose that she was involved in many other similar disputes.[45] During this critical period of law formation, when American courts were deliberating whether they would exercise any equitable jurisdiction over quitting performers, more than twice as many cases involved women performers as men.[46] Of only five reported cases during the entire century that permanently enjoined performers from performing elsewhere for the duration of the contract term, all involved women.[47] Three of the cases involved women of considerable stature in the theater. Two others enjoined women performers who were far less powerful and less independent of their theater employers. Moreover, in three of the five cases the courts enjoined actresses even when the contracts failed to contain any contract language or negative covenants purporting to reserve an exclusive right to the woman's services. These opinions indicate the courts' willingness to surpass even the language of the contracts in fashioning for the actresses a status subservient to their male employers' control.[48]

Beyond the quantitative evidence provided by the numbers of cases involving women is their distinctive qualitative nature. The ostensibly logical course of doctrine was frequently distorted in these cases in order to justify the issuance of injunctions against women performers and to deny their issuance in those few parallel cases involving men. In addition, the courts used language and imagery in describing the women and their claims that is subtly but distinctly gendered. The gist of the rulings was that if the lady's employer couldn't have her services, no one could.

Pomeroy's canon was constructed on *Daly v. Smith* and one of Lillian Russell's three cases, all of which evinced these qualitative distinctions to some degree. Decided in 1874, *Daly v. Smith*[49] involved Fanny Morant Smith, "a distinguished actress and a great artistic acquisition."[50] Mrs. Smith was a wealthy woman married to a rich New York industrialist and financially able to contemplate buying her way out of her contract. The opinion in the case is as biting in spirit toward the notion of Smith's free agency as the opinion in *Ford v. Jermon* is magnanimous.[51]

Through a series of incidents, Mrs. Smith had concluded that remaining with the theater manager, Augustin Daly, was harmful to her career. She had been left in the lurch when a previous theater season was canceled early, and she complained that the roles in which she was cast—as a character actress rather than a leading lady—were beneath her talents. Although she had signed on for another three years, she had come to believe that Daly's true motive in signing her was not really to produce her, but to keep her off the stage and away from rival theaters. Realizing her mistake, she had approached Daly to get out of the contract and posted a twenty thousand dollar surety bond against any damages for breach of contract for which she might have been liable. In other words, Mrs. Smith was prepared to pay damages to get out of the contract.

The judge's opinion indicates that his sympathies were entirely with the theater. It is perhaps not surprising that a powerful and wealthy actress like Mrs. Smith (or, in the later cases, Lillian Russell) did not evoke the court's sympathies the way that Mrs. Jermon had. Mrs. Smith would not be in danger of starving or going to beggar's prison[52] should she be foreclosed from performing at another theater. And yet her wealth stood her in no great stead with regard to an even-handed application of the usual legal rules. She was not given the benefit of her ability to pay off her breach of contract with damages.

Judge Freedman stated that he could conceive "of no reason why contracts for theatrical performances should stand upon a different footing than other contracts involving the exercise of intellectual faculties; why actors and actresses should, by the law of contracts, be treated as a specially privileged class, or why theatrical managers, who have to rely upon their contracts with performers of attractive talents . . . should, with the large capital necessarily invested in their business, be left completely at the mercy of their performers."[53] By proverbially "setting the stage" in this way, Judge Freedman accomplished two reversals of the customary equities between performers and managers. First, he sketched all the equities of unequal power or abuse of power as running in favor of the employer-theater owner, rather than the employee-performer. And second, he characterized the right to quit free from intervention by a court of equity as in effect a special privilege claimed by actors and actresses who sought to be placed on a different footing than others. Naturally, this suggested an intention to strip actors and actresses of an unwarranted special privilege.[54]

Judge Freedman continued by expressing almost a passing regret that he could not do more to order Mrs. Smith to perform the contract: "I am of the opinion that actors and actresses, like all other persons, should be held to a true and faithful performance of their engagements, and that whenever the court has not proper jurisdiction to enforce the whole engagement, *it should*, like in all other cases, *operate to bind their consciences, at least as far as they can be bound*, to a true and faithful performance."[55] This was largely a paraphrase of a similar statement made in *Lumley*.[56] Freedman's phrasing, however, makes two significant departures. First, where *Lumley* had delicately stated that binding consciences contributed to the wholesome tendency to maintain good faith, Judge Freedman's language stresses the maintenance of returns on the capital invested by the theater owner.[57] Secondly, Judge Freedman introduces the word "faithful"—"that persons should be held to a true and *faithful* performance of their engagements"—conjuring up a sense that employees were obligated to be faithful to their employers, a nuance not found in *Lumley*. Therefore, by attempting to quit, Mrs. Smith took on the pejorative mantle of being unfaithful.

In justifying the extraordinary use of equitable powers to restrain Mrs. Smith, Judge Freedman ignored her willingness to pay damages for breach. The usual justification necessary for equitable intervention is that the plaintiff is unable to obtain adequate relief at law. Instead, Judge Freedman rhetorically questioned why a theater manager must seek his remedy at law and "take the chance of proving his damages by legal evidence before a jury? Of what benefit would even a verdict be to him, in case the defendant is wholly insolvent?"[58] To protect a theater manager from an insolvent defendant, Judge Freedman concluded that courts of equity should be able to enjoin actresses from performing elsewhere. This was a shift in the judicial attitude regarding the significance of a performer's possible indigence and need to work to eat. The possible insolvency of the performer had led earlier courts, like Judge Hare, to pale at the notion of reducing them to beggars by equitable orders.[59] In this case, the hypothetical case of an insolvent performer led Judge Freedman to worry instead that the theater manager would go uncompensated.

In fact, Mrs. Smith was not insolvent and there was little risk the theater would go uncompensated. Yet Judge Freedman dismissed the significance of her sizable surety of twenty thousand dollars in real estate with the simple statement that "even if true, [these facts] are quite unimportant," concluding that no action at law could be adequate to do justice because "the resort to actions at law for damages . . . will, in most cases, fail to afford adequate compensation; and it is not always that the manager is deprived of his means of carrying on his business, but that his performers, by carrying their services to other establishments, deprive him of the fruits of his diligence and enterprise, increase the rivalry against him and cause him irreparable injury."[60] Not only does this statement establish a new compensable interest—the manager's loss of the fruits of his own diligence and enterprise—it also spells out a wholly new relationship as the critical relationship in the situation, that between the plaintiff theater and other theaters. No longer is the primary balancing of equities between the actress and the theater. Instead, the rivalry between one theater and another is considered the crucial protectible interest that tips the scales.

Moreover, the free labor principle, always somewhat malleable, had been molded to the benefit of the theater owner rather than the performer. According to Judge Freedman, it is the actress's attempt to quit that threatens to deprive the theater manager of the *fruits* of *his* diligence and enterprise, rather than the reverse, the theater's attempt to shut Mrs. Smith's career down. The free labor principle, the right to the fruits of one's labor,[61] had from its inception appealed to small entrepreneurs as well as laborers; in this case, the free labor principle had gone to the aid of capital in its disputes with labor and its rivalries with other capital interests. Instead of an injunctive order threatening to deprive the actress of the fruits of her diligence and enterprise and instead of the theater manager threatening to deprive the actress of her interest in advancing her career, it is the theater manager's interests that are threatened and need the court's equitable protection.

The court's method of inquiry in this case was constructed in order for Mrs. Smith to lose. By reserving consideration of the actress's equities to the end, Judge Freedman shifted the burden of proof to the defendant to get out from under the presumption of an injunction. And when the judge finally got around to considering Mrs. Smith's claim that remaining with Daly was injurious to her reputation, he quickly dismissed it with the strong language that the claim was "too preposterous to raise an equity in her behalf." His general assessment of her claims was that she was insincere. Her allegations, he said, seemed to "owe their origin to an afterthought, and that . . . was produced by a desire on her part to find some excuse for breaking her engagement." According to Judge Freedman, Mrs. Smith was a "shrewd lady of great business capacity and mature age and judgment" and it was safe to assume that "she made the best bargain for herself that could be got under the circumstances."[62]

Judge Freedman's treatment of Fanny Morant Smith's career interests is consistent with several other women's cases of the later period.[63] In contrast with men, women's reasons for wanting out of their contracts tended to be dismissed as lacking in credibility.[64]

LILLIAN RUSSELL: REPEAT LITIGANT AND ICON OF NINETEENTH-CENTURY AMERICAN WOMANHOOD

By 1883, the courts in these cases no longer recognized the free labor principle as a substantive policy. The litigation fate of one actress in particular seemed both to shape and to reinforce judicial and public attitudes about the consequences of the breach of employment contracts. Lillian Russell, both as a popular symbol and as an individual, was the ideal foil for the reinforcement of this more restrictive legal rule regarding women performers' freedom.[65] In the American consciousness, Lillian Russell was the larger-than-life symbol of American femininity. Her image adorned cigar boxes; her public presence was sweet, gracious, youthful, and above all submissive. Her losses in two major cases during the next decade reinforced the rule adopted in *Daly v. Smith*. More important, the opinions in Lillian Russell's cases suggest the influence of factors beyond the abstract application of a capital-protective legal rule. The opinion in Russell's second case in particular carried the rationale for the *Lumley* rule far beyond the terms of contract to the point of legal absurdity.

In 1883, early in her career, Lillian Russell became embroiled in a dispute with the manager of New York's Bijou Opera House, Colonel John McCaull. In the resultant litigation, Ms. Russell was sued not because she would not perform for the plaintiff theater but because she proposed to sing at other engagements as well.[66] McCaull, who had begun his career as an attorney for Ford's Theater, had drafted an iron-clad contract and sought to enjoin her from performing anywhere without his permission. He was quoted in the newspapers as saying that she could not sing anywhere without his consent.[67] Three different clauses in Russell's contract spelled out the theater's desire to maintain exclusive control over her singing engagements.

In stark contrast with *Jermon*, the *McCaull* court never considered whether it should look beyond the language of the tightly drafted contract to the substantive effect on the young actress. The court concerned itself only with interpreting the language of the agreement, and it betrayed no concern for who had the upper hand in drafting the contract's terms. Since Lillian Russell was not seeking to repudiate the contract, the issue of the right to quit was not squarely presented by this case. Nonetheless, the opinion was used as precedent in later cases in which actresses did seek to quit.

By the time of the second case, eight years later, Lillian Russell's position as the preeminent popular female performer had been established. By this time, she had broken off dozens of contracts. Her lawyers had also learned not to let her sign exclusivity clauses. In 1887, Ms. Russell was quoted in the press as saying that she never signed contracts with conditions in them.

One would not have expected history to repeat itself, at least not with the same actress represented by the same attorneys. But the second time litigation was actually pursued, it was assigned to Judge Freedman, the same judge who had decided Fanny Morant Smith's case. This time Judge Freedman ignored the language of the contract and turned the equitable rules into parodies of themselves.

In *Duff v. Russell*,[68] the rule that equitable relief was only available when legal remedies were inadequate was reversed. Legal remedies were said to be inadequate in such cases because the amount of damages could not be accurately estimated. In *Duff v. Russell*, however, the parties had actually reached a stipulated agreement about the amount of damages before trial. The parties agreed that Russell could proceed with the rival performance, but if the injunction was deemed valid at trial, Russell would pay Duff two thousand dollars. Clearly, the damages in this case could be accurately estimated. Judge Freedman, however, gave no more heed to the usual equitable rules in this case than he had in *Daly v. Smith*. He first recounted the facts of the agreed upon amount and then, with no apparent consciousness of the contradiction, stated that an injunction was appropriate because damages were incapable of determination.

The second distortion occurred with regard to the absence from the contract of any language purporting to prevent Lillian Russell from performing at other theaters. This omission, no doubt intended by Lillian Russell's attorneys, did not faze Judge Freedman. He was prepared to imply a restrictive clause. He stated: "As was shown in *Daly v. Smith*, the court is bound to look to the substance, and not to the form, of the contract. As the defendant had agreed to appear in seven performances in each week . . . it was not possible for her to perform elsewhere . . . without a violation of her contract with the plaintiff, and a negative clause was unnecessary to secure to the plaintiff exclusively the services of defendant."[69] Judge Freedman failed to recognize that when a defendant quit a contract that did not include an exclusivity clause it made no difference whether the contract called for seven performances a week or two. Nothing in the contract specified that she should not perform elsewhere when she quit. In *Duff v. Russell*, Judge Freedman's application of the *Lumley* rule to restrain Lillian Russell overreached even the rule's own stated limitations.

After *Duff v. Russell*, American courts went even further in preventing women from breaking off their employment contracts, regardless of whether the contract included a clause restricting the performer's opportunities elsewhere or reserving exclusive control of her services. It must be recognized that in these cases the women were held to their employers in a subservient status constructed largely by the courts, rather than by language to which they had willingly agreed. In *Hoyt v. Fuller* and *Edwards v. Fitzgerald*, courts issued injunctions preventing the women defendants from performing elsewhere even though their respective contracts failed to contain negative clauses. Neither of these women was as yet a highly paid star performer, as Fanny Morant Smith and Lillian Russell were. Loie Fuller had originated a new dance and had attempted to defend it against imitators.

Her vigilance in keeping the dance her own was used against her as an argument for the irreparable harm that would befall the theater managers if she performed it elsewhere, even though she had not conveyed any exclusive rights to them in her contract. Moreover, her contract lacked mutuality, in that the theater could terminate her services on short notice, but no provision allowed her to terminate her relationship with the theater. Although mutuality was supposed to be a precondition to equitable intervention, the court said, "The defendant cannot complain of that after obtaining employment on the strength of that special condition."[70] Unlike Mrs. Smith, who had been lauded as "a shrewd lady of great business capacity" such that she should be bound to the language of her contract, the court in this case held Loie Fuller to the one-sided contract language by implying that she should have considered herself lucky to get a contract at all.

In *Edwards v. Fitzgerald*, a dancer who received only an extremely modest salary was restrained in the absence of contractual language because although "her talents may not be so exceptional as to render it impossible to replace her . . . she has a charm peculiar to herself. The plaintiff would undoubtedly find it difficult to procure a substitute who would be likely to produce a similar impression." The question of uniqueness in women's cases had come to mean not just whether the performer was exceptional or irreplaceable, but whether someone could be found to produce the same charm or impression. The social construction of women, much more than of men, was to value them for their unique appearance or charm. Every actress or dancer was encouraged to distinguish herself by her looks, her grace, or her talent. As a result, almost any woman performer, except the most indistinguishable member of the background chorus, was susceptible to this definition of uniqueness. Any woman performer who the judge might find had a charm "peculiar to herself" was vulnerable to injunction, regardless of the language of her contract.

Moreover, the dancer's reasons for quitting were characterized as "flimsy in the extreme." The court concluded by asking rhetorically: "Is it not apparent that the success of the [producer's] entire enterprise is dependent upon the fidelity of his employees, and if that be wanting—upon the assurance that desertion will be checked by the strong arm of the law?"[71] These final words emphasize the newly constructed theme of one-sided fidelity: a loyalty of employee to employer superimposed on a gendered relationship. By contrast to these five cases of women performers, in the single case in which a woman theatrical producer sued a departing male actor in similar circumstances, the court did not imply a duty of loyalty, despite an exclusivity provision.[72]

THE CHANGING STATUS OF FREE LABOR:
JUDICIAL ATTITUDES, SOCIAL ATTITUDES,
AND LAW FORMATION

In these cases, judicial redefinition of the legal status of the performers as one identical with the generality of more menial employees
was consonant with the Victorian subjugation of women, and with the
stronger social disapprobation that attached to women who performed
in public than to men.[73] My claim is not that gender is the *only* explanatory factor. Far from it. Preferences of capital to labor obviously
played a role, as did legal formalism. My point is, rather, that gender
played a contributory role that should not be ignored. The free labor
sentiment was in decline at the end of the nineteenth century, even
in cases involving men. But actresses, by their precarious social position in a highly gendered society, served as a lightning rod for these
forces to touch down.

Over the course of the nineteenth century, the significance of the
gender factor changed. When the subject employee was a woman,
judges rarely responded to her as a fully free and independent laborer
in control of her labor. More often she was seen as a subordinate or
dependent person. However, the judges of different periods reacted
differently to this factor. In *Ford v. Jermon*, the actress was viewed
as an individual whose need to earn a livelihood justified equity's
sympathy and the sympathy of humankind. Mrs. Jermon evoked the
sympathetically benevolent protection of the judge, a sensitivity he
was also willing to extend to other working people in keeping with
the free labor sentiment of the day. In the later cases, the women's
subordination triggered a far less sympathetic reaction. Actresses by
the very act of performing in public defied the social norm that
the place for women was in the home, that the proper role of women
was as faithful mothers, wives, and daughters, obligated to serve.
When actresses broke their contracts, then, they received harsher
treatment at the hands of the court than did men. They were chastised
for their lack of fidelity and bound to their masters by equitable
orders.

In the post-1870 cases, forces subordinating labor to capital and
women to men supplemented each other. As a result, the actual degree
of subjugation of women performers transcended even the formal limits of the terms in their contracts and the limits of the doctrine's logic.
Rules of interpretation were ignored or unevenly deployed, depending
on gender, to reach different results. In the women's cases in particular,
formal legal logic was frequently distorted. Essential preconditions
were dismissed as irrelevant, burdens of proof were reversed, and coun-

terfactual circumstances posited in order to justify the issuance of injunctions against women performers.

Although the distribution of results and the deployment of arguments and rhetoric tells a gendered story, the rules in these cases were invariably stated in neutral terms. Courts never intimated that there could be one rule for actresses and a different rule for male performers. As the common law rules were abstracted from their gendered context and recited with declarative authority by treatise writers, they eventually took on gender neutrality and became applicable to men too. (So complete was the abstraction from the gendered context that in one case retelling the *Lumley v. Wagner* story, a judge who got it wrong referred to opera singer Johanna Wagner as "he"[74]). In this way, a women's rule, a rule that might have been seen as the rule for a subpopulation had it been articulated separately, became the canon for the entire class of unique employees under contract. Because the law was stated in gender-neutral terms, it could be applied to men as well as to women. It was recited in men's cases, despite the fact that during the nineteenth century male performers always successfully escaped the issuance of injunctions. After the rule was canonized in Pomeroy, with citation to the women's cases appended, the gender factor that contextualized these applications was stripped away. The three applications to women had built the decisional base. Later courts could say that there was no doubt as to the rule to be applied and there was no need to reconsider the policies underlying the rule.

After Pomeroy's treatise declared the *Lumley* rule to be the controlling rule for the United States, most courts ceased to give consideration to the differential impact of the rule on employers and employees in terms of their needs.[75] For employees, the primary means of avoiding an injunction was to argue that their services were not unique and therefore not indispensable to the employer. By this construction, the rule favored employers because it was the employers' need for access to a dependable flow of employee services that received the greatest protection under the rule, rather than the replacement of any capital lost. The employer's right to a continuing supply of labor services and its position vis-à-vis rival employers was the key, rather than the employee's right to gain freedom from an employer's control, which might become oppressive. Whether the contract exhibited an appropriate degree of mutuality and whether the unique employee was sufficiently well off to live without working or had to work to eat were no longer part of the equity court's deliberations. The injunction would be refused if the employer could obtain a fungible, substitute employee. By this means, ordinary wage earners were let off the hook, not because they had a right to quit and move on, not because there was a social value to their mobility to better jobs (a value the Republicans of the earlier era would have prized), but because they were merely ordinary. The courts never made a serious attempt to assess whether the employer's commercial loss could be adequately remedied by damages, even where the parties had stipulated the amount of loss.

Canonization of the *Lumley* rule caused specialized professional performers to lose something over the earlier partnership rule that required a mutual commitment on each party's side to justify equitable intervention.[76] Professionals could no longer expect to make claims on their employers reciprocal to the claims their employers had on them. This potential had been present even in the *Lumley* case. In Johanna Wagner's contract providing that she was to sing exclusively for Her Majesty's Theatre, the agent agreed to hire no other cantatrice to sing the roles assigned exclusively to her.[77] Each side had the reciprocal ability to block the other from proceeding without it. With the adoption of the *Lumley* rule, courts increasingly lost their willingness to examine whether the contract held the parties to mutual degrees of commitment. As a result, these unique professional performers were relegated to the status of employees, expected to be devoted exclusively to their employers but with no reciprocal claim on their employers' exclusive dedication to them.[78]

The rule grew out of cases primarily involving women at a time when women were increasingly testing the limits of their civic, domestic, and employment liberties and when these liberties were increasingly being constrained by social and legal strictures. Acting was one of the first professions with significant numbers of women, and actresses vastly outnumbered professional women in other fields. In certain respects the status of actress was the pinnacle of employment autonomy that women could hope to attain; it represented the greatest degree of employment autonomy, income, and life-style privilege that existed for working women in the nineteenth century. To discover that actresses were more constrained by the courts than were actors is to discover the legal bounds of women's employment liberty.

Eventually, the *Lumley* rule gained sufficient prominence to apply to all professional performers. To paraphrase the language of Thaddeus Stevens: ultimately the common law rule that oppressed women performers came to oppress men as well.[79]

CONCLUSION

My discussion of these cases exemplifies the advantages of a distinctive methodology of labor legal history. Without a conscious awareness that the nineteenth-century American performers subjected to the *Lumley* rule were women, one loses an important dimension of the legal history of labor that the gender factor might have contributed. At the same time that this analysis illustrates that the work experiences of women performers were different, it integrates those experiences into nineteenth-century labor law. Simply put, without the women's cases there would have been no nineteenth-century adoption of the *Lumley* rule.

The methodology thus exemplified is simultaneously race conscious and race unconscious, gender conscious and gender unconscious, class conscious and class unconscious. This methodology allows us to see slavery as at one and the same time a condition of workers *and* a condition of African-Americans. It sees actresses like Mrs. Jermon both as employees under contract *and* as white women employees under contract, accorded certain privileges but denied others.

The advantages of this methodology are that as one codes the factors cross-categorically, the possibilities for cross-analysis multiply. By such means the labor law of the nineteenth century may be fractured into a series of overlapping but distinguishable coded frameworks, a collection of separate but intersecting planes, each particular to a different conjunction of employment conditions and social relations. Rather than a monolith, labor law can be observed to be truly multidimensional and as a result can be better understood and evaluated. Otherwise invisible interactions among factors can be considered.

Once this large set of demographically specific subsets is deconstructed, the shape of the resulting space can be seen more clearly, the connections among the intersecting planes can be better understood, and new connections can be noted. We may highlight more clearly the constructed synapses of cultural and legal thought, the mental connections and disjunctions, the theories of legal difference and similarity, and finally, the analogies that occasionally transcend otherwise separate racial, gender, and occupational categories. In this way we can view previously hidden dimensions in the history of labor law and of labor relations.

NOTES

I wish to thank the Fund for Labor Studies for supporting this research. I would like to thank several readers for their helpful comments: Martha Chamallas, Matt Finkin, Herb Hovenkamp, Linda Kerber, Mark Linder, and Jean Love. I would also like to acknowledge the generous and insightful contributions of Mary Joe Frug to this work and to this way of thinking about law.

Finally I wish to thank my family for their unwavering support.

1. See, for example, Litwack 1979; Daniel 1972.

2. VanderVelde 1989.

3. 1 De G. M. & G. 604, 42 Eng. Rep. 687 (1852).

4. 2 El. & Bl. 216, 118 Eng. Rep. 749 (Q.B. 1853).

5. The fact that cases about women predominate is more than coincidence. Elsewhere I explore more fully possible explanations for this phenomenon and provide a complete account of the gendered context of this line of cases. See VanderVelde 1992.

6. There are few nineteenth-century cases that deal with the legal rights of working women. What we can know of the labor *legal* history of working women must hence be extrapolated from such glimpses as we can get in whatever settings they appear. Acting was one of the first professions with significant numbers of women because it was one of the only professions open to women in the nineteenth century. Actresses vastly outnumbered professional women in other fields. For most of the century, there were more actresses than women in law, medicine (including nursing), business, journalism, or any profession other than teaching. See Johnson 1984: 50. Thus, these cases represent the best evidence of nineteenth-century legal treatment of professional women.

7. In some cases, employers failed even to allege irreparable injury from the employee's departure. *Mapleson v. Del Puente*, 13 Abb. N.C. 144 (N.Y. 1883) (male opera singer) (action to compel specific performance) (no irreparable injury, singer's place has been filled by another); *Mapleson v. LaBache*, Superior Court, Special Term (October 1883); (opinion reprinted in *Mapleson v. Del Puente*, 147 n. (female singer) (action for injunction *pendente lite*, restraining defendant from singing for others, in violation of her contract to sing for the plaintiff) (injunction denied for plaintiff's failure to aver irreparable injury from defendant's refusal to sing for him, or that he could not easily have procured an artist competent to fill defendant's place).

8. *Dockstader v. Reed*, 106 N.Y.S. 795, 796 (1907).

9. The origin and proper scope of the enticement action was the key issue in the case. 2 El. & Bl. 216, 118 Eng. Rep. 749 (Q.B. 1853).

10. See generally Labatt 1913, chap. 113: 2596–2627; Wood 1886.

11. Linder 1989: 45–100.

12. For example, there are repeated references deploring the low status of European workers in the Congressional debates over the Thirteenth Amendment. See, for example, the comments of Senator Henry Wilson (28 March 1864) and of Representative McBride (10 January 1865) reported in the *Congressional Globe*, 38th Congress, 1st Session, 1319, and 2nd Session, 201. See also Steinfeld 1991; Tomlins 1989.

13. VanderVelde 1989: 459–76. The term "man" is a conscious choice, intended to evoke the masculine quality of the then-prevalent image of free labor.

14. VanderVelde 1989: 459–95.

15. Ibid., 485–95.

16. Presumably, the most significant right that the Thirteenth Amend-

ment conferred was the right of an employee to quit. The right to quit is the functional antithesis of being held to slavery. The ability to quit is said to be the minimal means of guarding against unduly oppressive labor conditions. Schmidt 1984: 892–900.

Generally, the right to quit is not conditioned on the need to provide justification or to reserve the right in writing. As a fundamental aspect of the ability to exercise volition over one's person and to control one's labor, the fact that an individual wants out of an employment relation is generally considered sufficient. When the right to quit is conditioned and how it is conditioned affects how truly free employees are to control their labor.

17. Pre–Civil War enticement actions involved nonprofessional bound workers, whether slaves, indentured servants, bound orphans, or apprentices. The single significant exception was *Boston Glass Manufactory v. Binney*, 4 Pick. 425 (Mass. 1826).

18. Pomeroy 1897. Pomeroy's first edition was published in 1879.

19. For a fuller account that presents all the evidence for this thesis and examines more completely the nuances, verbal transformations, and rich factual contexts of the cases that led to the adoption of the *Lumley* rule in the United States, see VanderVelde 1992.

20. Before *Lumley* was decided American courts considered the issue six times, and British courts considered it four times. American courts tended to cite both British and American cases without distinguishing between them. *Morris v. Colman*, 18 Ves. 437 (1812) (male playwright); *Clarke v. Price*, 2 Wilson 157 (1819) (male court reporter); *Kemble v. Kean*, 6 Simons 333, 58 Eng. Rep. 619 (1829) (male actor); *De Rivafinoli v. Corsetti*, 4 Paige Ch. 264 (N.Y. Ch. 1833) (male opera singer); *Hamblin v. Dinneford*, 2 Ed. Ch. 528 (N.Y. Ch. 1835) (male comedian); *Kimberley v. Jennings*, 6 Sim. 339 (1836) (male clerk, traveler, bookkeeper); *Barnum v. Randall*, 2 West L.J. 96 (N.Y. 1844) (suit against Randall the Giant); *Burton, Burke and Wife v. Marshall*, 4 Gill 487 (Md. 1846) (actress); *Delavan v. Macarte and Wife*, 4 West L.J. 555 (C.P. Hamilton County, Ohio, 1847) (woman equestrian); *Sanquirico v. Benedetti*, 1 Barb. 315 (N.Y. Sup. Ct. 1847) (male opera singer).

21. 18 Ves. 437 (1812).

22. Ibid., 438.

23. *Kimberley v. Jennings*, 6 Sim. 339 (1836)(express covenant not to work for competitor). See also *Hamblin v. Dinneford*, 2 Ed. Ch. 528, 529 (N.Y. Ch. 1835).

24. In *Kemble v. Kean*, 6 Sim. 333, 58 Eng. Rep. 619 (1829), the court stated, at 621, "Where the agreement is mainly and substantially of an active nature, and is so undetermined that it is impossible to have performance of it in this Court, and it is only guarded by a negative provision, this Court will leave the parties altogether to a Court of law, and will not give partial relief by enforcing only a negative stipulation."

25. *Clarke v. Price*, 2 Wilson Ch. 157: 270, 273 (1819), 164 ("If the contract is one which the court will not carry into execution, the court cannot indirectly enforce it by restraining [the defendant] from doing some other act"). *Hamblin v. Dinneford*, 2 Ed. Ch. 529, 533 ("Only relief would restrain actor, . . . but

this would leave the positive part of the agreement untouched").

26. *Martin v. Nutkin*, 2 P.W. 266 (cited in *Lumley v. Wagner*) concerned contracts that bells would not be rung at certain times. The promise not to act was the entire gravamen of the contract.

27. *Gillis v. Hall*, 2 Brews. 342 (1870)(one partner sold out to other partner with promise not to use name or manufacture similar items).

28. *Wm. Rogers Mfg. Co. v. Rogers*, 58 Conn. 356, 7 L.R.A. 779, 18 Am. St. Rep. 278, 20 A. 467 (1890)(suit to enjoin traveling sales manager who gained familiarity with customer list); *Chain Belt Co. v. Von Sprekelsen*, 117 Wis. 106, 94 N.W. 78 (1903)(suit to enjoin expert machinist, who it was alleged, had learned valuable trade secrets while in the employ of the plaintiff.)

29. Unlike the later period, the opinions of this period do not seriously grapple with the issue of the scope of equitable power. The slippage between what the court "can" do and what it "should" do is fluid and nonspecific in these cases.

30. An earlier case, *Burton v. Marshall* (1846), for example, involved the services of a woman actress, although as a married woman she was a *femme couvert* and her husband was the party to the contract for her services.

31. Ford appears to be John Thomas Ford, owner-manager of the Ford Theater in Washington, D.C., where President Abraham Lincoln was shot in April of that year. John Ford was also listed as the manager of the Holliday Theater in Baltimore and the Academy of Music in Philadelphia.

32. 6 Phila. 6 (1865), 7.

33. As Judge Hare also said, ibid., 6–7: "In order to render such a decree effectual, it would be necessary to appoint a master [of equity], whose duty should be to frequent the theatre and decide whether the mistakes or incongruities by which the part might be disfigured, were in contempt of the order of the court, or unintentional."

It is interesting to consider the significance of the theatrical context in which this case arose. The first reference to the theater occurred when the court confronted the precedential value of *Lumley*. Judge Hare said: "The fact that amidst the multitude of quarrels that have distracted the green room or disturbed the stage, there has been but one instance of such interference, may be thought to indicate that it should be regarded as a warning rather than followed as a precedent." The theater, Hare implied, was a quarrelsome sort of place, and judges are best advised to stay out of these affairs altogether. The court cited other cases from the green room "which show conclusively, that the objections to enforcing contracts for personal services specifically, apply with peculiar force in the case of those whose business is to amuse as well as instruct and whose labors are worth nothing if given grudgingly, without the spirit that should pervade and give life to art." At the end of the opinion, Judge Hare concluded: "We therefore dismiss this bill as without our province, and belonging to a sphere more likely to be marred than improved, by the most formal decree that counsel could devise or the court award." 7.

34. Ibid. [emphasis added].

35. VanderVelde 1989: 447–8.

36. In the words of one of their spokesmen, "The Republican party was not just the anti-slavery party it was the party of free labor." This free labor principle had animated many of the debates over the abolition of slavery. Ibid., 438–39 n. 6, 459–74.

37. Her status both as a professional employee under contract and as a member of a prominent theater family gave Mrs. Jermon greater employment freedom than most employees. Her services were unique, but the average laborer's were not; though not a star, she was a prominent actress. She operated in a market that favored the seller of services to a greater extent than the buyers' market that shaped most employment contracts. Her greater status vis-à-vis other employees was reflected in the fact that her employment was governed by a written contract, rather than indentures or an oral agreement.

38. *Ford v. Jermon*, 7.

39. McPherson 1988.

40. One previous case involving a male actor resulted in a preliminary injunction, but that was reversed by an appeals court that clearly found the lower court's order unsettling. *Hayes v. Willio*, 11 Abb. Pr. (N.S.), 167 (N.Y. 1871), rev'd on another point, 4 Dal. 259 (1872).

41. Johnson 1984.

42. On women in public, see Ryan 1990, particularly 3–5. For one well-known example of denial to women of access to the professions, see *Bradwell v. Illinois*, 16 Wall. 131 (1873).

43. Johnson 1984: 4.

44. *Butler v. Galletti*, 21 How. Pr. 465 (N.Y. 1861); *DePol v. Sohlke*, 7 Robt. 280 (N.Y. 1867); *Daly v. Smith*, 49 How. Pr. 150 (N.Y. 1874); *Hoyt v. Fuller*, 19 N.Y. Supp. 962 (1892).

45. For cases involving Lillian Russell, see *McCaull v. Braham*, 16 Fed. 37 (S.D.N.Y. 1883); *Duff v. Russell*, 14 N.Y.S. 134 (1891), affirmed 133 N.Y. 678, 31 N.E. 622 (1892). See also *Canary v. Russell*, 30 N.Y. Supp. 122, 9 Misc. Rep. 558 (1894). On Lillian Russell, see, generally, O'Connor 1972.

46. Between 1860 and 1900, seventeen cases were recorded where theatrical performers were sued by male theater managers. Of these, twelve involved female performers and only five involved male performers. *Butler v. Galletti* (1861 or 2)(female danseuse); *Ford v. Jermon* (1865)(female actress); *DePol v. Sohlke* (1867)(female danseuse); *Hayes v. Willio* (1872)(male performer); *Daly v. Smith*, 49 How. Pr. 150 (N.Y. 1874)(female performer); *Hahn v. Concordia Society*, 42 Md. 460 (1875)(male performer); *McCaull v. Braham*, 16 Fed. 37 (S.D.N.Y. 1883)(female performer); *Mapleson v. Del Puente*, 13 Abb. N.C. 144 (N.Y. 1883)(male opera singer); *Mapleson v. LaBache*, 13 Abb. N.C. 147n. (1883)(female singer); *Cort v. Lassard & Lucifer*, 18 Ore. 221 (1889)(acrobats, gender not specified, but probably male); *James W. Hill v. Margaret Haberkorn*, 53 Hun 637 (1889)(female performer); *Pratt v. Montegriffo*, 10 N.Y.S. 903 (1890)(male tenor); *Duff v. Russell* (1891 affirmed 1892)(female performer); *Hoyt v. Fuller* (1892)(female danseuse); *Canary v. Russell*, 30 N.Y. Supp. 122, 9 Misc. Rep. 558 (15 August 1894), 24 Civ. Proc. R. 109, 10 Misc. Rep. 597 (November 1894)(female actress); *Rice v. D'Arville*, 162 Mass. 559

(1895)(female opera singer); *Edwards v. Fitzgerald,* Law Journal (16 January 1895) cited in *Hammerstein v. Sylva,* 124 N.Y. Supp. 535, 539 n.1, 66 Misc. Rep. 550 (1910)(female dancer.)

There was also a single case where a female theater manager sued a male actor. *Louise Dudley Carter v. William J. Ferguson* (1890).

47. *Daly v. Smith* (1874); *McCaull v. Braham* (1883); *Hoyt v. Fuller* (1892); *Duff v. Russell* (1891, 1892); *Edwards v. Fitzgerald* (1895). A sixth case involving an actress, *Canary v. Russell* (1894), could also be classified as resulting in a permanent injunction. See VanderVelde 1992: 813 n.196. These contracts often ran for several years, so the effect of an injunction could be a serious impairment of the defendant's career and her ability to work. In cases involving men, in contrast, only one, *Hayes v. Willio* (1871), resulted in an equitable order, and that was quickly reversed on appeal. See above, n. 40.

48. *Duff v. Russell* (1891, 1892); *Hoyt v. Fuller* (1892); *Edwards v. Fitzgerald* (1895).

49. 49 How. Pr. 150 (1874).

50. Ibid., 161.

51. Chafee and Re 1967: 280. Chafee and Re cite *Daly v. Smith* as the beginning of the current of authority in favor of injunctive relief.

52. *Burton v. Marshall* (1846), 491–92.

53. *Daly v. Smith* (1874), at 160.

54. Judge Freedman never identified which cases held that working individuals should be prevented from working for competitors when they quit. In fact, most of the cases that he could have used as illustration are cases involving real property or intellectual property like trademarks or copyrights.

55. *Daly v. Smith* (1874), at 169 (emphasis added.)

56. "Wherever this Court has not proper jurisdiction to enforce specific performance, it operates to bind men's consciences, as far as they can be bound, to a true and literal performance of their agreements; and it will not suffer them to depart from their contracts at their pleasure, leaving the party with whom they have contracted to the mere chance of damages which a jury may give. The exercise of this jurisdiction has, I believe, had a wholesome tendency towards the maintenance of that good faith which exists in this country to a much greater degree perhaps than in any other." *Lumley v. Wagner* (1852), at 619.

57. *Daly v. Smith* (1874), at 160.

58. Ibid., 160–61.

59. *Ford v. Jermon* (1865), 7; *Burton, Burke and Wife v. Marshall* (1846); *Kimberley v. Jennings* (1836), 349–50.

60. *Daly v. Smith* (1874), at 163, 160–61.

61. For a discussion of the significance of the term, "fruits of one's labor," see VanderVelde 1989: 473–74.

62. *Daly v. Smith,* 166, 165, 164. Had Judge Freedman considered Mrs. Smith's equities at the outset, he would have needed to consider such other equitable principles as "One must do equity to seek equity," "One must approach equity with clean hands," and "Harsh contracts will not be enforced,"

equitable principles that would have kept the burden of proving an injunction more squarely on the party seeking it.

63. *Duff v. Russell* (1891, 1892); *Hoyt v. Fuller* (1892).

64. *Duff v. Russell* (1891, 1892); *Edwards v. Fitzgerald* (1895). For a full discussion of cases involving male performers, see VanderVelde 1992.

65. The biographical details in this section are drawn from O'Connor 1972 and Morell 1940. See also Russell 1922.

66. There was some evidence she had proposed to break off her contract to enter another engagement, but the gravamen of the lawsuit was that she wished to perform a series of Sunday concerts that would not have interfered with her performance schedule. *New York Times* (4 March 1883), "Lilian [sic] Russell Enjoined—The Trouble between Her and John A. M'Caull, of the Bijou Opera House."

67. *New York Times* (16 August 1885) "Five Years a Manager—Col. M'Caull's Experience with Comic Opera."

68. 14 N.Y.S., 134, (1891), *affirmed* 133 N.Y. 678, 31 N.E. 622 (1892).

69. Ibid., at 136.

70. *Hoyt v. Fuller* (1892), at 962.

71. *Edwards v. Fitzgerald* (1895), as quoted in *Hammerstein v. Sylva*, at 539.

72. *Carter v. Ferguson*, 58 Hun 569 (1890). And see VanderVelde 1992.

73. One *New York Times* article cites the hypocrisy of Lillian Russell's exclusion from a Chicago social club on the grounds that she was an actress when that same social club had accepted several leading men of the same profession. VanderVelde 1992: 813 n.193.

74. *H. W. Gossard Co. v. Crosby*, 132 Iowa 155, 6 L.R.A. (N.S.) 1115, 109 N.W. 483 (1906).

75. Pomeroy 1897: 384.

76. *Morris v. Colman* (1812), discussed at text accompanying nn. 21–22, above.

77. *Lumley v. Wagner* (1852), 605.

78. *Keith v. Kellermann*, 169 Fed. R. 196 (1909).

79. Trefousse 1969: 56.

5 Beggars Can't Be Choosers: Compulsion and Contract in Postbellum America

Amy Dru Stanley

In the late nineteenth century, anyone traveling on foot in an American city was likely to be accosted by a beggar asking for alms. Beggars had long been a familiar metropolitan sight, even in the New World. But according to contemporaries, they were more commonplace in the years after the Civil War than ever before. With hands outstretched, they lined the streets, roved the parks, lingered on stoops.

By all accounts, the most vexing specimen was the sturdy beggar, a man in the prime of life, telling a pitiful tale of need. Should he be believed? Would alms help him or sink him deeper in pauperism by teaching that he need not labor to live? Puzzling over the subject, the writer William Dean Howells described his own encounter with a street beggar in New York City. In the urban sketch, "Tribulations of a Cheerful Giver," he recounted being torn between the pulls of "conscience" and "political economy." In the "presence of want," Howells observed, "there is something that says to me, 'Give to him that asketh.'" But the question of alms was not so simple: "I have been taught that street beggary is wrong, and when I have to unbutton two coats and go through three or four pockets before I can reach the small coin I mean to give . . . I certainly feel it to be wrong." In the end, Howells confessed, he gave the beggar fifteen cents, without getting so much as a lead pencil in exchange.[1]

In following his conscience, Howells flouted the political economy of the marketplace. Such charitable transactions belonged to an antiquated world of paternal relations that were based on protection and dependence rather than competitive exchange—a world doomed, so

Americans believed, by the Civil War and the destruction of slavery. For his lapse, Howells suffered only misgivings. But if an officer of the law had witnessed the transaction, the beggar would have been subject to arrest and forced to labor in a jail or workhouse.

In itself, the problem of the beggar was nothing new. Tales of encounters with needy strangers reached back to the Bible, and tracts on the most economical way to deal with dependency appeared during the seventeeth century, alongside the first systematic texts on the acquisition of wealth and discipline of labor. In its late nineteenth-century incarnation, however, beggary did not just symbolize the ancient problems of improvidence and misfortune; it marked the new prevalence of wage dependency and the crisis of prolonged economic depression.[2]

Like the beggar, involuntary pauper labor had a long lineage. Criminal laws commanding beggars and vagabonds to work dated back to the sixteenth century, spurring the transition from villeinage to a market in free labor. Along with other English laws, these rules passed into colonial legal codes, and versions of them remained on the statute books of the American states. In the late nineteenth century, however, philanthropic reformers, pointing to a dramatic increase in begging, campaigned for harsher sanctions. Beginning just after the Civil War and continuing through the depression of the 1870s, state legislatures throughout the North enacted a new set of vagrancy laws formulated by philanthropists that made it a crime to beg and wander about without "visible means of support." The punishment was imprisonment and a term of compulsory labor. The new enactments augmented the existing vagabond laws, enlarging the penalties and tightening the procedures. Ironically, in an era of free labor's ascendancy, reformers shored up the tradition of forced labor for beggars. As Josephine Shaw Lowell, a charity official who promoted the new laws, tersely declared in 1876: "We come back to the old rule, the man who won't work, shall be made to work." The problem of dependency, she observed, "is a historical question, and there is nothing new in it except the new details."[3]

More was at stake, however, than simply "new details"; a new juncture had arrived in the hoary debate over dependency and forced labor. The punishment for begging devised by charity reformers did not only echo Elizabethan law; it also expressed the indigenous and contradictory legacy of slave emancipation. In the South, at the close of the Civil War, Yankee officials imposed penal sanctions against idleness and vagrancy, obliging former slaves to enter wage contracts, forcibly inculcating the habits of free labor. In the North, a similar conjunction of compulsion and contract swiftly appeared in rules against beggars. From Port Royal to Boston, it became a crime for propertyless persons to eke out a livelihood outside the market. For generations, reformers and moralists had warned that paternalistic almsgiving menaced free-market discipline. But the new laws against beggars posed a fundamental ideological problem. In a nation just purged of chattel slavery, and formally dedicated to the ideal of free contract, how could coercive labor codes be justified?

This essay explores how the authors of the vagrancy legislation, most of whom were philanthropists deeply imbued with antislavery beliefs, reconciled a venerable system of compulsion aimed at free but dependent people with the ascendant doctrine of liberty of contract. It diverges from themes central to previous studies of postbellum charity reform: the rise of professional charity, the transformation in theories of causal attribution, the discovery of mass unemployment. It also shifts the focus from the advent of tramps and the plight of transients to the disorder personified by the beggar, someone who got something for nothing.[4] Here, the problems of begging, contract relations, and forced labor take center stage, set against the backdrop of the abolition of slavery.

By tracing the paradoxical links between contract and compulsion, North and South, this essay offers a new vantage point on the complex meaning of freedom and unfreedom in postbellum America. As conventionally interpreted, contract doctrine conjures up the image of stern judges striking down protective labor laws in the name of the right to buy and sell freely. This essay offers a different view of contract principles in the late nineteenth century, dealing not mainly with judges' words but rather with the rhetoric of public debate over begging. It reveals how charity reformers invoked contract tenets to reconceptualize traditional obligations of Christian charity, and in so doing legitimated involuntary pauper labor utterly at odds with the ideal of contract freedom. Coercive labor laws did not vanish with the triumph of market relations and reappear only at the extraordinary moment of slave emancipation to guide the transition to free labor.[5] On the contrary, in northern states where industrial capitalism and wage labor held full sway—but where beggars still hovered outside the bounds of commodity exchange—criminal law delivered an unequivocal answer to the almsgiver's moral dilemma. The beggar's legal status exposed the ambiguities of contract freedom in the age of high liberalism.

This essay opens by examining the problem of begging, the legal cure prescribed by charity reformers, and conflicting constructions of the law. It then unravels the contradictory lessons imparted by slave emancipation. The final section discloses how the new punitive code

of charity transformed dependency into a contract relation, a transformation mirroring the transition from slavery to freedom.

I

"A fact it is," Henry E. Pellew, a New York City philanthropist,
declared in 1879,"pauperism has become incorporated into the social
life of this country!" As an officer of the Association for Improving
the Condition of the Poor, a group of charitable business and professional men, Pellew claimed to know intimately the changing character
of poverty. Speaking at the Conference of Charities, where philanthropists, public officials, and social scientists gathered yearly to devise
measures for dealing with the poor, he voiced the fears of a generation
of charitable reformers. The problem of dependency, Pellew announced, had "assumed alarming proportions."[6]

Other observers confirmed Pellew's bleak views. In newspapers,
in annual reports put out by public and private charity agencies, and
in investigative studies of city life, accounts proliferated of squalid
destitution and swarms of street beggars. Yet as a member of the New
York State Board of Charities ruefully noted in 1875, Americans had
always assumed that "the terrible enigmas of pauperism" existing in
"the old world, would never trouble the new."[7]

Even in America, however, the problem of dependency had deep
roots. Since the early years of the nineteenth century, philanthropists
had confronted the distress of the laboring poor who earned barely
enough wages to support themselves. But it was only after the Civil
War, when the wage system became predominant, that a majority of
the gainfully employed suffered its chronic uncertainties. Even during
the best of times, wage work left both skilled and unskilled vulnerable
to casual labor, pay below subsistence levels, and unemployment—
each an expression of the fluctuating rhythms of commodity production. Always living precariously, increasing numbers of laboring people
were never far from poverty and, in the worst of times, from complete
dependence on alms. Soldiers back from the South swelled their ranks;
as production faltered with the return of peace, unemployed men paced
the streets.[8]

Indigence and unemployment soared during the depression of the
1870s, the worst times the nation yet had seen. As in earlier decades,
the vast majority relying on alms were wage earners, with common
laborers and domestic servants outnumbering persons in other trades.
By some estimates, the long years of depression left two million unemployed across the country, roughly one in every six of those gain-

fully occupied in 1870. The poor lined up at soup kitchens, and growing numbers lodged at police stations and poorhouses. In Brooklyn, for example, nearly a tenth of the population received public outdoor relief during 1877. In the rising costs of alms, in crowded poorhouses, and in the spectacle of thronging beggars, charity agents saw signs that social problems once deemed uniquely European had taken root in America. "No one could have walked the streets during the past winter" without learning a "humiliating" fact, lamented a New York City philanthropist in 1874: "this city is rapidly travelling in the track of the worst capitals of Europe, in the direction of abundant street paupers." Labor advocates said practically the same thing. "Our republic is a sham," one workingmen's journalist declared in 1875. "It generates as many millionaires and beggars as any European monarchy."[9]

The beggar was the most conspicuous figure of dependency and, in contemporary opinion, the most loathsome: a suspect figure, who allegedly thrived on deception rather than work. In his 1877 address to the Conference of Charities, Francis Wayland, the dean of Yale Law School and an influential proponent of criminal laws against beggars, put in rhyme what public and private charity agencies phrased more soberly:

> He tells you of his starving wife,
>   His children to be fed,
> Poor little, lovely innocents,
>   All clamorous for bread—
> And so you kindly help to put
>   A bachelor to bed.

Most beggars were said to be "idle from choice," not necessity, and they were often classed with vagabonds, vagrants, and the legion of unemployed transients whom charity reformers anxiously denounced as "tramps" in the 1870s. Supposedly, the beggar only pretended to seek work, "coining his unblushing falsehoods as fast as he can talk," while violating the divine rule of labor that charity agencies took as their watchword: "He that will not work, neither shall he eat." Brazenly advertising their need, adroitly manipulating conscience, beggars extorted their unearned gain "by stratagem rather than by force," related Jacob Riis in his famous study of slum life. It was mainly such tricky beggars, averred Boston philanthropists, "who infest the streets, whine at your houses, beset your stores." The verdict of the New York City Police Chief was that the "tramp-beggar" with a "hoarse voice" and "half-starved countenance" was usually a "fraud."[10]

Measuring the true extent of beggary was no simple task. Beggars reputedly circled expertly from one charity agency to the next: "busy dependents," Charles Loring Brace disapprovingly called them, who survived by a "science of alms." One journalist contended that some six thousand beggars clustered in New York City in the late nineteenth century. But their numbers and true disposition were difficult to gauge because they revolved nightly among different station houses and ranged between city and countryside. No systematic count was taken of roving beggars. Nonetheless, diverse observers indicated that most were able-bodied young men and, even though pauperism was commonly ascribed to immigrants, that they were as often native-born as foreign-born.[11]

The problem of begging touched the lives of both rich and poor; it was not hidden away inside poorhouses but seemed to spread everywhere, like one of the proverbial plagues, a sign of economic and social chaos as alarming to labor reformers and city missionaries as to charity, police, and prison officials. But it was philanthropic reformers, presiding over private agencies and the new state boards of charity, who studied the problem most intently and framed the debate. Assailing indiscriminate alms, they enjoined "kind-hearted, gushy people" not to allow beggars to live without marketing their labor. They claimed that begging was "contagious." As a Boston philanthropist balefully declared in 1879, "Picture for a moment the return of the professional mendicant, laden with booty, into the same tenement house where other men and women are working hard and earning less. What influence can be worse for all who see that begging pays better than work?"[12] The lesson of charity reform was that traditional benevolent practices invited the laboring poor to live in idleness and tell fantastic tales, sapping their morals and productive capacity while burdening the public with their support.

In the eyes of charity reformers, there was a clearly etched "line of distinction" between laboring for wages and begging. The wage laborer was an independent person, self-supporting, one who participated in the vast social exchange of the marketplace and obeyed its rules. The beggar was a dependent person, who neither bought nor sold but preyed on others. The wage earner abided by the obligations of contract; the beggar eluded them.[13]

But in the eyes of laboring men, no such distinct line existed, either in fact or theory. They hardly found the beggar an admirable figure, and they deplored both the spread of pauperism and the cost of supporting dependent persons in poorhouses and by outdoor alms. Yet they contended that most beggars did not beg by choice but due to "circumstances," as Samuel Gompers said, "over which they had no control." Many workingmen were doubtful that wage labor signified independence. Furthermore, they pointed out that laborers repeatedly crossed back and forth from depending on wages to depending on alms, from inside the wage contract to outside it. For them, the beggar was neither a deviant nor a disingenuous figure, but one who personified, in an extreme way, the dependence and compulsions implicit in the wage contract itself. The beggar reflected the condition of a "large class," the labor reformer Ira Steward explained, the class of people without means to employ themselves, who "must either sell day works, or live upon charity, or starve to death."[14]

Such an interpretation was unacceptable to charity reformers, however. Their view of beggary derived from the "best thought of the day"—the teachings of classical economists and other liberal and scientific thinkers. Composing a constituency of state and city officials, prominent industrialists and businessmen, intellectuals, and moral reformers, most of whom had been abolitionists, they were heir to an intellectual tradition that dissociated relations of personal dependency from transactions based on voluntary contract—especially wage labor. By their lights, the wage earner embodied independence, the polar opposite of the slave. That indeed had been the ideological lesson of the Civil War and emancipation, the basis for vindicating the free wage system.[15]

To charity reformers, therefore, it defied all logic to suppose that wage contracts could generate a compulsion to beg. Although not unaware of the material causes of poverty, they found it inconceivable that dependence was systematically linked to wage labor. Workingmen claimed they were not "voluntary beggars," but the charitable concluded the opposite. Regarding wage work as the obverse of dependence, they postulated that beggars simply lacked compulsion to work.[16]

To the tenderhearted almsgiver charity reformers issued dire warnings and stern homilies. But to the beggar they did more than preach. Their organizations were dedicated to suppressing mendicancy and "voluntary idleness." And they collaborated with lawmakers in securing the enactment of new criminal legislation. At the yearly Conference of Charities, which met under the auspices of the American Social Science Association, philanthropists gathered to devise enlightened measures to confine beggars to prisons and workhouses and compel them to work in return for alms. To extract labor from unworthy paupers—as Franklin B. Sanborn, a charity reformer who had once been a radical abolitionist, bluntly affirmed in 1878—"work-houses are very convenient."[17]

II

Massachusetts was the first of the northern states to enact new rules against beggars. In 1866, the Republican-dominated legislature passed an "Act Concerning Vagrants and Vagabonds." The 1860 criminal code had punished beggars along with a motley band of jugglers, tricksters, common pipers and fiddlers, pilferers, brawlers, and lewd persons. But the new law dwelled more specifically on the crime of begging. It was promoted by the Board of State Charities, which explicitly called for "additional legislation" sentencing "sturdy beggars" to "enforced labor." Directed against idle persons without "visible means of support," the act punished at forced labor for not longer than six months in a house of correction or workhouse "all persons wandering abroad and begging, or who go about from door to door, or place themselves in the streets, highways, passages or other public places to beg or receive alms."[18] Notably, just a month before the new law took effect, Congress had enacted the Civil Rights Act, thereby nullifying the southern Black Codes, which punished freed slaves for vagrancy and idleness. At the very moment when Republican statesmen in Washington were enshrining the legal supremacy of free labor as a cornerstone of Reconstruction, their brethren in Massachusetts were engaged in constructing an apparatus of labor compulsions.

Within two decades, states throughout the North had enacted similar laws against nomadic beggars. Labor advocates bitterly opposed the legislation on the grounds that it violated the freedom of poor men honestly looking for work. Nevertheless, vagrancy or "tramp" acts, as they were sometimes called, were passed in state after state: in Pennsylvania in 1871, 1876, and 1879; in Illinois in 1874 and 1877; and in New York in 1880 and 1885. The New England states adopted a set of harsh measures during the hard times of the 1870s, and Massachusetts passed several additional statutes. Although the wording of the statutes varied somewhat, all made begging a crime punishable by arrest, imprisonment, and compulsory labor. The Illinois vagabond law of 1874, for example, sentenced beggars along with wanton persons to jails or workhouses for as long as six months, amending the 1845 criminal code, which had ordered beggars and other immoral and profligate persons to be hired out at public auctions for up to four months' service. A further revision in 1877 revoked the right of begging vagabonds to a jury trial. Under the New York act of 1880, roving beggars were punished at hard labor in penitentiaries, whereas the earlier rule had sent all but the "notorious offender" to local poorhouses. In some states, sentences extended as long as two years. The intent of the new laws, as Franklin Sanborn and Francis Wayland explained in 1880, was to "convert" the vagrant beggar into a "fast prisoner."[19]

In many cases, the statutes were the direct accomplishment of charity reformers. Among the central tasks the Conference of Charities assigned itself was showing how "legislation ought to travel." As one member declared, "suppression of vagrancy and street begging" was "probably the most important work" of charity reform. Even before the Conference of Charities organized the effort, both public and private philanthropic agencies vigorously promoted laws against begging, all entailing forced labor. By 1866, New York City charity officials had concluded that the only way to prevent sloth was "compulsory labor." A few years later, a commissioner of the New York State Board of Charities recommended that the laws must be "more stringent" regarding "vagabonds and professional beggars." In Illinois, charity, police, and prison officials all pressed for what one police chief called a "good vagrant law." And both the Boston Industrial Aid Society and the New York Association for Improving the Condition of the Poor, agencies with close ties to the Republican party, promoted penal laws and involuntary labor as a cure for begging. The New York State Charities Aid Association was especially dogged in pursuing punitive measures, pledging both to "abolish beggary" and to compel "lazy vagabonds to work,"and preparing bills for the legislature. Its membership comprised New York City's elite—merchants, industrialists, ministers, lawyers, professors, and physicians. On its board sat Frederick Law Olmsted and E.L.Godkin, as well as eminent charity reformers such as Theodore Roosevelt, Sr., Charles Loring Brace, Josephine Shaw Lowell, and Louisa Lee Schuyler.[20] Not only the best men of the day, but their daughters and wives, distinguished themselves as authors of the vagrancy statutes.

In Massachusetts, charity officials, lawmakers, and the police joined in extending the reach of the new legislation. In 1872, the secretary of the Massachusetts Board of State Charities, Edward L. Pierce, proposed that Overseers of the Poor should have the authority to extract some type of labor from alms seekers—"chopping wood, picking stones"—in return for food or a night's lodging. In 1875, as a member of the legislature, Pierce successfully introduced this measure, which subjected beggars who refused to work to conviction as vagrants and forced labor. Three years later the legislature was again enmeshed in revising the vagrancy law. It held hearings, which disclosed "extraordinary differences of opinion upon nearly every point." Charity agents endorsed harsher sanctions and the chief of the state detective force advocated summary prosecution of beggars and strict work compulsions; but labor reformers led by Ira Steward testified that vagrant laws were not "politic or humane" and instead proposed laws reducing the hours of work and banning labor-saving machines. The outcome was an enactment giving the chief detective the duty of ferreting out vagrant beggars and enforcing the law. Still again, in 1880, the legislature tightened the rules, with an act declaring begging *"prima facie* evidence" of being a tramp and imposing a penalty of up to two years' confinement in the state workhouse.[21]

Although charity reformers professed to transform dealings with wandering beggars, they acknowledged the importance of English precedents. They spoke approvingly of the Tudor codes that relieved the worthy poor while setting vicious beggars to work, and especially of the New Poor Law of 1834, which provided public alms to the able bodied only if they agreed to enter a workhouse. Josephine Shaw Lowell lauded the notion of a workhouse test: charity was ideal when so detestable that "persons not in danger of starvation will not consent to receive it."[22] Nevertheless, by commanding the arrest and forced labor of beggars as criminals, the vagrancy laws did not grant, even in theory, that formal right of choice.

Like the New Poor Law, however, the vagrancy laws belonged to a wider attack on paternalistic customs of charity. Doles of money, food, or kindling; soup kitchens set up on the streets; police-station lodgings—all these traditional forms of outdoor alms constituted an "unmitigated evil" that not only destroyed the "habit of industry" but also taught the poor to view dependency as "a right" rather than a stigmatized status. Intoning the dominant precepts of laissez-faire, charity reformers especially condemned public outdoor alms and maintained that sturdy beggars had no right to state support, not even through public works. They denounced all such entitlements as socialistic, a shameful form of state guardianship, a vestige of feudalism brought over from the Old World, which bred "degradation and dependence" and made the state's relation to the beggar virtually the same as "between master and slave."[23]

Precisely because the able bodied were not entitled to be dependent, many philanthropists claimed they should be left to starve or live by selling their labor. The primal law of both nature and religion, the charitable tirelessly instructed, was that no one had a right to eat without working. Yet even officials like Lowell, who applauded hunger as a stimulus to industry, recognized that genuine want existed and valued charity as "preventative of violence." Moreover, even if the state recognized no right to alms, cunning beggars moaning that "they were starving" would survive on the benevolence of the conscience stricken.[24]

The vagrancy laws offered a tidy solution to this intricate set of problems by converting the dependency of sturdy beggars into a criminal status. A commissioner of the New York Board of Charities stated the rule emphatically: "The policy of the law should be to treat as criminals those who levy upon the public for support while able to earn their own living." As the state was not legally or morally bound to give gifts of charity, reformers reasoned, it could justly grant the able bodied public alms only as an act of penal authority. There was no right to relief unless the poor suffered "punitive treatment" and fell under the "category of tramps, vagrants, and so forth."[25]

This supposedly new system of charity rested squarely on state coercion. Ideally, reformers averred, almsgiving was meant to be a purely private and voluntary moral obligation; but when public it had to be accompanied by coercion. To prevent the poor from gaining a right to "live upon others," argued Lowell, the state should support none "except those whom it can control." Others were just as categorical. Dependency must be "as far as possible, punishable," Henry Pellew contended in 1879: "nothing but coercion will avail."[26]

By punishing dependent persons the vagrancy laws also impinged on private relations of charity. Although no law forbade giving, the beggar committed a crime simply by asking. Nor did guilt vary with the cause of need. "Harsh as it may seem," explained Francis Wayland, even those searching for work must be convicted for begging: "when those who honestly desire employment, but can find nothing to do, are reduced to the necessity of begging from door to door, they must . . . be classed with those who are unwilling to labor."[27]

It did not matter, then, whether the genesis of dependency lay in the poor refusing offers of work or having none to accept; for beggars to subsist outside the matrix of contract obligations had become a crime. Here, philanthropists conjectured, was a foolproof way to transform beggars into independent wage earners—to compel them to obey the rules of the market and enter into transactions of voluntary exchange. Like their British predecessors, they presumed that when begging was outlawed and public alms made repulsive, the poor "might be taught to prefer" to sell their labor "for pay." Perhaps some of these reformers may have been pricked by doubt, torn between traditional ideals of benevolence and the harsh precepts of the market. But they made no public avowals of private uncertainty, nor did they appear to lack foresight into the consequences of the laws they proposed. They spoke of uplifting the poor and ultimately eradicating dependency, but in the meantime of punishing beggars with forced labor. In the workhouse, they claimed, "if discipline were very strict and hard labor were enforced . . . the inmates might prefer to earn an honest living outside."[28] Worshiping volition, they spoke in the same breath of compulsion.

In linking forced labor to the operation of the wage system, charity officials laid bare the place of compulsion in a free market economy. Presumably dependent by choice and debased by their own habits, wandering beggars appeared impervious to sanctions that presupposed inner discipline. As Edward Pierce put it, "The low nature of the vagrant lacks any principle or purpose impelling him to labor." And where nature was lacking, the best expedient was the "force of the criminal law."[29] Augmenting the fear of hunger and the moral syllogisms of reformers, the laws against begging gave free labor a foundation in legal compulsion.

III

The legal justification for punishing beggars received classic statement in Christopher G. Tiedeman's *Limitations of Police Power*, the most influential treatise on state authority written in the late nineteenth century. The crime of vagrancy, Tiedeman explained, lay not in idleness or listless wandering, for citizens were bound neither to "produce something" nor to have a home. Nevertheless, a man had a duty to "take care of himself." According to Tiedeman, the "gist of the offense" was having no means of support—becoming a "public-burden." Virtually all the vagrancy statutes contained the phrase, "without visible means of support," identifying the offending deed as dependency.[30]

As proof of lack of support, old and tattered clothes, even a "dilapidated condition," were not enough to convict. Nor was it always lawful to search a man's pockets before arresting him to discover that he had no money. Simply begging, however, was unimpeachable evidence of guilt. "If a man is found supporting himself in his journeyings by means of begging," Tiedeman declared, "no doubt that would be deemed sufficient evidence of not having proper means of support." Undoubtedly almsgivers were accomplices to the crime; yet the law dealt differently with those of means and those without. No "rightful law" could prevent almsgivers from dispersing their property, but the state could "prohibit public and professional begging, and, under the vagrant laws, punish those who practice it." It was "certainly constitutional" to put beggars in the workhouse.[31] Validating the principles of charity reform, jurists affirmed that in a nation where labor was free, dependent persons ought to be viewed as criminals.

Under the vagrancy statutes the process of justice was summary. On sight or upon a complaint, officers of the law had a duty to arrest all offenders and carry them to the nearest municipal justice or police court, where without money for bail they were locked up until the day of trial. No warrant was required for the arrest, and the suspects were usually tried without a jury. The New York City Board of Police Justices noted that the procedure of conviction "is very simple; indictment and jury trial are unnecessary, the justice must proceed summarily; he cannot organize a court of special sessions to try the prisoner." Reversing the ordinary rule, suspects were presumed guilty unless they could rebut police testimony with a "good account of themselves." Convicts were removed to "places of industry," where they were set at tasks such as hauling coal and brick, breaking stone, scrubbing, sewing, laying pipes, and making bricks, brushes, and shoes; or less often they were hired out under private prison labor contracts.[32]

Great discretion fell to the police. Officers could make arrests simply on suspicion, without even witnessing the beggar in the act. Often, in visiting the homes of the poor, charity agents brought the police along to bring beggars to judgment. "No class of person has better opportunities or facilities for learning the real necessities and true condition of the poor than those who are constantly patrolling the localities in which the poor live," police officials boasted: "mendicants are traced to their haunts, their claim to charity investigated, and . . . they are prosecuted." According to a New York City detective, a "few simple propositions" governed "this street begging business." No subtlety entered into law enforcement: "beggars of every class should be driven from the street, under penalty of imprisonment." In particular, the beggar with "brawny arms and perfect health" deserved punishment. "A good square look at one of these creatures . . . begets an impulse to kick him into the street."[33]

Quite often the police yielded to such impulses, kicking and beating suspected vagrants. Laboring men in New York City reported that they might simply be sitting on a curb, or lingering on stoops, when police officers assaulted and arrested them. One man was standing on Tenth Avenue when allegedly, "without provocation," an officer "came up and said, 'What are you tramps doing here insulting respectable people?'"and struck him "several violent blows on the head with his baton and kicked him." Even men who sat on the streets outside their own homes, showing no signs of being beggars, risked being accosted and arrested—like Max Moskovits, who was resting on his own stoop on Essex Street in the Lower East Side. "Get out of here you bastard," one officer reportedly threatened him, "or I will lock you up."[34]

The accused stood trial before a police court justice. Observers noted that the cases in this tribunal often took "less than a minute," with police officers reading the charges, and the magistrate delivering a verdict instantly as the prisoners came before him. If they could post bond of several hundred dollars, convicted beggars could bring appeals to the lowest state court. Yet very few appear to have exercised that right, and those who did usually were found guilty again. When a man was poor or common looking, a critic of the legal system remarked, he could easily find himself "behind prison walls without his knowing even upon what charge he had been put there and without having made the slightest defense." The commissioners of the Workhouse in New York City described the process of punishment as an ordeal of "humiliation and self-abasement" from the moment offenders were "huddled into the gloomy prison van at the Tombs, till they are . . . marshalled into gangs, . . . marched off to the place where they are to do penance, . . . and after being scrubbed and ventilated, assigned to hard work."[35]

Despite the reports of swift retribution, charity reformers complained that too often the vagrancy codes remained a dead letter. They claimed that the police were not zealous enough in making arrests and that judges acquitted the poor. As the chairman of the Boston Overseers of the Poor argued: "Our judges, we fear, acting under a tender regard for the personal liberty of those brought before them, hesitate to sentence to the workhouse worthless persons." Some judges did display notable regard for the liberty of the poor. In a series of rulings in 1877 and 1878, a judge in the criminal court of Cook County, Illinois, declared that the state vagabond act of 1877 violated the constitution by denying the right of trial by jury and discharged all prisoners bringing their appeals before him.[36]

Such cases were the exception, however. Courts throughout the country upheld the vagrancy laws, and though charity reformers were not satisfied with the tally, thousands were arrested and confined each year as vagrants. Crime statistics are notoriously imprecise; nonetheless, in this case they amply document how widely the force of law was brought to bear on the poor. During the 1870s and 1880s, both in New York City and Chicago, the police arrested thousands of persons annually on vagrancy charges. In 1877, vagrancy arrests in New York City rose above a million. Not all who were arraigned were convicted, but vagrancy was the most common minor offense after drunkenness, assault, and disorderly conduct, and it was well known that the police easily secured vagrancy commitments when lacking evidence of more serious crimes. Prison officials reported that the new laws "largely increased the numbers held as vagrants." Just after the Illinois enactment of 1877, for example, annual vagabond convictions in Chicago alone rose to nearly twelve hundred, more than double the number a year before. From time to time, philanthropists noted approvingly, the police swept the poor off the streets, "arresting in one day, through a sudden and simultaneous movement, some 500 street-beggars, and subjecting them, through the courts, to the legally appointed penalties." According to the police reporter Jacob Riis, over half the arrests for begging in New York City were likely to end in convictions.[37]

That any were punished simply for lacking means of support was for many workingmen evidence enough that the vagrancy laws were unjust. Just as they disagreed with philanthropists about the cause of beggary, so labor spokesmen also construed the rules of law differently than treatise writers, judges, and the police. Holding the poor in "penal servitude" violated the principle of voluntary labor, turning free citizens into slaves, they protested. It was a free man's irrevocable right to travel in search of work, and he should not be "enslaved in the penitentiaries" because he asked for alms along the way. A man was "not a law-breaker" because he begged from "necessity."[38]

Knowing firsthand the stimulus of hunger, laboring men gave testimony to the conflict between the ideal of free contract and the coercive provisions of the vagrancy laws. Necessity itself was a dreadful compulsion, they argued, which compromised the legal right to choose when, for how long, and for whom to labor. All too often poor men made "contracts only against their will . . . compelled by the force of circumstance." The vagrancy laws revoked even this formal right of free choice by enlisting punitive state power as an instrument of labor compulsion. In workingmen's judgment, the rule of consent enshrined in treatises on contract law ran contrary to statutes ordering beggars to be jailed and "compelled to work, whether they want to or not." Vagrancy codes, they claimed, had no place in a nation committed to freedom, but represented a throwback to bondage, a scheme "worthy the days of fugitive slave laws."[39]

To charity reformers' way of thinking, however, there was nothing inconsistent about endorsing both the principle of state coercion and the rules of the free market. Rarely did their publications fail to offer reverential discussions of the "natural laws" of political economy and the superiority of free labor institutions. Nor did they doubt that the genius of American institutions was to entitle "every man to act with perfect freedom," bargain for the "best price," and "refuse to sell his labor" and that "no law ought to be made in a free country to prevent his doing so."[40]

The key point was that even free persons could not choose to beg instead of agreeing to work for low wages. However much charity reformers espoused full liberty in bargain making, they deplored the existence of a "large class who make begging a trade [and] who will only do such work and at such wages as suit them." It was not forced pauper labor, they insisted, but rather begging and alms that transgressed the laws of the market, disturbing the "voluntary play" of commodity exchange and the beneficent workings of supply and demand.[41] By such reasoning, the vagrancy laws were made to appear as the guarantee, not the nullification, of voluntary transactions.

That reasoning gained credence in leading texts of political economy. Like legal theorists, liberal economists sanctioned the coercive aspects of the vagrancy laws, although they preached the gospel of free labor. It was of the "highest economical consequence," wrote Francis Amasa Walker in 1883, that "something of a penalty" be put on dependency. Three years later, in his landmark reformulation of classical economics, *The Philosophy of Wealth*, John Bates Clark expressly approved "work-houses for tramps." While celebrating America as a free society, purged of all bondage "since slavery was abolished in the Southern land," both economists and lawyers joined philanthropists in upholding the rectitude of involuntary pauper labor.[42]

IV

Although Yankees professed to the contrary, nowhere did the contradictory aspects of contract freedom emerge more plainly than in the southern states after the Civil War. Policies of free labor imposed by the North brought to light the coercive underside of market relations. Officials of the Freedmen's Bureau abjured slavery's paternal bonds and extolled the ideal of voluntary labor. Yet simultaneously they punished as vagrants freed people who refused to enter into wage contracts and set them to work. It was not only across the Atlantic in English poor law that charity reformers found an example; paradoxically, slave emancipation furnished a native model of forced labor. The abolition of slavery distilled fundamental problems of dependence and discipline, bequeathing a distinctive ideology and set of precepts to charity reformers in the North.

Throughout the proclamations of the Freedmen's Bureau ran a double message: an affirmation of the former slaves' right to liberty and a warning that freedom barred dependence. The bureau sought to dispel the notion that its mission was charitable, aiming its words both at freed people and at their liberators, who shunned the prospect of permanently supporting a population of free blacks. "Freedom does not mean the right to live without work at other people's expense," the bureau declared in 1865. "A man who can work has no right to a support by government or by charity." Although entitled to choose their employers and earn wages, former slaves were not free to refuse to labor. The bureau made explicit the double meaning of emancipation: "While the freedmen must and will be protected in their rights, they must be required to meet these first and most essential conditions of a state of freedom, *a visible means of support, and fidelity to contracts.*"[43]

The bureau's chief, General Oliver Otis Howard, stoutly denied that it was designed, as many charged, to "'feed the niggers in idleness.'" Rather, it took all proper steps to induce former slaves to work, scrupulously subjected all applicants for relief to a "rigid examination," and turned away all who were fit to labor. If the freedmen "failed to contract," Howard explained, "they incurred the odium of being a 'lazy, idle, and worthless race,' besides running the risk of starving." Although pledging to prevent a recurrence of bondage, Howard was consistent in neither his convictions nor his policies. "I repeatedly cautioned my officers against any substitute whatsoever for slavery, " he avowed. Nevertheless, he affirmed that "a little wholesome constraint" could not be avoided and even led to "larger independence."[44]

Agents of the bureau had great latitude in exercising "wholesome constraint." They did not hesitate to compel former slaves to enter into year long labor contracts binding them to plantation labor. Their strictures repeatedly juxtaposed the contrary principles of consent and coercion. In July 1865 an assistant commissioner for Louisiana issued an edict epitomizing the contradiction in bureau policy: "That freedmen everywhere be *enjoined to work*, and in doing so, they will, in all cases, enter into *free and voluntary contracts.*" Similar rules were promulgated throughout the southern states. In Georgia, for example, the bureau forced freed persons to accept jobs on plantations, and the duty of local agents was to "make contracts for them"—agreements as "binding . . . as though made with the full consent of the freed people."[45] Stationed in the South to guarantee free labor practices, agents of the national government created a system of compulsory contract.

Such measures culminated in penal rules against vagrancy. According to Howard, idleness was an intractable problem, and neither persuasion nor threats overcame the freedmen's reluctance to make contracts. And so he turned to legal sanctions against those who preferred to survive outside the contract system: "At last I urged for such freedmen the use of the vagrant laws" though "leaving out the whipping post." Instead, the penalty was a prison term, or bound labor on plantations and public works. A Mississippi agent provided the freed people in his charge a graphic explanation of the offense and the punishment: "The government hopes you will do your duty, and in return will secure you all the rights of freemen." But if "you are found idle you may be taken up and set to work where you will not like it." It was "nonsense" to think that by entering "a contract you will somehow be made slaves." Rather, he warned, "Your danger lies exactly in the other direction. If you do not have some occupation you will be treated as vagrants, and made to labor on public works."[46]

At the very moment the Freedmen's Bureau was perfecting its remedies for idleness and vagrancy, northerners were condemning the Black Codes being enacted by former slaveholders in legislatures across the South. Antislavery leaders catalogued the atrocities of the Black Codes—the rules requiring black people to sign annual labor contracts, prohibiting enticement, and outlawing vagrancy—attacking them as a return to "practical Slavery" and "compulsory labor." Ironically, however, victors and vanquished, ostensibly still struggling to implement opposing visions of emancipation, were adopting quite similar methods of labor compulsion. Yet as plain as the parallel was, Yankees appeared not to recognize it. Although bureau policies evoked criticism in the North, free labor advocates raised no sweeping protest that their emissaries were promoting measures resembling the Black Codes. Rather, leading exponents of Yankee habits of industry—"a hundred merchants" in the citadel of the Boston Board of Trade, as Wendell Phillips indignantly observed—backed coercion in the conquered states: "a stringent vagrant law that shall whip men to work."[47]

In northern eyes, the critical difference between bureau rules and the Black Codes was that the compulsions imposed by the bureau did not discriminate on the basis of race. At Howard's orders, the bureau extended existing vagrant laws "made for free people" to the former slaves, a policy nominally blind to color. Conversely, northerners stressed that the Black Codes inflicted unusual penalties on "account of color" and that the vagrancy rules especially operated "most iniquitously upon the freedmen."[48] Evidently, it was not the abstract principle of compulsion that inflamed antislavery opposition but its unequal application on account of race.

In supervising the transition to freedom, Yankee officials openly defended the propriety of forcing former slaves to work. "A vagrant law is right in principle," a bureau agent in Mississippi affirmed: "I cannot ask the civil officers to leave you idle, to beg or steal. If they find any of you without . . . means of living, they will do right if they treat you as bad persons and take away your misused liberty." Among the rights guaranteed to freedmen none gave them liberty to "saunter about neglecting their business," to be without a livelihood and take up begging. As a bureau officer solemnly told his staff, that restriction was intrinsic to free institutions: "the peace and good order of the community, and the success of free labor, depend largely upon the vigor and thoroughness of your action in relation to vagrants."[49]

The lessons of emancipation quickly traveled north, where they guided the cures devised for dependency. For like the former slave, the poor had neither masters nor property, and both subsisted by selling their labor or by depending on alms.[50] And many who became apostles of charity reform after the Civil War, and who had long opposed slavery, studied the progress of free labor in southern society. Not only did they survey the situation from afar; several journeyed and lived in the South, inspecting up close and helping to formulate the procedures for installing the wage system: compiling reports on relations between former masters and slaves, overseeing plantations, working as missionaries among the freed people. On returning north, where their own city streets were filled with beggars, they brought back more than recollections of burning sunlight and gangs of freed slaves picking endless rows of cotton.

The career of Edward Pierce suggests the itinerary of many philanthropists. A lawyer by training, Pierce supervised the wartime experiment with free labor at Port Royal, South Carolina, then served as secretary of the Massachusetts Board of State Charities, and soon after guided a vagrant law through the Massachusetts legislature. As he traveled the length of the country, his thoughts on freedom consistently allowed for compulsion. At Port Royal, Pierce had told the former slaves "if they were to be free, they would have to work, and would be shut up or deprived of privileges if they did not." He had envisioned "the workhouse or even the prison" as punishment. Yet Pierce also assailed the Black Codes, not only because they discriminated against freed people but because they made breaking a labor contract a crime. Back in Boston, however, in 1872, echoing ideas he had uttered at Port Royal, Pierce affirmed that criminal law must compel begging vagabonds to work, a punishment not "interfering with personal liberty." In the famous venture at Port Royal, Pierce worked closely with the Educational Commission of Boston, a group of reformers and professional men dedicated to elevating the condition of freed slaves. Like Pierce, the commission's first chairman, the Reverend Edward Everett Hale, went on to advocate vagrant laws and forced pauper labor. Hale became an official of the Boston Industrial Aid Society, which was devoted to suppressing street beggary and whose members belonged to the same circle as the Educational Commission.[51]

Other prominent charity reformers also had studied the transition from slave to free labor. Josephine Shaw Lowell traveled in the South with the Freedmen's Association after the war, and later became a principal exponent of workhouses. Even more striking was the route of the Yankee reformer Samuel Gridley Howe. In 1863, shortly before being appointed chairman of the Massachusetts Board of State Charities, Howe had toured the South as a member of the Freedmen's Inquiry Commission. The commission concluded that freed slaves must be "self-supporting," deploring both a paternalist "scheme of guardianship" and all restraints on their liberty—except for vagrancy laws. While the Freedmen's Bureau disseminated these precepts across the South, Howe reiterated them in dealing with beggars on his own home ground. Under his direction, the Massachusetts Board of State Charities proclaimed "punishment for vagrancy" the first rule of scientific alms and sponsored the vagrant law of 1866.[52]

Shaped by their southern experience, charity reformers both renounced paternal obligations to the poor and interpreted the compulsory aspects of contract freedom to require punishing beggars. They did not explicitly equate their undertaking with that of the Freedmen's Bureau. Yet other Yankees, even without the benefit of personal experience, frankly observed how apt a model slave emancipation offered for curing dependency. In 1878 the *Boston Daily Globe* urged that plans devised for the "lately emancipated negroes" should be used to solve "the great questions . . . of suppressing the vagrant practices of the idle." According to the *Globe*, "What was in 1865 considered as eminently practical, is equally so now."[53] The experience of war and emancipation not only honed efficient techniques of philanthropy, but schooled Yankees in schemes for forcing beggars to work. The task of reconstructing the southern labor system and installing contract practices recast conceptions of dependency, obligation, and labor compulsion. Just as the ideal of free labor was transported south, so its coercive aspects—articulated in rules governing the freed people—were carried back north.

V

What could not be so easily echoed in the North was the logic that justified compelling freed slaves to put their labor up for sale. Slave emancipation represented an apocalyptic moment; but problems of dependency appeared endemic in the North. Nor could Yankee reformers simply restate rationales that Englishmen had used centuries earlier to defend coercive poor laws, for they confronted an ideological problem unknown to their forebears. Their task was not simply to make beggars work, but to explain how a society rhetorically committed to voluntary relations of exchange could embrace a rule so at odds with the principle of consent.[54]

Before the emergence of the antislavery movement in the late eighteenth century, the system of forced pauper labor had required no special justification. It had coexisted in the Atlantic economy with other forms of bound labor that ranged along a continuum from indentured servitude to chattel slavery, and in both England and America spokesmen of the propertied classes used identical arguments on behalf of slavery and compulsory pauper labor. Members of Parliament and American slaveholders shared a common conception of labor discipline, and philosophers such as Thomas Hobbes and Francis Hutcheson expressly recommended enslavement as a punishment for vagabonds and idlers.[55]

Yet as antislavery beliefs came to prevail on both sides of the Atlantic, reformers and statesmen pulled apart the strands of arguments that once had been intertwined. It was not that abolitionists were uninterested in questions of labor discipline or even opposed to compulsory pauper labor or workhouses, but in advocating such measures they no longer conflated them with slavery. Instead they distinguished between systems of bound labor. The theory that beggars must be set to work endured. What shifted were the justifications, the styles of argument, that free labor exponents throughout the Anglo-American world used to defend traditional modes of coercion that fell short of outright slavery.[56]

In the aftermath of the Civil War, northerners turned to two lines of argument to explain the paradox that guarding ex-slaves' freedom impressed them into involuntary labor. On the one hand, they claimed that devices such as vagrancy laws and compulsory contracts were merely temporary expedients needed to mediate the transition from slavery to freedom. As O. O. Howard maintained, these were extraordinary measures, required to educate persons accustomed to bondage in the ways of the market and the wage system: "I would have been glad to have adopted precisely the same methods of regulating labor as obtained in the northern States, but neither the planters nor the freedmen were yet prepared for this." On the other hand, northerners resorted to a defense implying that former slaves would never be ready for complete freedom, citing racial inferiority as grounds for coercion. Although the rules of the Freedmen's Bureau did not discriminate by race, many who endorsed them fell back on longstanding apologies for involuntary servitude. According to Wendell Phillips, even Yankees could still be found arguing, " 'There is a race among us that obliges us to go back to compulsion.' "[57]

Neither of these arguments spoke exactly to the predicament of charity reformers in the North, for they faced a situation almost as different from circumstances in the South as from those in England in centuries past. The northern vagrancy codes were not intended as temporary expedients. Nor were they devised (as both the Tudor statutes and the Reconstruction measures had been) to promote the transition to commodity relations and the creation of a wage-earning class. Rather, they were designed for a society long accustomed both to free labor and to market transactions, in which hirelings were not in scarce supply but often too abundant, as in the depression of the 1870s. Nor did beggars, unlike the freed people, comprise a separate race; although philanthropists often equated paupers with immigrants and blamed their individual traits on *"poor stock,"* they did not classify them as a different species of being or presume their stock made them unsuited to free labor. The enactment of the northern vagrancy laws, therefore, represented a paradox similar but not identical to that posed by emancipation, and it had to be justified in different terms.[58]

Not even the most steadfast proponents of the laws could escape the problem: a society priding itself on having abolished slavery was forcibly extracting labor from dependent persons. Edward Everett Hale admitted the thorny questions at stake: the "difficulty under our system of personal liberty" of granting overseers of the poor "penal powers." The philanthropist Henry Pellew conceded that the "embryo" of such "difficulties" lay in the "supposed antagonism between free and enforced labor." Yet he claimed this was a specious objection, a "prejudice and misunderstanding" that would disappear with a "full discussion" of the advantages of coercion.[59]

It was the rule of exchange that charity reformers invoked to sweep away the "misunderstanding" regarding enforced labor. In defending the vagrancy acts they spoke most commonly in the idiom of the marketplace. As was the case in any bargain, so in almsgiving, they claimed, the beggar owed something in return: a share of labor—surrendered willingly or not—for a portion of food or a night's lodging. The New York Board of Charities stated the rule emphatically: "In the case of the able-bodied, no aid should be extended to them except upon their rendering an equivalent therefor, by their labor." Philanthropists intoned this injunction again and again. Images of commerce, the language of buying and selling, of equivalence, of payment, pervaded their discussions. The poor must be "made to work in payment for what they have received," declared the Charities Aid Association. The primacy of exchange had struck Edward Pierce as a student at Harvard; it was the theme of a prize-winning essay he wrote on contract law. As a charity official he returned to it, announcing that forced labor obliged the beggar "to pay his way." Both public and private philanthropic agencies affirmed the justice of requiring paupers to "render an equivalent." More important than the liberty of the poor, as Edward Everett Hale argued in 1877, was the principle inscribed in the vagrancy laws: "that in all cases, a return in work be extracted in proportion to the relief thus given."[60]

By compelling beggars to work in exchange for alms, charity reformers professed to be simply upholding the rules of the market. Every
sale, as Blackstone had written, required a *"quid pro quo,"* and it was
a settled rule of contracts that the law would only enforce agreements
entailing reciprocity, that a valid contract required "consideration."
Indeed, the rule of reciprocity marked the dividing line between economic and moral transactions. The notion of "proper exchange" was
foreign to the "field of morals," the economist Arthur Latham Perry
explained in 1868, but there was "nothing else but proper exchange
within the field of economy." To produce—in the "language of Political
Economy"—meant nothing other than to "render a service for an
equivalent." Through a deft translation philanthropists applied these
precepts to their project of reform, showing the worth of compulsory
labor. As Henry Pellew declared in 1878, "Even in giving out-door
relief the principle of obtaining some return, some *quid pro quo . . .*
should be insisted upon."[61]

The sturdy beggar who refused to pay a share of labor was a "swin-
dler," said charity reformers. Like a thief, he looked on the public as
a "vast, intangible body" to "plunder without remorse." Citing the
labor theory of wealth, charity reformers averred that every cent of
unrequited alms amounted to robbery, just as if the beggar had gone
pilfering from door to door. What made the pauper and the criminal
alike was that both took something for nothing, receiving "benefits,
without rendering an equivalent in return."[62] As an antidote to such
swindling practices, the vagrancy laws held beggars strictly to the rule
of exchange, transforming charity into a punitive bargain.

In insisting on the paramount importance of mutual exchange,
charity reformers adroitly translated the principles of contract into a
justification for involuntary labor. A contract ordinarily signified both
consent and reciprocity. By splitting apart these interlocking principles, charity reformers demonstrated how easily the ideal of contract—
when transposed into poor relief—could be made to stand for compulsion. It required no more than a rhetorical inversion, a facile shift
of words. Instead of naming slavery as a referent, the authors of the
vagrancy laws spoke in terms of "earning," thereby likening forced
pauper labor not to bondage but to wage work. It was wrong to give
the "slightest aid," Francis Wayland postulated in 1877, "which is not
earned by an equivalent amount of labor." According to such arguments, compulsory labor gave almsgiving the form of a wage contract.
As one charity official explained: if beggars chose not to work, the
"public has the same right to exact from them labor as it has to exact
labor from those to whom it pays wages."[63] Throughout the commercial world, agreement usually took priority over the notion of fair

exchange; but in the economy of charity, exchange annulled volition. Philanthropists used the language of contract—the rule of "rendering an equivalent"—to legitimate an exchange relation that plainly violated the principle of consent.

Like any other market transaction, then, the duty to the poor reduced to an exchange of commodities. The accomplishment of scientific philanthropy was not only to rediscover the virtues of vagrancy statutes and workhouses but to give a new ideological configuration to charity: to impose a commodity form on the obligation between almsgiver and beggar, to convert a dependency relation into a relation of contract. Charity, by tradition, was the very essence of a paternal relationship, remote from the world of sharp bargaining, and the beggar the exemplar of dependency. "Nobody but a beggar chuses to depend chiefly upon the benevolence of his fellow-citizens," Adam Smith had written. But using Smith's own vocabulary, philanthropists in America remodeled charitable benevolence in the image of a contract. The only choice they left beggars was to enter the matrix of exchange relations, to yield up their labor under a compulsory charitable contract. None was so unflinching in stating this hard fact or in renouncing the ethos of paternalism as Josephine Shaw Lowell. Even in dealing with the poor widow, the most pathetic figure of dependency, Lowell declared, it was always "a good thing to drive a hard bargain" rather than give "a dollar without . . . equivalent" and leave the widow to spend "her days in idleness and her nights in debauchery."[64] The rules of the market were no more a mystery to benevolent women than to benevolent men.

Sentiment held little place in the new code of almsgiving. Philanthropists continued to speak of uplifting and redeeming the poor, fusing an older rhetoric of Christian charity with the usages of political economy. But, for all their moral concerns, they disowned a paternal obligation to the poor, insisting that the strict law of quid pro quo must govern both public and private alms. They claimed that the best type of charity was personal, creating a bond between giver and receiver, but they conceived of that bond more in terms of contract than sympathy. This was precisely the model of obligation prescribed by theorists of liberalism, the creed of scientific thinkers who deciphered all social exchange according to the calculus of contract. As the sociologist William Graham Sumner explained the virtue in the harsh rule of equivalence, to be dependent—to make no return—was to renege on the rights of freedom itself. "A free man," wrote Sumner in 1883, "derogates from his rank if he takes a favor for which he does not render an equivalent."[65]

Out on the streets charity reformers distributed cards bearing the legend, "WHAT TO DO WITH BEGGARS," which warned, "DO NOT GIVE." In the words of Edward Everett Hale, charity reformers gave benevolence a new meaning: "they so worked on the public, that men began to believe that it is wicked to give money to a beggar."[66] Among rich and poor, philanthropists inculcated this creed, remodeling charity as a market relation, recasting the ideal of reciprocity into a justification for coercion. Here was the source of the almsgiver's dilemma, the sin of giving to a street beggar who gave nothing in return, which proved so troubling to good Samaritans such as William Dean Howells.

The vagrancy laws purportedly rescued beggars—against their will—from the abject status of taking favors without rendering an equivalent. For, according to the new political economy of charity, it was not forced labor but rather alms without work that threatened to reduce the poor to slavery. The object of the legislation, its authors insisted, was not to set beggars in bondage but to hold them fast within the world of exchange. It secured the supremacy of contract relations by bringing even dependent persons under their terms. The laws were "equitable enactments," affirmed the Association for Improving the Condition of the Poor, "based on contract and individual rights."[67]

In so arguing, charity reformers gave new moral legitimacy to labor compulsions that came perilously close to slavery. Under the vagrancy laws, the state enforced the sale of labor—through an involuntary exchange—wherever beggars contrived to avoid the natural sanctions of hunger and cold. In an age of supposedly untrammeled liberty in the marketplace, legal coercions were resurrected to assure the supremacy of wage relations. The system of unfree pauper labor dated back to premodern times. But in reconciling that tradition with the rules of the market, Americans in the late nineteenth century spoke in a distinctly modern language of contract.

NOTES

For their insights and criticisms, I am indebted to Susan Armeny, Betsy Clark, Nancy Cott, David Brion Davis, Leon Fink, Eric Foner, Willy Forbath, Lucy Gorham, Dirk Hartog, David Montgomery, Daniel Rodgers, Lewis Stanley, Sally Stein, Alan Steinberg, David Thelen, Chris Tomlins, Kristin Warbasse, and most of all Craig Becker.

The following abbreviations are used throughout these notes:
ACB—Associated Charities of Boston; BDPIB—Board of Directors for Public Institutions of the City of Boston; BIAS—Boston Industrial Aid Society; BOP—Boston Overseers of the Poor; CCC—Conference of Charities and Corrections; CRAS—Chicago Relief and Aid Society; HCCBI—House of Correction of the City of Chicago, Board of Inspectors; IBSC—Illinois Board of State Commis-

sioners of Public Charities; MBSC—Massachusetts Board of State Charities; MBSL—Massachusetts Bureau of Statistics of Labor; MCP—Massachusetts Commissioner of Prisons; NYAICP—New York Association for Improving the Conditions of the Poor; NYCCPCC—New York City Commissioners of Public Charities and Correction; NYSBC—New York State Board of Charities; NYS-CAA—New York State Charities Aid Association.

    1. Howells 1972 [1896]: 150–52, 160, 167.

    2. Ribton-Turner 1972 [1887]; Furniss 1920; Wermel 1938. On the crisis of the American economy in the 1870s-1890s, see Gordon, Edwards, and Reich 1982.

    3. NYSCAA *Fourth Annual Report* (New York, 1876), 102. On the English legacy, see Tawney 1912: 266–80; C. Hill 1958: 215–38; Dobb 1947: 224–39; Marx 1977, 1: 877–901. On the colonial reception of English poor law, see Rothman 1971: 20–29.

    4. On charity and poverty in late nineteenth-century America, see, generally, Boyer 1978; Bremner 1956, 1980; Ginzberg 1990: 133–212; Haskell 1977b; Kelso 1969; Schneider and Deutsch 1969; Tishler 1971; Trattner 1984; Watson 1971. M. B. Katz 1983 provides an illuminating critical perspective on this literature. On the rise of the "tramp" problem, see Harring 1977: 873–911; Monkkonen 1984; Ringenbach 1973.

    5. On the use of contract principles to strike down social legislation, see Fine 1967: 140–62; Forbath 1985: 767–817; Keller 1977: 343–70; McCurdy 1984: 20–33. For a contrasting analysis of the links between contract doctrine and humanitarian sensibility, see Haskell 1985: 547–66. Eric Foner has maintained that the "compulsory system of free labor" imposed on the freed slaves was an "anomaly" born of the crisis of the Civil War and emancipation, and that in the North vagrancy laws were not used to punish those without work as criminals. Foner 1988: 56, 208; 1983: 51.

    6. CCC *Proceedings of the Sixth Annual Conference* (Boston, 1879), 217.

    7. NYSBC *Eighth Annual Report* (New York, 1875), 128.

    8. Mohl 1971; Smith-Rosenberg 1971; Stansell 1986: 19–37, 44–54, 63–75, 193–214. On the wage economy and unemployment in the late nineteenth century, see Keyssar 1986; M. B. Katz 1983.

    9. CCC *First Annual Conference* (1874), 31; *National Labor Tribune*, 24 April 1875; Tishler 1971: 20–21. On the numbers of the unemployed, see J. Cook 1880:55; Keyssar 1986: 1–4, 342–43. On soup kitchens and station-house lodgings, see, for example, Rogers et al. 1874: 74–83. On outdoor relief, see CCC *Sixth Annual Conference* (1879), 202. On alms seekers' occupations, see, for example, MBSL *Eighth Annual Report* (1877), 192–93.

    10. CCC *Fourth Annual Conference* (1877), 119–20; *Eighth Annual Conference* (1881), 132; BIAS *Fortieth Annual Report* (1875), 7; NYAICP *Thirtieth Annual Report* (1873), 73; Riis 1971 [1890]: 192; ACB *Third Annual Report* (1882), 12; Walling 1972 [1887]: 449. On rising concern over tramps in the 1870s, see Ringenbach 1973; M. B. Katz 1983: 157–237. Denning 1987: 149–66.

    11. Brace 1967 [1872]: 384; Thomas Knox, in Campbell 1969 [1891], 584. On the identity of vagrant beggars, see MBSC *Fourth Annual Report* (1868),

130; Leavitt 1886:198; Harring 1977: 875–76; M. B. Katz 1983: 166. On charity reformers' association of pauperism with immigrants, see NYSBC *Ninth Annual Report* (1876), 134.

  12. CCC *Eighth Annual Report* (1881), 132; Stewart 1911: 133; "Address of Robert Treat Paine, Jr." (1879), in ACB *Publications* (Boston, 1879–1903), 8. And see Thelen 1986: 103–8.

  13. NYAICP *Thirtieth Annual Report* (1873), 77. On the distinction between wage laborers and dependent paupers, see Steinfeld 1989.

  14. U.S. Congress 1885, 1: 371 (testimony of Samuel Gompers). Ira Steward, "Causes of Increased Wages" (undated manuscript), Ira Steward Papers.

  15. NYSCAA, *Fifth Annual Report* (1877), x. On the equation of freedom with contract relations in the postbellum era, see Stanley 1988: 471–500.

  16. *National Labor Tribune*, 10 November, 1877; IBSC *Fourth Biennial Report* (Springfield, 1877), 98, 204–8.

  17. NYSBC *Twelfth Annual Report* (1879), 230.

  18. "An Act Concerning Vagrants and Vagabonds," *Mass. Stats.* (1866), chap. 235, pp. 229–30; *Mass. Gen. Stats.* (1860), chap. 165, sec. 28, p. 820; MBSC *Second Annual Report* (1866), xcviii-ix.

  19. CCC *Seventh Annual Conference* (1880), 278. On the vagrancy laws, see Leavitt 1886: 190–200; CCC *Sixth Annual Conference* (1879), 24–26; *Illinois Rev. St.* (1845), 175–76, (1874), 392–93 and *Laws* (1877), 87–89; *New York Rev. St.* (1859), 2: 879, and *Laws* (1880), chap. 176, and Harring 1977; Ringenbach 1973: 11–29; Keyssar 1986: 253–54; Rodgers 1978: 226–28. Some of the laws exempted "residents" and provided for fines as an alternative to jail. On labor reformers' opposition to the laws, see Michael Davis 1984: 141–65.

  20. CCC *Seventh Annual Conference* (1880), 23; *Eighth Annual Conference* (1881), 131; NYCCPCC *Seventh Annual Report* (1867), xxix; NYSBC *Eighth Annual Report* (1875), 102; Chicago Board of Police, *Report* (1876), 12; NYSCAA *First Annual Report* (1873), 7; *Third Annual Report* (1875), 24.

  21. MBSC *Eighth Annual Report* (1872), 29–30, *Twelfth Annual Report* (1876), 93–94; "An Act Concerning Vagrants," *Mass. Stats.* (1875), chap. 70, pp. 648–49; "Report and Bill Concerning Vagrants," in Massachusetts House of Representatives, *Legislative Documents* (Boston, 1878), No. 100: 1–2, 10, 19–20; *Boston Daily Globe*, 18 and 23 January, 1878; "Report of the Chief of the State Detective Force of the Commonwealth of Massachusetts for the Year 1877," in *Massachusetts Public Documents* 1877 (Boston 1878), No. 37; *Mass. Stats.* (1878), chap. 160, p. 115; *Mass. Stats* (1880), chap. 257, p. 232.

  22. Stewart 1911: 160. On claims of radical change, see NYSBC Ninth Annual Report (1876), 29. On discussion of English legal precedents, see, for example, CCC *Fourth Annual Conference* (1877), 102–4. On the English Poor Law Amendment Act of 1834, see Himmelfarb 1984: 147–76; M. E. Rose 1986: 9–14; Polanyi 1944: 101–4, 163–66.

  23. NYSBC *Seventeenth Annual Report* (1884), 157; W. B. Rogers 1874: 78–79; NYAICP *Thirty Second Annual Report* (1875), 67; BOP *Fourteenth Annual Report* (1878), 6. On Gilded Age social thought and the disavowal of paternal obligations and state responsibility, see Fine 1967.

24. NYSBC *Seventeenth Annual Report* (1884), 143–44; IBSC *Fourth Biennial Report* (1877), 98, 200.

25. NYSBC *Eighth Annual Report* (1875), 102; *Fifth Annual Report* (1872), 37; CCC *Fifth Annual Conference* (1878), 56.

26. NYSBC *Seventeenth Annual Report* (1884), 160; CCC *Sixth Annual Conference* (1879), 220; Lowell 1884; Ely 1889: 92–93. On the vast expansion of state power implicit also in the reformed English poor-law system of the nineteenth century, see Himmelfarb 1984: 164–68.

27. CCC *Fourth Annual Conference* (1877), 118.

28. NYSCAA *First Annual Report* (1873), 23; NYSBC *Eleventh Annual Report* (1878), 211. On the connections that the authors of the Tudor poor laws drew between "free" labor contracts and antivagrancy legislation, see C. Hill 1958: 221–22.

29. MBSC *Eighth Annual Report* (1872), 20.

30. Tiedeman 1975 [1900]: 149, 143–44. (This is the second edition of the treatise better known by the title cited in the text, first published in 1886).

31. Ibid., 144–45, 149–50.

32. NYAICP *Thirty Sixth Annual Report* (1879), 14; Tiedeman 1900: 99–100, 142, 146; Walling 1972 [1887]: 388, 449. On the types of penal labor enforced in houses of correction and workhouses, see, for example, HCCBI *Sixth Annual Report* (1877), 28.

33. Boston Chief of Police, *Annual Report* (1873), 49; Walling 1972 [1887]: 194, 387, 449; Warren 1970 [1875], 211, 198. On charity agencies' use of the police to investigate the poor in their homes, see, for example, NYSBC *Ninth Annual Report* (1876), 131.

34. Complaints of George Satterwhite (24 December, 1893) and Max Moskovits (11 November, 1892) in New York Senate, "Examination of Trials by the Police Board from January 1, 1891 to May 1, 1894," (New York, 1 May, 1894), 87, 99, New York Historical Society. On the police in this era, see Monkkonen 1981.

35. M. H. Smith 1869: 167; *Arena*, 2 (August 1890), 330–31; NYCCPCC, *Eighteenth Annual Report* (1877), ix. On the appeals process in Massachusetts, see, for example, Suffolk Superior Court, Criminal Case Files, Box 76B (1874–75), case nos. 2190, 1090, 3060; Box 78B (1877–81), nos. 2045, 2030, Massachusetts State Archives. On the infrequency of appeals in vagrancy cases, see Tiedeman 1900: 146. On the expanding power of the police and the state in the nineteenth-century criminal justice system, see Steinberg 1989.

36. MBSC *Twelfth Annual Report* (1876), 178; *The People, ex rel., Hattie Brown,* in *Chicago Legal News,* 8 December, 1877, 96 and *In re Scully and O'Leary,* in *Chicago Legal News,* 12 November, 1878, 27–28.

37. Massachusetts Commissioner of Prisons, *Seventh Annual Report* (1878), 14; NYAICP *Thirtieth Annual Report* (1873), 74; Riis 1971 [1890]: 194. On courts' affirmation of the constitutionality of vagrancy laws, see *Chicago Legal News,* 29 June, 1878, 329–30, and 1 February, 1879, 162; Tiedeman 1900: 147. On the imprecision of criminal statistics and the extent of vagrancy commitments, see NYSCAA *Fifth Annual Report* (1877), 11. On the tendency of the police to secure vagrancy convictions when lacking evidence of other of-

fenses, see Massachusetts House of Representatives, *Legislative Documents* (1878), No. 100, 7. Recent studies suggest that the vagrancy laws were not rigorously enforced in the late nineteenth century, but these studies do not examine the relevant criminal statistics; see Keyssar 1986: 138, 411 n. 59; Tishler 1971: 22. On vagrancy convictions relative to other offenses, see generally Wines 1888: 506; Wines 1895: 355; MBSL, *Eleventh Annual Report* (1880), 170–71, 182–85. On annual arrests and convictions for vagrancy, see Chicago Board of Police, *Annual Report* (1872–85); HCCBI *Annual Reports* (1872–85), especially *Fifth Annual Report*, 20, and *Sixth Annual Report*, 21; Police Department of the City of New York, *Annual Report* (1866–86); Children's Aid Society, *Thirty Sixth Annual Report* (New York, 1888), 12; "Report of the Secretary of State on the Statistics of Crime for 1886," (New York), 223; CCC *Fifth Annual Conference* (1878), 59; Ringenbach 1973: 11; Boston Chief of Police, *Annual Report* (1870–87); MBSL, *Eleventh Annual Report* (1880), 142–69; MCP, *Annual Report* (1875–80); BDPIB, *Tenth to Twenty-Seventh Annual Reports* (1867–84). For charity officials' accounts of the admirable effects of strict enforcement of vagrancy legislation, see CCC *Fourth Annual Conference* (1877),xxiv. Although begging is not the focus, for a discussion of the high rate of vagrancy/disorderly conduct convictions in antebellum Philadelphia and the discretion of magistrates, see Steinberg 1989: 123–28, 178.

38. *National Labor Tribune*, 4 September, 1875, 10 November, 1877; *John Swinton's Paper*, 26 April, 1885.

39. U.S. Congress 1885, 1: 1155 (testimony of John Jarrett); *National Labor Tribune*, 13 April, 1878; *Workingman's Advocate*, 15 January, 1876.

40. NYAICP *Thirty Second Annual Report* (1875), 68; NYSBC *Eighth Annual Report* (1875), 126; BIAS *Thirty Eighth Annual Report* (1873), 10.

41. BIAS *Thirty Ninth Annual Report* (1874), 6; NYAICP *Twenty Seventh Annual Report* (1870), 45.

42. F. A. Walker 1883: 423; J. B. Clark 1886: 196; Atkinson 1887: 103.

43. Bureau of Refugees, Freedmen and Abandoned Lands, "Orders of the Commissioner and Assistant Commissioners," House Exec. Doc. 70, 39th Cong., 1st Sess., 155, 139. On the bureau's views of poor relief and dependency, see Foner 1988: 152–53.

44. O. O. Howard 1907, 2: 214; "Report of the Commissioner of the Bureau of Refugees, Freedmen and Abandoned Lands," House Exec. Doc. III, 1, 39th Cong., 2nd Sess., 1, 772; Howard 1907, 2: 246–47, 221, and see 310, 312.

45. "Orders of the Commissioner," 10 (emphasis added), 65, and see 149, 58.

46. Howard 1907, 2: 247; "Reports of Assistant Commissioners of the Bureau of Refugees, Freedmen and Abandoned Lands," Senate Exec. Doc. 27, 39th Cong., 1st Sess., 36–37. And see "Orders of the Commissioner," 174, 139, 28–29, 52. On the vagrancy regulations and the compulsions of the free labor contract system, see T. Holt 1982: 283–313; Litwack 1979: 319–21, 366–71; Foner 1988: 153–70.

47. *National Anti-Slavery Standard*, 30 December, 1865 ; *Liberator*, 24 November, 1865; *National Anti-Slavery Standard*, 24 February, 1866 ("Speech

of Wendell Phillips, Esq."]. The antislavery press did assail General Joseph S. Fullerton, the bureau chief in Louisiana, for using military law to enforce a system of "compulsory contracts." See *National Anti-Slavery Standard*, 18 November, 1865. But this singular indictment was prompted by Fullerton's exceptionally outspoken disregard for freed people's liberty. Though enforcing identical policies, bureau officials in other states met with no such criticism. In defending the Black Codes, however, southern whites underscored their similarity to bureau regulations. See Foner 1988: 208. On abolitionists' support for the Freedmen's Bureau, see McPherson 1964: 178–91, 341, 349–50. On the Black Codes, see Foner 1988: 198–205, 208–10; Litwack 1979: 366–71.

48. "Orders of the Commissioner," 52; "Report of the Commissioner," 741. And see Hyman 1967: 281, 218–19; O. O. Howard 1907, 2: 278; Foner 1988: 149–51, 153–55.

49. "Reports of the Assistant Commissioners," 36; "Orders of the Commissioner," 53.

50. On definitions in early English law of vagabonds as lordless men, bound neither to the land nor a master, see F. Pollock and Maitland 1923 [1898], 1: 30.

51. Stevens 1896: 72, 85, 152–54; MBSC *Eighth Annual Report* (1872), 20, 30. On Pierce's career, see Rhodes 1903–4: 363–69; Hoar 1897: 197–210. On Pierce's role at Port Royal, his work with Hale and the Educational Commission, and the contradictory strains of policy toward the freed slaves, see W. L. Rose 1964. For Hale's summary of the goals of the Industrial Aid Society and his support for vagrancy laws and forced pauper labor, see BIAS *Fiftieth Annual Report* (1885), 5–12; CCC *Fourth Annual Conference* (1877), 108–10.

52. Hyman 1967: 201–2, 113–15; MBSC *Twelfth Annual Report* (1876), lxxiv, *Fifth Annual Report* (1869), xvii. On Lowell's southern travels, see Stewart 1911: 48–49. On the Freedmen's Inquiry Commission and Bureau policies, see T. Holt 1982: 293–95. On Howe's role in establishing the Massachusetts Board of Charities, see Haskell 1977b: 92–97.

53. *Boston Daily Globe*, 19 January, 1878. Historians have focused on the expert administrative techniques charity reformers honed from the experience of Civil War and Reconstruction. See, for example, Frederickson 1965: 98–112, 211–25. My interpretation stresses the primacy of emancipation and the schemes for enforcing voluntary wage labor that charity reformers inherited from the national government's policies toward freed people.

54. Despite the simultaneity of British abolition and poor-law reform, the architects of the English Poor Law Amendment Act of 1834 did not face precisely the same ideological predicament as American charity reformers. British reformers aimed not principally to put the able bodied to work, but rather to discriminate between paupers and those who were merely poor by means of a work test that gave the able bodied the formal choice to enter the workhouse or starve or beg. See Himmelfarb 1984: 160. The American vagrancy laws provided not for a work test but for compulsory penal labor.

55. On the parallels between rationales for slavery and compulsory pauper labor in England and America in the seventeenth and eighteenth centuries, see

Morgan 1975: 319–27, 338–39; D. B. Davis 1975: 263–64; Furniss 1920: 42, 67, 80–116.

56. On tensions in English and American abolitionism toward the problem of labor compulsion see D. B. Davis 1975: 241–54, 260–66, 357–59, 453–67. Davis stresses the significance of antislavery ideology in legitimating new forms of industrial discipline in a free market economy; my concern here is with the problem that antislavery doctrine posed for legitimating enduring methods of coercing the poor to work.

57. "Report of the Commissioner," 772; *National Anti-Slavery Standard*, 24 February, 1866. On the coercive policies of the Freedmen's Bureau as temporary remedies, see Foner 1988: 208. On racial explanations for these policies, see Fields 1982: 165; T. Holt 1982: 303. On racial justifications for slavery, see E. S. Morgan 1975: 316–37; D. B. Davis 1975: 299–306. For a comparative discussion of the paradoxical union of compulsion and freedom in the labor systems constructed in the wake of slave emancipation worldwide, see Woodward 1988: 22–27.

58. MBSC *Second Annual Report* (1866), xxii. On coercive labor legislation during the long transition to capitalism (a situation reversed in the northern regions of the United States in the late nineteenth century), see Dobb 1947: 23–25, 231. On charity reformers' tendency to employ Darwinian hereditary theories, see M. B. Katz 1983: 94, 103, 134–35, 177. However, it was not until the 1890s that racial determinism dominated social scientific thought; see Higham 1970: 131–57.

59. CCC *Fourth Annual Conference* (1877), 107, *Fifth Annual Conference* (1878), 57.

60. NYSBC *Ninth Annual Report* (1876), 29; NYSCAA *Thirteenth Annual Report* (1885), 17; E. L. Pierce 1853–54: 257–79, 385–400, 449–59; MBSC *Eighth Annual Report* (1872), 30; CCC *Seventh Annual Conference* (1880), 245, *Fourth Annual Conference* (1877), 110. On the "business rhetoric" of charity reformers, see Ginzberg 1990: 197–98.

61. Blackstone 1979 [1765–69], 2: 442–46; Perry 1868: 44, 91; CCC *Fifth Annual Conference* (1878), 57.

62. NYSBC *Twelfth Annual Report* (1879), 260; CCC *Fourth Annual Conference* (1877), 48; IBSC *First Biennial Report* (1871), 18.

63. CCC *Fourth Annual Conference* (1877), 119; NYSBC *Eighth Annual Report* (1875), 100. On the preeminence of principles of consent over notions of fair exchange in nineteenth-century contract doctrine, see Horwitz 1977b: 160–210. On English poor-law reformers' conception of the wage contract, see Himmelfarb 1984: 162–63.

64. A. Smith 1937 [1776]: 14; Lowell 1884: 93.

65. Sumner 1972 [1883]: 39. On the conjunction of market principles with personal ideals of charity and home visitation, see CCC *Fourth Annual Conference* (1877), 46–51, *Fifth Annual Conference* (1878), 53–72. While attentive to the predominance of market theories of contract relations, Katz suggests that charity reformers clung to older notions of personal deference and paternal obligations, without noting how deeply the newer contract principles influ-

enced their conceptions of philanthropy, see M. B. Katz 1983: 200–201.

66. ACB *Third Annual Report* (1882), 21; BIAS *Fiftieth Annual Report* (1885), 11.

67. NYAICP *Twenty Eighth Annual Report* (1871), 59. On the theory that the degradation of the pauper was worse than that of the slave, see F. A. Walker 1876: 88.

6 Metaphysics and Reality in Late Nineteenth-Century Labor Adjudication

Karen Orren

In the last quarter of the nineteenth century, the American labor movement mounted an assault against the massive system of power, authority, and governance that had ordered relations in the workplace for several centuries. That system, elaborated and enforced in the ancient law of master and servant, had failed to be removed by either democratic or industrial revolutions but remained embedded in the structure of the Constitution, limiting both legislative policy and private collective action. Its eventual displacement was, after the Civil War, the most important political change since the nation's founding.

Except when seen against this background, and in particular against the lineage of the old labor system, union activities in the late nineteenth century· remain in historical limbo. Despite the recovery of the variety of workers' outlooks and strategies, and the recreation of those decades as a crucible of movement discourse, the period is still reckoned a defeat, the failure of voluntarism against the combined power of employers and judges.[1] In contrast, this essay argues that the unions' collective actions were a monumental historic success. By outreaching the categories of the ancient law, by defying the law's capacity to predict and order employment in accord with the accumulated wisdom of centuries, they undermined the rationale upon which the labor system rested.[2]

As with all feudal law, based on custom and precedent and accreted and enforced in judicial holdings, the law of master and servant was a *metaphysical* structure. By that I mean that its rules were formal, detached from their original settings, placed in a framework of concepts, the reasonability of which was defined through a process of exposition by professionally trained intellects. On the other hand, the rules corresponded to a *physical* reality that had coincided with their origins in the ancient workplace and was replicated in persons and places and acts—the hirings and dismissals, the payment and non-payment of wages, the intrusions and bodily injuries—in court cases over centuries. Indeed the greatest abstraction in this reenactment was the idea of the contract, which was not an agreement arrived at by the parties but the presumed acquiescence by the worker in the law's own designation of the relation, its incidents and obligations. The strike, the picket line, the boycott: these were not only an assault *on* the old system, but a movement *out from under it*, each action a demonstration that the old principles no longer held.

In this essay, I attempt to lay out the structure of the nineteenth-century labor system and establish its ancient pedigree; to place late nineteenth-century adjudication of the union's collective actions directly within, and continuous with, this structure; and to demonstrate how these actions, the *practices* of trade unionism—not the development of alternative legal discourses—presaged the end of the old regime. Finally, I connect the labor movement to certain broader cultural currents that mirror its development.

PRINCIPLES

The law of master and servant as it regulated American labor relations in the nineteenth century implemented the two essential principles of medieval social organization. The first principle was *hierarchy*, the personal relation of lord and man, prescribed in rules of obligation and deference, in designated realms of rank and function. The second principle was *protection*, the shielding of this relation in its diverse forms from intrusion by outsiders, persons the law often referred to as "strangers." These principles, both descended from a time of political fragmentation, complemented one another: the order of the one, the services and morality it generated, was to be shielded from the disorder and injury of actions unconstrained by other hierarchies.[3]

The two principles are observable at every stage of the nineteenth-century employment relation. Let me begin just before actual entry into the contract: American workers, like their ancestors in the Middle Ages, were free to choose among available masters, but that they have a master was a requirement of law. In every jurisdiction in the country it was a crime for a person who had no other means of support not to be working or looking for work. This crime, the crime of vagrancy,

addressed within the comprehensive framework of the Statutes of Labourers (1349) but much older in common law, was enforced in the
colonies and grafted onto the laws of the new American states.[4] Providing fines, hard labor, and imprisonment for their violation—in summary, judgment by a magistrate with no provision for appeal—the
vagrancy laws over the centuries presented the identical configuration
of meanings and policies.[5] Christopher Tiedeman in *The Limitations
of Police Power* (1886) begins his remarks on vagrancy: "The vagrant
has been very appropriately described as the chrysalis of every species
of criminal."[6] A vagrancy statute promulgated under Edward VI (1547)
reads: "Foreasmuche as Idleness and Vagabundrye is the mother and
roote of all theftes, robberyes and all evill actes and other mis-
chiefs . . ."[7] Characteristically, the law of vagrancy was not merely
prescriptive but predictive, justified by dangerous behaviors ascribed
a priori to those outside the workplace hierarchy.

   Hierarchy and protection were likewise implemented at the point
of entry in the employment contract. To assume the relation of master
and servant in its full sense, the employee had to be *sui juris*, which
meant that he or she had no obligations incompatible with the service
about to be undertaken, a requirement that excluded lunatics, married
women, members of the armed services, and infants.[8] The relation was
based on the *person* of the employee, not simply his or her labor, which
under the law could not be provided by a substitute.[9] The workplace
hierarchy, activated by the will of the employer, was thereby accorded
absolute deference, safe against other outstanding claims that might
interfere in the future.

   Inside the contract, the principle of hierarchy asserted itself
through its first rule, which was obedience. Disputes over obedience
per se are not common in the recorded case law, for the rule was plain
and seldom contested: any violation was grounds for immediate discharge. The leading English precedents well into the late nineteenth
century included firing for a refusal to travel a mile away until after
a long-delayed dinner was eaten; and for a visit to a dying mother
against the master's orders.[10] Employers were not required under the
law to give reasons for either their orders or their dismissals; indeed,
in suits for back wages, reasons would be accepted by the courts ret-
roactively, even if the reasons had not been known to the employer
at the time of the employee's discharge.[11] The only limit on the master's absolute right of command—imposed through the legal recovery
of wages, there being no remedy of reinstatement available—was that
an order not fall outside the type of labor contracted for and that the
worker not be exposed to physical dangers not expected at the time

of hiring. The reason of the master's will was established a priori, by virtue of his or her authority.

The worker's will appeared in the old law also, but always pejoratively, as in "willfully abandoned the service," and "willful disobedience." If an injury to a member of the public was caused willfully, that is, not in a bona fide exercise of obedience, masters were not liable for damages, any more than they would have been had the injury been from a machine or animal, for which fault must be assumed only in the absence of due care.[12] Similar assimilation of the worker to a machine or animal, that is, to property, may be seen in other ancient doctrines, which demonstrate again the law's anticipation of disruptions from outside. One, stemming from the ancient disability of villeinage, *quicquid acquietur servo acquietur domino*, gave the master legal right to retain earnings due his laborer for outside work should these somehow come into his hands.[13] Another, *per quod servitium amisit*, entitled the master to compensation for physical injuries to the employee that resulted in an interruption of services.[14] Both doctrines bore unmistakable marks of their medieval origins: in *quicquid acquietur servo*, of ownership as tangible possession; in the *per quod* action, the anomaly that American judges, based on authority leading back to 1371 and often against their personal sentiments, denied all damages in cases of an employee's death.[15]

At their perimeter, work relations were fortified by a number of bulwarks, including the ancient rights of the master and servant to commit a battery in defense of each other.[16] For later developments, however, the most important was the prohibition against enticement. The Statutes of Labourers provided for both criminal and civil proceedings against any person who knowingly persuaded or induced a servant away from his employment; by 1355, an action of trespass on the case was available as an independent civil remedy under common law. In the United States, enticement was an underlying wrong in such early conspiracy prosecutions as *Commonwealth v. Pullis* and *People v. Fisher*; Justice Shaw in *Commonwealth v. Hunt* took pains to distinguish the facts at bar from circumstances of enticement.[17] Usually cited as the leading American case, *Boston Glass Manufactory v. Binney* was argued on the basis of sixteenth-century precedent, which in turn cited fourteenth-century authority.[18] Shortly after the Civil War, the enticement action was extended by courts in the United States to the growing body of workers employed "at will."[19]

The enticement action again illustrates the interplay of hierarchy and protection. The principle of hierarchy is evident in the total eclipse of the worker's will in the determination of illegality: enticement was one of the few torts where intervening will did not affect liability.[20] Nor was what the employee might have been legally entitled to do him- or herself of any material interest: an eighteenth-century case often cited by American courts held an army recruiter guilty of enticing a man who had entered his employment under an invalid contract of slavery.[21] As for the enticer, it was necessary only to prove there was an intention to interfere; beyond that, motives were irrelevant. The tort did not require, for example, that enticement be for one's own benefit.[22]

The ultimate protection of the relation of master and servant was constitutional. The feudal law was judicial law, and as the American federal system received English common law into its own constitutions at a time when labor relations were still under the jurisdiction of the English courts, labor relations remained in the constitutional domain of American courts. Within this scheme, legislators, even before the doctrine of substantive due process, were but another species of intruder. The absence of effective administrative machinery, which has been offered as the reason why early protective legislation went unenforced, cannot explain the perversity of the judges' interpretations. The Supreme Court of Connecticut, for example, read the eight-hour statute in that state to mean that a worker could not, without a special agreement to the contrary, claim compensation for more than eight hours, no matter how long he may have worked.[23]

APPLICATIONS

Confronted by the labor movement's collective actions across the broad front of American workplaces, employers and judges relied on the protections of the master and servant law. As workers broke their contracts and shouted and hammered away at the old order, they were convicted of conspiracy, trespass, assault and battery, and breaking the peace.[24] The main illegality in injunctions and damage awards and the underlying wrong in most convictions for criminal conspiracy, however, was the tort of enticement. While the particular word "enticement" became something of an embarrassment, it was nonetheless in response to the act or purpose of persuading employees to leave their jobs, or interfering with the master's employment of workers under hire, that the judges regularly found it was illegal to gather together, to come onto property, to picket, and the rest.

The enticement tort in its simplest form, arising from an action by a single group of workers at a particular workplace, vividly reflected the physicality of the old law: the crossing of physical boundaries, the entry into factories, the speeches and shouting and other actions taken to stop ongoing work. To pick one case among dozens, in Michigan, *Webber v. Barry* proceeds from a declaration that invokes, typically, the ancient language of trespass: defendant with "force and arms broke and entered the plaintiff's said close" and "prevented said employees from continuing at the work of manufacturing lumber and salt." No one, says the judge, had the right to enter the premises of another (not to mention, shut off the steam) for the purpose of "inducing persons . . . to leave their employment," whether with the object of higher wages or shorter hours or for any other reason.[25]

Over the decades, as unions diversified their tactics and widened their actions to include more and various employees scattered over larger territory, the enticement action extended its range along with them. On the reasoning that the employment relation had been intentionally disrupted, damages were awarded and injunctions granted for interference by strikes, picketing, and boycotts;[26] when there was physical violence and when not;[27] when the tort was caused by an individual and when by a union;[28] when the purpose was to obtain higher wages and to secure a closed shop;[29] when the interference was with existing employees and with prospective employees;[30] when the plaintiffs in court were employers and when they were workers who had been discharged.[31] In its own name, as well as in more up-to-date formulations as interference in another's contract, the enticement tort endured straight through to the tentative victories of collective action before the New Deal.[32] Whereas the worker's will was to no avail inside the contract, as an accused enticer outside, his or her intentionality—wilfulness—was the gist of the tort.

The prevalence of the enticement action may perhaps best be indicated by those rare Gilded Age decisions that were decided in labor's favor. For example, in the *Johnston Harvester* case, arguably the leading prolabor precedent until the next century, the judge uses his opinion to review the enticement doctrine as it was applied in other states and avers that he is "disinclined to extend . . . the doctrine of recovery for enticing away servants where, both in fact and theory, the person enticed is a free agent to come and go as he will."[33] In the same (thin) line of prolabor decisions is *National Protective Association v. Cumming*, decided against discharged employees who sued a union of building trades on the theory that the existing legal authority, which supported their action, was "entirely consistent with the policy of the statute law of England, but hostile . . . to the spirit of our institutions."[34] My point here is not to question the soundness of the judges' opinions, but to show how they confirm the tenacity of the ancient law.

In enticement cases, as in master and servant relations generally, judges resisted inroads that came by way of the legislature and were designed to relieve the unions of penalties for their interference. For example, in Pennsylvania conspiracy to strike had been expressly eliminated as a crime by statute; yet the judge still enjoined a building trades strike according to his duty to protect the workplace, in this case a building under construction:

> If the legislature to-day abolished indictment for wilful and malicious trespass, or abolished the writ of estrepement, tomorrow courts of equity would still be bound under the Declaration of Rights to protect the citizen in the peaceable possession and enjoyment of his land, even if to do so they were compelled to imprison the lawless trespasser. . . . So the same courts are still bound to protect the humblest mechanic or laborer in his right to acquire property.
>
> Trades unions may cease to work for reasons satisfactory to their members, but if they combine . . . to prevent an employer from employing others by threats of a strike, they combine to accomplish an unlawful purpose, a purpose as unlawful now as it ever was, though not punishable by indictment.[35]

Threading through the enticement decisions is the division between insiders and outsiders. Insiders were the unmarked category of persons in the master-servant relation, *sui juris*, a category that extended during this period to embrace workers toward whom the employer had, as a kind of property right, a "probable expectancy" of hiring.[36] Outsiders were employees who had abandoned the work, along with the unionists and others who had induced them. Outsiders engaged other distancing features, such as secrecy, being from out of town, or speaking a foreign language.[37] Outsiders were not legally "interested" but only "sympathetic."[38] Interference in the employment contract was regularly equated with business "taken from the owner and assumed by . . . irresponsible strangers."[39]

The categories of insiders and outsiders, being abstract, reflected the intellectual structure of the law; still, there remained a close correspondence to the physical circumstances being litigated, workmen at their jobs, conspiring off the worksite, strikers barging in, picketers shouting "scab," and so forth. The element of a priori reasoning appears more starkly in the personal attributes judges regularly ascribed to errant employees. The very word *enticement* conjured up, as it had historically, a total picture of immorality—subject and object, instigator and victim, purpose and method—within the wider telos of an ordered society.[40] Striking workers were "wanton," "malicious," "intermeddling," all suggesting unbridled mischief tending to criminality, evident also in the vagrancy statutes; one decision speaks of the "vicious and lawless always to be found among the idle."[41]

As indicated by this last quotation, the law of master and servant, like the law of vagrancy, was not only descriptive; it was predictive. Oliver Wendell Holmes, Jr., once argued that the common law consisted of predictions of what judges would do.[42] But the prediction worked in two directions; the common law rested heavily on what its doctrines predicted people would do in various circumstances and then proceeded to regulate behavior accordingly. That these predictions were given full weight in determining the legality of workers' actions may be seen, for example, in the Massachusetts case of *Plant v. Woods*, where the equity judge turns aside defendants' pleas that they have neither committed nor planned violence:

> Even if their connection with the injurious and violent conduct of the turbulent among them or of their sympathizers be not such as to make them liable criminally or even answerable civilly in damages to those who suffer, still with full knowledge of what is to be expected they give the signal, and in so doing must be held to avail themselves of the degree of fear and dread which the knowledge of such consequences will cause in the mind of those—whether their employer or fellow workmen—against whom the strike is directed.[43]

Given the predictive dimension of the old law, it is not surprising that one of the labor movement's greatest affronts in the eyes of the judges was its introduction of uncertainty, the disquieting feeling that society was "sleeping upon the fires of a volcano."[44] This uncertainty threatened an industrial economy dependent upon—and composed in large part by—the existing order of labor. Thus the omnipresent prediction of social calamity: "Carried to their logical conclusion, the owner of property would lose its control and management. . . . Enterprises employing labor would cease. . . . Idleness and want would follow."[45] It was this uncertainty, I think, not a devotion to republicanism, that lay behind the judges' repeated scorn for workingmen's "secret codes of law," arrangements made out of bounds, irresponsible, uncontrolled.

That the nineteenth-century master and servant law was predictive as well as descriptive is captured in the familiar idea that this law was "constitutive" of the employment relation, defining its proper content and expecting behavior to conform, with the anticipated consequences for violation of the rules. Here I will comment only on one more constitutive feature of this law, which is the location of the relations of employment in a realm separate from the relations of commerce. It has been argued that the common law embodied a double standard, permitting businessmen to do certain things in the way of competition, to break their own and others' contracts, a privilege that was denied workers.[46] The validity of this special treatment claim aside, there had never been doubt historically that workers were not competitors, except perhaps when they sold themselves to employers, an act performed, as we have seen, according to its own set of rules. Judges had successfully administered this distinction between workers and competitors for centuries, before and since the advent of markets under capitalism, without confusion. In an early period, under statutory wage setting, workers were not allowed to compete for wages when prices were largely unregulated. More recently, as shown in the nineteenth-century vagrancy statutes, American workers might not withhold their labor, something that traders in other commodities were legally free to do.

Put differently, judges declined to collapse this diversity of workers and businessmen, or of "insiders" and "outsiders," into a single undifferentiated category of competitors, in the manner urged, for example, by Justice Holmes and thus, in effect, to replace the model of work relations that from time out of mind had guided their decisions. Competition was beyond what the Massachusetts high court, answering Holmes's dissent in *Berry v. Donovan*, defined as the unions' "regular line of their business as employees. . . . [Competition was] outside of the province of workingmen." Insofar as union members acted from motives of competition, as they claimed, those motives were illegal. Echoing sentiments embodied in the law of master and servant from as far back as can be traced, the court opined that if laborers were permitted to behave like competitors and intervene in markets to their own advantage, the result would be "industrial wars," with employers "forced to yield to all their demands"—the end of the business system.[47]

FAILURE

The failure of the old labor system was a consequence, in the end, of its unreliability, the incompetence of its principles any longer to predict or even describe with reasonable accuracy the social behavior it had the constitutional authority to regulate. The failure occurred not out of the law's illogic, but rather through unions' collective actions that outreached its categories. This discrepancy, between the structure that was law and the reality of action, must be insisted upon against an interpretation of what happened in terms of one political program or "discourse" embraced by employers and courts defeated by a different political program or discourse embraced by labor and its supporters, although it was in part that as well. The latter reading overlooks the stakes of the conflict and, thus, the political significance of the outcome. At stake was governance by ancient principles, by a priori understandings of what was the case and what would occur, imposed by judges, as opposed to governance according to the changing vectors of social action, registered directly and through legislation.

What in fact happened has been further clouded by the idea that labor law in the late nineteenth century was the prime example of an innovative style of legal reasoning known as classical or formalistic jurisprudence. For example, Ellen Kelman has argued that labor law at that time was "an almost entirely new field of law." It therefore was a "testing ground" for formalistic categories that, besides masking judges' proemployer bias through a rhetoric of neutrality, were also unintelligible and circular.[48] Against the historical background of labor regulation, however, such views will be seen to be inapposite. Labor law was a very old field. The formalist metaphors of legal rights, based on property notions of clear demarcations over which people might not stray, were not only natural to but historically coincident with the medieval origins of the labor system, dedicated to defining and protecting the workplace hierarchy from outside disruption. Due in large part to the persistence and constitutive properties of master and servant law, labor relations in practice had remained sufficiently constant for the old concepts to retain their cogency.

Placed within the old framework, distinctions that otherwise might seem unintelligible make sense. Distinctions between "immediate" and "remote" causes and "direct" and "indirect" purposes were compatible with the territorial character of labor regulation and with the line separating insiders and outsiders.[49] Strikes to enforce existing closed shop agreements, for example, were comfortably categorized as direct and legal, while strikes to obtain closed shop agreements were indirect and illegal, especially when, as was virtually always the case, a new closed shop involved discharging existing employees. Measures to strengthen bargaining power frequently entailed outside activities and organizers; they were indirect, with palpable interference in the relations of those inside, whose relation to the situation was deemed direct. Strikes that sought higher wages or the enforcement of existing contracts were an inside affair, direct and, therefore, legal. If the starting point of this reasoning had been a level playing field, then these distinctions might seem, as Kelman says, "indefensible."[50] However, judges started with a hierarchical playing field and a law anciently constructed to preserve it.

Similarly, the charge of circularity against standards like the "natural laws of business" and "malice" is not so much incorrect as beside the point. These standards were imposed a priori rather than extracted from facts, but they were a priori in a particular way. As common law, they were the ingrained sediment of experience over centuries, and justified and recommended on that basis. "Enticement," like "vagrancy," had its morality built in; it was by definition both contrary to the natural laws of business and malicious. Justice Holmes would have emptied the law of these predispositions, but he never persuaded the majority in any state or federal court to his view. The final result, then, with the eventual legitimation of labor's collective actions through statute, was to pull down this old and by now decayed edifice of reasoning. In the meantime, the unions displayed its unreasonability, as meant here and within the common law, by their practices.

The courts' doctrines were eroded, first of all, by the success of collective actions—strikes and threats of strikes—that the courts, if asked to decide, would have found illegal.[51] Agreements between employers and groups of tradesmen had a long and unchallenged tradition in American industry, however; and for those employers determined to resist, the old legal system was still intact. What finally brought things to a crisis point was the unions' tactic of the consumer product boycott.

As long as secondary boycotts had contained the ingredient of quitting work, courts continued to adjudicate on the enticement pattern, stretching it to give companies targeted what was, in effect, a legal interest in uninterrupted work by the employees of its supplier or customer firms, or in the case of the railroads, employees on connecting lines.[52] The consumer boycott, with no accompanying action to quit or interfere with work of others, presented the courts with an entirely new set of problems. The novelty was not in the manifestly peaceful nature of the action, since courts were long accustomed to discerning presumptive violence down the line. Nor was it in depriving the company of its customers, which had long been an incident of interfering with work relations and had been held illegal right along with such interference.[53] But the consumer product boycott formed an alliance between union members and members of the public, some of whom were personally connected to the labor movement, were "friends" of labor, or were acting on a momentary impulse. Before, the judges had declined to collapse different social activities into new universal categories like "competition" and had distinguished among diverse strike actions, which were in any case all historically suspect. Now, they had to disaggregate actions—purchasing and nonpurchasing, from one vendor rather than another—that were universal and highly approved of culturally in order to explain why, under certain circumstances and for certain persons, they were illegal.

The courts' approach, both in England and in the United States, was to look behind the acts of purchasing and nonpurchasing and persuading others to do likewise to the motives of the organizers. These were found to have knowingly caused harm and were therefore deemed "malicious."[54] By this term the judges did not refer to factual malice, that is, the subjective feeling of ill will, which was the colloquial meaning. They meant legal malice, which designated an intentional act that caused injury performed by a person who had no right to do it. This was an entirely external quality, bestowed a priori on acts and persons that by an objective standard fell into the category of wrong, as had been the case with vagrants and enticers. In fact, this method sparked legal debate on both sides of the Atlantic and prompted the first wave of prolabor legislation introduced in the Congress, but these were a gloss, not the cause of events.[55] (It was perhaps unfortunate for the American judges that they had conjured up one of the truly hallowed phrases in the nation's political mythology, "with malice toward none.") Here I will briefly indicate how a reliance on the old formalities, but now without the underlying social realities to match, brought the old structure to a condition of decay, even as it continued to function.

Courts took several tacks. One, for example, used a kind of distinction between insiders and outsiders in response to workers' insistence that far from intending harm, by selectively distributing their purchasing power they aimed to benefit those merchants friendly to their cause. Unionists, said the court in a case arising from a boycott of advertisers in a targeted newspaper, might have entirely peaceful intentions, but their "communications were addressed to the public and indiscriminately circulated. They were not intended only for members of the order by whom a technical signification would be given to the word 'boycott,' but to the general public who would read them and give the word its accepted [threatening] meaning."[56] Here, in other words, the legal malice of the insiders results from the factual malice of the outsiders. This kind of reasoning was not unprecedented: union members had often been made culpable through the putative violence of infiltrators in their ranks. But the approach was further strained when the acts in question, even in their anticipation, were identical.

A different move was to create through rhetoric the impression of self-evident wrongdoing that historically adhered to the old workplace offenses. For example, using the direct and indirect distinction, the circuit court issuing the *Danbury Hatters'* injunction recited the bill of allegations bridged by such queries as, "Are they not acting in combination, not merely for the ultimate purpose of advancing their own interests as workmen, but for the direct and immediate purpose of injuring the complainants in their business and property?"[57] Since the organizers of the boycott were not employees, they could not "directly" affect employees' working conditions; they instead maliciously organized a national boycott with a far-flung "system of picketing and espionage" that the court was at pains to depict as carrying out the "indirect" purpose of the action. The point, again, is not logic or illogic, but that the power of such a priori arguments was considerably diminished once the action was divorced from the old workplace settings. Put differently, the new law was no more formal than the law had been for hundreds of years, but it became through the unions' actions a good deal more abstract. Seen in this light, the important change in the late nineteenth century was not how legal formalism vitiated the rights of workers; it was how the actions of workers vitiated the ancient system of legal formalism.

RE-VISIONS

The upheaval overall had transformative effects on American politics and culture. The political effects were largely postponed for several decades while agencies of the state wrestled with the problem of bringing order to industrial life without taking changed labor practices into account.[58] The cultural effects, on the other hand, can be observed apace, as what had been timeless truths about society gave way to the new realities. A major cultural effect was the event itself, the startling eruption of strikes and boycotts, at once tactics and expressions of the revised arrangements of authority the unions were creating. To this event ideas about legality and morality, stability and change, citizenship and civility inevitably attached. Indeed, I would go so far as to say that without an appreciation for the passing of the labor system as it had existed since time out of memory, certain cultural aspects of the period seem incoherent.

In the few pages that remain, I wish briefly to address this issue with reference to one such incongruity, one that the historian David Hollinger has identified as "the problem of pragmatism in American life."[59] Although it is currently enjoying something of a revival, pragmatism is one of those St. Elmo's fires in the national past that for a time burned brightly—no less radiantly than "the American mind"—and then receded without refutation or remark. Looking back, it has been difficult to see what all the excitement was about, how pragmatism offered more than an amorphous set of precepts already long a part of the democratic tradition.

If my interpretation of the ancient ordering of the workplace is correct, however, it suggests the following solution. Labor organization was an earthquake under what remained of feudal society, and it shook the world of the late nineteenth century in the same way that the religious and commercial and their associated political revolutions shook their worlds in the seventeenth and eighteenth centuries. More to the point, the unions shook society along the very same fault lines as those earlier revolutions did, along the lines between authority and will, hierarchy and equality, law and action, segmentation and flow. Voluntarism, democracy, energy, openness: these characteristic themes of pragmatism had been reiterated throughout the stages of liberal development. However, only the persistence of the old labor regime, not as a geological site one might visit on a field trip, but as a system of personal relations inhabited by a sizable portion of the population for most of their waking hours and one that underlay the existing system of industry, makes understandable why these themes took hold upon the philosophical imagination as strongly as they did. Afterward, with the old order significantly flattened, it seemed that pragmatism had added little new to the visible terrain.

Certain secondary connections between the philosophy of pragmatism and the labor movement are well known, starting with the bromide that American labor is itself "pragmatic." Several of the labor movement's intellectual supporters—Herbert Croly, Walter Weyl, Walter Lippman—were enthusiastic students of William James and John Dewey.[60] The two most important figures in the realist assault on labor law, Oliver Wendell Holmes and Roscoe Pound were, respectively, friend and disciple of James.[61] My view, however, goes deeper into this association, into the concepts of pragmatism at their root rather than their application, and argues that they arose when they did because they mirrored and explained and pointed a direction in a changing society. This might seem like a fairly common-sense proposition except that most discussions of pragmatism's sources proceed from the standpoint of religion and science, fields treated socially only with respect to their effects, not their causes.[62] For that matter, the presence of post-Kantian epistemology and Darwinian science at the intellectual foundations of the pragmatist project does not in any way conflict with a greater specification of the more ordinary human activities that the new approach to truth and inquiry was intended to energize and sustain.

Intriguing pathways in and out of the circle of absolute intellect lead to the "labor question." It was before the Metaphysical Club, whose six or seven fellow members at the time included Charles Peirce and James, that Holmes first aired his ideas on the common law; this would have been before James published his work on psychology and while Dewey was still a student at Johns Hopkins, but probably after Peirce had published his first article on pragmatic thinking.[63] Another member of the club, Nicholas St. John Green, who died in 1876, was a leading commentator on the subject of the master's liability for the acts of his servant, and he tracked and anticipated changes in that law.[64] These early dates suggest an engagement with the subject of labor years before the popular reception of pragmatism (James coined the word in 1898), by which time figures like Dewey and James were invited to comment on sundry issues of the day and Holmes was a judge. In the event, the first article Dewey wrote on the law, in 1916, criticized the equation of reason with custom as applied to relations of master and servant.[65]

All of this is mere anecdotal support for the remarkable affinities between the outlook and terminology of pragmatism and the questions being fought out in the labor cases before the American courts. These are worthy of extended treatment, yet are so obviously suggestive that they need only be mentioned to establish the general point. Each of pragmatism's precepts contradicted a parallel idea in the common law, divined by professionals, justified by tradition, prescribing relations and behaviors distilled from the experience of centuries. Reasoning, according to Dewey, was the process by which a hypothesis is developed "until it receives a form in which it can instigate and direct an experiment that will disclose precisely those conditions which have the maximum possible force in determining whether the hypothesis should be accepted or rejected."[66] Inquiry into discrete causality "only abstracts some aspect of the existing course of events in order to re-duplicate it as a petrified eternal principle by which to explain the very changes of which it is the formalization."[67] Knowledge consisted in the mind's tendency of "subordinating environment to itself rather than passively accommodating itself to a coercion working from without."[68] Logical thought with its divides and categories sapped life of its vitality and clogged what James saw as the "inextricable interfusion of human experience."[69]

The social implications were likewise adverse to the courts' position. Against the common law's a priori morality, "moral truths that are not recreated in application to the urgencies of the passing hour, no matter how true in the place and time of their origin, are pernicious and misleading, i.e. false."[70] History could not justify social order when history itself was "nothing but the story of Men's struggles from generation to generation to find the more and more inclusive order."[71] Pragmatism rejected the individualism associated with the market and the rights of workers so long as they were not exercised in harmony: its philosophical hold on reality was attributable to the fact that it was "essentially a *social* philosophy, a philosophy of 'co,' in which conjunctions do the work."[72] Democracy's "substitution, for *a priori* truth and deduction, of fluent doubt and inquiry, meant trust in human nature in the concrete; in individual honesty, curiosity, and sympathy."[73] Constitutions were no bar to change, for politics could not admit of "closet solutions." Only experiments, and the outcry and appeasements they bring, could discover "by what sort of conduct the maximum good can be gained and kept in this world."[74]

I don't wish to give the impression that these American philosophers pondered the news of industrial strife each morning as they prepared to go to their respective studies. My argument is that the formalism in pragmatism's so-called revolt against formalism had a particular historical content.[75] It would seem a minimal claim that a philosophy insistent that all knowledge was both historical and social was alert to the explosive social drama of its own time. In a talk to women students in the mid-1890s, James describes in a romantic, Tolstoyian passage how, after spending a week at the assembly at Chautauqua Lake and thinking that heroism had vanished forever, he rediscovered the "daily lives of the laboring classes . . . and a wave of sympathy greater than I had ever felt before with the common life of common men began to fill my soul." James tells his listeners that each one will be caught up in the perplexities of the "labor question," by which he referred to "anarchist discontents and socialistic projects, and the conservative resistance which they provoke." When the conflict was past and society arrived at a new and better equilibrium, the "same eternal thing"—ideals allied to courage and endurance—would still comprise the "solid meaning of life."[76]

For James and Dewey and the other philosophical pragmatists, a new order of labor relations was not a goal as it was for their admirers on the *New Republic*. Rather, the "labor question" infused the society in which they lived, and the changing realities that exemplified the philosophical dilemmas of knowledge and inquiry with which they were concerned were the same changing realities that reached beyond the idealizations of the old law.

NOTES

1. Recent work incorporating these themes includes Fink 1987; Hattam 1990; and Forbath 1989.

2. This argument comprises part of the study in Orren 1991. See also Orren 1987.

3. On hierarchy and protection as feudal principles, see Bloch 1961, 1: 148–62.

4. On vagrancy laws generally, see Lacey 1953; Perkins 1958. Vagrancy laws withstood most constitutional challenges until the late 1960s. For the shift, see Lahan 1968. The statutes anticipated that a considerable part of the work force would be drawn from those who were vagrants and forbad the giving of alms to able-bodied beggars, who might otherwise be induced to labor.

5. Antebellum court procedures and their English background are discussed in *People v. Eliza Phillips*, 1 Edm. Sel. Cas. 386 (N.Y. 1847).

6. Tiedeman 1886: 116–17.

7. 1 Edw. 6, c. 3. The statute is recited in Ribton-Turner 1887: 89–92.

8. Wood 1877: 5.

9. *Stanton v. Bell*, 2 Hawks 145 (N.C., 1822).

10. *Spain v. Arnott*, KB 2 Starkie 256 (1817); *Turner v. Mason*, 14 M. & W. 112 (1845).

11. *Harrington v. First National Bank of Chittenango*, 1 T. & C., 361 (N.Y. 1873). For a later case on this same principle, see *McCauley v. Press Publishing Co.*, 155 N. Y. S. 1044 (1915).

12. *M'Manus v. Crickett*, 1 East 105 (1800), which in turn cites sixteenth-century precedent. For a later leading case, see *Courtney v. Baker*, 60 N.Y. 1 (1875). In the late nineteenth century, courts inquired whether the action was in the scope of the servant's authority, rather than whether it was pursuant to a specific order.

13. See the discussion in Wood 1877: 195–98 and cases cited at 196, n. 3. For a midthirteenth-century statement of the principle, see Henrici de Bracton, *De legibus et consuetudinibus Angliae libri quinq* (London: apud Richardum Tottellum, 1569), 29–55.

14. The leading case in the late nineteenth century was *Ames v. Union Railway*, 117 Mass. 541 (1875). Early precedents in this line go back to *Gray v. Jefferies*, Cro. Eliz. 55 (1587) and *Barham v. Dennis*, Cro. Eliz. 77 (1600).

15. The leading case into the late nineteenth century was *Baker v. Bolton*, 1 Camp. 493 (1808). For one nineteenth-century exception to this rule see *Sullivan v. Union Pacific Railroad*, 1 Central Law Journal (U.S. Cir. Ct., Neb.), 595 (1874). This decision is useful for its review of the common law and American precedents on the subject (which, the judge remarks, "it requires some courage to disregard").

16. See Wood 1877: 290–91; Bacon 1860, 6: 551 and precedent cited.

17. *Commonwealth v. Pullis*, reprinted in Commons 1910–11, 3: 61–248, at 63–64, 234; *People v. Fisher*, 14 Wend. 10 (Sup. Ct. N.Y. 1835), 20; *Commonwealth v. Hunt*, 4 Metcalf 111 (Mass. 1842), at 130.

18. 4 Pick. 425 (Mass. 1827). The decision in *Boston Glass* turned on whether employers might legally arrange employment contracts with competitors' employees, in this case skilled glassworkers, to take effect after the existing term of employment had expired. The court ruled in the affirmative, but restated the principle of noninterference with ongoing employment relations. The early precedent cited is *Adams and Bafealds Case*, 1 Leonard 240 (1591). *Adams and Bafealds Case* relies on precedents from the reigns of Edward III, Edward IV, and Henry IV, the earliest from 1373, holding that the enticement action is nonstatutory.

19. *Walker v. Cronin,* 107 Mass. 555 (1871). An older English case holding that journeymen shoemakers working by the piece were servants in common law is *Hart v. Aldridge,* 1 Cowp. 56 (1774). The plaintiff there, who prevailed, gives a historical review from the early fifteenth century in support of the position that the law made no distinctions among workingmen according to either manner of hiring or "capacity" (trade).

20. See Lahan 1980: 1510.

21. *Keane v. Boycott,* 2 H. Bl. 511 (1795).

22. For an application of this doctrine to the marriage relation see *Smith v. Kaye,* 20 T.L.R. 262 (1904).

23. *Luske v. Hotchkiss* 37 Conn. 219 (1870). See also *Bartlett v. Street Railway Co. of Grand Rapids,* 82 Mich. 658 (1890). The argument that the absence of administrative means was responsible for the null effect of labor statutes is in Friedman 1973: 492.

24. Conspiracy convictions remained common during the period following the civil war. See, for example, *Carew v. Rutherford,* 106 Mass. 1 (1870); *State v. Stewart,* 59 Vermont 273 (1887); *Erdman v. Mitchell,* 207 Pa. St. 79 (1903); *Coeur d'Alene Consolidated & Mining Co. v. Miners' Union of Wardner,* 51 Fed. 260 (1892). On a simple trespass see *Patchen v. Kelley* 19 Nev. 404 (1887). For an example of an assault and battery case, see *Zeiger v. Nolan,* 1 City Ct. R. Supp. 54 (N.Y. 1884). For a breach of peace case against a labor organizer, see *Commonwealth v. Silvers,* 11 Penn. Cty. Ct. Rep., 481 (1892).

25. 66 Mich. 127 (1887), 132–33, 131.

26. On picketing, see *Vegelahn v. Guntner,* 167 Mass. 92 (1896). Strike and boycott cases are discussed below.

27. On a strike without physical violence, see *State v. Stewart* (1887). The tactic involved was the listing of "scab shops" in a union newspaper.

28. Many cases involved both. For an enticement conviction of an individual which the New York Supreme Court, based on sixteenth-century precedent, refused to reverse on a plea that the damages awarded were excessive, see *Haight v. Badgeley,* 15 Barb. 499 (N.Y. 1854). A notorious case involving union organizers was *Hitchman Coal & Coke Co. v. Mitchell,* 245 U.S. 229 (1917).

29. On the illegality of a strike to obtain a closed shop see *Plant v. Woods,* 176 Mass. 492 (1900).

30. On "probable expectancy" see *Jersey City Printing Co. v. Cassidy,* 63 Eq. 18 Dick. Ch. 759 (N.J. 1902).

31. Plaintiffs in *Erdman v. Mitchell* (1903) had been fired as a result of a union's action to enforce a closed-shop agreement.

32. See, for example, *American Steel Foundries v. Tri-City Central Trades Council,* 257 U.S. 184 (1921). This was a victory for limited ("pink tea") picketing, where the court states: "The principle of the unlawfulness of maliciously enticing laborers still remains and actions may be maintained therefor in proper cases" at 209.

33. *Johnston Harvester Company agt. Peter Meinhardt,* 60 N.Y. Prac. Rep. 168 (1880), 175–76.

34. 170 N.Y. Rep. 315 (1902), at 332.

35. *Erdman v. Mitchell* (1903), 92.
36. *Jersey City Printing Co. v. Cassidy* (1902).
37. *Coeur d'Alene Consolidated & Mining Co v. Miners' Union* (1892); *Hitchman v. Mitchell* (1917). For an extensive treatment of judges' attribution of miscreant behavior to unionists, see Avery 1989.
38. *Barr v. Essex Trades Council*, 53 Eq. 8 Dick. Ch. 101 (N.J. 1894) 115. In *Old Dominion Steamship Co. v. McKenna*, 30 Fed. Rep. 48 (1887), at 49, the judge pointedly mentions the demand that the company "pay southern negroes the same wages as New York longshore-men."
39. *Barr v. Essex Trades Council* (1894), 113.
40. Cf. J. Wycliff: "Fals prelates that don by the conseil and enticement of hem that sechen erthelich thinges," *Apocalypse* iii, *Bible*, Pref. 8 (1380); J. Milton: "Here to every thirsty wanderer by sly enticement gives his baneful cup," *Comus*, 524 (1634). All of the usages provided in the *Oxford English Dictionary* (1971 edition) are of the same coloration.
41. *Barr v. Essex Trades Council* (1894), 111.
42. Holmes 1881.
43. 176 Mass. 492, 497.
44. *State v. Stewart* (1887), 286.
45. *Coeur d'Alene Consolidated & Mining Co. v. Miners' Union* (1892), 263.
46. Lahan 1980: 1532ff. See also Gregory and Katz 1979: 65–68. William Forbath presents a related idea, namely that labor uncovered "contradictory commitments" in the common law between protecting competitive freedom and protecting property and contractual interests. Forbath 1989: 1207.
47. 188 Mass. 353 (1905), 358, 360, 359.
48. Kelman 1983: 2.
49. This physical, territorial quality was characteristic of medieval law generally, for analogous historical reasons. In an essay written in the 1870s, Nicholas St. John Green provides an erudite refutation of the aptness of such metaphors, and thereby eloquent testimony to their use. See his "Proximate and Remote Cause," in N.St.J. Green 1933: 1–17.
50. Kelman 1983: 45.
51. During a period extending from 1881 until the start of World War I, and with the exception only of the antiunion drives and economic contraction in 1906–8, strikes more often than not were won, or they ended in compromise. See P. K. Edwards 1981: 15, 42, 12–51, 84–133 passim; D. Montgomery 1980: 92.
52. *Purvis v. United Brotherhood*, 214 Pa. 348 (1906); *Hopkins v. Oxley Stave Co.*, 83 Fed. Rep. 912 (1897); *Toledo, A.A. & N.M. Ry. Co. v. Pennsylvania Co.*, 54 Fed. Rep. 730 (1893).
53. For an early seventeenth-century case of this kind, see *Garrett v. Taylor*, Cro. Jac. 567 (1620.)
54. The closely watched English case on this issue was *Allen v. Flood* [1898] AC 1.
55. The connection of this intellectual stir to the origins of the Clayton Act is discussed in Justice Brandeis's dissenting opinion in *Duplex Printing v.*

Deering, 254 U.S. 443 (1921), 485. American comments include Huffcut 1898; J. Smith 1907; Lewis 1905; J. B. Ames 1905. The English background is discussed in Dicey 1904.

56. *Barr v. Essex Trades Council* (1894), 121.

57. 139 Fed. 71 (1905), 79.

58. See Orren 1991: chap. 5 for early attempts at railroad regulation under the Interstate Commerce Act, based on the assumption that stability could be brought to the industry through controls on management alone. Only in the Transportation Act of 1920 were labor relations made an intrinsic part of the regulatory framework. Also see Orren 1982 on the contradictory interplay between monetary policy and labor organization before the Full Employment Act of 1946.

59. Hollinger 1980: 88–107.

60. Forcey 1961.

61. Pound's debt to James may be seen in Pound 1908. For Holmes's views on labor law see Holmes 1894. On the two men's relations to the later movement known as legal realism see G. E. White 1978: 116–129, 209–211.

62. See, for example, Kuklick 1977. The same emphasis remains in the more politically informed interpretation of James Kloppenberg. See Kloppenberg 1987.

63. See Patterson 1940: 174.

64. N.St.J. Green 1933: 127–37. This excerpt was a note to the 8th edition of Joseph Story's treatise on the law of agency, published in 1874.

65. Dewey 1929: 790–97.

66. John Dewey, *Logic: The Theory of Inquiry,* quoted in Hook 1939: 96.

67. Dewey 1976–83, 4: 11.

68. Ibid., 4: 180.

69. James 1925: 124.

70. Dewey 1976–83, 4: 74.

71. James 1896: 155–56.

72. James 1909: 72.

73. Dewey 1976–83, 4: 39.

74. James 1896: 157.

75. The phrase, "revolt against formalism," is of course from M. White 1961.

76. James 1899: 275, 297–99.

7 The *Danbury Hatters'* Case

Daniel R. Ernst

When William Humphries, a defendant in the *Danbury Hatters'* case, took the stand on September 20, 1912, *Loewe v. Lawlor* was already more than nine years old. The quarrel between the hat manufacturer Dietrich Eduard Loewe and individual members of the United Hatters of North America had been the subject of an earlier five-month trial, two decisions by an intermediate appellate court, and a unanimous opinion by the U.S. Supreme Court holding that the Sherman Anti-Trust Act prohibited the boycott alleged in Loewe's complaint. Of the many trade unionists who protested the Supreme Court's decision, none had been more outspoken than AFL President Samuel Gompers, himself a defendant in another boycott suit. Gompers attacked the decision in the *American Federationist*, in congressional testimony, on the hustings for William Jennings Bryan in 1908, and as the second trial wore on in 1912, while stumping for another Democratic presidential candidate, Woodrow Wilson. Each time, leaders of the National Association of Manufacturers, the American Anti-Boycott Association, and other antiunion organizations defended the case in no less passionate terms.[1]

So when the hatters' lawyer, Frank Mulholland, commenced his examination of William Humphries, the arguments on both sides were already clear. Earlier stages in the litigation had established the illegality of the boycott under the Sherman Act. Now Mulholland called the seventy-two-year-old hat finisher to the stand simply to determine whether he should be held responsible for the actions of the national officers in conducting the boycott. Like the great majority of the original 250 co-defendants, Humphries had never been an officer in the United Hatters and had never been employed by Loewe. Daniel Davenport, the senior member in Loewe's litigation team, had named Humphries in his complaint simply because he was on the union's membership rolls and owned a house and a savings account that could be attached under a Connecticut statute. Like his co-defendants, Humphries had signed over to the United Hatters title to these assets in exchange for the union's promise to conduct the defense and to reimburse him in the event of an adverse judgment.

The jury of Connecticut farmers must have considered Humphries a sympathetic defendant. Born in Ireland in 1840, he had come with his parents to the United States at the age of nine. He had worked in the hatting industry since 1854, interrupting his labors only to "wear the blue" of the Union Army. He had taken little interest in the boycotts ordered by the leaders of the national union. He testified, "I am willing to acquiesce in the matter because I didn't take any part in electing them." Indeed, Humphries, like many of his co-defendants, had taken little part in *any* aspect of union affairs. He "didn't know the national officers . . . either by sight or by name." He rarely read the United Hatters' *Journal*. "I couldn't see very good," Humphries explained, "and I hadn't time to do it." As an honorary member of his local union since his fiftieth birthday, Humphries was excused from appearing at its meetings and almost never attended them.[2]

To an uninstructed member of the general public, the idea that this unexceptionable working man should be held responsible for the acts of a distant leadership must have been surprising. Humphries himself thought the idea incredible: "I never was a party to a conspiracy to interfere with Mr. Loewe or anybody else," he insisted. "I never was a party to any conspiracy of any kind."[3] Yet according to the law of agency, Humphries and his co-defendants *were* responsible. Shortly after the United Hatters had called out his work force in July 1902, Loewe sent to every hatter in Danbury's city directory and published in the local paper a notice warning "the members of All Labor Unions" that he would hold them responsible for the unlawful acts of their leaders. Given this notice and the regular coverage of the boycott in the Danbury *News*, a jury could hardly conclude that Humphries lacked the personal knowledge that made his continued payment of dues an implicit ratification of the leadership's actions.[4]

Nor did they. The jurors who heard Humphries testify awarded Loewe the full amount he sought (after first inquiring whether they could return a still larger verdict). Once they completed their labors, the good men of the jury burst into the doxology. Appellate courts were equally stern. "A soldier who with his regiment charges the enemy's line can hardly be heard to assert that he did not know a battle was in progress," declared Alfred C. Coxe, chief judge of the Second Circuit.[5] Oliver Wendell Holmes, Jr., reviewing the record for the U.S. Supreme Court, thought it "almost inconceivable" that the individual defendants did not know of the boycott.[6]

Humphries's testimony revealed that a great chasm had opened up between legal theory and industrial reality. In theory, Humphries was the master of the national leadership of the United Hatters. In fact, he was an insignificant and somewhat apathetic constituent of that corporate, if formally unincorporated, body. By eliciting testimony showing that the union had assumed the cost of the litigation, Loewe's lawyers implied that the individual hatters would not personally suffer from an adverse judgment. But the individual defendants did suffer: they could not sell or mortgage their homes while attached, and they were not certain that the national union could or would live up to its promise.

For Humphries this plight was all the more bewildering because he and Loewe had always been on cordial terms. Humphries knew Loewe very well—knew him personally—from their joint service on the board of Danbury's hospital. Even after the strike and boycott, Humphries frequently met Loewe, and Loewe "always was glad to see me." Why, then, were they locked in this great, seemingly endless lawsuit? To find out, Humphries simply walked up to Loewe during a recess and asked the employer why he had attached his home and bank account. Loewe, obviously dismayed, replied, "If I had the doing of it, I wouldn't have attached your property." Loewe also said "he was very sorry," Humphries testified, "and he said, 'It will never cost you a cent.' "[7]

I suppose one could dismiss Loewe's regrets as a class warrior's momentary failure of nerve when brought face to face with the human costs of his avarice. That view would be consistent with the leading interpretation of *Loewe*, which treats it and the larger law of industrial disputes of the Progressive Era as a successful attempt by a united capitalist class to enlist the courts in an antiunion crusade. This is an old view, dating back to Samuel Gompers's denunciation of the courts as "the pliant tools of corporate wealth." It accords with much recent scholarship that identifies the business corporation as the preeminent shaper of economic policy in the Progressive Era. If the visible hand of the corporation was so influential in the fashioning of public policy on railroads, antitrust, industrial accidents, and banking, then one might well assume it was no less important a force in the law of industrial disputes.[8]

Yet to treat *Loewe v. Lawlor* as an unambiguous victory for the rising forces of corporate capitalism is to misread the case in two important respects. First, the case is better viewed as part of the denouement of proprietary capitalism and Victorian culture than the appearance of a new industrial and cultural order. Loewe personally owned the boycotted company, identified closely with it, and intended to leave it to his children. In stating his case against the union, Loewe and his lawyers emphasized the personal traits that made him a successful employer and citizen and not (as a corporate manager might) his contribution to the welfare of consumers or the industry as a whole. Loewe had prospered because he possessed the independence, diligence, thrift, and calculation needed to thrive in the competitive marketplace, which he considered (in Richard Hofstadter's words) "a kind of disciplinary machinery for the development of character."[9] The boycott threatened Loewe with personal ruin, and, incidentally, denied the general public the opportunity to buy his low-priced hats; yet its potential for subverting a vital inculcator of economic morality was by far its greatest danger.

Loewe's suit placed him at odds with the emerging industrial order in a second respect. Throughout the early twentieth century employers in competitive industries experimented with ways of stabilizing prices and profits in their industries. In coal, clothing, and other industries with high labor costs, collective bargaining with a strong national union presented employers with a plausible vehicle for administering their product markets. This "regulatory unionism" (as Colin Gordon has dubbed the phenomenon) was the context for many of the great labor cases of the early twentieth century—including the *Danbury Hatters'* case. Rival manufacturers were arrayed alongside trade unionists in the combination against Loewe. His suit illustrates division among capitalists, not unity.[10]

In his moralistic understanding of economic behavior and commitment to personal independence, Loewe had more in common with William Humphries than with a manager of one of the new corporate behemoths. Through hard work and fair dealing the hat finisher Humphries and the former hat finisher Loewe had become property owners and citizens in a country both believed in deeply—a belief evidenced in Humphries' case by service in the Grand Army of the Republic and in Loewe's by the American flag and American eagle prominently featured in his advertising.[11]

Loewe's response to Humphries, then, reveals his genuine confusion at finding himself locked in mortal struggle with a man who had been no less faithful to the tenets of economic morality than Loewe had himself. By the end of the *Danbury Hatters'* case, others experienced Loewe's confusion as they discovered that individualistic notions of fair dealing provided little help in separating villains from victims in industrial disputes. While the proprietors and their allies continued to insist on the timeless truth of what Henry F. May has called the "old, rigid certainties" of Victorian morality, middle-class liberals, newly professionalized social scientists, and progressives within the business community articulated new ways of explaining labor strife in the new industrial order.[12]

THE HAT TRADE

Understanding the circumstances that brought Humphries and Loewe face to face in a Connecticut courtroom requires us to take a long step backward from 1912 into the late nineteenth century. By 1880, the hatting industry had divided into two branches: stiff hats, such as the derby, and soft hats, such as the fedora. Some large companies, like the John B. Stetson Company, E. A. Mallory & Sons, and Henry H. Roelof & Company, produced both stiff and soft hats and kept all stages of production within their own factories. Many more firms specialized in producing one or the other variety. Stiff hatting centered in two Connecticut towns, Danbury and South Norwalk; soft hatting centered in Newark and the Orange Valley of New Jersey. Firms also specialized in various stages of the production process. Some firms "made" partially shaped hat bodies and sold them through merchant houses to "commission shops" for "finishing" into either stiff or soft hats.[13]

As a rule, firms in the hatting industry did not experience the managerial revolution Alfred Chandler described in *The Visible Hand*. Instead they typified the proprietary capitalism Philip Scranton has chronicled in Philadelphia's textile industry.[14] The industry did include an exceptional giant or two. Stetson, for example, was incorporated, owned its own distribution network, and employed 2,150 workers in a large factory complex. Stetson's workers enjoyed the latest in welfare capitalism, such as a company-sponsored Sunday school and a home savings club. The company could afford these benefits thanks to its solid and stable profits—more than $380,000 in 1899.[15] But the typical hat firm looked nothing like Stetson. It was managed and financed by a single proprietor or a handful of partners. Quite often these men had been hatters themselves before scraping together the several hundred dollars needed to start business as a commission shop. Firms generally employed fewer than a hundred workers in a single factory and marketed their output through independent chains of wholesalers and retailers.[16]

The lack of profits to be had in the industry was a constant lament.

The trade journals rarely missed a chance to urge manufacturers to resist price cutting, sometimes employing pithy aphorisms like "Whatever is worth having should be of sufficient account to charge in the bill" and "There's always room at the top."[17] The established manufacturers agreed. A gathering in late 1902 lamented "an almost entire absence of profits in their business" and blamed the "unintelligent competition" of the "lower, profitless grades" of hats for their plight.[18]

Now and then the manufacturers contemplated the kind of horizontal combination that flourished during the merger movement of 1895–1904. For example, in the summer of 1901 the trade journals reported efforts by an unnamed New York City law firm to convince proprietors to sell out to a holding company. Nothing came of this scheme, perhaps because of diseconomies of scale and the variability of fashion in the trade and perhaps because of years of mistrust among the hat manufacturers. "There is probably no industry in the country where there is so much petty jealousy and underhand influences at work," a trade journalist wrote in dismissing the idea of a "Hat Trust." "Each manufacturer is sitting up nights in the effort to design some plan to circumvent his competitors."[19]

One consequence of this scheming was that wages did not keep pace with the rising cost of living at century's end. Many manufacturers had only recently left the workers' ranks and sympathized with calls for higher wages. None, however, would pay more if it meant being undersold by a rival. Thus, a trade journal claimed that "no manufacturer cares whether he pays $1.50 or $2 a dozen for finishing hats provided that his neighbor is made to pay the same rate for a similar grade. Both can make a corresponding advance in the selling price, and since one cannot undersell the other both can get the advance."[20]

Such sentiments were by no means unique to the hatting industry. "In my opinion the trouble is caused by each local union being permitted to make a scale of prices," declared the proprietor of a New York cigar-making firm in 1886. "In consequence some localities can manufacture cheaper than others. My judgment is this, make a uniform price for the entire United States; give men good pay, but make everyone pay alike for manufacturing the same article. I am a friend of labor and would like to see it well paid."[21] To take such employers at their word, Adolph Strasser and Samuel Gompers made uniform trade agreements a cornerstone of the cigar makers' "business unionism" during the Gilded Age.[22]

In the fall of 1885, the leaders of the hatters unions reached the same conclusion and invited the hat manufacturers to discuss "the present state of the trade, and the way to improve it, and the condition of those engaged in it." Edmund Tweedy, the proprietor of one of Danbury's largest firms, took the lead in recruiting manufacturers for a meeting with the union. His address to his fellow employers alluded to the labor strife of the day and to conditions in the hatting industry. "It is safe to say that in many a factory . . . the wheels have been turned for the sole benefit of the workers, while the owner has been content if the end of the year found him in no worse financial condition than the beginning." Tweedy conceded that "the workmen in our trade have not been satisfied with their share of the profits of the business," but he also observed that, with few exceptions, "the same remark will apply to the employers."

The hatters had taken an astonishing first step, Tweedy claimed, by inviting their employers to organize themselves into an association. The workers sincerely believed that "by mutual interchange of views, and by concert of action, it is possible to improve the condition of trade, remove many of its difficulties, and make it more profitable to all parties." Tweedy was well aware that many of his fellow employers regarded unionization as "a foretaste of the torments that await the wicked." But if "injurious competition" could be curtailed through the proposed organization and concerted action, Tweedy believed the benefits for the industry would be immense. By surrendering some measure of individual freedom, the hat manufacturers would taste "a paradise on earth."[23]

New Jersey hat manufacturers, among whom were many of Tweedy's "injurious" competitors, rejected his proposal, but the Danbury proprietors established their own association to "maintain harmonious relations with our employes and unite with them in the adoption of such measures as will tend to improve the condition of the business and promote the general welfare of all employed in it." Despite these good intentions, the Danbury hat manufacturers grew restive as the New Jersey firms made serious inroads into their share of the market. The business collapse of 1893 provided them with an opportunity to break with the union. "The soft hatting industry has nearly left us and stiff hatting is rapidly losing ground," they complained in an open letter to the hatters in July 1893. The nonunion New Jersey firms could pay lower wages and use better machinery than the union permitted them. "We have the factories and the men," the employers asserted, "but the conditions surrounding the employment of men, owing to the restrictions of trade unions here, are such that it is impossible to successfully compete." After a lockout of almost ten weeks, eleven of Danbury's hatting companies, including C. H. Merritt & Son and D. E. Loewe & Co., reopened as independent shops.[24]

As the nation recovered from the depression of 1893–96, the hat finishers and hat makers merged their two organizations into the United Hatters of North America and commenced a new campaign of strikes and boycotts to organize the industry.[25] A major turning point was the capitulation in August 1900 of the largest soft-hatting concern in New Jersey's Orange Valley, F. Berg & Company. After Berg "went fair," the union quickly organized the remaining soft-hatting firms in the Orange Valley and Newark.[26]

As early as November 1900 Loewe had discussed unionization with James P. Maher, president of the local hat makers association and national treasurer of the United Hatters.[27] "I told him that I did not care to meet any people that did not belong to Danbury," Loewe recalled. The national leadership "were not Danbury people and had no interest in Danbury affairs." The following March, Loewe again met with Maher and Martin Lawlor (a local hat maker and national secretary of the United Hatters), but he broke off negotiations after learning that many of his employees would not be given union cards were he to go fair. On April 22, Loewe defended his decision in a letter to the national leadership, "care of James Maher," and braced himself for a strike and boycott.[28]

This surely would have immediately ensued but for a spontaneous walkout three days earlier at Henry H. Roelof's Philadelphia factory. The national leadership suspended its plans for Loewe in order to mount a national boycott of Roelof's goods at an expense to the union of some $23,000. Roelof, a confirmed opponent of trade unionism, responded with civil and criminal conspiracy suits, but finally came to terms with the union on July 19, 1902. Less than a week later, the United Hatters called out Loewe's workforce. Even though Loewe's workers had never complained to the union about their employer, even though Loewe begged them to stay with tears in his eyes, they left rather than be blacklisted by the union and barred from the industry. Among those leaving was the son of Loewe's partner, a union member who was not later named a defendant in the suit.[29]

In the days after the walkout, Loewe met with Maher and John Moffitt, president of the United Hatters, who had convened a meeting of the general executive board in a Danbury hotel. While these negotiations were in progress, a thousand workers struck another giant soft-hat firm, the Waring Hat Company of Yonkers, New York. This time, however, Loewe was given no reprieve, for when Maher and Moffitt left Danbury for Yonkers, they left behind a committee to continue discussions. Loewe broke off the negotiations with the declaration, "If I am to die, I am going to die my way." On August 7, 1902, the board authorized the national officers to proceed with a boycott of Loewe's hats.[30]

"MILLION AGAINST ONE"

In hyperbolic moments, the open-shop press depicted Loewe as larger than life, "the man of the hour" heroically defending individual liberty "in the face of tremendous odds and impending disaster." To one of his lawyers, he was "an obstinate German, who would much rather be ruined and free than . . . prosperous and subject to a commercial slavery." In 1902, Loewe himself explained his actions as the discharge of a duty to "the business, to the people still in the factory, to the town of Danbury." At a victory banquet in March 1908, he modestly protested, "You are making too much of me altogether. I have been doing my duty, trying to do so, at least, and if in doing my duty I have been able to help the cause along a little, I am glad of it, but I don't think I have done any more than that."[31]

Loewe's sense of duty flowed from the experiences of his own life. To more than one observer this "proletarian who, by the opportunities of this country, rose to the rewards of his native abilities" epitomized the workings of the free labor creed.[32] Born in Germany in 1852, Loewe had come to the United States in 1870. A short stint as a railroad laborer brought him to Danbury, where he became a journeyman hat maker in Tweedy's factory in 1871. Over the next several years he learned the more specialized skills of hat finishing, and by 1879 he had become a foreman in the finishing department of a different firm. That year he established his own commission shop with an initial investment of $180. Between 1885 and 1896 Loewe and his partners produced both stiff and soft hats on commission, but starting in the latter year he abandoned his line of stiff hats and commenced selling soft hats under his own name through several large wholesalers and his own store in New York City.[33]

By the turn of the century the firm, while no giant, had nonetheless become a significant producer in the soft hat industry and a real threat to the newly unionized New Jersey concerns. Loewe's principal wholesaler recalled that his dealings with the manufacturer "gradually grew to quite a nice business in 1900. Then it grew quite rapidly up to 1902, when it was a very satisfactory business to us, and, I hope, to Mr. Loewe." Loewe's balance sheets told the same story: his profits in 1900 came to $25,000 (6 percent of his net sales). In 1901, the last full year before the strike, they totaled $28,000, an increase of 12 percent.[34] At the time of the strike, Loewe's payroll of 246 workers placed him ahead of most Connecticut hat firms, although well behind Berg, Roelof, Stetson, and Waring.

In large part Loewe's business had grown because he used more apprentices on his best-selling line than union regulations permitted.

The Danbury locals never complained to the national hierarchy about conditions in Loewe's factory. In fact, the members of the local winked at this infraction, because it gave work to the children of union members who could not otherwise "obtain a livelihood in their native town."[35] But this local arrangement jeopardized the efforts by the national leadership and union employers to realize Tweedy's paradise of stable wages and profits.

Loewe was convinced that a return to union work rules would destroy his business. "Our experience of 1885 to 1894 is still in our minds," Loewe explained to Maher in April 1901, "and the knowledge then obtained convinces us that the increased cost would drive the production of our most popular grades of hats from Danbury, just as the increased cost of production occasioned by the unionizing of all the factories in 1885 drove the soft hatting from this town to other districts." Union conditions would force him to fire many valued employees who would not be "white-washed" into the union. As Loewe recalled, "I knew that all the employees were satisfied—and we as a firm were satisfied—with the way the business was running, and I felt that Danbury as a town was satisfied, and I couldn't see why it should be necessary to change the conditions. I wanted to be left alone."[36]

But Loewe couldn't be left alone, not if prices, profits, and wages in the hatting industry were to stay at comfortable levels. The divergence between the interests of a single, marginal firm and the larger industry became apparent when Loewe met with Maher shortly after the strike commenced. "If I should acquiesce in your demands to unionize the factory," Loewe explained, "I would soon have to make a higher class of goods here, and I would not find a market for them, or, in other words, I would soon die of dry rot." But Maher was adamant. "The manufacturers had tried for many years to control this industry," he insisted. It was now the union's turn.

"It would seem that you are called upon to right the wrongs of the hatting industry," Loewe retorted. "Well," Maher replied, "in a way. You may call this a trust, and perhaps it is a trust, but it is the only thing for us to do to get a good living out of the industry."[37]

That Loewe was not misstating his position became clear once the boycott commenced. Perhaps the most revealing evidence of both the marginal nature of his firm and the efficacy of the United Hatters' boycott comes from the letters Loewe received from his wholesale merchant in Richmond, Virginia. In December 1902, Thomas D. Stokes wrote Loewe about his recent meeting with a delegation of local labor leaders. In response to their demand that he stop marketing Loewe's hats, Stokes pointed out the dilemma Loewe would face if he unionized his firm. Based on his general knowledge of the trade, the merchant estimated that unionization would raise Loewe's costs by more than 10 percent. Should Loewe maintain the quality of his hats, he would have to raise his prices to those of the Berg firm. "I explained to them that in this event we would not need both factories," Stokes reported to Loewe. Because he already bought a special line of hats from Berg, "we no doubt would have to place our business with him to your detriment." Should Loewe attempt to maintain his prices, the quality would slide to an unacceptable level, and, once again, Stokes would take his business to Loewe's competitors.[38]

Despite his initial resolve to stand by Loewe, Stokes quickly capitulated to the unionists' demands. Richmond retailers had been warned that if they continued to sell Stokes's merchandise they would be placed on an unfair list. "Since this was done our trade has virtually amounted to nothing in Richmond," wrote Stokes. Because he had "no chance whatever of winning out single handed," Stokes reluctantly canceled his outstanding orders.[39]

Similar efforts targeting Loewe's other distributors were equally effective. In 1901, Loewe's profits totaled $28,000; his balance sheet for 1902 revealed a loss of $17,600, and losses continued in the following years. Small wonder, then, that at the May 1903 convention of the United Hatters, President Moffitt ended his review of recent triumphs against such giants as Berg and Roelof with a confident report on the Loewe boycott. It was "progressing satisfactorily," he announced, and he predicted it would be concluded just "as successfully as have been the other fights of like nature in recent years."[40]

What confounded Moffitt's prediction was the establishment in August 1903 of the American Anti-Boycott Association (AABA). Since 1901, Loewe had regularly discussed his predicament with his friend and fellow nonunion hat manufacturer, Charles H. Merritt. Merritt had been president of the Danbury manufacturers' association, which had bargained collectively with local unions before the 1893 lockout. The experience had left Merritt (as an obituary put it) "unalterably opposed to the arbitrary principles and coercive methods of the dominating union leaders." Loewe and Merritt came up with the idea of an organization whose sole purpose would be to resist boycotts by lawsuits and other legal measures—in effect, a proemployer legal defense fund.[41]

To help solicit members they recruited Daniel Davenport, a Bridgeport lawyer who had recently distinguished himself in a state constitutional convention. In May 1903 the AABA formally commenced operations with Merritt as president and Davenport as general executive agent. One of the association's first acts was to authorize Davenport to commence suit on Loewe's behalf. He was assisted by

Merritt's son, Walter Gordon Merritt, who had just received his law degree. The younger Merritt devoted a large portion of his practice to the affairs of the AABA. After his father's death in 1917 he assumed the effective leadership of the organization.[42]

DANBURY'S DUPES

A full account of the *Danbury Hatters'* case would relate the progress of the litigation on its first trip to the Supreme Court, how the justices came to conclude that the Sherman Act applied to trade unions, and how the decision provoked the AFL into a campaign to exempt organized labor from the antitrust laws.[43] Here I want to confine myself to a discussion of one consequence of those events.

Long before Dietrich Loewe's confrontation with the United Hatters, middle-class moralists and jurists had reconciled the existence of trade unions with the individualistic assumptions of Victorian culture. They did so by insisting that legitimate trade unions were nothing more than voluntary associations of free and independent worker-citizens. This theory led them to approve actions by labor leaders to the extent that they behaved as the freely designated agents of the rank and file. Should those leaders exercise corporate power over the membership or other workers, however, the limits of legitimate trade unionism would be crossed.[44]

Viewed in its industrial context, the *Danbury Hatters'* case shows how an independent employer used the tenets of Victorian culture to resist a union-sponsored scheme for industrial coordination. It remains to be seen how these same assumptions fared when Loewe attempted to hold individual hatters like William Humphries accountable for the actions of the national leadership. The case did not spark a general reconsideration of the relative merits of competition and cooperation among capitalists. But did it lead contemporaries to question the assumptions underlying the Victorian theory of the labor union?

For two years after the Supreme Court's decision upholding the verdict in the second trial, the AABA, United Hatters, and AFL blustered and feinted as Davenport and Merritt moved to collect the judgment they had won for Loewe. The AABA steadfastly insisted that contracts between the individual defendants and the United Hatters legally obligated the union to pay the judgment. Moreover, they argued that the AFL agreed to help the hatters under a 1908 resolution pledging "moral and such financial support as may be necessary in the pending contention." A levy of about thirty-five dollars on each member of the United Hatters would raise the needed sum, the AABA pointed out, and if every member of the AFL was taxed the individual contribution

would drop to just fifteen cents.[45] An open letter from Loewe emphasized his patience in collecting the judgment; behind the scenes Merritt
and the union officials haggled over a settlement figure.[46]

For their part, the leaders of the United Hatters and AFL took the
steps needed to raise the funds. They insisted, however, that the money
was for the relief of the individual defendants rather than "blood
money" for Loewe and his lawyers. Samuel Gompers wrote the United
Hatters' president in July 1910 that the AFL's resolve did not contemplate the payment of the judgment, that the AFL did not have enough
money to pay the judgment, and that even if the federation had the
funds they could not be devoted to such ends. When the Supreme
Court upheld the second verdict in the case, Gompers told the press,
"I feel awful in regard to how the men will take this when their homes
are sold to pay this terrible judgment," but he announced no program
for their relief. (A newspaperman retorted, "There is nothing to prevent
those who feel that the boycott is a sacred right from chipping in a
few cents a piece" to save the hatters.)[47] Nevertheless, the AFL raised
the bulk of the funds needed to satisfy the judgment. In 1910 the AFL
voted a two-cent assessment on the members of its affiliated unions,
and it later declared January 27, 1916 (Gompers's birthday) "Hatters'
Day," on which union workers were to donate an hour's earnings to
the cause.[48]

The leaders of the United Hatters adopted a similar course. In
February 1915, they and Gompers petitioned Congress to satisfy the
judgment on the theory that, as the labor provisions of the Clayton
Act recognized, the Sherman Act had been erroneously applied to organized labor. Although a hearing was held, the unionists went away
empty handed. A resolve of the May 1915 convention denied that the
union was legally obligated to pay the judgment, but it also authorized
an annual 1 percent assessment on each member's earnings.[49]

Still the two sides could not come to terms, and it seemed possible
in the summer of 1917 that the AABA would have to execute its liens
on the hatters' homes—"homes of old people, homes that were loved"
(as Walter Gordon Merritt wrote in his autobiography). The bad publicity this would generate was one consideration inclining the AABA
toward compromise; another was pressure from the creditors of
Loewe's firm, which had gone into receivership during the litigation.
As Merritt recalled, "The bankers' committee was at my elbow urging
compromise, but I did not wish to end what seemed to me to be a
noble battle with an anticlimax of haggling; and so, surrounded by
glowering glances of disapproval from the banking fraternity," he insisted on the full amount of the balance due. This he received on July

12. Of the $234,192 paid to Loewe on that date, the AFL had raised $216,024.[50]

Behind the hemming and hawing of the union leaders was their desire to avoid establishing in practice what by law did not exist: the corporate responsibility of unions for liabilities incurred by their officers. The New York *World* charged that the AFL and United Hatters were quite prepared to sacrifice "their dupes in Danbury" rather than recognize the principle that "labor organizations, like other combinations, may be held responsible for their acts." Samuel Gompers admitted his desire to avoid setting a precedent during congressional testimony in 1915. Asked why the AFL did not come to the aid of the hatters, Gompers responded that to do so would be to invite a host of lawsuits.[51]

Yet the legal responsibility of the union—as well as compensation for Loewe—was precisely what the AABA sought in bringing the suit. Unless that principle were established, Merritt insisted, the employer would have no adequate protection against an army of unionists arrayed against him. Fortunately the courts had held the defendants individually responsible, telling them, in effect, "you cannot safely continue a member of an organization doing wrong; you must reform it or leave it." Merritt predicted that conservative, property-owning members of the rank and file would insist that their leaders obey the law. Friends of labor, in contrast, charged that the AABA hoped that these unionists would leave the labor movement altogether and place workers at the mercy of their employers.[52]

Another route was possible, however: labor unions could incorporate and thereby limit the liability of their members. In the 1880s organized labor had sought and won the passage of laws providing for the incorporation of trade unions. At the time, many in the movement believed that the statutes were needed to remove any doubt about the lawfulness of unions or their efforts to improve the wages, hours, and working conditions of their members. When nineteenth-century judges upheld unions and these aims, the incentive to incorporate disappeared, to be replaced by fears that incorporation would place unions at the mercy of a hostile judiciary. Thus, Gompers opposed incorporation in a debate with Louis Brandeis in 1903. "Do you blame us if we fear to place further power in the courts and judges of our country?" he asked his audience. "You must excuse us, if you please, if we decline your invitation to step into your parlor."[53]

Despite their refusal to incorporate their unions, labor leaders increasingly found themselves defending their organizations in court. The procedural barriers against common law damage suits did not prevent employers from petitioning equity courts for injunctions against unions in their common name. Moreover, in many states employers sought and won statutes making voluntary associations suable. And in the *Coronado Coal* decision of 1922, Chief Justice William Howard Taft interpreted a provision of the Sherman Act broadly enough to bring unincorporated trade unions under that statute. The great power of labor unions and the difficulty of suing individual members required this result, Taft wrote; otherwise, individuals and society would have no remedy against the oppression of labor organizations.[54]

Gompers denounced *Coronado*, charging that it marked the triumph of big business in its "long campaign for trade-union incorporation."[55] Labor's protests notwithstanding, Taft's opinion in *Coronado* had one great virtue: it sought to accommodate legal doctrine to industrial change. Its frank acknowledgment of collective industrial power would have better served the actual parties to the *Danbury Hatters'* case than the individualistic logic of agency law. Continued adherence to the tenets of economic morality produced real hardship on both sides of the dispute.

Consider Dietrich Loewe. True, Loewe received in full his judgment of more than $250,000, but the money went to his creditors: his firm was in receivership when the judgment was satisfied. The business closed for good in 1926, paying creditors forty cents on the dollar. In 1927, in poor health and nearly blind, Loewe was living on an annuity raised by several manufacturers' associations. When he died at the end of 1935, he left no family business for his grandson, a union hatter, to inherit.[56]

Among the defendant hatters were men who believed as staunchly in unionism as Loewe did in his duty to remain an open shop. When Lyman Beecher Stowe was dispatched to Danbury by the *Outlook* in the summer of 1915, he asked one defendant, "a defiant little man upwards of sixty," if he believed the United Hatters would compensate him for his losses. "He fairly shouted at me," Stowe reported. " 'Of course we'll be taken care of by the union. Guess you never belonged to a union, or you wouldn't ask such a question? Don't you know that's the whole idea—the whole philosophy of . . . unionism?' "[57]

Stowe's conversations with other defendants, however, revealed a rank and file alienated from its leadership. A "big, lethargic-looking German" told Stowe in imperfect English that he joined the union "to keep my job same as the others." At first he attended meetings of the union, but, he recalled, "I couldn't understand what they was talkin' about, so I finally says, 'I leave it to them as can talk and I won't go no more.' So when this trouble started I hadn't been near no meetin' for years, and I didn't know nothin' about the union." The hatter ignored the attachment of his home, because, as he figured it, "There ain't no law as can hold me responsible for things what I ain't never heard about." When Stowe explained that the law presumed that the individual defendants were principals who controlled the union leadership, the hatter interrupted: "Well, then, if they presume that they presume just the opposite from what is the truth. Yes, we pay them, but we don't control them—they controls us!"

Another defendant had also stopped attending union meetings long before the start of the boycott. "I found that I could talk myself black in the face without anybody's paying attention. I found I had no real voice in their matters and that it was just a waste of time and breath." This hatter believed that the union was run by a "ring," and he had harsh words for then-president John Scully, whose "backing an' fillin' an' quibblin' " over settling the case was "very unmanly." "Why don't he take his medicine an' acknowledge we're beaten and try to come to terms so we can get out of it the best we can?" the hatter asked. Scully should have met regularly with the defendants; instead, the hatter complained, "he paid no more attention to us than if we was children." "We were never consulted about the boycott or about the trial, or about anything," he fumed.[58]

In the end, of course, the union saved the defendants' homes and helped pay for repairs that, following the advice of the union's lawyers, the defendants had put off during the litigation. Many hatters and their dependents suffered nonetheless. A hatter who had vowed to ignore the attachment of his house finally asked to discuss the matter with local officials. He apologetically explained, "The old woman was worried about losin' her home an' wanted I should come round an' inquire." The attachments kept a second defendant, it was said, from raising the money needed to treat a tubercular daughter, who subsequently died. The wife of a third defendant wrote the union that when her husband died after a year's illness, "our savings vanished. . . . My only support was gone." She tried to lease the house, but the threat of foreclosure deterred renters. "I finally was obliged to offer it for less than half the rent as an inducement rather than close up the place."[59]

Perhaps the saddest tale involved Nathan Hoy, the man who immediately preceded William Humphries on the witness stand in the fall of 1912. Hoy was sixty-six years old when he testified. He had never worked for Loewe, he explained, although he had known the employer "just to speak" for twenty-five years. Like Humphries, Hoy had long since stopped going to union meetings when the strike broke out. He denied that he was an active member of the United Hatters: "I never considered myself really a member of anything that I couldn't have my say in when there was a meeting going on." When Walter

Gordon Merritt asked why Hoy had taken no steps to defend himself after Loewe filed suit, the hatter replied that he had left the matter "entirely to those that caused the trouble. I hadn't caused trouble."

Merritt then turned to the task of establishing that Hoy had personal knowledge of the boycott. He first asked Hoy if he recalled receiving the circular Loewe sent out threatening suit. Hoy could not, nor (he testified) could "the lady of the house." Merritt then inquired whether Hoy had seen Loewe's notice in the Danbury *News*. Once again, the old hatter was uncertain. "There is somebody that is connected with me that likes to get the paper first," he explained, "and if I get the paper first, it is stale news to her. Consequently, I sit down and smoke while she reads it to me."[60]

Five years later, the "somebody connected" with Hoy wrote the United Hatters for assistance in making repairs to her home. "Mr. Hoy having full confidence in your promises took your advice and let the property run down and I am left with it on my hands in a deplorable condition," Mrs. Hoy explained. Yet the state of her house was the least of her troubles. Far greater was her loss of "the best of husbands through this attachment. The Dr says the worry and injustice was the first cause of the disease that resulted in his death."[61]

The plaintive voices of Danbury's workers and widows were all but drowned out by the shrill speechifying and lawyering of the AABA, the AFL, and the United Hatters. A good reporter like Stowe—Harriet Beecher Stowe's grandson—heard them and saw the tragic consequences of the case for the "innocent, industrious, frugal, and elderly workmen" of Danbury. But the culprit eluded him. "Who is to blame?" Stowe asked. "What is to blame?"[62]

THE CULTURAL CRISIS OF PROPRIETARY CAPITALISM

Stowe was not alone in his confusion. As the *Danbury Hatters'* case wound its way through the courts, many other middle-class Americans experienced the same difficulty. Loewe's career exemplified basic tenets of Victorian culture—belief in the moral value of economic competition, in the blessed absence of permanent social classes in America. As an editorialist declared, Loewe "was not a Trust; he was not a grinder of the faces of the poor. . . . He operated his factory with due fellow-feeling for those toward whom he had come in time in the position of employer instead of co-laborer."[63] But if Loewe was not the villain of the *Danbury Hatters'* case, who was? The aged, honest workingmen of Danbury?

Such questions led the thoughtful progressive to doubt the continued value of individualistic economic morality in deciphering the industrial strife of the day. The solution Stowe and his influential editor, Lyman Abbott, settled on was the incorporation of trade unions, a remedy that would bring to labor the order that the new corporations and trade associations had brought to capital.[64] They had grasped a point obscured by the rhetoricians of individual liberty whether among employers or in the judiciary, or for that matter in the labor movement. Regardless of their formal legal status, unions had in fact become corporate bodies. Neither the free labor creed, nor the law of agency served as a sure guide to the industrial realities of the early twentieth century.

As an independent proprietary capitalist, Dietrich Loewe resisted the forces of industrial concentration and cooperation. If the first decade of the twentieth century was an industrial watershed in the American past, then Loewe and Danbury's hatters are better understood as part of the passing order. To mistake Loewe's pyrrhic victory in any other way would simply be to append an ironic ending to a tragic case.

NOTES

I am grateful to Andrew King, Philip Scranton, and Christopher Tomlins for their comments on earlier versions of this paper.

1. *Loewe v. Lawlor*, 208 U.S. 274 (1908). See P. Taft 1957: 266–68, 295–98; Merritt 1951: 37–39.

2. Record, *Loewe v. Lawlor*, 235 U.S. 522 (1915), at 1215, 421, 1217, 1218, 1227; U.S. Census of Individuals, 1900, vol. 3, E.D. 56, sheet 2, line 2, s.v. "William Humphries."

3. Record, *Loewe*, 1220.

4. Merritt 1951: 14–15.

5. Ibid., 21; *Loewe v. Lawlor*, 209 F. 721, 728 (2d Cir. 1913).

6. *Loewe v. Lawlor*, 235 U.S. 522, 535 (1915).

7. Record, *Loewe*, 1216, 1219, 1120; Devlin 1984: 71, 73. This conversation took place during the first trial. Humphries testified about it in the second trial.

8. Kolko 1963; J. Weinstein 1963; Sklar 1988; Livingston 1986. For a succinct and thoughtful summary, see Rodgers 1982: 119–21. Gompers quoted in Tomlins 1985: 62.

9. Hofstadter, 1965: 199–200. See also Hofstadter 1955: 10–11.

10. Faulkner 1951: 170–75; C. Gordon 1990; Ulman 1966: 123–28, 489–566; Ramirez 1978; Fraser 1983: 214–18.

11. *Hat Review*, 31 (August 1903): 49.

12. May 1949: 104. See Hawley 1979: 6–11, 66–71; Ross 1979: 121.

13. Bensman 1985: 34–41.

14. Chandler 1977; Scranton 1983, 1989.

15. *Hat Review*, 27 (January 1900): 27–28; *American Hatter*, 30 (March 1901): 58; Pennsylvania Department of Factory Inspection 1902: 132; Scranton

and Licht 1986: 155–70. I am grateful to Philip Scranton for this reference.

16. Bensman 1985: 35, 39; *Statistics of Manufacturers* (Twelfth U.S. Census, 1900), 1: 537; *Hat Review,* 29 (December 1901): 18; New Jersey Bureau of Statistics 1903: 15.

17. *Hat Review,* 30 (March 1903): 42; ibid., 27 (May 1900): 38. See also ibid., 28 (July 1901): 26; ibid., 31 (October 1903): 11.

18. *American Hatter,* 32 (January 1903): 39.

19. *Hat Review,* 29 (August 1901): 65; *American Hatter,* 31 (August 1901): 50. For a price-fixing agreement among Danbury's leading stiff-hat firms, see *American Hatter,* 32 (March 1903): 18. On horizontal combination in the merger movement, see Lamoreaux 1985.

20. *American Hatter,* 30 (September 1900): 45.

21. New York Bureau of Labor Statistics 1887: 723.

22. Derber 1970.

23. Connecticut Bureau of Labor Statistics 1891: 131, 133, 134, 135, 137; Bensman 1977: 224–35.

24. Bensman 1985: 155–57, 171–78; Connecticut Bureau of Labor Statistics 1891: 139–49, 163; "Explanatory Circular Issued by the Members of the Fur Hat Manufacturers' Association of Danbury, Conn.," 20 November 1893, Box HRD-17, United Hatters of North America (UHNA) Papers; Bensman 1977: 342–59.

25. See generally, Bensman 1985: 185–89, 198–201; Robinson 1948: 78–79.

26. *American Hatter,* 30 (September 1900): 28, 45, 48; ibid., 30 (November 1900): 41; *Hat Review* 28 (September 1900): 62; UHNA Proceedings, 1900, 1903, in Record, *Loewe,* 17, 33–36.

27. That month another prominent Danbury firm, E. A. Mallory & Sons, went fair after negotiations over the fate of "a number of employees who were under the ban of the union." Danbury *Evening News,* 9 November 1900, in Record, *Loewe,* 1120.

28. Record, *Loewe,* 978–99; Robinson 1948: 81–82.

29. Bensman 1985: 202; Record, *Loewe,* 39–43, 459–60, 1095; Danbury *Evening News,* 9 April 1902, in Record, *Loewe,* 1120; South Norwalk *Evening Sentinel,* 2 June 1902, in Record, *Loewe,* 1138; personal interviews cited by Devlin 1984: 73.

30. The hatters' version of the meeting had Loewe declaring that "if he died he would never come to the trade." Record, *Loewe,* 1017–22; *Journal of the United Hatters,* 4 (September 1902): 12–14; *American Hatter,* 30 (November 1901): 1.

31. American Anti-Boycott Association 1904; American Anti-Boycott Association 1908a: 33; American Anti-Boycott Association 1908b: 5, 27; Record, *Loewe,* 1021.

32. New York *Post,* 16 September 1903, quoted in *American Hatter,* 33 (September 1903): 31.

33. Record, *Loewe,* 965–68; *National Cyclopedia of American Biography,* 15: 373, s.v. "Loewe, Dietrich Eduard"; Ives 1902–3: 641–42.

34. Record, *Loewe,* 976, 981, 1068–74, 1077. By way of contrast, for the

fiscal year ending 30 November 1899, the Stetson firm reported net profits of $384,830. In that year, Loewe's profits amounted to a mere $12,000. *Hat Review*, 27 (January 1900): 27–28. At the time of the strike, Loewe had $130,000 invested in the firm (some of it borrowed); in contrast, the Roelof firm announced an initial capitalization of $2 million when it incorporated in 1903. Record, *Loewe*, 976; *American Hatter*, 32 (January 1903): 44.

35. Record, *Loewe*, 981.

36. Dietrich E. Loewe to National Officers of the United Hatters of North America, 22 April 1901, reprinted in *American Industries*, 1 October 1903, 5–6; Record, *Loewe*, 984.

37. Record, *Loewe*, 1017, 1019.

38. Stokes to Loewe, 2 December 1902, in Record, *Loewe*, 516.

39. Stokes to Loewe, 20 January 1903, in Record, *Loewe*, 525–26.

40. Record, *Loewe*, 1068–74; United Hatters of North America, 1903: 20.

41. Loewe, *Record*, 1025; *American Hatter* (1917): 96; Merritt 1951: 8.

42. Ernst 1989b: 57–60.

43. See ibid., 142–61; Ernst 1989a.

44. See Tomlins 1985: 32–59.

45. *Danbury Evening News*, 22 April 1915, reprinted in AABA, *Danbury Hatters' Case* (n.p., n.d.), 1–2; AABA, *June Bulletin: Collecting the Danbury Hatters' Judgment*, 7 June 1915; E. E. Witte, "Danbury Hatters' Case," p. 4, Box 120, Edwin E. Witte Papers.

46. Thus, in October 1915 the union suggested that Loewe settle for one-third of the judgment, and Merritt countered with an offer of either (1) "a fair valuation of the property and bank accounts now available for the satisfaction of the judgment" or (2) the sum of the original verdict of $74,000, "all subsequent damages not covered by the verdict for which the unlawful operations of the Hatters' Union are responsible," and the expense of the litigation. Walter Gordon Merritt and Daniel Davenport to Martin J. Cunningham and William F. Tammany, 20 October 1915 (copy), Box HRD-17, UHNA Papers.

47. Gompers to John A. Moffitt, 16 July 1910, vol. 158, Gompers Letter Books; *Literary Digest*, 16 January 1915 (vol. 50 no. 86); *New York Times*, 21 January 1916.

48. The 1910 assessment raised $98,756; the first Hatters' Day and a second, held on 15 June 1916, raised another $164,509. A final reckoning placed the total cost of the suit to organized labor at $421,477. Robinson 1948: 92–94.

49. This raised another $50,382. Robinson 1948: 93; Stowe 1915: 613.

50. Merritt 1951: 24; *Carpenter*, 37 (November 1917):19.

51. *New York World*, 24 April 1915, reprinted in AABA, *Danbury Hatters' Case*, 3; House Committee on Appropriations, *Danbury Hatters' Judgment*, 63d Cong., 3d sess., 1913, 16.

52. Merritt 1910: 276, 275; Megaarden 1915: 423. Megaarden was an associate of Alton B. Parker, the Democratic presidential candidate in 1904 and Gompers's lawyer in the *Buck's Stove* case. Alton B. Parker to Rosa L. Guard, 7 May 1913, *The American Federation of Labor Records: The Gompers Era*, reel 65.

53. *Boston Globe*, 5 December 1902 (copy), in *AFL Records*, reel 126. See Tomlins 1985: 86–87.

54. *United Mine Workers v. Coronado Coal Co.*, 259 U.S. 344, 388–90 (1922). See Witte 1932: 141–44; Kutler 1961.

55. *A.F. of L. Weekly News Letter*, 10 June 1922, quoted in Witte 1932: 137 n.1.

56. *Milwaukee Sentinel*, 11 December 1927; *New York Herald Tribune*, 13 September 1935; *Hat Life* (January 1936), Box HRD-17, UHNA Papers; Robinson 1948: 94.

57. Stowe 1915: 612.

58. Ibid., 613–14.

59. Ibid., 612; Catherine Hunt to Martin Lawlor, 3 September 1917, Box HRD-19, UHNA Papers.

60. Record, *Loewe*, at 1230–40.

61. Mrs. Nathan C. Hoy to Officers of the United Hatters of North America, 11 July 1917, UHNA Papers.

62. Stowe 1915: 615.

63. New York *Post*, 16 September 1903, in *American Hatter*, September 1903 (vol. 33 no. 31).

64. *Outlook*, 94 (19 February 1910): 370–71. See generally Sklar 1988; Lamoreaux 1985.

8 Law and the Shaping of Labor Politics in the United States and England

William Forbath

In addition to being the nation's portliest president, William Howard Taft was a high court judge. A state, then a federal, judge, and ultimately tenth chief justice of the U.S. Supreme Court, Taft was the leading architect of American judicial activism in labor strife.[1] In the spring of 1894, as the United States circuit judge for the Sixth Circuit, Taft presided over some of the crucial proceedings in the judicial repression of the great Pullman Boycott.[2] He interrupted his court business to deliver the commencement address at the University of Michigan Law School. His subject was "The Right of Private Property," and he warned that that right was "at stake" in "the social conflict now at hand."[3]

By the conflict at hand Judge Taft did not mean merely the Pullman Boycott. He pointed to a broader attack on property, and especially on "corporate capital," in the nation's politics as well as in its industries. The chief aggressors, according to the judge, were "labor organizations . . . blinded by the new sense of social and political power which combination and organization have given them." Congressmen, state legislators, and local "peace officers" all encouraged "the workingman to think that property has few rights which, in his organized union, he is bound to respect." With the connivance of such pandering politicians, labor organizations under leaders like Debs were pressing the nation toward socialism.[4]

The present seemed bleak, but Judge Taft remained optimistic about the future. The current drift toward "state socialism" would be reversed. The main "burden of this conflict" was bound to "fall upon the courts," he declared, and the courts would prevail. He contrasted America's situation with England's. There "the assaults of socialism on the existing order" would surely prove more enduring than here. England had bequeathed to her colonies the common law, with its high regard for "security of property and contract." But England lacked our Constitution. In England "parliament has always been omnipotent." In the United States, courts had been able to insulate the rights of contract and property "much further . . . from the gusty and unthinking passions of temporary majorities." In the United States these rights were "buttressed" by a "written Constitution" against "anarchy, socialism and communism." The American judiciary, in other words, had constitutionalized many of the basic common law rules of the industrial game and, by doing so, removed them from the political arena. In time, Judge Taft assured his audience, the American labor movement would come to its senses. "Longer experience" with our "complicated [constitutional] form of government" and with staunch judges like himself would enlighten the unions as to the futility of radical politics.[5]

To our ears the judge's confidence sounds misplaced. Did it not require a nineteenth-century habit of mind to believe that constitutions molded a working class's political outlook? To be sure, what Taft regarded as "socialism"—what we would call social democracy—became the creed of the twentieth-century labor movement in England and not in America. But could that have had much to do with "our written Constitution"? Don't Judge Taft's ideas simply betray his lack of a modern sociological imagination?

I think not, and in this essay I suggest that Judge Taft was largely right. We—particularly those of us who till the fields of legal and social history—now tend to look to deep sociological factors for our theories of causation. But in our readiness to appreciate how social groups and classes mold the law, we tend to overlook how the legal order molds those very groups as they clash and compromise over it. By comparing American and English labor's experiences with their countries' legal orders during the decades around the turn of the century, I aim to show how America's constitutional scheme and the unique powers of courts within that scheme shaped the distinctive character of the nation's labor movement.[6] More broadly, this comparative discussion will suggest how profoundly courts and judge-made law have molded our political culture and identities.

Comparative history is said to work best when it begins with similar contexts and concurrent events in the histories of two societies and proceeds from such sameness to the exploration of revealing differences.[7] A comparative approach seems promising here because of the profound similarities in the contexts—both institutional and cultural—of labor activity in the two countries. First, the two legal systems had much in common. The courts of both countries worked in the same common law tradition. Indeed, the judiciaries of both nations launched an almost simultaneous wave of attacks on strikes and boycotts in the 1880s and 1890s, and they elaborated a common body of rules and precepts to restrain workers' collective action.

Second, the two nations' labor movements also had structures and traditions in common. For example, the two most important labor leaders in turn-of-the-century America, Samuel Gompers and John Mitchell, were English immigrants, as were hundreds of lesser-known union leaders. They brought with them ideas and models from English trade unions. In England, conversely, the pioneers of industrial unionism and "independent labor politics" drew inspiration from their American counterparts.

Third, when confronted with mounting judicial attacks, the labor movements on both sides of the Atlantic responded alike. Each sought legislation that would repeal hostile judge-made law and legalize peaceful industrial protest. They strove for a regime of strict laissez-faire regarding workers' concerted activities. In both countries, moreover, labor met with legislative success. Here, however, the fruits of comparison begin to appear. In England, where, as Judge Taft reminded us, there was no institution of judicial review, the courts grudgingly acquiesced in their own demotion. Parliament had the final word, and labor's political victories were preserved. In the United States, by contrast, the courts swept aside one court-curbing statute after another.

The importance of this relatively subtle constitutional difference, and of the different results it generated in this case, emerges in the subsequent divergences in political strategy and vision on the part of the two movements. During this period—the late nineteenth and early twentieth century—each movement was embroiled in a battle over the political soul of trade unionism. On one side were those who championed "independent labor politics" and wished to pursue broad, class-based social and industrial reforms; on the other were those who held that labor should steer clear of politics as much as possible, other than to reform the ground rules of private ordering. In England those who championed broad reformism prevailed; in the United States they lost. The comparison I am drawing suggests that the two movements' different experiences with courts and legislatures did much to shape these divergent outcomes.

THE INSUFFICIENCY OF THE "DEEPER" FACTORS

The traditional account of American "exceptionalism" is familiar. Both in its general form and in specific comparisons of English and American experience, the account has been roughly this.[8] The unique social context of the United States produced a working class that lacked "class consciousness" and, instead, was individualistic. From the dawn of industrialization, American workers have been wedded to individualistic strategies for bettering their lot and have largely resisted efforts to improve their condition as members of a class. Even American trade unionists have always been "pragmatists," not "class conscious" but "job conscious."[9] Accordingly, socialist and class-based reform politics have been the province of intellectuals and agitators on the margins of political life.

The picture of the American working class on which this traditional account rests was first drawn in scholarly fashion in the 1910s and 1920s by the founders of American labor history, John Commons and the "Wisconsin School," and particularly Commons's brilliant student Selig Perlman. Commons, Perlman, and scores of other scholars after them sought to explain the phenomenon widely known as American "exceptionalism"—American workers' apparent deviance from other countries' working-class history, their supposed lack of class consciousness. Some emphasized the privileged economic condition of American workers in the nineteenth and twentieth centuries, their affluence and mobility. Others singled out the unique ethnic and religious divisions within the American working class. Generally, accounts of American "exceptionalism" have underscored both these factors and also pointed to the unusual pervasiveness of liberalism and individualism in American life, to America's tenacious two-party system and to its distinctively "weak" and fragmented liberal state.

As a result of the work of the "new labor historians," however, the received accounts will no longer do. Launched in the 1960s and by now a venerable tradition itself, the new labor history's detailed reexamination of nineteenth-century working-class life and politics has undermined the classic picture of the American working class as distinctively conservative, cautious, and individualistic. The new labor historians have rediscovered that the history of the workplace in industrializing America is one of recurring militancy and of class-based, as well as shop- and craft-based, collective action. Measured by the scale, frequency, and duration of strikes, workers' disposition toward collective action was greater in the United States than in most European nations, and considerably greater than in England, during the late nineteenth and early twentieth centuries.[10]

The new labor history also shows that the mutualism that American workers displayed at work frequently carried over into their communities and their political and cultural lives. As Sean Wilentz and others have argued, the political ideas, cultural values, and forms of associational life that characterized the nineteenth-century workers' movements in the United States, in England, and on the Continent, were far more similar than the traditional story allows.[11] Broad and radical reform politics characterized the mainstream views of the Gilded Age labor movement.[12] The more cautious "pure and simple" union philosophy of Samuel Gompers was also active, but as a minority perspective in this era of American labor history. Most Gilded Age observers agreed that American unions were *more*, not less, wedded to political radicalism than their English counterparts.[13]

Thus the key question that the work of the new labor historians poses, but has yet to answer, is this: If late nineteenth-century American workers and trade unionists were so radical, then why, by the early twentieth century, did most of them end up supporting unions and political parties that were more conservative than those embraced by their counterparts abroad? If the American labor movement was not born with a comparatively narrow, interest-group outlook or an inveterate bias against broad, positive uses of law and state power, then how did that outlook and bias become dominant in the labor movement by the early 1900s?

Of course, the old sociological explanations still beckon as potential answers to this newer question. But, again, the work of the new labor historians suggests that many of these social factors can no longer bear any great explanatory weight. For example, the view that American workers enjoyed unparalleled opportunities to rise into the middle class figures prominently in most traditional explanations for American "exceptionalism." One can imagine the same view incorporated into an account of the demise of class-based reform politics. However, the mobility story's empirical foundations have proven shaky. Sophisticated recent quantitative histories of the American working class have shown that the bulk of America's working class was no more mobile (into the middle class) than England's. Nor did any significant portion of the nineteenth-century industrial working class actually ever "go West" from urban shops and factories into farming, as traditional accounts have assumed. Even mobility *within* the American working class (from unskilled to skilled work) was far more varied and uneven than was thought.[14] Moreover, it now seems clear that the typical forms of social mobility for nineteenth-century American workers, and, more important, their typical *aspirations* for it, were not incompatible with seeking material gains for themselves *as workers*—

rather than as the individualistic incipient entrepreneurs that the mobility story always describes.[15] Thus the mobility story probably must relinquish its place as a key factor accounting for the peculiarities of American labor politics.

Ethnic division is the other principal factor in traditional accounts. In any revised account, ethnic and racial cleavages will surely remain central. However, as Wilentz observes in surveying the field, "the familiar arguments that American exceptionalism arose from some unique divisions within the American working class are no longer as compelling as they once were." Indeed, the new labor history demonstrates that in many contexts "ethnicity could be more of a reinforcement to class solidarity than a distraction from class antagonisms."[16]

Thus, most of the key reasons for the divergence between the political paths of the American and English labor movements must be located elsewhere, not in the character of the working-class or labor movement so much as in the character of the state and polity; less, that is, in labor and more in the arenas in which labor made and remade its visions and strategies. Perhaps, then, we should return to Judge Taft's quaint emphasis on courts and constitutions.[17]

THE TWO FORMS OF GOVERNMENT

The powers it conferred on the courts were a critical—perhaps *the* critical—politics-shaping aspect of the American Constitution. The courts, however, did not operate in a vacuum. As Taft insisted, the American Constitution's safeguards against "socialism" consisted not only in the unique role of the courts but in the entire "complicated form of government."[18] Thus we cannot fully assess Taft's prophecy about the role of the American Constitution in twentieth-century working-class history without considering England's and America's entire forms of government. In addition to the powers of the judiciary, three aspects of the nineteenth-century American state and polity seem central: federalism, the nature and role of political parties, and the absence of an administrative state elite. Along each of these three dimensions the English state and polity differed sharply, with important implications for the interplay of state and class formation. For now I will simply sketch these three other significant differences. I will then turn to comparing labor's experiences with the courts in the two countries. There we will see these other differences in play, complementing and reinforcing the difference between judicial and parliamentary supremacy.

The framers hoped that the far-flung and federal nature of their new republic would help avoid the formation of a class-based political "faction" of have-nots in the national arena.[19] Their hope was realized. By the 1830s the United States had become the world's first nation with a mass franchise: by that decade, virtually all white adult males enjoyed the vote. Thus throughout the era of industrialization propertyless male industrial workers were voters. Yet, as Ira Katznelson has recently reminded us, the "diffuse federal organizational structure of the United States took much of the charge out of the issue of franchise extension, for there was no unitary state to defend or transform."[20] American labor reformers had to contend with multiple and competing tiers of policy-making authority. This structural exigency raised the costs and reduced the efficacy of labor reforms.[21] So doing, it strengthened the case for voluntarism.

The English state, by contrast, was unitary. During the nineteenth century, as England became an industrial nation, the making of public policies toward industrial workers happened increasingly at the center of government, as did the administration of those policies.[22] The structure of government enabled the country's dispersed and localized unions and labor reform associations to meld their political claims.

Just as the United States was the first nation with a mass franchise, so the nineteenth-century American political party was the world's first mass-based party. Yet, the ties it forged with worker-constituents were often intensely local and particularistic. As working people were incorporated into the polity, their party loyalties generally hinged on local patronage and neighborhood, ethnic, or religious bonds—not on the broader bonds of class.[23] Indeed, during the decades when this institutional matrix emerged and was consolidated, the industrial working class had barely been born. While not immutable, these non-class-based, particularistic, and patronage ties to the two old parties had staying power.[24]

In 1894 the head of the Tailors' Union, John Lennon, argued this way against the prospects of independent labor politics: "We have in this country conditions that do not exist in Great Britain. We have the 'spoils' system which is something almost unknown in Great Britain and on account of it we cannot afford to try at this time to start a political party as an adjunct with their unions."[25]

"Spoils" or local patronage was not a currency available to England's political parties by the time that country's male workers were fully enfranchised. In the mid-1870s England undertook major civil service reforms. Therefore, the English parties could not adopt local patronage as a means of drawing in the new mass of working-class voters.[26] Accordingly, England's Liberal and Conservative parties relied upon class-based programmatic appeals in competing for workers' votes in a way that the Democrats and Republicans in the United States did not.[27] Like the unitary structure of the English state, this leaning toward programmatic reforms strengthened the hand of the English trade unionists who championed broad reformism.

Late nineteenth-century England's professional civil service did more than cut off the possibility of patronage-based "machine" politics as a way of mobilizing working-class voters. It also supplied the socialists and progressives in the English labor movement with valuable allies in the corridors of state power. The upper tiers of the professional civil service constituted a powerful *nonjudicial* state elite—a substantial group of high-placed policy makers with institutional autonomy, permanence of office, and interests as well as a tradition of their own. This alternative, and often reform-minded, state elite vied with the courts for primacy in governing industrial affairs and provided significant support for the English trade unionists who championed a more statist politics. Indeed, as we shall see, many reform-minded members of this administrative elite worked hard to *persuade* often reluctant English unions to champion their reform proposals; in this respect they did not merely lend credibility to, but actually helped create, a more statist outlook among English trade unionists.[28]

In contrast, institutional space did not exist in the nineteenth- or early twentieth-century American state for an organizationally autonomous administrative state elite. There was, of course, no lack of reform-minded, university-educated professionals in the United States who were ready and eager to do the same policy-making and state-building work undertaken by their English counterparts.[29] In a handful of states—and across a narrower range of industrial issues—they managed to do so. But administrative posts with power and influence comparable to England's high officialdom did not exist in the United States. The state and federal constitutions had been designed to frustrate those who would centralize and expand executive policy-making authority and administrative capacities, encouraging instead the emergence of what political scientist Steven Skowronek has called a "state of courts and parties."[30]

Late nineteenth- and early twentieth-century America saw an unholy but highly successful alliance between the judicial elite and party bosses against civil service reformers and would-be welfare state builders. The party pols saw the reformers' efforts to create a professionalized civil service and a centralized welfare state as threats to the localized, patronage forms of government on which their power rested. To the courts the reformers' vision of the modern administrative agency undermined the separation of powers as well as judicial prerogatives. They concluded that it lay outside the constitutional pale.[31]

The victories of this alliance in upholding the old scheme of government deprived the era's labor movement of the kinds of powerful state-based allies enjoyed by their English comrades. The lack of such allies, in turn, made broad reform politics less availing in the United States.

The reformers' defeats also deprived the labor movement of a corps of factory and mine inspectors and labor law administrators comparable to England's. Already in the 1860s England's factory inspectors had earned the admiration of no less a critic than Karl Marx.[32] By the 1890s, England had roughly 140 full-time factory and mine inspectors covering roughly 190,000 workplaces.[33] In sharp contrast to the United States, their jobs were insulated from changes in political administration; their occupation had become a reformist profession, with its own schools and traditions.[34]

At the turn of the century most labor laws in most American states remained in what a classic study calls "the pre-enforcement stage"; they either were hortatory and had no penalty provisions or, at best, required enforcement by private civil actions rather than by state officials. More advanced states relied on the affected employee or his union to try to prevail on the ordinary state attorneys to prosecute their complaints.[35] Seventeen states were in the "enforcement stage" at the turn of the century; they had factory and mine inspectors. Throughout the nation, all of 114 inspectors covered some 513,000 workplaces; many of them were merely policemen on special assignment, and many others were less than full-time inspectors.[36]

Small wonder, then, that in turn-of-the-century America, English immigrant miners and factory workers could be heard bemoaning the paucity and powerlessness of American mine and factory inspectors.[37] Even in the most progressive states, factory and mine inspectors often were scarce in comparison to England and lacked many of their English colleagues' enforcement and rule-making powers; "the courts remained the fundamental agency for securing compliance."[38] Accordingly, courts held greater sway over the interpretation, administration, and enforcement of labor laws, and they tended to nullify by hostile construction many of the reforms that they didn't strike down.[39] This too helped make the "progressive" vision of state-based industrial reform seem unavailing to many American trade unionists.

These, then, were the contrasting state structures and traditions within which judicial supremacy operated upon labor's political choices in America and parliamentary supremacy swayed labor's politics in England. I turn now to those developments.[40]

THE AMERICAN STORY

The mainstream of the American labor movement in the late nineteenth century hewed to the idea that workers could use the ballot to transform the face of industry. Largest of Gilded Age (1880s–90s) labor organizations was the Knights of Labor; the Knights strove to meld trade union and political endeavors, appealing to the "laboring classes" as both producers and citizens. The organization reached out from a base among coal miners and artisans to a constituency that embraced the burgeoning mass of unskilled factory workers. In addition to waging strikes and boycotts, the Knights created labor parties and ran and elected candidates to local and state government. Unifying all these activities was the project of preparing the "toiling classes" for self-rule. Workers read traditional republican principles to mean that in an industrial society the very survival of republican government demanded using governmental power to quell the "tyranny" of corporations and capital. Toppling "corporate tyranny" entailed a host of legislative reforms: hours laws and other workplace regulations, the abolition of private banking, public funding for worker-owned industry, and the nationalization of monopolies.[41]

During the Gilded Age the American Federation of Labor also emerged. Many of its founders were trade union leaders like Samuel Gompers, who shunned the ranging reform ambitions of the Knights; they also diverged from the Knights by insisting that unions were best built on a craft basis rather than by embracing all who toiled in a given industry. Gompers was the preeminent spokesman for this somewhat narrower trade union philosophy. During this era, however, the outlook associated with Gompers was far less distinct from the competing vision embodied in the Knights than it later became. Indeed, a great many AFL unions and union activists in this period shared the Knights' vision of inclusive unionism, their broad reform ambitions, and their faith in lawmaking and the ballot.[42]

By the turn of the century, however, Gompers's outlook had become the predominant one. The Knights of Labor were defunct, and the AFL was the nation's leading labor organization. Government bludgeoning of one major strike after another had left the AFL leadership wary of inclusive unionism and broad-based sympathetic actions. Soon the AFL would also begin to assail many varieties of labor laws and social and industrial "reform by legislation," and the republican rights talk of the Gilded Age movement would give way to a liberal, laissez-faire language of protest and reform.

This new antistatist labor outlook did not preclude involvement in national as well as state politics; to the contrary, the early twentieth-century AFL became increasingly involved in electioneering and lobbying. But its initiatives focused on *voluntarist* goals—above all, to halt hostile judicial interventions in labor disputes.[43] Increasingly, the organization's dominant unions set their faces against the broader, class-based reform politics and inclusive unionism that had marked the earlier era.

What part did the courts play in these developments? In spite of the obstacles that we have canvassed—the federated form of American government, the patronage and particularistic cast of political parties, and the absence of a strong administrative state apparatus and elite— the Gilded Age labor movement's successes in electing local and state candidates and passing labor reforms meant that in some late nineteenth-century industrial states, the laws regulating hours and workplace conditions and enlarging workers' freedom of collective action compared favorably with England's.[44] These successes seemed to vindicate the view that politics and legislation were powerful engines of industrial reform.

Once legislative reforms were passed, however, it was the courts that determined how they would fare; and during the 1880s and 1890s the state and federal courts were more likely than not to strike down the very laws that labor sought most avidly. By the turn of the century, judges had voided roughly sixty labor laws.[45] These constitutional cases figured prominently in the battles that raged through the 1890s between the champions of broad and minimalist labor politics. One such debate occurred at the 1894 AFL Convention,[46] concerning whether the AFL would embrace "independent labor politics" and adopt a "political programme," which had been proposed by some of the federation's socialist unions.[47] The program included the goal of a legal eight-hour workday. Speaking to that point, Adolph Strasser of the Cigarmakers declared: "There is one fact that can't be overlooked. You can't pass an eight hour day without changing the Constitution of the United States and the Constitution of every state in the Union. . . . I am opposed to wasting our time declaring for legislation being enacted for a time after we are all dead."[48]

Henry Lloyd, a widely known journalist, a key figure in the Labor-Populist alliance, and a champion of broad labor reform responded by describing the depth of support for a legal eight-hour day at a recent labor conference that he had attended in England. Unimpressed, Strasser retorted, "Is it not a fact that in England there is no constitutional provision [to stymie an eight-hour law]?" Then Strasser pointed proudly to the craft unions like his own Cigarmakers, who had gained the eight-hour day "by themselves . . . pass[ing] and enforc[ing] [their own] law without the government."[49]

Invalidated labor laws were both powerful evidence and a potent symbol of the recalcitrance of the American state. The courts seemed so formidable partly because judicial review of labor laws was bound up with a broader judicial power. We have noted the extent to which courts controlled the interpretation, administration, and enforcement of reform legislation. Not only could judges strike down labor laws; they could also nullify them by hostile construction. And nullify they did. Typically, they treated labor legislation as ill-considered tinkering with a governmental domain that belonged by right to the judiciary and the common law.[50]

Judicial review of reform legislation arose at a key moment of collective decision making in labor's political history. During this moment the courts helped turn minimalist politics from a minority outlook of cautious craft unionists like Strasser and Gompers into what seemed the surest path to most of the labor movement, a movement that would come increasingly to be dominated by craft unionists like themselves.

The thrust of a Gompers's or Strasser's voluntarist outlook was this: Labor should improve its lot through organization and collective bargaining. The less it relied on the state and the more it attained in the private realm of market relations, the better.

But the courts did not simply leave alone this private realm of market relations. First, of course, it was the common law that defined the metes and bounds of workers' marketplace conduct. In the early nineteenth century, the legal bounds on workers' "combinations" and strikes were more generous in the United States than elsewhere.[51] Nonetheless, the antebellum American courts set sharp limits on what counted as a legally tolerable strike or as allowable strike activities, limits that changed remarkably little over the course of the nineteenth century. Moreover, the application of these legal restraints grew dramatically harsher and more pervasive. Beginning in the 1880s, the courts vastly enlarged their role in regulating and policing industrial conflict. Also at this time, the characteristic form of legal intervention changed, and the labor injunction was born. By a conservative reckoning, at least forty-three hundred injunctions were issued between 1880 and 1930. This figure represents only a small fraction of the total number of strikes in those decades but a sizable proportion of the larger strikes and a significant percentage of sympathetic and secondary actions. During the 1890s, for example, courts enjoined at least 15 percent of recorded sympathy strikes. That percentage rose to 25 percent in the next decade, and by the 1920s 46 percent of all sympathy strikes were greeted by antistrike decrees. As injunctions multiplied, the language of judge-made law became pervasive in industrial strife. Antiunion employers and state officials constantly spoke a court-minted language of rights and wrongs. Again and again trade unionists attributed the repression of strikes and protest to judge-made law—even when no injunction was in sight.[52]

As the legal repression of labor protest and collective action intensified, the mainstream of the labor movement relinquished positive regulation or reconstruction of industry as its central political project. The prime object of labor's political energies became simply escaping the burdens of semi-outlawry. Thus the AFL strove to legalize all the peaceful forms of collective action that stood under judicial ban. It contested judge-made law everywhere: in the courts, of course, but equally in the legislatures and in the public sphere. In the course of this decades-long campaign, trade unionists began to speak and think more and more in the language of the law, abandoning a republican vocabulary of protest and reform for a liberal, law-inspired language of rights.[53] They no longer proposed to use legislation to quell the "tyranny" of capital. "Labor," they would declare, "asks no favors from the State. It wants to be let alone and to be allowed to exercise its rights."[54]

The protracted nature of this struggle to end legal repression returns us to the significance of the courts' power to hobble labor legislation. From the 1890s through the 1920s, labor prevailed on legislatures to pass many statutes loosening the judge-made restraints on collective action; in all, the states and Congress passed roughly forty court-curbing reforms during these decades—reversing substantive labor law doctrines, instituting procedural changes, and narrowing and, in some instances, flatly repealing equity jurisdiction over labor.[55] At least twenty-five of these statutes were voided on constitutional grounds, and most of those not struck down were vitiated by narrow construction.[56] Until the national emergency of the Great Depression and the constitutional revolution waged by FDR and the New Dealers,[57] courts had both the power and the will to trump these measures. So, during these four formative decades, as the number of antistrike decrees multiplied and the burdens of outlawry persisted, the AFL's political energies were riveted on gaining this indispensable—but negative, laissez-faireist—reform, and the AFL's voluntarist perspective hardened.[58]

To be sure, the debate between minimalists and radicals continued. The anticapitalist republicanism of the Gilded Age labor movement was carried into the twentieth century by the Socialist party and others, and socialist and "progressive" labor leaders were prominent in many important AFL unions throughout the period. Moreover, the relative autonomy of the state federations of labor meant that broad reform politics remained dominant in some industrial states. Nevertheless, from 1900 onward most American trade unionists agreed with Gompers that it was folly to try to remake industry by legislation; legislation was a distressingly unreliable engine of reform, and the only things that labor ought to seek from government was what it could not gain otherwise: above all, repeal of the judge-made restraints on collective action. Even those with a broader reform vision than Gompers's had to concede that this goal was labor's political sine qua non, and for the AFL leadership, it became the defining theme of an increasingly rigid, antistatist politics. Thus the recalcitrance of the American state of courts and parties got labor stuck in this stage of "negative" reform and minimalist politics—a stage that, as we shall now see, the English labor movement in this same era left behind.[59]

THE ENGLISH STORY

The Common Law and the Common Beginning

American and English courts worked within the same common law tradition. They restricted workers' collective action through an almost identical body of rules and precepts. All the key common law doctrines of American labor law hailed from or developed simultaneously in England.[60] But despite this profound similarity in legal systems, English courts played a different role in regulating workers' collective action during the nineteenth and early twentieth centuries. The English judiciary shared policy-making initiative and power with Parliament, and Parliament was the more powerful actor. There were, to be sure, persistent tensions, and as we will see, English courts were no less ill disposed than American ones toward legislative measures that loosened the legal reins on workers. But Parliament held the trumps.

In the first decades of the nineteenth century English labor law was more hostile to unionism than American. It was also more statutory. In contrast to the United States, modern trade unionism and both craft and industrial workers' collective action emerged in England under a legal regime forged chiefly by the legislature. Inspired by events in France and their domestic reverberations, the Combination Acts of 1799 and 1800 criminalized unions along with many other associational activities of the lower classes. Other statutes also prohibited combinations in specific trades. In addition, unions were (under broadly defined circumstances) criminal conspiracies "in restraint of trade."[61]

With the easing of upper-class anxieties, Parliament repealed the

Combination Acts in 1824 and thereby ended the English state's efforts flatly to bar combinations among artisans and laborers.[62] For the next half-century English trade unions existed in an often precarious position of semilegality, prone to the vagaries of judicial interpretation of the law of criminal conspiracy. Statutory reforms had increased employers' reliance on conspiracy law.[63] As unionism extended beyond traditional crafts, strikes became an increasingly common aspect of labor organization. The courts greeted these developments by enlarging the bans of conspiracy doctrine to cover more and more kinds of strikes and strike activities.[64]

Ousting the Criminal Law

In the late 1860s, this burgeoning law of labor conspiracies inspired the newly formed Trades Union Congress to turn to politics. Founded in 1868 by the national leaders of such major unions as the engineers, the carpenters, and the bricklayers, the Trades Union Congress (TUC) became England's enduring labor federation.[65] At the time, however, most English trade unionists were wary of centralization. Other efforts at forming national union federations had failed.[66] If they wanted to overcome the workers' ingrained particularism and jealous independence, the ambitious leaders who founded the TUC had to demonstrate the new federation's worth. They did so by successfully lobbying against repressive judge-made and statutory labor law.[67] Led by the new Parliamentary Committee of the Trades Union Congress, the unions in 1871 secured from Parliament the Trade Union and Criminal Law Amendment Acts. Then in 1875 Disraeli's government, prompted by competition for the votes of the newly enfranchised upper layers of the working class, met the unions' demands for greater protection from the courts with the Conspiracy and Protection of Property Act. The 1875 act contained what English labor lawyers ever since have called the "golden formula": acts by two or more persons, done in the context of a "trade dispute," were not liable to prosecution unless the acts were crimes if done by individuals.[68] The 1875 act created a broad immunity indeed; it "marked the end of the significance of criminal law in labour relations" in England.[69]

Broad as these immunities were, the "golden formula," along with the 1871 acts' immunity for labor from restraint of trade prosecutions and legalization of picketing, was virtually identical to provisions of several statutes passed by American state legislatures in the 1880s and 1890s.[70] Courts struck down or sharply vitiated all of these late nineteenth-century American statutes, and the era saw the harshest (and most frequent) labor conspiracy convictions in the nation's history.[71] In contrast, in England criminal prosecutions against labor virtually ceased after the 1875 act.[72] This is what was remarkable from an American perspective: not the legislature's liberality—American legislatures had matched that—but the judiciary's acquiescence in the sharp revision of judge-made law.

Parliament's decision and its judicial aftermath taught English labor that Parliament could rule the courts in the setting of state policy.[73] The 1875 act and its aftermath of judicial restraint would also figure as crucial precedent in the next chapter of Parliament versus the courts, involving civil injunctions and damage suits.

The "Collectivist" Alternative

The legislation of 1875 brought in its wake a full-blown alliance between the TUC leadership and the Liberals. Labor "formed," in Engels's acid phrase, "the tail of the 'Great Liberal Party.' "[74] By 1886 the TUC boasted ten "Lib-Lab" members of Parliament. Their views on the uses of law and state power were laissez-faire and anti-interventionist, more adamantly so than those of many middle-class MPs in the Liberal party.[75] Born of the self-help ethos of strong craft unions and of the English working class's long exclusion from politics and its mistrust of government paternalism,[76] it was an outlook that closely resembled that of Gompers and his AFL craft union allies across the Atlantic.

In the United States, as we have noted, this laissez-faire creed remained something of a minority viewpoint in the 1880s. In contrast to their English brothers, American workingmen had long enjoyed the ballot, and, as David Montgomery has shown, the Radical Republicans of the Reconstruction era had imparted to most American trade union leaders a strong belief in "reform by legislation." The Radicals, their ideology, and their Reconstruction programs had taught labor's advocates the potentialities of an active democratic state for transforming oppressive social and labor relations.[77]

Thus at the beginning of our period, the more radical and more statist alternative enjoyed stronger support in the United States. But it found adherents in England too. In both countries, it was the trade unionists who led the less skilled who tended to insist that mere laissez-faire was not enough, that positive state support and regulation were necessary. A broad view of the uses of law and state power generally went along with a broader, more inclusive unionism. In the United States this more radical vision belonged to the Knights of Labor and to the socialist and progressive wing of the AFL. In England it was associated with the "new unionism" of the less skilled and unskilled workers, which emerged in the 1880s, led by working-class socialists like John Burns and Tom Mann, who led the great London dock strike of 1889 and founded the Dockworkers' union.[78] These new unions stood outside the pale of the "labor aristocracy" that dominated the TUC.

Just as unionists associated with the inclusive Knights created local labor parties and ran labor candidates for local elections, so Burns and Mann were founders of the Independent Labour Party, the small socialist party of late nineteenth-century England. In retrospect it is ironic that their brightest inspiration lay in the success of the Knights in America.[79]

The Employers' Counteroffensive

In the mid-1890s, English labor leaders of all political stripes began to speak about a threatened "Americanization" of English industry.[80] The phrase rested on a fear that giant American-style trusts and combinations were emerging in England. The specter of "Americanization" also had a more specific set of referents—one suggested by English trade unionists' constant talk of "Homestead" and "Pullman." These American comparisons were used to characterize what English labor historians have called "the employers' counteroffensive" of the 1890s.[81] Prompted by the rise of the "new unionism," particularly by the new unions' tumultuous strikes and radical politics, and also by mounting international competition, the employers' counteroffensive was marked by the renewal of judicial activism against striking unions. This, above all, made "Americanization" an apt description. The courts' renewed involvement in labor strife took a form that was already familiar by virtue of stories from America: stories of injunctions, heavy damage awards, and the use of judicially sanctioned violence against strikers.

As in the United States, a series of antiunion high court decisions encouraged the creation of employers' associations devoted to organized strikebreaking,[82] and the new employers' associations, in turn, encouraged greater resort to the courts for antistrike decrees and damage judgments. *Temperton v. Russell*,[83] decided in 1893, was the first of these hostile decisions. It involved a refusal by plasterers and stoneworkers to work on materials bound for an antiunion construction firm. By ruling for the building firm, *Temperton* announced the applicability of civil conspiracy doctrine in circumstances in which the 1875 act precluded a finding of criminal conspiracy.[84] In so doing, the case introduced a vast new uncertainty about the bounds of concerted action, since it signaled that the "golden formula" did not insulate traditional tactics from civil liability. Other civil cases followed, similarly holding actionable union conduct that was immune from criminal sanctions under the 1875 act. The employers' counteroffensive was marked by grim nationwide lockouts against long-established craft unions like the engineers as well as against the newly organized Dockers. Accompanying these lockouts was the employers' increasingly massive and systematic recruitment of strikebreakers. The picket line was often the striker's only chance to speak to strikebreakers—whether to exhort, cajole, or shame, or to menace. Yet the lower courts had begun routinely to enjoin picketing.[85]

The most important case upholding the judicial repression of picketing was *Lyons v. Wilkins* (1896). The opinions of both the trial and the various appellate judges suggest that their views on the allowable bounds of labor protest were roughly identical to those that characterized most American federal and state court judges at the time.[86] *Temperton, Lyons,* and the cases that followed inspired alarm over how far the borders of allowable protest and mutual aid would narrow. Americanization seemed to be approaching with a vengeance.

Taff Vale

Then came the 1901 House of Lords decision in *Taff Vale,* which upheld an injunction and damages award against Welsh railway workers and their union.[87] The Taff Vale strike was emblematic of the employers' counteroffensive against the new unionism, involving a struggle for recognition waged by the Amalgamated Society of Railway Servants (ASRS), which embraced both skilled and semiskilled workers. In resisting the strike, an obdurate railway management had turned to the services of a recently founded employers' association that operated a national network of "Free Labour Exchanges." When the Free Labour strikebreakers first arrived at the Cardiff station, they were met by a large band of pickets. At the head of the pickets was Richard Bell, the Amalgamated general secretary. Bell distributed to the imported workers a leaflet notifying them of the strike and offering them return fares.[88] At least a third of the workers were browbeaten into accepting the offer and returned to London and Glasgow.

The Law Lords held that Bell's and the picketers' "besetting" of the strikebreakers at the station was illegal under *Temperton.* The Lords also held that not only could strikers and their leaders be held liable for such conduct, but so too could union treasuries. Henceforth, unions might be liable for heavy damages for any of the kinds of boycotts, strikes, and strike activities that were falling under judicial bans.[89]

After *Taff Vale* even the most conservative of the "old guard" were persuaded of the need for vigorous action to repeal the judge-made law of industrial conflicts.[90] But during the years immediately following the decision the Conservative government resisted all talk of restoring the "golden formula." Meanwhile, the Liberals seemed downright indifferent to labor's plight, as the party's leaders temporized, uncertain how far they wanted to redraw the boundaries of allowable collective action. Within a few years, the Liberal party lost the allegiance of hundreds of local unions and trade councils, as these groups turned away from restrained Lib-Lab politics toward supporting independent labor candidacies.

Taff Vale and the courts trebled the number of trade unions that affiliated with the Labour Representation Committee, predecessor of the Labour party.[91] This dramatic growth of the LRC was a triumph for the radicals and socialists, but it did not overnight transform the character of labor politics. Many old guard unions that had affiliated with the LRC were quite unsure where they stood on the question of collectivism. Still wary of broad reform ambitions, they were wedded only to the goal of creating a sufficiently strong bargaining position to force the next Liberal government to undo the effects of the *Taff Vale* decision.[92] The radicals' desire to forge a long-term alternative to liberalism would have to await the outcome of the immediate struggle.

Both desires—the immediate one for repeal of *Taff Vale* and the long-term one for a collectivist alternative—were, however, educated by experiences that made them seem attainable. It was hardly reckless for trade unionists to believe that if pressed, Parliament could swiftly quell the courts. The 1875 act, and the effective immunities from conspiracy and restraint of trade prosecutions that it created, had not only taught labor a lesson in the efficacy of reform by legislation; they also meant that labor could cast "repealing *Taff Vale*" as restoring Parliament's own rule with respect to an issue Parliament had already once decided. Thus Labour MPs spoke constantly of the need for legislation "to restore to the trade unions an immunity which for thirty years they have enjoyed"[93] and "to prevent workmen being placed by judge-made law in a position inferior to that intended by Parliament in 1875."[94] In 1906 the Liberal prime minister, Campbell-Bannerman, would champion the Trade Disputes Act precisely in the language of restoring the "old borders" and Parliament's authority over labor law.[95]

Even with respect to the long-term goal of a collectivist alternative to liberalism, the more radical trade unionists had good reasons to believe that the state was relatively amenable to their new program. Here the role of the high civil service is central and the contrast with the United States becomes marked, for the latter lacked both a central administrative apparatus and a nonjudicial state elite. As I have pointed out, by the 1890s England's high civil service in offices like the Board of Trade contained "new liberals," who keenly supported not only new protective legislation like minimum wages laws, but also the expansion of the state's responsibilities (and administrative capacity) to embrace ambitious "collectivist" welfare measures like old age, health, and unemployment insurance. Indeed, around the turn of the century high-placed progressive adminstrators were negotiating with labor leaders about the part unions might play in administering various forms of state-based social insurance.[96] The Board of Trade had begun "sending speakers to trade councils and other organizations and appointing trade unionists to the Labour Department."[97] In England, the idea of a national government won over to classwide social "reform by legislation" had none of the utopian quality it bore in the United States.

Enlightened politicians and administrators also had no doubt that they, and not the courts, were the proper policy makers respecting strikes. Even during the grim 1890s and into the early 1900s, while *Taff Vale* remained good law, they stood for a policy of government support for trade unionism. From 1901 through 1905 the Board of Trade's high officials advocated reforming labor law "so as to minimize the scope for judicial involvement."[98]

Thus in weighing whether to invest their political fortunes in independent labor politics, trade unionists knew that significant state actors had already made an investment of their own in the labor movement. The question was whether fielding independent labor candidates would force the Liberals' hand.

The answer turned out to be yes. In the face of Liberal temporizing the LRC put fifty independent candidates in the field in the general election of 1906. And in the face of this showing virtually all Liberal and a significant number of Conservative candidates committed themselves to the TUC's Trade Disputes Bill. The bill became law that year.[99] Section 1 restored the "golden formula," applying it to civil conspiracy law, so that henceforth any act done in concert, in contemplation or furtherance of a trade dispute, was not actionable unless it was illegal if done by an individual without concert. Section 2 repealed the courts' bar on peaceful picketing, immunizing pickets from civil and criminal prosecution. Section 4, the most controversial, specifically repealed *Taff Vale* by ruling out tort actions for damages or equitable relief against unions for wrongs committed by either officers or members; section 4 embodied, in Kahn-Freund's words, "the British solution of the problem of the labor injunction."[100] Thus the 1906 act gave English labor an extraordinary freedom from legal restraints. According to Sidney and Beatrice Webb, "most lawyers, as well as all employers, regard[ed the extent of these immunities] as monstrous." Nevertheless, Parliament had spoken, and apart from some minor skirmishes, the courts acquiesced in labor's new freedom of collective action.[101]

CONCLUSION

"The Legislature cannot make evil good," declared the judge who had authored *Taff Vale* in a 1908 opinion construing the monstrous new act, "but it can make it not actionable."[102] Not all the high court judges were as outspoken. Some insisted on greater stoicism in the judicial administration of the disturbing new immunities.[103] However, other Law Lords besides the author of *Taff Vale* sometimes made plain how they would have treated the act if, like their American counterparts, they had enjoyed the power of judicial review.[104]

By 1906 American judges had struck down four statutes containing provisions similar to those in the 1906 English act and left none standing.[105] The English judges lacked that power. Accordingly, labor gained another dramatic lesson in the efficacy of reform by legislation. The year that the TUC's Trades Disputes Bill became law—1906—marked the official founding of the Labour party.[106] More important, it marked a turning point in the evolution of English labor politics.

Ending the legal repression of trade unionism lent enormous impetus and authority to the radicals and socialists who had led the battle for independent labor politics. Over the next several years, this impetus and authority would enable them to mobilize the ambivalent "old guard" unionists—and, thereby, the TUC—in support of the new party and its "collectivist" program of social reforms. Reading the labor press and the speeches of Labour candidates in the years following 1906, one finds the proponents of a broad reform program appealing again and again to Labour's swift triumph over the courts. The stump speakers and publicists of the new party pointed to this victory and called on their uncertain comrades to look anew at Parliament as a vehicle of working-class aspirations. Now that labor had secured its legal status in the industrial arena by gaining collective laissez-faire, it was no longer treacherous, but timely instead, to focus upon other, positive reforms. And the acquiescence of the Liberals and the administrative elite in adopting labor's own version of labor's rights supplied a balm for the old fears of government-sponsored reforms. Those fears were bred of a dependency on middle-class advocates and representatives; the party vowed to break that dependency and to press forward with the rest of its program—old age pensions, unemployment insurance, an eight-hour day.[107]

The old guard might have responded to these progressive appeals as did their counterparts in early twentieth-century America, resisting any fundamental break with their voluntarist, antistatist outlook. However, the victory over the courts meant that labor's industrial liberties were no longer in jeopardy; the political sina qua non had been gained in England, and the manifest support of the powerful progressive state elite in that battle—and the promise of its support in battles to come—made it seem a wise wager to depart from the voluntarist heritage and embrace a broader and independent labor politics.

Embrace it they did. The party's membership doubled between 1906 and 1911. And during those years Parliament passed an eight-hour day for miners; a noncontributory old age pension scheme; provision for the first trade boards, which would administer a minimum wage; and finally sickness and unemployment insurance schemes. Prodded by the unions and the Labour party, and guided by the progressive state-builders in the permanent civil service, "it had laid the foundations of the welfare state."

In the United States achieving a secure legal status for trade unionism consumed several decades. A constitutional revolution had to occur before that sina qua non could be attained. During the Gilded Age the movement's mainstream had been disposed toward broad regulatory and redistributive politics. But its experiences with what Judge Taft called our "complicated" constitutional form of government—a continent-sized, fragmented, federalist state dominated by obdurate constitutional courts and tenacious, multiclass parties—drove it toward a narrow, antistatist outlook. It spurned "socialism," as the judge prophesied it would, and embraced instead a labor variant of the courts' own laissez-faire Constitution.[108]

NOTES

This essay has benefited from many thoughtful readers and critics. I would like especially to thank the participants at the conference on "Labor Law in America" from which this book emerged. In particular, Chris Tomlins proved a wise and painstaking editor. At UCLA, Robert Goldstein gave the piece his keen and careful attention. Thanks also to Leon Fink, Michael Klarman, Kathy Stone, and Jonathan Zeitlin. Research funding came from the UCLA Academic Senate and research assistance from Marty Barash, Jim Guerette, and Margaret Talbot. The themes developed here are discussed at greater length in Forbath 1991a.

1. See Avery 1989; Hurvitz 1986; Pringle 1939.
2. See Avery 1989: 18–35; Pringle 1939: 127–38.
3. See W. H. Taft 1894: 215, 216.
4. Ibid., 227–29, 233.

5. Ibid., 218–19, 233.

6. Thus this comparative essay offers a new approach to the problem addressed, and new arguments in support of the thesis set out, in Forbath 1989 and, more expansively, in Forbath 1991b.

7. Bloch 1953; Sewell 1967.

8. The following brief examination of the American "exceptionalism" debate distills the more detailed discussion and argument in Forbath 1991b.

9. The phrases are from Perlman 1923.

10. See Edwards 1981; Montgomery 1980; Brecher 1972.

11. See Wilentz 1984a: 3–4 (citing authorities); Zolberg 1986: 397–456.

12. See Forbath 1989: 1121–23 and works cited.

13. Fink 1983.

14. See Shergold 1982; J. Holt 1977.

15. See Henretta 1977; Chudacoff 1982; Conk 1978.

16. Wilentz 1984a: 5; Foner 1978; Gutman 1976: 234–60; V. Greene 1968: 207–15; J. Freeman 1983.

17. Recent works by two labor historians and a political scientist have approached the origins of American labor voluntarism in a way similar to mine, emphasizing the roles of law, state, and polity and drawing attention to the English experience. I have found all of them helpful. See Fink 1987; Oestreicher 1988; Hattam 1987; Hattam 1990. In particular, Victoria Hattam's work and mine have important themes in common. For discussion of these—and also of those points on which we part company—see below nn. 58, 59, and 65.

18. W. H. Taft 1894: 218.

19. See Madison 1961.

20. Katznelson 1985: 257, 273.

21. Commons and Andrews 1936: 48–63; Kelley 1905; USCIR 1915: 38. For a compelling account of some *radical* potentialities of American federalism, see Valelly 1989.

22. The Public Health, Factory and Mines Acts passed from midcentury onward engendered a dramatic growth of England's central government. See Sutherland 1972; Thane 1984.

23. See Shefter 1986. For a contrasting account that underscores the salience of class-based issues in the development of the urban political machine, see Bridges 1984.

24. See Kleppner 1979; Kleppner 1970; Oestreicher 1988.

25. American Federation of Labor 1895: 8.

26. This argument, about the relative timing of mass suffrage on one hand and civil service reform on the other, draws upon Shefter 1978 and 1977. See also Orloff and Skocpol 1984: 68–69.

27. See Shefter 1978. See also Keller 1980.

28. See Gilbert 1966: chaps. 5–7; Heclo 1974: 84–90; Orloff and Skocpol 1984: 737.

29. Almost every student of American labor and social reform has noted that nineteenth- and early twentieth-century American reformers were keenly attentive to the work and examples of their English counterparts. See, for example, Baker 1925: 204, 334, 350; Andrews 1938: 142. On the topic of English

social reformers' influence on American colleagues, see A. Mann 1956: 672–92; K. O. Morgan 1976.

30. See Skowronek 1982: 47–55; Forbath 1989: 1126–30.

31. See Skowronek 1982: 150–54.

32. See Marx 1977, 1: 401, 609.

33. Abraham and Davies 1902: 12; *Report of the Chief Inspector of Factories and Workshops*, 1896: 323–28.

34. For a knowledgeable American's account of the differences between English and American factory inspectors, see Price 1914: 24–25, 81–82.

35. E. Brandeis 1935: 626–32.

36. See Kingsbury 1971 [1911]: 233–35.

37. See, for example, USIC 1900–1902, 12 [*Relations and Conditions of Capital and Labor Employed in the Mining Industry*]: 56 (testimony of John Mitchell), 201–2 (testimony of George Clark). For trade unionists in other trades comparing the factory laws and inspectorates of the United States with those of England, see USIC 1900–1902, 7 [*Relations and Conditions of Capital and Labor Employed in Manufactures and General Business*]: 112–13 (testimony of George E. McNeill), 198 (testimony of Henry White).

38. See E. Brandeis 1935: 633. On the size, powers, and responsibilities of New York's factory inspectorate, see Baker 1925: 281–84. See also, generally, USIC 1900–1902, 14 [*Relations and Conditions of Capital and Labor Employed in Manufactures and General Business, no. 2*]: 251 (testimony of Thomas Lappin); Pennsylvania Department of Factory Inspection 1890–1902; Barnard 1907; Illinois Department of Factory Inspection 1894–1900; Beckner 1929; E. Brandeis 1935: 626–32; Brock 1984: 148–184; Mess 1926.

39. Forbath 1989: 1148 n. 168.

40. The story that follows, of American labor's experiences with the nation's legal order, is one that I have told elsewhere in great detail. See Forbath 1989.

41. For a more detailed account of the outlook and activities of the Knights see Fink 1983; Forbath 1985; 1989: 1120–22 and works cited therein.

42. See Forbath 1989: 1123.

43. Ibid., 1123–25.

44. Compare Abraham and Davies 1902 (England) with Kingsbury 1971 [1911] (Massachusetts); USIC 1900–1902, 5 [*Labor Legislation*]: 356–421 (New York, Pennsylvania). On the extent of labor's political and legislative successes during the 1880s and 1890s, see Forbath 1989: 1132–47.

45. See Forbath 1989: 1133 n. 78, 1237–45.

46. American Federation of Labor 1895.

47. In a plebiscite vote in 1894 a majority of the AFL's constituent unions endorsed the program. It was rejected at the 1894 convention, although most accounts agree that the defeat resulted from the "parliamentary sleight-of-hand" of Gompers and other federation leaders. See Shefter 1986: 257; see also Rayback 1959; Commons et al. 1966 [1918] 2: 511–13.

48. American Federation of Labor 1895: 19–20.

49. Ibid., 21.

50. Forbath 1989: 1148; USCIR 1915: 38.

51. During the first three decades of the nineteenth century, the courts and the laws of England, France, and Germany all flatly condemned strikes or combinations to raise wages or contest working conditions as criminal combinations or conspiracies. See Hepple 1986; Fox 1983.

52. Forbath 1989: 1448–76; 1448–80, 1249–53; 1185–95, 1201–2.

53. Ibid., 1202–14.

54. Ibid., 1205 (quoting Gompers). From the 1890s until the New Deal, an astonishing number of trade unionists immersed themselves in equitable, common law, and constitutional doctrine. They turned out thousands of editorials, speeches, and pamphlets assailing "government by injunction" and created, in the process, an alternative rights rhetoric and constitutionalism revolving around "liberty of contract" as well as the First and Thirteenth Amendments. See Forbath 1989: 1208–14.

55. Frankfurter and Greene 1930: 136–98; see also Forbath 1989: 1220–22.

56. See Forbath 1989.

57. See the superb account in Ackerman 1990.

58. Here my interpretation differs substantially from Victoria Hattam's. To my way of thinking, Hattam's admirable 1987 dissertation mischaracterizes the political outlook and behavior of the early twentieth-century AFL. As a result, she misses some key aspects of the role of law in shaping that organization.

Hattam's assessment of the AFL is informed by case studies of two pre-AFL organizations and their legislatively successful but judicially nullified efforts to secure court-curbing legislation narrowing the grounds for conspiracy prosecutions of strikers and boycotters. As a consequence of such experiences, Hattam contends, when the AFL arrived on the scene it abandoned politics, eschewing the electoral and legislative involvements of its predecessors in favor of "pure and simple unionism." Hattam 1987: 125–68. The conclusion that the AFL early abandoned the pursuit of reform by legislation is, however, not borne out by an examination of its history. With vigor equal to and resources greater than the pre-AFL organizations she describes, the AFL and its state federations continued to electioneer and lobby for immigration restrictions, various kinds of protective legislation, especially for women and children, and above all, court-curbing measures removing the harsh legal restraints on collective action. These were the visible hand of AFL voluntarism. In particular, court-curbing measures, which Hattam focuses on for the pre-AFL era, were a reform goal that the AFL simply could not afford to abandon. Broader reform ambitions receded, but the long legislative campaign against the courts continued and intensified. Indeed, ironically, labor's outlook fell more under the sway of the law. See Forbath 1989.

59. Here again Professor Hattam and I differ, as she has indicated in a recent article (Hattam 1990: 129, 129n). There, however, she contrasts her account with my work in a way that I think is misleading. My work has not "focus[ed] exclusively on the AFL," nor "reified the nature of judicial power," nor looked solely to the "structure and capacity of the American legal system" while neglecting "the *interaction*" of labor organizations and social move-

ments with the courts. Indeed, I had thought my work examines those inter-actions as carefully as any. See Forbath 1985, 1989. The actual differences between us are, I think, more subtle but also more substantive.

The AFL, in Hattam's view, stood for "trade unionism," always hewing to Gompers' outlook and striving to carve out a place in the emerging industrial order for craft unions and collective bargaining. The Knights of Labor stood for "producerism" and largely rejected unionism and collective action. Spurn-ing strikes and boycotts, the Knights strove instead to restore the propertied independence of small producers through antimonopoly legislation and public control of currency and credit. Of these two main currents of Gilded Age labor politics, it was only the "trade unionist" stream than ran up against the courts. Therefore, Hattam concludes, "the courts' power to shape the American work-ing class" was "contingent" (83). It hinged on the demise of the Knights and their vision, a demise attributable to factors other than the legal order.

Hattam and I differ, first, in our understandings of the two organizations. The Gilded Age Knights of Labor was indeed heir to the "producerism" that Hattam aptly describes, but she implies that their alternative America was one in which workers somehow would return to individually owned shops. This overlooks that the Knights' producerism was entwined with a more col-lectivist outlook, one that registered a full generation or more of experience in the nation's factories. They envisioned an economy of cooperative and pub-licly owned industries, not one composed of individual producers.

By the same token, although at points Hattam seems to claim otherwise, it was quite possible for a Gilded Age worker to be both a "producerist" *and* a "trade unionist." Most Knights were both; their goal of a future "Co-operative Commonwealth" did not prevent them from being staunch trade unionists in the present. Thus, although Hattam suggests that the Knights were largely indifferent to workers' rights to strike and boycott, in fact they made protection of these rights the chief aim of countless campaigns. Similarly, just as pro-ducerists could be trade unionists, so could many AFL unions champion a broad producerist politics. The AFL was never ideologically monolithic, as Hattam herself acknowledges, least of all in its first two decades, when the union philosophy associated with Gompers vied constantly with the more inclusive unionism and more ambitious vision of labor reform which I have sketched. Despite her interest in historical contingency, Hattam seems in-advertently to slight the most robust alternatives to Gompersism in the Gilded Age.

I also question Hattam's insistence that the courts played no significant part in the Knights' demise. In scores of industries and locales court-sponsored suppression drove old-stock skilled workers away from the class-based soli-darities they had formed in the Knights with the unskilled and the new im-migrants, and into the more exclusive organizations and restricted spheres of action that characterized the AFL craft unions. See Forbath 1991. To say that the courts played this role is in no sense to deny that the "power of the courts to shape the American working class" was "contingent." That power *was* contingent, not only as regards the Knights, but also as regards the AFL, an arena that Hattam seems to exempt from contingency. In both contexts, as we shall see, the contingency of the courts' power is illuminated by the English comparison—by, for example, the lightness of America's industrial working class when weighed against the whole voting population compared to the greater political weight of England's working class, and by the fact that the Democrats and Republicans in the United States were both culturally and structurally far less constrained than England's two main parties to compete for industrial workers' votes through class-based appeals. Had factors such as these been otherwise, the political will necessary to rein in a uniquely powerful judiciary probably would have emerged much sooner.

60. See Kahn-Freund 1964.

61. Wedderburn 1965: 207–10.

62. The best account of the repeal of the Combination Acts remains Webb and Webb 1920: chap. 7.

63. See Macdonald 1976: chap. 2.

64. See Wedderburn 1965: 207–10; Webb and Webb 1920: 248–49. The most richly detailed assessment of the development of English trade union law and of the vagaries of the English judiciary's interpretations of Parliamentary reforms is to be found in a recent American law review article—too recent for me to have used it here as fully as I would have liked. See Klarman 1989. Klarman confirms a few key points. First, his account supports my view that English courts were markedly similar to the American judiciary in their use of strained constructions to vitiate prolabor statutory reforms. Second, Klarman agrees that judicial hostility played a central role in shaping the collective laissez-faire outlook of organized labor in England, much as it did in the United States.

Finally, Klarman remarks on the tenacity of this laissez-faire outlook among English trade unionists. Having ousted the courts, English labor preferred continued judicial nonintervention over legally recognized rights to organize and to employer recognition. So too did the AFL decades later, after Congress had passed the Norris-LaGuardia Act of 1932; hence the AFL's initial opposition to, and swiftly renewed hostility toward, the National Labor Relations Act of 1935. See Tomlins 1985. But it would be wrong to read Klarman more broadly. Klarman does not appear to claim, and certainly does not show, that as a result of its experiences with the courts, the English labor movement remained permanently hostile to government involvement in other "traditional trade union functions," such as hours and wages regulation and unemployment or health insurance. In fact, as we shall see, English trade unionists tended to remain hostile to such welfare state measures only as long as they perceived the courts as ruling the roosts of state policy and state power.

65. For a sustained and subtle interpretation of the pre-1880 English labor movement's similarities with organized labor in America, see Hattam 1987: 169–94. It is worth underlining here that the leading unions of the early TUC were powerful craft organizations like those that dominated the AFL. Indeed, they supplied Gompers, an English immigrant who had grown up in London's trade union world, with a model of the "business unionism" that he pioneered in the United States. The English unions' key features from Gompers's perspective were their greater measure of "businesslike" centralized control over

matters of union finance and the calling of strikes, their high dues, and their sizable treasuries. See Gompers 1925, 1; Kaufman 1973. On the TUC's founding see Webb and Webb 1920; Fox 1983; Clegg, Fox, and Thompson 1974.

66. See Cole 1953; Clegg 1972: 396.

67. Webb and Webb 1920: 78–103; Clegg, Fox, and Thompson 1974: 41–42.

68. Wedderburn 1965: 212–13. Thus the act eliminated such vague offenses as "molestation" and "intimidation" insofar as these had been construed to include peaceful boycotting and other forms of secondary pressure and such demands as the closed shop; the act also expressly legalized peaceful picketing.

69. Kahn-Freund 1967: 55.

70. Forbath 1989: 1220.

71. Ibid.: 1241–43. See also Hattam 1987; Kuritz 1950. Criminal conspiracy prosecutions of unionists finally ceased in the United States in the 1900s, but not due to labor's legislative efforts. Instead, they were cast aside when both employers and state officials concluded that the injunction was a more efficacious weapon. See Forbath 1989.

72. See Kahn-Freund 1967: 55. On the few occasions after 1875 in which they were called on to address the question, appellate courts consistently ordered the dismissal of conspiracy indictments and the reversal of conspiracy convictions against trade unionists. See *Connor v. Kent*, 2 Q.B. 549 (1891) (reversing magistrate's conviction of three local trade union leaders for threatening strike to enforce closed shop, demanding firing of three nonunion workers); *Curran v. Treleaven*, 2 Q.B. 560 (1891) (same); *Gibbon v. Lawson*, 2 Q.B. 557, 558 (1891) (upholding dismissal of indictment by magistrate). *Gibbon, Connor*, and *Curran* appear to be the last cases in which the question of the criminality of peaceful strikes and boycotts had to be addressed at the appellate level; they were preceded by a decade in which no such cases were reported.

73. Fox 1983: 229–30; see also Phelps-Brown 1983: 58–59.

74. Quoted in Clegg, Fox, and Thompson 1974: 50.

75. Pelling 1979: 153; Webb and Webb 1920: 373, 374.

76. See Pelling 1979: 62–82.

77. See D. Montgomery 1974.

78. On the creation and character of the new unions see Webb and Webb 1920: 358–422; Clegg, Fox, and Thompson 1974: 55–96.

79. Pelling 1964: 80; Pelling 1956 (quoting Burns, Mann, Thorne).

80. Pelling 1964: 196–97; Saville 1960: 345; Clegg 1972: 396.

81. On the "employers' counter-offensive" see Clegg, Fox, and Thompson 1974: 126–79; Saville 1960: 317–50; Fox 1983: 174–221.

82. See Saville 1960: 323.

83. 1 Q.B. 715 (1893).

84. See Saville 1960: 344 n. 3 (quoting Sir Frederick Pollock's supplementary note on *Temperton* appended to his 1892 *Memorandum on the Law of Trade Combinations*, which appears in Royal Commission on Labour 1894: 157–63).

85. Saville 1960: 344–45.

86. *J. Lyons & Sons v. Wilkins*, 1 Ch. 811 (1896); 825–26.

87. 1901 A.C. (Eng.) 426.

88. Bealey and Pelling 1958: 60.

89. 1901 A.C. (Eng.) 426.

90. See Bealey and Pelling 1958: 74.

91. See Webb and Webb 1920: 604; Bealey and Pelling 1958: 95.

92. Hinton 1982: 32.

93. William Hudson, Labour MP, Newcastle-on-Tyne, during Parliamentary debates on the Trade Unions' Disputes Bill, quoted in *Labour Leader*, 670 (6 April 1906).

94. TUC-sponsored motion in Parliament, 14 May 1902, quoted in Bealey and Pelling 1958: 93.

95. Quoted in Phelps Brown 1983: 37–38.

96. Gilbert 1966: chap. 5–7; Heclo 1974: 84–90; Thane 1984: 899.

97. Thane 1984: 899.

98. Fox 1983: 252.

99. 6 Edward VII. c. 47.

100. Kahn-Freund 1967: 68.

101. Although they bowed to the act's exiling them from the world of industrial relations, the courts did not go gently. They turned their ire on the new Labour party, whose potential strength the act had revealed. In 1908 the Court of Appeal ruled that unions could not impose "levies" on their memberships to pay the salaries of labor representatives in Parliament—MP's received no salary from the government. With scant support in either statutory law or precedent, the court held, and the House of Lords affirmed, that the unions' political levies were *ultra vires. Osborne v. Amalgamated Soc'y of Ry. Servants*, 1 Ch. 163 (1909) (C.A. 1908); 1910 A.C. 87 (1909). In 1913 Parliament again came to the unions' rescue, passing the 1913 Trade Union Act, which legalized such levies, with some protection for dissenters. This act's principles still govern trade union spending. 1913, 2 & 3 Geo. 5, chap. 30, sec. 3. These developments are well chronicled in Klarman 1989: 1536–47.

102. *Conway v. Wade*, 1908 A.C. 844, 856 (Farwell, L.J.).

103. See, for example, *Dallimore v. Williams and Jenson*, 30 Times Law Reports 432, 433 (1 May, 1914) (A.C.). In *Dallimore*, Lord Sumner reversed a jury verdict against officials of a musicians' union as barred by the act. He reproached "the learned [trial] Judge" for assailing the act and telling the jury "that a person who availed himself of the defence afforded by the Act was setting up a dishonest defence." These remarks were "inopportune, detrimental to the defendants' case, and, perhaps worst of all, irrelevant." 433.

104. The lord chancellor, for example, declared during the House of Lords' legislative debates on the bill that it "legalized tyranny" and was "contrary to the . . . Constitution." Quoted in Klarman 1989: 1542. In *Conway v. Wade*, 1908 A.C. 844, 857, Kennedy, L.J. stated, "It was possible for the Courts in former years to defend individual liberty . . . because the defence rested on the law which they administered; it is not possible for the Courts to do so when the Legislature alters the laws as to destroy liberty, for they can only administer the law." See also *Luby v. Warwickshire Miners' Association*, 1912 L. 203.

105. Forbath 1989: 1220–22.

106. See Fox 1983: 276–79; Clegg, Fox, and Thompson 1974: 364–422.

107. *The Case for the Labour Party,* for example, was a handbook that supplied stump speakers with arguments to win support for the new party. Published in 1909, the handbook underscored the fledgling party's legislative achievements and promises; above all, it emphasized the party's role in reforming *The Legal Position of Trade Unions.* For similar arguments in trade union newspapers, see, for example, "Well-Done!" *Labour Leader* (6 April 1906), 668. See also "The Cotton Operative and Politics," *Labour Leader* (22 January 1909), 57 (the cotton operative, traditionally "narrow" and "backward" in his politics, was inspired by the party's practical parliamentary triumphs over the courts to "begin to look at Parliament as the instrument of his social and industrial progress.").

108. Ironically, a laissez-faire state policy toward peaceful collective action turned out to be exactly what American labor never got. (Or, rather, such a national policy existed only during the brief interregnum between the passage of Norris-LaGuardia in 1930 and the Wagner Act of 1935, which, of course, created a national administrative agency with substantial regulatory powers over collective bargaining and labor conflict). See Tomlins 1985.

English labor, by contrast, got such a laissez-faire state policy toward strikes and concerted action in 1906; and neither the English labor movement nor the Labour party ever relinquished its commitment to that policy. It endured, with little interruption or exception, until 1979, when Margaret Thatcher came to the premiership committed to fundamental change in the nation's labor law. The changes wrought by Thatcher's government were Americanization once again, and with a vengeance: detailed state regulation of union affairs and sharp limits on strikes and collective action. As Klarman observes, "the Thatcher Government's recent trade union legislation constitutes an unmitigated rejection of collective laissez-faire . . . [and] it seems increasingly likely that the . . . [old] British system of industrial relations . . . now has" vanished for good. See Klarman 1989: 1596–1601.

9 The Workers' Unemployment Insurance Bill: American Social Wage, Labor Organization, and Legal Ideology

Kenneth Casebeer

We indorsed the Frazier-Lundeen Bill not because we are Communist, which we are not, but on the merits of the Bill. . . . What difference does it make who endorses a Bill so long as it is in favor of the working people!
—James O. Cox, H. N. Cassell, and E. H. Helterbraun,
Billings, Montana, to William Green, 16 January 1935,
Papers of the Office of the President, AFL

Unemployment remains the defining experience of the Depression, the searing fear of loss of job and livelihood. "Our economic condition as workers . . . has grown steadily worse. We have had practically no work for five years, being unable to meet the interest of our mortgages, and of paying taxes, a great many have lost their homes and a lifetime of savings."[1] The Depression's meaning now, however, is often reconstructed differently; changes in law and state associated with crises are more prominently remembered. Today, battles over the legislative details of enacting unemployment insurance appear to have been waged solely by professional, academic, and political elites in orderly conferences and hearing rooms.[2] Absent are the millions in fear and in pain. This account rediscovers their voices and politics in the rank-and-file struggle for an alternative legal approach to unemployment insurance, foregone but nonetheless present, politically plausible, and contemporaneously of considerable consequence.

The fight for the Workers' Unemployment and Social Insurance Bill thus becomes a component of contingent political construction of a particular type of social wage consciousness—ours. Deceptively simple, HR 7598 provided in pertinent part:

> **Sec. 2.** . . . immediate establishment of a system of unemployment and social insurance for the purpose of providing insurance for all workers and farmers unemployed through no fault of their own in amounts equal to average local wages. Such insurance shall be administered by workers and farmers and controlled by them under rules and regulations prescribed by the Secretary of Labor . . . through unemployment insurance commissions composed of the rank and file members of workers' and farmers' organizations. . . . In no case shall the unemployment insurance be less than $10 per week plus $3 for each dependent.
>
> **Sec. 3.** . . . establishment of other forms of social insurance . . . for loss of wages because of part-time work, sickness, accident, old age, or maternity.
>
> **Sec. 4.** The benefits of this Act shall be extended to workers and farmers without discrimination because of age, sex, race, or color, religious or political opinion, or affiliation, whether they be industrial, agricultural, domestic, or professional workers, for all time lost.[3]

The fight for passage of the Workers' Bill encompasses many narratives. It is the story of a rank-and-file movement endorsed by union locals representing more than a million members, pushing conservative union leaders to formulate an AFL economic security response. It is the story of the progress in Congress of the bill of Farmer-Labor Congressman Ernest Lundeen, which went farther toward becoming law than any other predecessor to Social Security. It is the story of an incipient social movement, connecting significant radical activists otherwise never linked personally or through their organizations: Lundeen himself; labor leaders Harry Bridges and Mother Bloor; social reformer Mary Van Kleeck; Communist party organizer Herbert Benjamin; Urban League officer T. Arnold Hill.

This tangle of multiple narratives supports three distinct strands of argument. First, the recognition and respect due the Workers' Bill and its partisans in itself justifies this historical recovery. Second, the issue of unemployment insurance generally, and the Workers' Bill specifically, provides a lens through which to understand the transformation of American Federation of Labor voluntarism into New Deal partnership and also to understand one catalyst of the CIO schism with the AFL. Third, the argument challenges the inevitability of the present structural consciousness defining collective bargaining law and labor law generally, which centers on the private management of investment insulated from bilateral voluntary control of wages, hours, and working conditions.[4]

The story is thus a small picture of how structure and culture meet in the process of the state as it both reflects and shapes the organization of work. The argument follows the labor history of David Montgomery,[5] expanding worker's politics from shop floor control to the social consequences of economic, social, and technological change. It also follows the legal history of E. P. Thompson,[6] emphasizing the contingency of legal and political content upon conscious, continuous, and pervasive mass-based social activity and conflict. The account expands the legal form of American exceptionalism described by William Forbath before the 1930s and by Joel Rogers postwar.[7] Agreeing with Forbath that exceptionalism did not mean the absence of a distinct labor politics, it shows how the content of organized labor's politics formed in response to rank-and-file and unorganized worker pressures, not merely in response to an antagonistic state. Agreeing with Rogers that the structure of labor law built through World War II created the conditions for a rational politics of organization which ensured the weakness of labor organization as a political force, it holds that this was not an inevitable outcome. First, this structure developed at least in part by virtue of a distinct politics internal to organized labor during the early New Deal. Second, worker politics during the Depression found voices other than unions and causes other than the organization and control of work.

More than showing the absence of a labor or social democratic party, organized labor's earlier antagonism to the state and its later alliance with a pluralistic centrist party frame what is particular about American worker politics. Depression era workers often demanded the resources to protect family and home in social wage terms. Dialectically, the social democratic moral vision of the radical rank and file became subordinated, but not lost, in organized labor's politics and the content of legislation.[8] A different version of workers' politics than prevailed could have linked a social wage to organizing mass production industry, which might have more easily generalized to a labor party. So also, recognition of a mode of collective bargaining more defined by full economic power of strikes, primary and secondary boycotts, and consumer actions—a mode precluded by judicial retrenchment of the National Labor Relations Act and the Taft-Hartley amendments—might have expanded bargainable "conditions of work" to include conditions of investment, breaking the separation of investment and employment. Instead, Senator Robert Wagner's collective bargaining vision succumbed to the legal ideology of an always con-

servative AFL leadership and a later CIO leadership increasingly dis-
tanced from the rank and file: preference for unemployment reserves
and industrial peace rather than social wage, worker democracy, and
worker control over production. Half a loaf.

Finally, focus on the contested origins of unemployment insurance
constructs an argument about legal ideology. When approached from
a broad understanding of the state, such as the structure or totality of
power organizing social relations, the legitimation by law of social
conditions and actions necessarily assumes a contested moral vision.
Legal consciousness that fails to acknowledge the contested contingency of power in social relations is in and of itself exclusionary politics.

AFL VOLUNTARISM

The story begins in the classic antistate ideology of craft-based
labor organization under Samuel Gompers. Since capital managers naturally obtain work through contract at the lowest possible wage, organization by crafts created the maximum possible holdout leverage
for organized employees. Elite and skilled workers could control not
only the terms of their work but also the return to their contribution.
Any government intervention into the gains from withholding labor
either limited the economic weapon or sapped the will to use it. Moreover, since skills defined scarcity, sufficient return could be extracted
to support pooling against risks such as loss of job.

Until his death Gompers believed that the state by inclination
and inevitable effect would reduce workers' standards of living and
therefore their very freedom. Unemployment insurance made the
means for life and thus liberty *dependent* on government supervision
of the conditions of leaving employment in order to be eligible for
insurance, often in partnership with a coercive employers' leverage
over employment terms. "The whole of activity to organize, to assert
and to live our own lives would be subject to every petty or high official
. . . according to the government's conception of what is and what is
not voluntary unemployment."[9]

AFL policy could still be reconciled with a retooled voluntarism
under Gompers's successor, William Green, but both the context and
direction of antistatism changed significantly.[10] As of 1930 and 1931,
the AFL and President Green were still clearly opposed to unemployment insurance even as they supported some governmental efforts to
ease joblessness through the formation of a national employment service, statistical studies of the problem, and increased public employment. At the September 1930 quarterly meeting of the executive coun-

cil, Green announced a public platform of voluntary agreements between employers and workers in seasonal industries for setting up insurance funds, shorter workdays and weeks to divide available work, and stabilization of production to guarantee the worker a regular yearly wage. As late as February of 1931, Green could still resemble Gompers: "We do not want to destroy our economic movement through the substitution of force and state domination growing out of the enactment of hasty and ill-considered legislation."[11] Green would even assert unemployment was unnecessary. "If industry had paid wages corresponding with the increasing power of individual and collective production, working people would have bought the things which industry produced and thus we would have employment." Finally, Green retreated to bedrock: "The basis of all improvement in our economic and social well being is found in the growth, strength and expansion of organized labor. Unemployment plans suggested by some well meaning people would, if put into effect, effectively destroy the organized labor movement."[12] Yet by July 1932, Green was reporting to Senator Robert Wagner, "At the July meeting of the Executive Council I was instructed to draft a plan for unemployment reserves. . . . Relief had become so imperative an issue that we ought to consider legislative means for providing stable incomes for wage earners."[13]

The 1931 convention of the AFL was pivotal to a more subtly evolving voluntarism. In Boston the previous year the executive council had agreed to be instructed to study the problem of unemployment and various proposals in response, including insurance, but had also vigorously reasserted voluntarism. The executive council report to the 1931 Vancouver convention ignored insurance. An emergency program demanded maintaining wages, shortening hours, adding workers by each employer, public building, employment agencies, preference for workers with dependents, and financial relief from public funds. The long-term program called for employment stabilization through corporatist national planning, which would include organized labor as a partner, and aimed at balancing work time and wages with productivity increases so that "workers shall share in industrial progress by advances in real wages and greater leisure and recognition of worker equities in their jobs."[14] In short, the leadership maintained voluntarism's twin goals of private control over benefits as a necessary tool of organization strategy and economic leverage over real wealth to improve living conditions while combining them with a pro-state policy to stabilize macroeconomic conditions and, as an adjunct to planning, state power to stand behind increased labor organization and rationalization.

However, labor's protopartnership with business and state for stabilized growth required that business supply job security and climbing living standards. Instead, an ambivalent capitalist class retained increased profits while preempting the necessary counterrationalizing labor organization by undermining organizing strategies. "Firms are establishing benefit features paid for by low wages and working conditions imposed on the workers. These methods are making it very difficult for our organizations to organize their employees."[15]

AFL proposals developed by concession. The council continued its reactive stance in the August 1931 meeting. Green believed the call for relief was simply diverting attention from the federation's approach of increasing jobs and sharing work, although Vice President Wharton concluded that divided work meant earnings so far reduced that they would not enable workers to make a living wage.

> Failure of industrial management to provide and maintain work
> opportunities through the distribution of the amount of work
> available upon a nation-wide basis is resulting in the crystalliza-
> tion of public opinion in support of Unemployment Insurance
> legislation. . . . The American Federation of Labor wishes very
> sincerely that the enactment of such legislation could be
> avoided. It prefers work and the creation of work opportunities
> to the payment of relief to those who are idle, but men, women,
> and children must not suffer from hunger and want merely be-
> cause willing workers are deprived of the opportunity to work.[16]

Minutes of AFL Executive Council meetings show the council gave grudgingly little time to substantive discussion of proposals to deal with unemployment.[17] In stark contrast, after 1931 the minutes record considerable attention in the council to the Communist source of rank-and-file proposals for the Workers' Bill.

THE RANK AND FILE INSIDE THE AFL

As chair of the Resolutions Committee and thus of floor debates at the 1931 AFL convention, Third Vice President Matthew Woll controlled the defense of the executive council's report and program against rank-and-file resolutions.[18] The charged atmosphere of the debates connected industrial organizing and economic conditions. Delegate Duncan of the Seattle Central Labor Council challenged the efficacy of the leadership's organizing strategy, amending the executive council's report to force American Federation of Labor commitment to unemployment relief. "I want men to get the sustenance from somewhere so that they can stand up like real men and say, 'No, I am getting enough to get by on, I don't have to undermine my fellows, I

will stick to my unemployment insurance until I can go to work with
my fellows and maintain my self respect.'" The relationship between
unemployment and the more fungible jobs of industrial workers made
the ability of workers to remain outside the labor pool more important
to organizing and later protecting their strikes. This would become
key to the unions that would later form the Committee on Industrial
Organization, such as the Textile Workers and the UMW. The Typog-
raphers' Charles Howard, a CIO founder whose philosophy of unionism
fit the CIO troublingly, objected sympathetically that workers could
predict that capital would use superior political power to force the tax
burden onto employees. He also could not imagine disbursement being
turned over to trade unions. Conservative Andrew Furuseth, president
of the Seamen, lamented the impact of the injunction on the strength
of union self-protection through economic power, but sharply repudiated Duncan in an anti-industrial echo equating industrial government and revolution. "I certainly do feel that the proposals, innocently
but in fact, are transmitted in some way from those who are planning
the destruction of existing governments and establishing an industrial
government in its place." But Delegate Hunter of the UMW responded
by detailing both the number of miners unemployed and the impact
on union power: "It means that the coal operators take advantage of
that situation to break down the conditions of the men who are working in the mines. They know they can get plenty of men and they
impose conditions upon the miners that are almost unbearable."
Hunter estimated that 90 percent of the miners favored unemployment
insurance. Vice President Olander, who would succeed Woll on Resolutions, appealed that liberty not be sacrificed to alleviate some hunger. Seemingly forced to intervene, President Green acknowledged the
need for government to aid the destitute but pleaded with the convention not to commit to insurance, "which involves very fundamental principles, principles upon which our great union rests." Insurance
risked voluntarism, since "you must report, you must subject yourself
in every way to the control of law."[19]

Presentation of the earliest version of the Workers' Bill to Congress, December 7, 1931, climaxed the National Hunger March, organized by Herbert Benjamin's Unemployed Councils. This "bill" was
in the form of five demands: (1) a federal system of unemployment
insurance to be immediately adopted guaranteeing full wages for full
or part involuntary unemployment; (2) this to be available to all categories of wage labor without discrimination by race, sex, age, origin,
or political opinion; no person to be deprived of benefits for refusing
to take the place of a striker or to work for less than union rates; (3)
full funding from war preparation appropriations combined with

sharply progressive taxation on all incomes above $5,000 with no levies on workers; (4) administration by elected worker committees; and (5) social insurance for loss of wages through sickness, accident, old age, or maternity.[20]

Workers frustrated by their leaders formed a natural constituency and a perfect political and economic opening for the Communists. At this point, however, affiliations blurred. On January 27, 1932, Carpenters Local 2717 called a conference of eighteen New York locals to establish the New York AF of L Trade Union Committee for Unemployment Insurance and Relief. A painter who had become unemployed as a result of the Depression, Louis Weinstock, was named secretary. As an independent group consisting only of union members within the AFL, the New York committee explained that its purpose was to initiate a rank-and-file referendum for the repudiation of the 1931 AFL Vancouver convention's rejection of unemployment insurance and its betrayal of twelve million unemployed workers. "The standard of living of American workers must be maintained. Breadlines and starvation must be done away with. Unemployment Insurance is a life necessity."[21] The committee itself claimed to have proposed the Workers' Unemployment Insurance Bill although it was in draft identical to the hunger marchers' wish list.[22] Condemning voluntarist arguments as against worker interest, the committee attacked Green, Woll, and company. "These fakers dare to speak about the pride of workers, at a time when with the legal assistance of the AF of L affiliation, the bosses have reduced millions of American workers to bread lines and flop houses. . . . They have the effrontery to say it is the workers who do not want Unemployment Insurance."[23]

Pressure on the AFL leadership indeed mounted. In the February executive council meeting, President Green had worried, "The call from the mining sections of the country is terrific. . . . Now, what are we to do? How are these workers to express themselves except through the American Federation of Labor? They are calling for relief. . . . My position at the convention had nothing to do with the relief of the hungry; compulsory unemployment insurance was a union wrecking agency. I do not know what we can do when the people are hungry."[24] Yet as late as July 2, 1932, Green wrote in the AFL Weekly News Service, "Labor abhors unemployment insurance. Unemployment can be prevented by making the work week and the work day short enough so that all workers shall be employed in the future."[25] At the July meeting, Vice President Duffy of the Carpenters called attention to a communication from the Chicago District Council of Carpenters for AFL formulation of an acceptable insurance plan. In response, President Green recalled local pressures; he had "submitted to the council information in regard to the formation of the Communist movement in New York, known as the New York AF of L Trade Union Committee for Unemployment Insurance and Relief. A number of our organizations, through a misunderstanding, became associated with it. They are in favor of a plan for unemployment insurance. We may have to face the situation some way and make a definite declaration because of the growing demand to do something."[26] On October 18, 1932, just before the Cincinnati convention, the council worried about the New York committee's intention to enter the convention hall by force of numbers and "create whatever disorder they can while there. Their demand is for unemployment insurance."

The New York committee issued a second pamphlet calling for a rank-and-file convention to be held in Cincinnati concurrent with the AFL convention.[27] Two hundred and fifty rank-and-file delegates from across the country met in Cincinnati's Carpenters Hall. A delegation of twenty-five people was sent to the AFL to seek floor access to press for unemployment insurance. Upon discovering the AFL was using a nonunion hotel, the rank and file used one hundred pickets around the hotel before attempting to present their delegation's credentials, which were refused. Thereupon, pickets and delegates entered the hall's public balcony. In order to present their demands for unemployment insurance, Weinstock climbed on a large chandelier and shouted out his message. The Cincinnati afternoon paper headlined, "Rump Convention Disrupts AF of L Convention."[28]

At the AFL convention itself, the more industrially organized unions pushed for action on unemployment relief. Citing introduction of machine technology, the fifty-seventh convention of the Amalgamated Association of Iron, Steel and Tin Workers called for AFL pressure on Congress. Decrying the hardship of increasing and permanent unemployment, the thirty-second convention of the United Mine Workers did the same, accompanied by their own extensive study of insurance. "Independent occupation no longer furnishes a livelihood to the great industrial masses. . . . If this economic structure determines the dependency of labor, it must also bear the obligation of providing employment for labor or caring for it while unemployed. . . . The unemployed labor reserves upon which industry thus relies, constitutes a just item of industrial cost." The UMW leaders directly attacked the AFL leaders' fear that employers would have no incentive to stabilize production, arguing that full employment or its equivalent maintained living standards, while increased purchasing power accelerated the demand necessary to business growth. The report concluded pointedly, "It seems foolish to say that unemployment insurance will operate against the organized labor movement. The great purpose of union labor is to bring to all workers the American standard of wages and working conditions. . . . The pressure of [the unemployed] for jobs, coupled with the fear of many of those employed that they may lose their jobs, constitute the real barrier to the organization of all industrial workers." When Thomas F. McMahon, president of the United Textile Workers, introduced a resolution for insurance at the expense of the state and employers to be administered in part by committees on which labor is represented, old line delegates Andrew Furuseth and John P. Frey, of the Metal Trades Department, could only lament the passing of Gompers-style voluntarism. "We did not go to the unorganized who were suffering from industrial injustice and tell them, 'If you join our union we will secure certain legislation for you.' We believe that we have to do something which would impress the non-unionists with the necessity for a vigorous, virile, militant organization in the economic field."[29] President Green finally closed the debate by invoking the escape clause of the Vancouver convention—business neglect will force us to support insurance—insisting that any insurance protect the right and incentive to belong to a union.

Although the 1932 convention voted to support a historic change in direction, incredibly, the minutes of the executive council for 1933 record no discussion of unemployment insurance. Meanwhile, the rank-and-file organization, dropping New York from its title, called for another parallel convention for the 1933 AFL meeting in Washington. At this Second Annual Rank and File Conference, Frank Mozer, Philadelphia Plumbers Union 690, was elected president, and Louis Weinstock reelected secretary-treasurer. The agenda of the organization was broadened to include all other rank-and-file issues: racketeering, exemption of unemployed dues, injunctions, right to strike, and so forth. Subsequently, a third pamphlet was issued concerning organized labor's complicity with the NRA, seeing too little too late in the AFL convention decision to begin chartering federal unions. "Progressive elements in the AF of L unions have long advocated industrial unions, and opposed the system of craft trade unions as a system that divides the forces of the workers in the shop, job or industry and makes it easier for the employers to defeat the workers. The AF of L leaders have been strong adherents of craft unionism. Now, however, after a wave of organization, and the fear of the employers that militant independent unions would come, the AF of L is expected to organize the workers and keep them from struggling."[30]

Once again, a delegation of twenty-five of the rank and filers presented credentials to the AFL convention and was rebuffed. However, one R. Suny, an AFL delegate representing the Cleaners, Dyers, Spotters, and Pressers, who also attended the rank-and-file meeting, introduced the Workers' Unemployment Insurance Bill on behalf of his union as a resolution at the AFL Convention. In the brief convention floor debate on the Worker's Bill, Thomas Kennedy of the UMW asked if nonconcurrence meant that the Committee on Resolutions believed Senator Wagner's alternative unemployment insurance bill was also unconstitutional in its federal aspects and was assured it was not. Kennedy would later write of his more generalized skepticism, "Of course, I am aware that some of our reactionary groups, as always is the case, have raised the question of unconstitutionality against a National System. No worthy course or movement for human welfare has ever been free from such indirect and insincere attacks."[31]

While unsuccessful at entering the AFL convention, the rank-and-file committee did get the attention of the executive council. At the January 1934 meeting, it agreed to receive a delegation. Frank Mozer began by claiming twelve hundred locals and twelve state federations. Mr. Coleman of Aeronautical Workers Union 18286, Buffalo, New York, challenged, "If the American Federation of Labor expects to remain as a leader of the workers it must do something and do it now." Louis Weinstock called for support of the Workers' Bill. Mr. Kuhlman, Painters, asked for ending suspensions for nonpayment of dues, noting that the AFL had lost 400,000 members since 1932. Mr. Stein of the Quarry Workers No. 70, Bangor, Maine, said that "the Federation is built on craft lines and that less than fifty thousand are in about eight different organizations and they should be in one." Mr. Peter Paul, UMW, Girardsville, Pennsylvania, followed by warning, "[In] one instance of 25,000 miners marching from one town to another demanding unemployment relief, John Lewis sent a telegram to them not to strike but the miners went out on strike."[32] The executive council offered no substantive response to the specific proposal of the Workers' Bill and instead bristled at the accusation of widespread racketeering and rigged elections. President Green concluded the meeting by raising the Constitution as a barrier to any federal legislation.

In the September 1934 executive council, Vice President Duffy once again reported that many locals had "unknowingly" supported resolutions circulated favoring the Workers' Bill. Regarding the San Francisco convention, "We will have to expose them because they will have the communists in here. They had them in the Washington convention and introduced resolutions but the convention voted them down. At some session they will probably want to storm the hall as they did in Cincinnati and other places demanding the right to be heard. They are not coming into the convention; they are not going to be heard."[33] The council considered a recommendation of the Committee on Resolutions designed to limit the danger of outside organizations introducing resolutions during the convention and requiring advance submission and screening.

Resolutions in opposition to the executive council's nonspecific support for state unemployment reserves were introduced in the 1934 convention in San Francisco, particularly from industrial unions. David Dubinsky and the ILGWU "resolved that the American Federation of Labor, in fifty-fourth convention assembled, in the city of San Francisco, continue unremittingly its drive for the passage of a compulsory Federal unemployment insurance law; and . . . further resolved, that the administration of the insurance funds created by this law be left to each and every industry and that the workers in each industry should have a paramount voice in its administration."[34] Delegates Stubbe and Johnson of Automobile Workers Federal Labor Unions introduced resolutions attacking the adequacy of the Wagner-Lewis bill to establish unemployment reserves and supporting the Workers' Bill as the only real unemployment insurance. The council's report was adopted without floor debate.

By its highpoint in early 1935, the AF of L Trade Union Committee had collected endorsements from three thousand locals, five international unions, six state federations—Arkansas, Colorado, Iowa, Montana, Nebraska, Rhode Island—and thirty-three central labor unions, including Pittsburgh, San Diego, Minneapolis, St. Louis, Albuquerque, Queens and Nassau counties, Providence, Salt Lake City, and Milwaukee.[35] The red baiting from President Green's office, which had begun in 1932, increased in harshness as these numbers grew. In 1933, Hutcheson's Carpenters dissolved New York Carpenter's Local 2717, the local that called the first meeting of the AF of L Trade Union Committee on Unemployment Insurance and Relief, and transferred their members to other local carpenters' unions in the city. The same fate befell Local 1151 in Philadelphia, which had sent out a referendum on the Workers' Bill to all carpenters' locals.[36] When on August 4, 1934, George Butler communicated the unanimous endorsement of the Workers' Bill by Local 252 of the Oil Field, Gas Well and Refinery Workers and objected to the worthless Wagner bill, Green replied, reiterating support for the Wagner-Lewis bill, "I presume you are not aware of the motive behind the circulation of this [Workers'] bill among the labor organizations of this country. The bill was prepared by Communists, who, as it is well known, are opposed to unemployment insurance. They simply had introduced an impossible bill in order that the real bill would be defeated."[37] Butler countered,

> We of local 252 don't understand your motive by branding this bill, as being prepared by communists, we read both bills before

the body, HR 7598, bill is a thousand times better and suitable to the American laborer, than the half baked Wagner Lewis bill, which saddles the bill on the workers pay envelope. . . . Was there any cry from the American worker of communism when high finance, big business, industry, rail roads, banks who received a governmental dole not of ten dollars a week but millions upon millions. . . . Take off that plug hat of reactionism and get into overalls. . . . We are not going to beg your leadership to change your opinion of HR 7598, bill which is a just bill for the American laborer but demand you to support this bill which is not impossible but just.[38]

William Green sent letters to endorsing locals labeling the Workers' Bill a ploy of the Communists as demonstrated by its unconstitutionality. Rank-and-file President Frank Mozer responded, "Some of the locals sent the letters back to William Green, telling him that unemployment was also unconstitutional, and that Green was not doing very much to alleviate this condition."[39] W. W. Britton, president-secretary-treasurer of the Metal Polishers International, wrote Green asking for proof that the Workers' Bill was communism that he could give to members angry at being asked to pass a local rule prohibiting reading of AF of L Committee on Unemployment Insurance and Relief literature. "I have issued an order to our local President not to permit the discussion of this matter on the floor of the meeting any more, and the threat of taking charge of that organization by the International and placing our own officers in the chair."[40] Green responded, "The Lundeen [Workers'] bill was prepared by the communists and is being urged by the 'Daily Worker,' the official organ of the Soviet Government in the United States."[41] To one of the central labor unions endorsing the bill, Green wrote, "House Bill 2827 [successor to 7598] is sent out by the communists. . . . No contribution should be made by any labor organization to this group."[42] To the Yellowstone Country Trades and Labor Assembly, he wrote, "Some twelve years ago the Third International at Moscow, Russia, called upon the Communists in this country to advocate unemployment insurance. It was to be used as a slogan in the campaign to organize Communists. At the same time it was made known that an impossible bill should be prepared as the Committern [sic] was opposed to unemployment insurance."[43] The President of the Montana state federation, one of the state federations to endorse the Workers' Bill later in 1936, wrote Green to tell him, "The boys were a little peeved at your letter as they took it you were insinuating that they were mixed up with the communists."[44] In contrast, after the formation of the CIO, but before expulsion, Green treated a UMW local's endorsement more gingerly. "The American Federation of Labor convention which was held last October did not endorse any specific bill."[45] Based on its "communist philosophy," the executive council in October 1935 did disapprove a resolution supporting the Workers' Bill sent by the Committee on Resolutions of the 1934 convention to the council for action.

The Workers' Bill was introduced in resolutions again in the 1935 and 1936 conventions but was not debated save to the extent of Vice-President Woll's insistence on supporting the Social Security Act with appropriate amendments. By this time, in any case, issue-by-issue conflict between craft and industrial interests had given way to all-out conflict over the necessity that organized labor deal with the mass production industries.

THE CIO AND THE WORKERS' BILL

Together with Sidney Hillman's Amalgamated Clothing Workers of America (ACWA), which had its own internal unemployment insurance plan, four other international unions—the Miners, ILGWU, Textile Workers, and Mine, Mill and Smelter Workers—had actively opposed the AFL leadership program on unemployment insurance at AFL conventions between 1932 and 1934. The Textile Workers and the Mine, Mill and Smelter Workers specifically endorsed the Workers' Bill. James Robinson, secretary of the latter, delivered the International's stark endorsement, "Whereas, we believe that the final solution of the unemployment problem is the seizure of power by the workers and the production for use instead of for profit . . ."[46] By the time John Frey brought expulsion charges against the twelve unions of the Committee on Industrial Organization in July of 1936, a third backer of the Workers' Bill, the Iron, Steel and Tin Workers, had joined the CIO.

For Lewis and the CIO, dealing with the causes of unemployment meant also dealing with the causes of union power decline. *"In the great mass production industries and those in which the workers are composite mechanics, specialized and engaged upon classes of work which do not fully qualify them for craft union membership, industrial organization is the only solution.* Continuous employment, economic security and the ability to protect the individual worker depends upon organization upon industrial lines."[47] Moreover, failing to change organization meant worsening conditions. "With great mass unemployment, people are driven to accept low wages. The pay of union men is forced down by the competition of those who must work for less to secure a job. The many changes taking place in methods and materials are undermining old ways of doing things, so that even the most skilled worker cannot be sure that his craft will not be swept away by new inventions."[48]

The door swung both ways. As industrial unions recognized the problem of unemployment, so unemployed worker activists became important to the CIO. "Many leaders of the CIO came directly out of the unemployed movement, and it appears that many in the rank and file had similar training."[49]

The connection between unemployment, insurance, and industrial organization was always prominent in the minds of the organizers of the rank-and-file committee. Louis Weinstock recalled, "By 1934, we had a new country actually in the labor movement. We had the mobilizations of millions of unemployed people, who became organized in [the] unemployment movement, who were ready to become union people. This struggle for unemployment insurance coincided with the struggle for organization of the unorganized into industrial unionism. There was a struggle going on in this country way back since [the] 1920s to change the nature of the American Trade Union movement from craft unionism to industrial unionism."[50]

This intent was prominent in the *Rank and File Federationist*, a monthly newspaper published between 1933 and 1935 by the AF of L Trade Union Committee for Unemployment Insurance and Relief, and edited by Weinstock. An article by A. Baskoff in number 6 reported AFL "sabotage" of mine strikes, the Toledo Autolite strike, and disruption of the longshore jurisdictional battle, concluding, "The issue of craft versus industrial unionism forms one of the most colorful chapters of American Labor history. Sincere farsighted progressive elements in the AF of L have always fought for industrial unionism. . . . This AF of L Committee is definitely in favor of Industrial Unionism and is ready to support the rank and file in the AF of L in the fight for industrial unionism."[51] In number 8, Weinstock berated Green for not supporting the West Coast strike. Joseph Ryan is quoted, "Conservative Union leaders sanctioned the general strike to force a showdown and terminate the activities of Harry Bridges, radical longshoring leader."[52] Number 10 reports on the 1934 AFL convention and its rank-and-file parallel, which added industrial unionism and full participation for black workers to the Trade Union Committee program. The committee convention elected Harry Bridges, ILA, president, and Louis Weinstock secretary of the organization. In volume 2, number 5, following the 1935 AFL convention, the editorial attitude on John L. Lewis shifted drastically to his favor as a result of the celebrated punching of Carpenters' President Hutcheson over industrial organizing: "This palace battle is caused by two main factors—first, the continuing impact of the six year economic crisis upon the AF of L membership and the

American working class as a whole, and second, resulting from this, the growing disbelief of the AF of L membership—especially newly organized workers in basic industries—in the honesty and ability of the top leadership of the AF of L and its principal affiliated unions."[53] The last issue, number 6 of volume 2, pushed for formation of a labor party.

By late 1935, the need for the publication had been superceded by events. By the time an action instigated by the executive council in the Federal Trade Commission for trademark infringement was decided on November 24, 1936,[54] prohibiting use of the names *Rank and File Federationist* (vs. *American Federationist*) and "AF of L Trade Union Committee for Unemployment Insurance and Relief," the newspaper had ceased publication. Already in 1934, the AF of L Trade Union Committee had begun to urge in their convention support of the coalition National Congress on Unemployment and Social Insurance. When lobbying continued for the Lundeen bill after passage of the Social Security Act, the committee participated as part of a broader social insurance movement. According to Weinstock, a union-only organization "was not necessary anymore, because this was already the time when [the AFL] seriously considered the fight for unemployment insurance and industrial unionism, and John L. Lewis already appeared on the scene."[55]

SOCIAL MOVEMENT

More than seventy municipal governments in cities and counties,[56] including city councils such as Minneapolis, endorsed the Workers' Bill during its congressional lifetime as the Lundeen bill from 1934 to 1937. Numerous local chapters of mutual benefit societies wrote Senator Robert Wagner to ask him to support the Lundeen bill, not all ignorant that he was the sponsor of the competing reserves plan, the Wagner-Lewis bill.[57] The Fraternal Federation for Social Insurance claimed twenty-five thousand members in endorsing the Workers' Bill; also locals of the Workmen's Sick and Death Benefit Fund, the International Workers' Order, the Adolph Ullman Aid Society, and others. Immigrant ethnic organizations, made up largely of unorganized mass production workers and families, uniformly preferred the Workers' Bill; the Swedish Brotherhood, the Czech Society, the Russian Workers Club of Hamtramck, Michigan, the Polish Republic Society of Milwaukee, Wisconsin, Yugoslav Organization of Monessen, Pennsylvania, eighteen Lithuanian organizations, the Organization of Italian Descendants—Cleveland, the Union and League of Roumanian Societies of America, all wrote directly to Congressman Lundeen.[58] Organizations for the unemployed did too, not suprisingly since Wagner-Lewis would not make eligible those who had already lost their jobs. The United Shoe and Leather Workers Unemployed Council with ten thousand members wrote Wagner, as did many locals of the Workers Unemployed Union, whose advisory board included Sidney Hillman, David Dubinsky, and David Saposs.

Black workers, who were hit hardest by the Depression, received the least (and discriminatory) relief and were more often industrial and unorganized workers, found appeal in the principles of the Workers' Bill. More than 50 percent of black workers were engaged in farm and domestic labor and were therefore excluded from the Wagner bill. T. Arnold Hill, executive secretary of the National Urban League, wrote: "There must come before the congress of the United States, legislation that will guarantee, for all workers regardless of age, occupation, color, sex, or political belief, full compensation for all loss of time occasioned by involuntary unemployment, industrial accident, and sickness. Minimum standards must be set below which this compensation must not fall. Costs must be placed not upon workers, but upon Government and Capital; and workers must not be excluded from administering the benefits of such a plan." Blacks had reason to fear discrimination from the states. "Such an unemployment insurance scheme has special meaning for Negro workers. The establishment of uniform benefits regardless of race would be a step toward ending the whole system of segregation. Uniform benefits would put the Negro in a better position to bargain for higher wages and thus help eliminate the present differential between wages of white and Negro workers doing the same work."[59]

Similarly, women could look to benefits during maternity for the first time. "Mother" Ella Bloor testified:

I think very few of us who are in the cities realize the poverty that the women are suffering, especially the young women in the farm districts, on account of not only the drought and the usual conditions there, but especially the fact of maternity in these isolated places. . . . We found in the women's section of the Unemployed Congress, which took place in Washington recently, when I met with those women two or three times, that they were especially interested in this part of the bill, about maternity . . . not only the farm women, but working women everywhere. At this caucus of women in connection with the Congress, several women spoke, and they said they felt we must have a bill such as this, which makes no distinction between men and women in its benefits. In other clauses of the bill it just says "workers" and "farmers;" it never says "male workers."[60]

A poll of readers taken by the New York *Post* after printing the contents of the Wagner-Lewis, Lundeen, and Townsend bills, reported tallies of 1,391 votes cast—1,209 Lundeen, 157 Townsend, 14 Wagner-Lewis, 7 none. Of 1,073 employed—957 Lundeen, 100 Townsend, 7 Wagner-Lewis, 5 none. "The Post calls attention to the relatively high proportion of supporters of the Lundeen Bill who are at present employed, a noteworthy fact, indicating the growing consciousness of the need for security among workers still able to support themselves. The voters, employed and unemployed, came from every group and class. . . . The Administration's Wagner-Lewis measure drew the votes of almost exactly one in a hundred."[61]

Neither organization nor indoctrination can explain this support for the Worker's Bill. As the direct pleas written to Congressman Lundeen indicate, this was a mass movement. "The reason I am writing you is, that we Farmers and Industrial Workers feel that you are the only Congressman or Representative that is working for our interest. We have analyzed the Wagner-Lewis Bill and also Townsend Bill. But the Lundeen H.R. (2827), is the only bill that means anything for our class. . . . The people all over the country are awaken up to the facts that the two old Political Parties are owned soul, mind and body by the Capitalist Class."[62]

THE WORKERS' BILL IN CONGRESS

When Congressman Ernest Lundeen, Farmer-Labor party of Minnesota,[63] introduced the Workers Unemployment and Social Insurance Act (H.R. 7598) February 2, 1934, it differed substantively from the principles of the AF of L Trade Union Committee's version only in omitting the latter's guarantee of benefits regardless of citizenship. Both rank-and-file organizer Louis Weinstock and Ernest Lundeen credit Mary Van Kleeck, director of industrial research for the Russell Sage Foundation, with actually drafting the Workers' Unemployment Insurance Bill.[64] Lundeen kept an undated and unsigned preliminary draft of the Van Kleeck version. The preamble begins, "Congress recognizes the right of all useful members of society to enjoy the opportunity to secure and enjoy the essentials of life and accordingly undertakes to guarantee such opportunity to all workers who are deprived of their ordinary means of livelihood in consequence of mass unemployment, accident, sickness, old age, maternity, or any other cause that prevents workers from engaging in their normal wage-earning pursuits."[65]

The mechanism for guaranteeing the social wage was more ingenious than insidious. "Where the benefits exceeded the prevailing wage, this differential would withdraw workers from the labor market and by making labor more scarce would raise the wage rate until it at least equalled the unemployment benefits. The benefits to the unemployed could thus be used as a lever to compel industry to pay a living wage to those who were employed. In a sense, therefore, this proposal meant that the benefits could be used to finance a tacit strike to make the scale of benefits the scale of wages."[66] Instead of reserves to subsidize capital by underwriting labor pools, guaranteed living standards subsidized labor by underwriting wage floors.

Lundeen firmly believed that the purpose of insurance was a social wage, or income security, which he contrasted to unemployment reserves as security of existing employment: "In my opinion the Wagner-Lewis bill is a piece of medieval barbarism. For the fifteen million people now unemployed it provides absolutely nothing. In no provision does it recognize the responsibility of the federal government to provide its citizens with social security. The supporters of the bill to date have not dared to bring it out of its Committees."[67] Senator Wagner was less certain in return, preferring his own but answering an endorser of the Workers' Bill: "I am always ready to say that I have never seen an unemployment insurance bill that I did not prefer to no bill."[68]

President Roosevelt pulled the rug from beneath the Wagner-Lewis bill in forming the Committee on Economic Security in 1935 in order to put old age and disabled and dependent children insurance into an omnibus social security program. The Lundeen bill, however, was already comprehensive. By operating through the states, the administration's Social Security Act both avoided the federal constitutionality question and made it unnecessary to develop a social theory of the related causes of income insecurity, thus treating such insecurity as problems of individual misfortune. In contrast, the Workers' Bill not only tied the needs of the aged and disabled to their economic basis, but forced recognition of the social nature of the costs of the production system and of the reproduction of the labor force. This in turn demanded national action in order to maintain the economic system's health by guaranteeing the purchasing power of all the producers of the system's wealth—the social wage. "The system must provide compensation for the loss of income suffered, by guaranteeing an income equal to average earnings, but in no case less than a minimum standard of living."[69] Van Kleeck outlined this premise flatly opposed to the individualism of voluntarism, as follows:

By the very definition of the term, therefore, individual case treatment is excluded as a remedy, and it is recognized that the needs created by involuntary mass unemployment are also "mass needs" reflected in lowered standards of living both for the individual and the community. This suggests the necessity for *social* insurance as opposed to *individual* insurance, and it makes necessary the *integration* of insurance against "unemployment" . . . whether the cause of unemployment be located . . . in a general industrial depression; or whether it be due to the recognized general hazards to security, namely, industrial accidents, sickness, maternity, and old age. . . . *Social insurance should not be split into categories.*[70]

Politically, the Lundeen bill could not be ignored.[71] Edmund Witte, the Wisconsin professor who headed the staff of the President's Committee on Economic Security, concluded, "[The Lundeen bill] enabled the Administration to use its bill as a scarecrow to get action on its bill. Also expected to have great influence in the future."[72] Reintroduced in 1935 as H.R. 2827, the Workers' Bill received a major boost when William Connery of Massachusetts, chair of the House Committee on Labor, endorsed it.[73] The subcommittee conducting the main hearings on H.R. 2827 in 1935 voted 6–1 favorably on the bill. On March 8, 1935, the full Labor Committee voted 7–6 to report the bill to the floor—Chair Connery, Subcommittee Chair Dunn, Lundeen, Lesinski, Gilder, Truax, and Marcantonio favorable. The bill, however, seemed destined to languish in the House graveyard, the Rules Committee. Lundeen needed 212 votes to discharge it to the floor. An extensive campaign during March yielded a total of 166 signers; among the most active petition gatherers were William Connery and a young Illinois representative, Everett Dirksen.[74] In April, Lundeen tried to attach the Workers' Bill to the Social Security Act as an amendment from the floor. Paul Douglas treated the fifty-two votes in favor of the amendment as an indication of little broad based support, but Lundeen was upbeat. "We won a victory in bringing the Workers' Bill, H.R. 2827, before the House for a vote. On a standing vote we had fifty-two Congressman for the bill. If we had been given an opportunity for full discussion on the bill, we would have had many more votes. . . . We have presented the first complete program for social insurance ever introduced."[75]

During the hearings on H.R. 2827 in 1935, the AF of L Trade Union Committee witnesses repeatedly emphasized security against technical change in the production system. Secretary Louis Weinstock began by noting that 26 percent of the members of AF of L labor unions were totally unemployed. Wage standards were falling even faster than employment, with 1933 payrolls down 55 percent from 1929, while employment was down 34.3 percent. "As a result of the excessive lay-offs, speed-up increased in the shops." With employment dropping at the same time as gross productivity increased, labor union member-ship, the premise of economic self-protection, dropped sharply. Gains of new members did nothing to protect the old members now un-employed. Not needed for the work, the surplus employee needed a living standard guarantee. Legislation "must protect the standards of the employed, it must offer security against illness and old age, and against a condition where millions of children are under nourished and starving, where families must live in overcrowded slum firetraps and are faced with evictions and lack of shelter."[76]

Union endorsements of the bill followed the industrial unionism theme. The Iron, Steel and Tin Workers endorsed the Lundeen bill because of rising productivity and falling employment in the industry. "This proves to us that even with increased production, with a pick-up in steel, they will never be able to put the steel workers back to work," argued spokesman Roy Hallas, adding, "A large number of them are thinking of their own Labor Party."[77] F. Elmer Brown, Typogra-phers, based his call for social insurance on the inability of the craft organizations to maintain their holdout power: "It is the only bill which places the responsibility for unemployment where it belongs— upon the federal government and the owners of the tools and natural resources of the country." Confronted by scientific management and the redivision of labor, the power of the craftsman had settled to the level of the production worker. Union members had no greater ability to provide self-insurance. "For many years the printing trades unions have administered unemployment relief, sick benefits, and old age pensions to their members. Funds for these social features have been collected from the membership. However, technological development, in which the workers shared but little, with other maladjustments in our social system, have compelled the unions either to abandon these practices or curtail them to such a degree as to render them almost of no value."[78]

THE STRUCTURE OF LABOR LAW

In explaining the desirability of the Workers' Bill's social wage approach to insurance, the Labor Committee report relied directly on the testimony of its draftsperson, Mary Van Kleeck. "Other proposals [serve] merely to rearrange worker's income, decreasing current earn-ings in the interest of building up reserve funds against future unemployment. These funds enter into channels of investment, which really constitute increase in the debt burden of American industry and still further throw out of gear the purchasing power of the people in relation to productive capacity." In the Workers' Bill, "stability of the worker's dollar implies the possibility of purchasing always a suitable quantity of the necessities of life. And whether the dollar be measured in the value of metal or in terms of a commodity, both farmers and industrial workers must be able to count upon the stability of their income on one hand and, on the other hand, on the stability of the elements of the standards of living which this country makes possible."[79]

Outside the hearings, Van Kleeck further elaborated on the possibility of establishing a new legal understanding of property as use value related to production, thus guaranteeing living standards. "Given so great a productive capacity that goods must be destroyed, it is a reasonable demand that the unemployed be given the purchasing power which as the surplus of resources shows, has not been paid in wages to the unemployed in sufficient quantity to buy the goods produced. From this point of view, unemployment insurance is a kind of deferred wage bill." Just as this meant redistributive funding, it also meant workers' entitlement to exercise control. "As such it is to be administered by workers for the same reason that they control their own wages after they are paid."[80]

The opposed ideas animating the alternative insurance proposals—that workers should control a portion of credit or investment streams in the definition of the social wage versus the alternative of unemployment reserves, which preserve management access to investment or credit streams at the expense of privately defined wages—throw into sharp relief the key structural provisions of American labor law. The extension of the social wage undermines the idea that the terms of production are necessarily defined by bilateral wage agreements in which costs and risks of production and reproduction of the labor force are voluntarily assumed. Rights are defined equally in alternative to or supervention of contract within the relations of the state and social organization. Worker controls over production are not limited to contract, property in the job is established, and, concomitantly, investment is no longer reserved by contract prerogative and property right to capital. In contrast, a reserves plan such as adopted in the Social Security Act requires direct wage reductions to pool for future loss, or indirect funding by taxes passed on in prices to worker-consumers. "As in the past program of the New Deal, restoration of business is the point of attack, rather than income, which appears to be the decisive factor in the maladjustment between production and consumption."[81]

Van Kleeck justified the constitutionality of a federal program in proto-Keynesian terms. Increasing purchasing power would free the flow of interstate commerce by removing gluts on the national goods markets, a problem that individual states could not solve given prisoner dilemma or competition problems. Thus current unemployed workers must be protected as much as currently working but at-risk employees.

The drafters of the other Wagner act also originally intended to increase and stabilize demand by making redistribution a tool of recovery. The National Labor Relations Act framers believed increased organization would end recognition battles stopping production loss, while increased labor power would redistribute wealth by forcing higher wages and control over conditions of employment.[82] However, just as the future Labor Board and the federal courts would instead emphasize the industrial peace made possible by government of the workplace under the collective bargain, thus reducing the economic power of union organization necessary to redistribution,[83] so the Social Security Act was also never completely under Senator Wagner's control. Wagner and his aid, Leon Keyserling, both preferred a federal program, not only for uniformity but also to establish minimum standards of purchasing power. Yielding to Roosevelt, the Social Security Act was the only New Deal legislation Wagner sponsored without complete control over drafting.[84]

Indeed, in explaining her opposition to the proposed National Labor Relations Act, Van Kleeck predicted judicial and administrative retrenchment of the act's redistributive potential, precisely because workers were denied control over investment. "Fundamentally I believe it is impossible to equalize the bargaining power of employers and employees, since necessarily the decision to produce at all and in what quantities and by what processes—such, for instance, as increase in mechanization—rests with the employer." Van Kleeck saw the seeds of industrial peace forced on unions.

> Strikes which have for their purpose gradual increase in the workers' power in a period when fundamental economic change in the ownership of industry can clearly be envisaged may only seem to check the rising power of the opponents of human rights in exchange for obligations which are likely to be merely the least common denominator of industrial practice. . . . It seems to me to be self evident that a strike for any purpose

listed in the bill as an 'unfair labor practice,' including a strike
for the making of a trade-union agreement or against the discharge of a union member or on other points involved in the
forming and establishment of a strong union, would necessarily
have to be discouraged on the ground that these are matters
within the jurisdiction of a statutory federal body, the National
Labor Board.[85]

By using state benefits determinations and reserves funds, much
of the purchasing power rationale for recovery is diminished. In fact,
the results can be perverse. "Unemployment reserves are incapable of
mobilization when needed and any attempt to mobilize them will only
result in further intensification of depression."[86] Moreover, by limiting
benefit periods, those persons permanently unemployed by technology
or depression must retrain for new jobs; benefits will not sustain them
if their skills or labor are no longer necessary to management in full
control over investment in technology or changes in the division of
labor. The administration programs simply ameliorated the normal
contractual order, leaving workers "forced to maintain themselves in
idleness, awaiting the time when the industrial system will need them
for renewed production."[87]

In a sense the reserves plan primarily supports business by sub-
sidizing labor pools of skills defined by eligibility standards outside
the control of workers. The existence of these skilled pools removes
the need for employers to guard themselves against labor supply fluc-
tuation by contracting for fixed durations or by modifying their investment control over the firm's division of labor. The at-will contract,
another American particularism, thus is made more viable, independent of its simultaneous protection by contract law.[88] Moreover, given
employer leverage over at-will employees who can be fired for good
reason, bad reason, or no reason at all, organization is made more
difficult, and once accomplished, bargaining over the division of labor
in the enterprise and its relation to the division of union and nonunion
jobs also is more difficult. The social security approach to labor pool
reserves, and to individualizing risk within insurance pools, fits precisely the collective bargaining policy of private governance within
industrial pluralism that eventuated in Taft-Hartley.

Furthermore, the Wagner-Lewis unemployment reserves bill increased the state's potential to undermine workers' economic power.
"The insecurity of the working class is further emphasized by the drive
of big business against trade-union organization. If employed workers
strike to prevent further wage-cuts or to advance present rates, their
lack of reserves undermines their power of endurance in a strike; and

from the masses of unemployed are drawn willing strike breakers, while all the apparatus of the blacklist and discrimination against workers for trade-union activities is put into action." Van Kleeck did not trust the NLRA's unfair labor practice machinery to prevent such control over workers. Only a more fundamental industrial change of approach to both control of investment *and* social insurance could provide worker security. "The programs which have been described all center in provisions for mere compensation for insecurity. Except as they stimulate and coordinate organized action by workers in all occupations, they do not touch the essential elements of a program for security. Basically this calls for the development of a planned economy founded upon the maximum utilization of America's productive capacity . . . assuming as a prerequisite the socialization of all industry."[89]

CONCLUSION

In the 1930s, workers were vitally engaged in the politics of law. If they did not prevail, still they were heard, and the content of social security, then and now, can be fully understood only in reaction to them. Understanding legal consciousness requires more than revealing the social meanings taken as natural in the use (often instrumental) and consequences of legal action or texts. For those discovered meanings to have more than abstract content there must also be consciousness of the alternatives and contexts, both historically situated and present, through which particular meanings become socially known and which frame their production and continued deployment. Especially if the production of ideas is no different in principle from the production of the material, meaning-laden world, legal consciousness includes the dialectic of the relations—read, as required, struggle—of social action correlated to law.[90]

To read the history of labor organization as exceptional depends upon comparisons of social history as if fully constructed by dominant power and institutions, including those prevailing in law. This involves two intellectual mistakes. First, the history of American labor politics as exceptional depends upon a historical determinism incompatible with workers' revealed actions. Second, the history of labor law as exceptional depends upon a distorted view of the making and interpretation of law. Neither the mistakes nor what actually happened are accidental. American labor law and labor politics *are* particular, and especially so in their interrelationship. Organized labor, however divided, allied politically with progressive scientific management to elect industrial pluralism as a structure of collective organization privatizing economic planning and legally preserved in the separation of investment and employment. At the same time, organized labor acceded to individualized risk pooling for social injuries, simultaneously rationalizing labor reserves. But these outcomes carry more than one layer of historical meaning. They represent rejection of a different legal-political ideology, but rejection in the context of an opposed and present alternative—that of social democracy and a social wage. Thus, to make America exceptional is to hide the political struggles immanent and visible in the very role of law; it pretends methodological virtue in legally forgetting what cannot indefinitely be ignored. The voices our history has lost echo in the misery the law and state still allow.

NOTES

Thanks to Martha Mahoney, Dan Ernst, Joel Rogers, Steve Diamond, Chris Tomlins, and Rob Rosen for discussion of earlier drafts, and to Joel Klaff for research assistance. The support of a grant for archival research from the Fund for Labor Studies is gratefully acknowledged.

1. Robert Larson, Secretary and Business Agent, United Brotherhood of Carpenters and Joiners of America Local 66, Jamestown, New York, to Senator Robert F. Wagner, 23 January 1935, Wagner Papers.

2. On Keynesian pump priming, see Weir 1988. On urban-liberal coalition, see Huthmacher 1968; on capitalist crisis, see Piven and Cloward 1971: 104–11.

3. H.R. 7598, 73rd Cong., 2d Sess., 2 February 1934.

4. Atleson 1983.

5. D. Montgomery 1987.

6. E. P. Thompson 1975: 258–69; 1963; Dawley 1989: 154.

7. Forbath 1989; J. Rogers 1990.

8. Fraser 1989: 78. On militancy and labor law, see J. Green 1972; Goldfield 1989.

9. *Report of Proceedings of the 41st Convention of the AFL,* 1921: 377.

10. Tomlins 1979.

11. Green to Charles W. Anderson, secretary, City and County Employees Joint Council, Minneapolis, Minnesota, 17 February 1931, AFL, Papers of the Office of the President.

12. Green to John M. Gancz, secretary, Lodge 7, International Association of Machinists, 19 February 1931, AFL, Papers of the Office of the President.

13. Green to Senator Robert Wagner, 21 July 1932, AFL, Papers of the Office of the President.

14. *Report of Proceedings of the 51st Convention of the AFL,* 1931:17.

15. AFL Executive Council Minutes, September 1930: 82, George Meany Archives.

16. William Green, Labor Day Address, AFL Official Information and Publicity Service, 5 September 1932, 3, George Meany Archives.

17. See also M. L. Farber 1959.

18. On unemployment insurance at the AFL convention, see P. Taft 1959: 19.

19. *Report of Proceedings of the 51st Convention, AFL,* 1931: 379, 378, 383, 396, 397.

20. A. W. Mills, organizer, Unemployed Council Committee for the National Hunger March, to Senator Robert Wagner, 3 December 1931, Wagner Papers. On the Unemployed Councils generally, see Leab 1969; Rosenzweig 1983.

21. A.F. of L. Trade Union Committee for Unemployment Insurance and Relief 1932: 15.

22. Herbert Benjamin confirmed that the bill was sponsored by both. Hearings on H.R. 7598, House Committee on Labor, 12 February 1934: 9.

23. A.F. of L. Trade Union Committee for Unemployment Insurance and Relief 1932: 7.

24. AFL Executive Council Minutes, 1932: 34, 36.

25. Green, *AFL Weekly News Service,* AFL, Papers of the Office of the President.

26. AFL Executive Council Minutes, 1932: 71–72.

27. A.F. of L. Trade Union Committee for Unemployment Insurance and Relief 1932.

28. Louis Weinstock Oral History (D. Bernhardt, comp., Tamiment Library, New York University): 20–26.

29. *Report of Proceedings of the 52nd Convention of the AFL,* 1932: 326, 327, 334, 342.

30. A.F. of L. Trade Union Committee for Unemployment Insurance and Relief 1934a: 42–43.

31. Kennedy, Secretary-Treasurer, UMW, "Unemployment Insurance," National Conference on Economic Security, 14 November 1934, AFL-CIO papers, clippings file, George Meany Archives.

32. AFL Executive Council Minutes, 1934: 92, 95.

33. Ibid., 54.

34. *Report of Proceedings of the 54th Convention of the AFL,* 1934: 599.

35. A.F. of L. Trade Union Committee for Unemployment Insurance and Relief 1935: 33–39.

36. U.S. Congress 1934: 22.

37. Green to George W. Butler, 4 September 1934, Ernest Lundeen Papers.

38. Butler to William Green, September 1934, Ernest Lundeen Papers.

39. A.F. of L. Trade Union Committee for Unemployment Insurance and Relief.

40. Britton to William Green, 16 January 1935, AFL, Papers of the Office of the President.

41. Green to W. W. Britton, 23 January 1935, AFL, Papers of the Office of the President.

42. Green to G. Heath, secretary, Kalamazoo Federation of Labor, 30 December 1935, AFL, Papers of the Office of the President.

43. Green to E. H. Helterbraun, 15 December 1935, AFL, Papers of the Office of the President.

44. James D. Graham, president, Montana State Federation of Labor, to William Green, 2 January 1936, AFL, Papers of the Office of the President.

45. Green to Bert Graham, president, UMW Local 3506, Russellton, Pennsylvania, AFL, Papers of the Office of the President.

46. Robinson to William Green, 27 August 1935, AFL, Papers of the Office of the President.

47. Committee for Industrial Organization, 1935: 7 [emphasis in original].

48. Committee for Industrial Organization, 1936: 5.

49. Rosenzweig 1983: 169, 182.

50. Louis Weinstock Oral History: 27–28.

51. *Rank and File Federationist*, 1, no. 6, 1934: 5.

52. *Rank and File Federationist*, 1, no. 8, 1934: 3.

53. *Rank and File Federationist*, 2, no. 5, 1935.

54. Federal Trade Commission, 24 November 1936, George Meany Archives.

55. Louis Weinstock Oral History: 30.

56. National Congress for Unemployment and Social Insurance, 1935: 2.

57. Communications from benefit societies, ethnic organizations, unemployed councils to Senator Robert Wagner, Wagner Papers.

58. Enest Lundeen Papers.

59. Ibid.

60. U.S. Congress 1935: 129–30.

61. New York *Post*, 2 April 1935, Ernest Lundeen Papers.

62. Jesse L. Keyser to Ernest Lundeen, 15 February 1935, Ernest Lundeen Papers.

63. For the role of the Farmer-Labor Party in Minnesota politics, see Valelly 1989.

64. On Mary Van Kleeck, see Alchon 1985. Harvey Klehr credits the drafting of the Workers' Bill to the Communist party, based on an interview with Herbert Benjamin and various claims of sponsorship during the hearings. See Klehr 1984: 284–89.

65. Draft, Workers' Unemployment and Social Insurance Law, Ernest Lundeen Papers.

66. Douglas 1939: 80.

67. Lundeen to "Dear Friend," 22 March 1935, Ernest Lundeen Papers.

68. Wagner to T. B. Hallock, secretary, Workers' Unemployed Union, Local 4, New York City, Robert F. Wagner Papers.

69. National Congress for Unemployment and Social Insurance 1935: 4.

70. Van Kleeck, Address before the National Congress for Unemployment and Social Insurance, 5–7 January 1935, Ernest Lundeen Papers [emphasis in original].

71. Quadagno 1984. But see also D. Nelson 1969.

72. Edmund Witte Papers.

73. Connery to Benjamin E. Waite, 7 January 1935, Ernest Lundeen Papers.

74. Ernest Lundeen Papers.

75. Lundeen to Walter Frank, 27 April 1935, Ernest Lundeen Papers.

76. A.F. of L. Trade Union Committee for Unemployment Insurance and Relief 1935: 8–9, 11.

77. Testimony of Roy Hallas, president, Revival Lodge 169, Amalgamated Association of Iron, Steel and Tin Workers, Clairton, Pennsylvania, in U.S. Congress 1935: 20.

78. Testimony of F. Elmer Brown, ibid.: 23, 24.

79. Van Kleeck, Committee on Labor, 5 February 1935, Ernest Lundeen Papers.

80. Van Kleeck 1934: 123.

81. Ibid., 121.

82. For development of the ideas behind the Wagner Act, see Casebeer 1987, 1989a.

83. Klare 1978.

84. Leon Keyserling, interview with the author, 3–4 March 1985.

85. Van Kleeck to Senator Robert Wagner, 12 March 1934, Leon Keyserling Papers.

86. Report on H.R. 2827, House Committee on Labor, 5, 15 March 1935.

87. Van Kleeck, Address, National Congress for Unemployment and Social Insurance, Ernest Lundeen Papers.

88. For development of the relation between contemporary unemployment insurance and the at-will contract, see Casebeer 1985.

89. Van Kleeck 1936: 12, 13.

90. Casebeer 1989b.

10 The Regulation of Homework and the Devolution of the Postwar Labor Standards Regime: Beyond Dichotomy

Eileen Boris

The labor standards regime forged in the New Deal era defined the worker as male. As the labor force participation of mothers with small children soared in the 1980s, however, the working mother became a national policy issue.[1] At the same time, industrial homework, or paid labor in the home for an employer, resurfaced as a political question, provoking renewed debate over the bans on industrial homework under the Fair Labor Standards Act (FLSA). These two issues—the working mother and industrial homework—were not unrelated because mothers with small children predominated among homeworkers.

This essay situates the 1980 debate in its historical context. In the early 1940s, industrial homework was prohibited in seven garment-related industries. The bans, administrative rulings by the Department of Labor's newly formed Wage and Hour Division, were the culmination of a half-century-long crusade to save the home from the factory by removing paid labor from family dwellings. They served as a crucial mechanism sustaining the key provisions of FLSA itself: minimum wages, maximum hours, and child labor limits. The bans were upheld by the Supreme Court in 1945.[2]

Before we can understand the debate over homework we must recognize its dependence on women's unpaid domestic labor and the social construction of gender that justifies women's position in both the family and the labor market. Recent feminist theory has challenged the dichotomies embedded in the practice of homework and the labor standards enacted to undermine that practice. It has shown how the division of the world into male and female, public and private, work and home, is a man-made and not a natural phenomenon. As the philosopher Carol Pateman has explained, "The private or personal and the public or political are held to be separate from and irrelevant to each other; women's everyday experience confirms this separation yet, simultaneously, it denies it and affirms the integral connection between the two spheres. The separation of the private and public is both part of our actual lives and an ideological mystification."[3] Though theorized in liberal political thought as separate spheres, the home and the workplace actually are interconnected. Not only is the home one form of workplace, but power and status in the home influence the position of women, especially mothers, in other spaces—the office, factory, school, court, and legislature.

The homework debate reflects, even as it exposes, this dichotomous mindset in our labor standards regime, a mindset that has made those labor standards simultaneously inadequate to meet the needs of working people and vulnerable to right-wing attack. This essay, then, addresses two forms of dichotomy: the regulatory dichotomy between home and workplace created by FLSA and the ideological dichotomy upon which that regulatory division into home and workplace rested. My critique of both regulatory and ideological dichotomy stems from a historical analysis of the continuous pressures for and against homework, a context influenced by economic, legal, and social factors.

FLSA—and by extension the entire postwar labor standards regime for which it stood as the linchpin—addressed labor standards at the workplace. Only in banning homework did it consider the ways that the workplace related to the home. Its basic assumptions overlooked the underlying reasons for homework and thus failed to confront why women, particularly married women with children, were homeworkers. In particular, it failed to take into account the divisions of labor by sex, race/ethnicity, age, and kinship position that characterize both homes and other workplaces. The labor liberals who crafted FLSA assumed that the home was properly a separate realm from the workplace, that the private world of the family needed protection from intrusion by the all too public market.[4] To them homework was an evil, in large part because it represented the invasion of the home, the site of domesticity and the family, by the factory, the site of work. Such a characterization elided the unpaid labor of child care, housework, and sex/affective production[5] engaged in by women, particularly mothers, in the home. This of course was the very labor that rationalized homework in the minds of employers. Employers sought to profit from the sexual division of labor that limited the options of some women and made homework appear attractive to those whose unpaid workload or cultural values kept them at home.[6]

The current debate over homework starkly reveals the dichotomy built into the law and our thinking about the relationship between home and workplace. This essay asks us to recognize and move beyond dichotomy, not by accepting the right-wing demand that homes again become simply one more place for worker exploitation, but by reformulating our understanding of labor standards.

PROTECTING MOTHERHOOD: THE ORIGINS OF FLSA

The Fair Labor Standards Act represented a new strategy for an old crusade: the ending of sweated labor, reinterpreted during the 1930s as state provision of "the minimum standard of living necessary for health, efficiency, and general well-being of workers."[7] Significantly, the living standards upon which the Roosevelt Department of Labor calculated such minima assumed a nuclear family unit with a blue-collar male breadwinner and a wife who did all her own housework.[8] This assumption continued one strand of thinking prominent among a generation of women social reformers who pioneered labor legislation: the creation of a family wage for men so that mothers could remain at home. Single women could benefit from labor standards; indeed, they needed aid to become self-supporting. However, the mother overwhelmingly subsumed all of womanhood in reform thought. Reformers understood that social welfare and labor standards were intertwined; policies at the workplace would affect home life. Ridding the workplace of exploitative conditions would keep the home free from paid labor and thus able to perform its function as a place of nurturance.[9]

FLSA was the climax of a nearly half-century-long quest for protective labor standards which had taken the form of a campaign for maximum hour and minimum wage laws for women and child labor restrictions for minors.[10] Yet FLSA referred to workers, not women. The gender-neutral language was a consequence of the act's constitutional grounding in the commerce clause, which gave the federal government authority to regulate interstate activities. Through this justification, with its emphasis on the state's right to protect the economy from unfair practices, labor standards proponents sought an escape from the "gender trap" that historically had associated labor standards with the protection of women and children—although this line of reasoning had been seriously stymied in the 1920s both by *Adkins v. Children's Hospital*, which struck down Washington, D.C.'s model minimum wage law,[11] and by activist women's disagreements over the Equal Rights Amendment (ERA).[12]

Previous legal decisions had encouraged the development of gendered, as opposed to class-based, legislation. Conservative interpretation of the Fourteenth Amendment championed "freedom of contract," which applied only to the actions of adult men.[13] Such reasoning had led New York's highest court to strike down a law prohibiting cigar making in tenement houses, the first major regulation of industrial homework, because "it cannot be perceived how the cigarmaker is to be improved in his health or his morals by forcing him from his home and its hallowed associations and beneficent influences, to ply his trade elsewhere."[14] While the 1898 Supreme Court decision in *Holden v. Hardy* sustained an hour limit for miners,[15] suggesting that state interference in the labor contract would be tolerated when a trade was dangerous and detrimental to the health of the worker, less than ten years later *Lochner v. New York*, which negated a law limiting the hours of bakers,[16] set an unreasonably high standard of proof when it came to male workers.

In contrast to the Supreme Court, state courts during the late nineteenth and early twentieth centuries inched toward upholding labor legislation. Yet their decisions were gendered, with standards for women and children different from those for male workers. Courts accepted laws that applied to large numbers of men—like those providing workmen's compensation—out of a sense of universal entitlement, sometimes based on contract rights. When it came to women and children, however, courts relied on their public/legal status as dependent and powerless and their presumed biological status as weaker to justify what came to be known as protective labor legislation.[17]

This trend culminated in the Supreme Court's 1908 decision *Muller v. Oregon*, which sustained a maximum-hour law for women.[18] The court upheld the use of police power to protect the welfare of women, seen as mothers or potential mothers, by collapsing the category "female worker" into the category "mother," suggesting a unity between family status and workplace, private and public, gender economy and political economy. It categorized "women" differently from "men," thus sustaining a dichotomy based on biology.[19]

Such reasoning led reformers like Florence Kelley of the National Consumers' League (NCL) to structure a new campaign for the minimum wage around the state's interest in protecting women.[20] Gaining labor standards for some workers would be the entering wedge for improving the conditions of all workers. Legal strategy here reinforced the belief of women reformers that female vulnerability—which stemmed from both women's unorganized position in the labor market and their additional responsibility for home and children along with wage labor—necessitated state action. Yet while reformers, led by the woman-centered NCL, sought to advance the status of wage-laboring women, they often defined them in terms of the family and as mothers. Only the most perceptive of reformers viewed women's lives holistically. Because they considered women's family labor and wage labor as part of a continuum, they argued that mothers needed more leisure and less work.

Nonetheless they sought to separate the home from the workplace. Industrial homework, a prominent form of sweated labor particularly in the garment trades, was the one evil of modern industrial life that the NCL, the Women's Trade Union League (WTUL), and other labor reformers found particularly dangerous because this form of wage labor invaded the domestic realm, breaking down the separation of private from public. It degraded home life, forcing mothers to sweat their own children and allowing fathers, who appeared lazy, to place the burden of breadwinning upon these overburdened housekeepers. It encouraged mothers to earn instead of care for their children and children to labor instead of attend school or play outdoors; that is, it stunted childhood and perverted motherhood. Moreover, homework stood in the way of the family wage for men and minimum wages for those women, often without men, whose poverty compelled them to earn. It lowered the wages and working conditions of factory workers while giving "chiseling" employers an unfair advantage over those who paid decent wages for reasonable hours. Its dirty and diseased products threatened the homes of consumers. Thus homework had a double impact: it lowered labor standards and destroyed the home in the process.[21]

Before FLSA, reformers fought for labor standards in the name of motherhood and the family and against exploitation and inefficiency. Minimum wages and maximum hours, it was thought, would eliminate homework. Yet the persistence of paid labor in the home could undermine such laws by shifting work from the factory to such a lower-waged space. Hence more than one hundred of the codes under the National Recovery Administration (NRA) restricted homework as a means to enforce wage, hour, and child labor standards; protection of the family wage for men and motherhood for women was given in justification for such actions.[22] After the Supreme Court declared the NRA unconstitutional in 1935, the women of the Labor Department—many of whom had served an apprenticeship in reform under Florence Kelley and maintained close ties with the NCL and the WTUL[23]—turned to state laws and joint federal-state administrative efforts to curb homework. They were joined by those unions most affected by competition from low-wage homework, particularly the International Ladies' Garment Workers Union (ILGWU) and the Amalgamated Clothing Workers of America (ACWA).[24] New York's model law of

1935 linked the "public interest of the community at large in . . . [the] health and well-being" of women and minors with "the protection of factory industries" from the unscrupulous competition of homeworkers.[25] To save the home from the factory, the factory would have to be protected from the home.

THE PLACE OF THE HOME UNDER FLSA

The legislative history of FLSA can only be described as tortuous. The Senate and House versions differed significantly in their basic mechanisms and were amended repeatedly over nearly a two-year period. Prohibition of industrial homework went in and out as a specified element.[26] Within days of the introduction of the bill, the ILGWU was advising its sponsor Senator Hugo Black (D., Alabama) that "there should be . . . a provision that Industrial Homework shall be prohibited on findings of oppressive labor practices."[27] Secretary of Labor Frances Perkins, a key member of the women's reform network, firmly supported such an addition, calling for a board to prevent "circumvention of the Act . . . through the use of agents, independent contractors, subsidiary or controlled companies, or home or off-premise employees."[28]

Whether homeworkers, who were generally understood to be "women and minors," could be classified as "employees," and thus subjected to the bill, troubled those within the administration. "Independent contractor" was thought to be "the legal status of most 'homeworkers'." An independent contractor would not come under the definition of an employee as one who was "suffered or permitted to work." Although by 1937, the Social Security Administration, the Bureau of Internal Revenue, and state unemployment compensation boards all had ruled that homeworkers fell within the employer-employee relation, until the Supreme Court considered the matter such decisions rested, according to Roosevelt administration counsels, on "some 'natural' justice, rather than considered and supported legal opinions."[29] Women predominated in this shadow population. Yet because there was strong pressure to prohibit interference with the objectives of FLSA, their work site, the home, would be covered—though not specified—in the final version of the act. The act also included both fixed statutory wages and an administrative board to review those industries selected to receive the mandated minimum wage more rapidly than the statute proposed—a board that would be used to save the factory from the home by restricting homework.[30]

The first interpretive bulletin of the Wage and Hour Division, organized within the Department of Labor to administer FLSA, declared that the employee relation, not the site of labor, determined coverage under the act.[31] Hearings were held in January 1939 to determine whether special or additional records were needed for homework, and new regulations were announced a month later. Based on a handbook system, these required that the employer keep data on each worker and agent or contractor, recording for each work week information that would help determine hours worked and rates of pay. Homeworkers were to retain their own book.[32] Home and work were being linked, though not because administrators desired such an association, but because they expected to find it impossible for employers and homeworkers to keep accurate records. The idea was to use the handbooks as evidence that homework was a practice that by definition violated FLSA hour and wage mandates.

Representatives of industrial associations, appearing before the special record-keeping hearings in 1939, justified homework on grounds that it was performed by women, often rural and sometimes handicapped, in the home. "It is not a vocation; the money is not primarily earned for purposes of livelihood support, but it is a form of supplemental income," claimed the executive director of the National Knitted Outer Wear Association. Women working only a few hours in their spare time accounted for the average earnings of only a few dollars a week. It would be "almost impossible to assume that they would keep a record of every five minutes they spent knitting, between taking care of the baby or cooking the meals at home." For its part, the National Association of Leather Glove Manufacturers put forward a view of homework as a logical component of a woman's life cycle:

> She may come in to a factory, say, at 18 or 21. She may stay in there until she reaches the age of 24 or the age when she decides she is going to get married. If she is a very good operator naturally the factory dislikes to lose her, so some arrangements are made whereby she can continue to work for the factory and at the same time run her home. Arrangements are made whereby she can get a machine and do work at home. Then again, she may be marrying one whose income she feels is not sufficient to maintain her at the standard she would care to live and she would like to do this home work and get this supplemental income, and she more or less notifies the factory that she is now a home worker and would be willing to accept work in her home.

While male trade unionists and women New Dealers rejected employers' characterizations of such work as supplemental rather than necessary, they agreed that homeworkers were usually mothers, rein-

forcing the association of such women with the home. They recognized, however, that employers structured homework industries so
that these women had few other options and, in addition, so that
unionization would be impeded. Moreover, they felt that homework
mocked the idea of home. The ILGWU's lawyer put the argument in
time-honored form: "We are used to thinking of home as the man's
castle, a place to live in, and I think we have a 'Home Sweet Home,'
a very sentimental song, but" the long hours, low wages, and child
labor of the "Typical Home Worker" were rewriting that title to "Home
Sweat Home." The home location of homework posed a danger to
FLSA, Clara Beyer of the Division of Labor Standards asserted, because
you could not control hours or even the number of people engaged in
the work.[33]

What trade unionists and administrators saw as "little neighborly
groups who come in and sit around together and work and chat,"
making it impossible to calculate an adequate minimum wage, industry representatives described as part of the leisurely routine of small
town life. A woman "might start at eleven o'clock and after lunch she
would begin about two in the afternoon. The women from the church
come over there and sit around and talk until five o'clock at night."
In fact, over the years, investigators reported deliberate falsifications
of record-keeping books. In some cases homeworkers used books filled
in advance by their employers that would make piece rates come out
exactly to a forty-hour week at minimum wage.[34]

Not all accepted the ruling that the home stood within the jurisdiction of the Wage and Hour administrator. While some employers
attempted to circumvent FLSA by classifying their workers as "independent contractors" or creating "cooperative" schemes, others contended that the act never meant to apply to homework.[35] First in 1939
and again in 1949 and 1955, congressmen proposed amendments to
exempt rural homeworkers from FLSA—a provision suggested (but
then dropped under a flood of negative public comments) by Secretary
of Labor Raymond Donovan during the renewed 1980s debate. Always
coupled with the concern to safeguard employment in such areas, these
rural homework exemptions neglected the national extent of the
homework system, discriminating on the basis of residence. They
would undercut federal efforts to regulate because employers could
move homework operations to such uncovered areas.[36]

Conservatives argued for such exemptions in terms of the needs
or desires of rural *women*, not economic or geographic factors alone.
Tennessee Representative John Cooper (D.) introduced an amendment
in 1949 to allow women in his district to continue to crochet baby
bonnets at home. His amendment used gender-neutral language, re-

ferring to "rural person," but because Cooper accepted the home labor of his constituents as natural he did not have to specify its gendered nature. Implicitly understanding the social circumstances of home-work—its function as an income-generating activity for farm women without other means to earn cash—such amendments or their spon-sors never questioned the association of underpaid labor with women.[37] Opponents agreed that they were talking about women, but were more reluctant to undervalue the labor of rural women. As one New York state labor official and member of the women's reform network argued, "The needs of farm women are as great as those of their city sisters. Their labor has the same intrinsic value as that of other workers in the productive process."[38]

This history of employer subterfuge and congressional wrangling prefigured direct challenges to the authority of the administrator over the regulation of labor standards for the home. Under the act, the Wage and Hour administrator had the power to determine minimum wages until the statutory level of 40 cents an hour came into effect in 1945. During World War II, with labor and materials in short supply,[39] the administrator prohibited industrial homework in seven industries— jewelry, gloves and mittens, knitted outerwear, button and buckle, women's apparel, handkerchiefs, and embroideries—in the belief that otherwise FLSA could not be sustained. These industries shared key structural conditions that encouraged homework: seasonal cycles, un-dercapitalized firms and low initial capital requirements, fierce com-petition, unstable markets, hand or simple machine processes. Unions had organized the larger employers in each industry, and this partial organization on the part of both unions and associations of firms with union contracts provided the political pressure for homework restric-tion. In addition, the garment unions, particularly the ACWA under Sidney Hillman, were prominent members within the New Deal co-alition. Employer misuse of existing state and federal handbook sys-tems offered further justification for allies in the Department of Labor to gain tighter controls over homework.[40]

Restricting homework meant "no work shall be done in or about a home, apartment, tenement, or room in a residential establishment . . . except by persons who have obtained home work certificates." As with the NRA, the elderly and disabled or their caretakers could gain a certificate to perform homework. Regulations required such persons to have been engaged in homework in the industry before the date of restriction. By the end of 1945, certified homeworkers represented merely 15 percent of the number estimated to have existed before restriction.[41] By 1950, Wage and Hour had granted a mere 4,369 ap-plications for certificates, with another 1,570 for the glove and mitten industry handed out by New York for the federal agency.[42]

During the wartime hearings before the administrative bans, homework supporters sought to wrap themselves up in the flag of patriotism while embracing the sentimentality of mother love. The 1942 testimony of Fulton County (New York) glove sewer Mrs. Emma Nellis, president of what was apparently an employer-instigated "Homeworkers Federation," typified such arguments:

I'd overthrow that ban again
For there is [sic] stamps and bonds to buy
I say, we'll lift that ban once more
Give those homeworkers a try.

She most dramatically presented a discourse that, with minor variations, had characterized employer arguments during the NRA period and again would dominate the 1980s controversy. Claiming authority from her experience as a homeworker for more than twenty years who had also worked in the factory and was a mother, Nellis declared, "As the [homework] order considers invalids, we consider mothers with tiny children in the same class. Yet no consideration is given to the children. We are told to put them in day nurseries, children's homes, or institutions. What kind of a country would we have if we were all brought up without the benefit of our own homes? . . . Could it be possible that you think the head of an institution and the institution itself can take the place of a mother and a home of your own?" Nellis recounted the stories of women met during house-to-house canvassing for the federation, which numbered 1,119 members and purported to represent thousands more. Women with five and eight children each begged for the continuance of homework; they lived beyond bus lines, could not find competent girls to babysit, and feared they would be unable to provide necessities or higher education for their children. Forced into factories by New York state administrative orders, these women were, according to Nellis, "frantic" and "nervous" as their children roamed the streets. Nellis's comment about one such mother summarized the reliance of homework defenders on cultural associations of women with mothers and mothers with the home: "This woman doesn't want or ask relief; all she wants is her Homework and we think she certainly needs to be in her own home."[43]

In contrast, labor standards defender Clara Beyer—who felt about homework, it was said, "like the preacher . . . towards sin"[44]—over and over again emphasized the inefficiency of such labor, its connection with child labor and exploitative working conditions, its erosion of the minimum wage, and its waste of resources during wartime. Numerous investigations, she argued, proved "that the presence of children in the home does not prevent women from doing factory work." Indeed, studies tracing the impact of homework curtailment in New York state revealed "the presence of children in the family was not a deterrent in finding outside employment."[45] In the midst of World War II, when mothers were taking defense jobs and child care became a public need,[46] women reformers dropped their previous opposition to the paid labor of mothers except under desperate circumstances. They understood that, given economic incentives, mothers would leave the home for the factory, even without adequate child care. They refused to be swayed by their own domestic preferences for such women, for they judged homework more damaging to social life than even maternal employment. In contrast, their male counterparts in the Wage and Hour administration had trouble seeing beyond the homeworker as "the married woman with small children that she can't leave and she can't afford to have anybody take care of. . . . Perhaps she may need, very much need, to get that or some other sort of work that she could do."[47]

Homework opponents within the DOL had the political power to counter even the sympathetic responses that defenders elicited in some male administrators; with the support of the clothing unions and state departments of labor, they won administrative bans between 1941 and 1944. Employers, however, challenged the authority of the administrator, and a suit initiated by embroidery manufacturers reached the Supreme Court. Here what was at stake was not "the question whether home work is desirable or undesirable from a social point of view or as a form of economic organization" (the questions once foremost in the minds of women reformers) but "whether the home work system . . . furnishes a means of circumventing or evading a wage order." That is, legal arguments advanced by the administration considered the social context of homework only as evidence for the impossibility of adequately regulating wages and hours.[48]

Precisely why these families turned to homework or what possible alternatives existed for them never entered the regulatory discourse. That turned on the narrow question of whether the administrator indeed had overstepped his authority, a question that the Supreme Court answered by agreeing that homework was not a separate industry but "conducted largely by the same employers who maintain factory establishments or by 'contractors' who are in competition with such employers." The bans would not bring undue unemployment, it was said, because employers would transfer work into factories. The gender of homeworkers—their need for protection because they were women and minors, as earlier statutes had argued, or the reluctance to leave the home for the factory that many of these caretakers of dependents and their defenders felt—played no role in this opinion. Despite the argument of plaintiffs that the rulings were "experimental social legislation" rather than a "method of enforcement" and thus beyond the coverage of the statute, the court accepted the narrower parameters of the administrator.[49] Congress in 1949 incorporated these homework restrictions as section 11 (d) of FLSA, finally providing explicit language on homework regulation. Despite other amendments to FLSA, none in relation to homework passed over the years; nor did the administrator make any additional rulings of note until the Reagan era challenge to 11 (d) itself.[50]

The social realities behind homework continued to deny the terms of the legal system. During the 1950s, for example, business services became a growth area for homework. A 1958 study of homework under FLSA, the only one conducted after the restrictions were set in place, found that a mere 22 percent of the more than twenty-two thousand homeworkers surveyed felt they could adjust to factory labor, while 50 percent claimed a "need to stay home to care for young children" as their reason for homework. This was particularly true in the nonrestricted industries because, as we have seen, permits for the restricted industries were limited to those by definition unable to leave the home. That 69 percent of homeworkers in nonmanufacturing industries listed child care as their reason for homework and seven thousand of them were typists suggests that a changing political economy of white-collar work had found a flexible labor force in such mothers.[51] Indeed, Milton Derber, a noted professor of industrial relations and opponent of the "evils" of homework, concluded his own 1958 survey with a defense of the "useful social function" behind legitimate (that is, "properly supervised" so not to disregard any labor standards) homework: It provided work for both the disabled and "the housewife and mother who is generally preoccupied with the concerns of her family but who may wish to supplement the family income."[52]

Such an ideology of "sexual romanticism"[53] dominated early postwar thinking and justified nonindustrial, home-based labor. In the conservative political climate of the 1950s, when 95 percent of all women married, functionalist sociology designated the family as the site of women's work. Employers continued to discriminate against women in hiring and pay; state funding for child care ended in 1948, and the legal system gave preference to men. New standards increased time spent on housework, and household appliances brought some tasks, like clothes washing, back to the home, but technology generally provided more time for the venerated work of mothering. Moreover, suburbanization in these years took white housewives away from the location of employment. Yet despite these factors, women increasingly entered the paid labor force: one third of white women and one-half of black women worked during the child-bearing years from twenty-five through thirty-four. From the 1950s into the late 1960s, many white women, in particular, would work before marriage, leave with the birth of their first child, and return to nondomestic paid employment after their last child started school.[54] Homework certainly would have fitted into this life pattern; part-time work did, growing from one-quarter of women in the labor force in 1950 to one-third a decade later, with three-fifths of them married.[55]

The social and demographic factors that encouraged homework for white women in the clerical and business service sector also curtailed the labor supply for older forms of homework. Along with the continuing political strength of the garment unions in the 1950s and early 1960s, employer shifting of some product lines abroad, and technological and market changes,[56] this growth in female labor force participation suggested a decline in industrial homework.

Yet litigation from the 1950s through the 1970s failed to recognize the social sources of homework and its dependence on the sexual division of labor. Courts continued to address just the scope of FLSA.[57] The separation of home from waged workplace became as unstated an assumption as the responsibility of mothers to remain at home for their children. That second assumption, accepted by many women themselves, conflicted with the needs of their families for additional income, which in the early postwar world, as during previous decades, could undermine the first. Critics of homework, especially in the trade union movement, failed to consider such a contradiction; it was not part of their ideological or political agenda. They continued to celebrate legal victories against home-employing firms without asking, for example, why homeworkers continued to knit bootees.[58] For the public at large, and policy makers themselves, homework had become a non-issue, a relic of the past.[59]

THE WORKING MOTHER AND THE DEREGULATION OF HOMEWORK IN THE 1980S

During the 1980s, the working mother stood at the center of the renewed political debate over the regulation of homework. Whether seen as a potential welfare recipient, a harried half of a dual earner couple, an isolated farmwife, or a victimized immigrant, mothers have been both the subjects of this controversy and the objects of policy making. Rarely have they been actors in their own right. The deregulation campaign reflected national tension over the issue of mothers and paid labor as well as ideological disagreements over the role of the state in the economy, the relationship between family/home and work/ wage earning, and the feminist challenge to the sex segmentation of social life. Deregulators emphasized freedom or lack of it under the homework rules; for defenders of the bans, homeworkers became victims of the marketplace rather than the state. This debate also represented an attempt by certain sectors of capital to increase U.S. competitiveness through the creation of low-wage jobs for women. Deregulators first justified their policies in the name of the traditional family, but in a period when liberal feminism had influenced public discourse, some defended homework in the name of women's rights— specifically, the right to choose the domestic realm as the site of one's labor.[60]

Recent research on the demand for homework has suggested that, as in the past, for employers in undercapitalized and seasonal industries, homework can represent an opportunity to save on labor costs and overhead and also to adjust to fluctuating markets. For small-batch production, homework can be more efficient than a factory location. As a result, particularly in the "sick" garment industries, the deregulation of homework has become central to the conflict between employers and unions: as the garment unions weakened and economic and political refugees from the Americas and Asia entered the work force during the 1970s, garment manufacturers found that they no longer needed to turn abroad for cheap labor. Perhaps even more important than this economic development, however, was the promise of white-collar, home-based labor through word processing and other computer applications. Fear of future restrictions against computer homework undoubtedly fueled the impulse to deregulate the old garment trades.[61] Thus in an important sense, the recent battle over industrial homework has become the first round in a struggle over what former Secretary of Labor Ann McLaughlin has called "open collar" labor,[62] in which computers facilitate the decentralization of labor.

The possibility of labor cost economies, then, has fed the deregulators' dream of opening up entrepreneurial freedom, reminding us that the way employers structure the labor market is far more influential in determining its character and operation than worker preference. In another sense, the revival of the homework debate has belonged to the transformation of the labor market into a two-tier economy in which homework represents one form of contingent labor.[63] In either case, however, homework exists as a response to employer needs and perceptions as much as to the pressures some women face in their struggle to earn wages and to mother simultaneously. As historian Alice Kessler-Harris has explained in another context, a "vision of a labor market operating in response to the needs of women and the family . . . lacks any sense that employers, too, make choices in terms of their preconceptions about workers."[64]

The contemporary challenge to FLSA restrictions on homework in the seven garment-related trades grew out of a routine 1980 Wage and Hour investigation in Vermont that mushroomed into a conservative cause célèbre when a candidate for the Republican nomination for senator embraced the plight of knitwear companies and their homeworkers. The Vermont knitters captured national attention by portraying themselves as mothers assaulted by the state. The new Reagan administration responded in May 1981 by proposing to lift all FLSA homework restrictions. After a challenge by the ILGWU and the states of California and New York, the D.C. Circuit Court of Appeals held that lifting all bans would be "arbitrary and unreasoned," forcing another policy. The Department of Labor then devised a certification system (similar to earlier handbook systems) for knitted outerwear alone, which became effective in December 1984. Because of political opposition, it took from August 1986 until January 1988 to eliminate the ban on another five of the industries, an act which the ILGWU, Amalgamated Clothing and Textile Workers, Service Employees International Union, the states of New York and Illinois, and some employer associations challenged in court.[65] In December 1989, the U.S. District Court of the District of Columbia sustained the administration. Although the certification system in knitted outerwear has been a dismal failure, the court reasoned under the Administrative Procedure Act that the administration showed "reasoned decision, based on the record, that a certification system would be superior to a total homework ban in enforcing" FLSA.[66] The public comment period for rescinding the last restriction, on the large women's apparel industry, ended on May 5, 1989. The Bush administration had not then formally lifted this remaining ban on homework under FLSA but was expected to do so.[67]

These political changes occurred in a social context that made them appear liberatory, hiding their exploitative potential. By the last years of the 1980s, with a majority of mothers in the labor force and an upsurge in female-headed households, homework had emerged as a solution to the family-work dilemma. In a society that lacked adequate dependent care, it promised to end the overwork of the wage-earning mother forced to juggle family and market labor with commuting to work and transporting children to day care.[68] In announcing the deregulation of industrial homework in five industries on November 10, 1988, Ann McLaughlin declared, "The changing workforce demographics demand that we provide employment opportunities that allow workers the freedom to choose flexible alternatives including the ability to work in one's own home. Women, for example, have entered the workforce by the millions; homework adds a measure of worker flexibility and economic freedom."[69] The *Wall Street Journal* editorialized that this form of labor "increases family choices in work and child care. . . . The recision of the federal ban on homework represents a victory for American families."[70]

Despite such talk of "families," despite a discourse where "women" are subsumed under "families" and men desire an opportunity to stay home and parent, men's greater earning power would more likely predict which parent would "hold down work while looking after the children at home" even if gender socialization does not.[71] But speaking of "families" has been part of a disingenuous appeal to the dual earner couple that allows them to project their situation of relative resources and relative privilege onto the single or welfare mother and approve homework for her as a choice made out of freedom rather than from necessity. Moreover, homework has appealed to them because it promises to reduce welfare, so that the *Wall Street Journal* in the same editorial declared, "Single mothers, in particular, will have a potential source of income that won't entail costs for travel and child care."[72] Such discussions conflate the different forms of home-based labor—the traditional garment industries where immigrant women of color toil with the new clerical homework where white women predominate; the small business entrepreneur and independent contractor with the employee. Forgotten in this extolling of homework as a relief for women's double day is how it all too often has substituted for dependent care or living labor standards.[73]

The supply of homeworkers probably has existed in part because of a national failure to propose realistic solutions for working mothers, more so because of the influx of non-English-speaking groups desperate for any work. But despite the terms under which it has been discussed, homework deregulation has not fulfilled the goal of balancing home and family. Women have reported on the difficulty of watching their children and getting in their work hours.[74] Instead, deregulation has met the desire of some capitalists to weaken both trade unionism and state control over private business enterprise. The language of gender has provided the terrain for class conflict, even as some mothers, particularly in rural and immigrant districts, find homework their only option if they need wages.[75]

In the recent debate, the working mother has overshadowed economic factors, like labor standards. While the ILGWU has continued to speak of low wages, in the process stereotyping the homeworker as an exploited, ignorant immigrant,[76] deregulators have successfully focused on white, seemingly middle-class women, setting the terms even

for feminists, like Phoebe Jones-Schellenberg of the Wages for Housework campaign, who have attacked the suggestion that homework is
"advantageous to working women." By "using feminist rhetoric for
'choices' and 'opportunities in the workplace,'" she charged at a 1989
hearing, deregulators "claim to be responding to women's demands
for flexible hours and child care. In fact, just the opposite is the case.
Industrial homework imposes on women two jobs for way below the
price of one—a second job at below minimum wage on top of the first
job of unwaged housework and child rearing." Even if that wage topped
the low minimum of $3.35 an hour at the time, homeworking women
still would find themselves subject to a continuous workday, where
"the phone rings, someone comes to the door, the baby cries, the pot
boils over, you forget to record your time," whether they worked on
dresses or insurance claims.[77] Such a description of the homeworker
hardly differed from those given by employer representatives in 1939.
Yet it was precisely such home interference with labor standards that
FLSA sought to eliminate.

BEYOND DICHOTOMY

Discussion in the 1980s, both in the media and before government
committees, presented homework in the language of home, family,
and women's status.[78] The courts, however, restricted their opinions
to the scope of FLSA or administrative procedures.[79] Thus while deregulators made emotional and gendered arguments for homework as an
employment option, the ILGWU, in particular, had to fight on narrow
legal grounds.[80] The ILGWU failed to capture the public imagination
and in fact gave the impression that the labor movement was insensitive to the needs of working parents, even though some unions have
been pushing for child care as a contract benefit. Only when the
ILGWU began to use as its spokesperson Susan Cowell, who became
a vice president of the union during the course of the homework campaign, did it effectively counter administration rhetoric. Cowell plainly
told the public that homework was no solution to the problem of child
care, thus undermining the strongest appeal of its defenders.[81]

In the 1930s, all sides in the homework debate had glorified the
home but differed on whether homework served as a savior for the
family or a commercial invasion of motherhood and of the lives of
children. By the war years, some opponents were willing to reject the
argument that mothers could not leave their children for employment
in other places. In the 1980s controversy, some defenders of homework
still clung to the ideal of traditional womanhood but, after the revival
of feminism, were apt to speak of women's rights in terms not very

different from the *Adkins* court of the early 1920s, which saw the Nineteenth Amendment as breaking down any barriers to women's freedom of contract. Meanwhile, trade unionists defended homework restrictions in terms of protecting labor standards, citing how Reagan cutbacks on Department of Labor personnel made it impossible to monitor FLSA in existing areas, never mind nonrestricted homework.[82]

Although employees who worked at home fell under FLSA coverage, labor standards sought to raise wages and improve conditions in factories and later offices, hospitals, and other workplaces deemed "proper." The home as the center of the private sphere, it was thought, never should have belonged to the world of work, and it was this dichotomy of public/private, work/home, that guided policy makers even though the women reformers among them especially understood the interconnection of the two realms. This understanding in fact propelled them to end homework because of its negative impact on domestic and family life. Indeed, we could argue that homework was included under FLSA—before actual restrictions—with the hope of eradicating the practice by undermining the wage and hour advantages of homework employers. Thus the goal was to end home-based labor so that its monitoring would be unnecessary.

By relegating homework to a realm that would wither away, however, the 1950s generation of policy makers ignored the interconnection between homes and other workplaces. Although those who formulated the homework rules understood the social conditions behind homework, none even then directly confronted how the sexual division of social life, which valued mother care of children, organized the labor market so that some women would be available for homework. Policies for the workplace became disconnected from those for the home or family. FLSA assumed that in raising the male breadwinner's wage, it was improving the quality of life of families. But even at the time, women could not always count on men or did not want them; women also needed living wages, especially those who labored in service industries and agriculture, predominantly women of color, who were left uncovered by the interstate commerce limits of the act.[83] Indeed, such dualistic thinking ignored the historic reality faced by African American and other women of color who had never experienced a "public" separate from a "private" sphere, who more often than not had no choice but to leave the home in order to work.[84]

Part of the problem came from an ideological division of social policy into welfare or family policy, which dealt with women and children, and economic policy, which was for men. Welfare appeared as an alternative for the homeworking mother from the progressive era, when mothers' pensions first became part of the reform agenda.

As Mary Anderson, chief of the U.S. Women's Bureau, suggested in the 1930s, "The only thing to do about homework is to abolish it and to arrange for higher wages for the breadwinner in a family so that his wife and children do not have to supplement the family income by doing homework, or, if there is no regular breadwinner, to provide pensions or relief."[85] This gendered welfare system, where women received aid for their children and men gained unemployment, further separated the concept of labor standards from that of women's realm of home and family life.[86]

Despite its origins, then, minimum wages by the 1980s appeared to be a workplace and not a welfare issue. But the new demographics of the workplace—which by 1989 led some corporate leaders to question the separation of workplace from family or personal issues—challenges such a dualism. Family policy intersects with workplace issues.[87] Indeed, we must see child care and parental leave as labor standards and not merely family legislation, and occupational safety and minimum wage provisions as family legislation and not just labor standards. Family members are workers; what occurs in one place affects the other. To take one example, toxic chemicals in the workplace not only hurt workers but injure potential parents of both sexes; banning women from such workplaces has pushed them into lower-paid, female-dominated occupations and ultimately reaffirms existing power relations in the market as well as in the home. Forcing employers to clean up the workplace or devise seniority guarantees to workers of *either* sex unwilling to risk exposure to such chemicals would recognize the link between home and work, private and public, without advantaging men over women in either.[88]

Feminist theory argues that family and state, home and work, private and public are false dichotomies that sustain hierarchy. As political scientist Rosalind Petchesky has put it, "far from being separate from the private sphere of family and childbearing, the public realm of the state depends on that sphere and tries to shape it."[89] That is, women's work in the family, as well as power relations among family members, not only becomes a crucial factor (along with race and class) in shaping her position in the labor market but is itself contingent on public policies from taxation and immigration to welfare. Homework and its regulation exemplify this process. A deregulation policy that would undermine labor standards hardly serves the needs of working women who might discover in home-based labor a way to ease their double day, but who might also find that shifting the location of labor comes with a price. By sustaining the association of women with the home, policy makers place a barrier in the way of reorganizing social life to recognize the work and family obligations of us all.

NOTES

Thanks to Phyllis Palmer and Vivien Hart, for continued discussion on the Fair Labor Standards Act, and to Nelson Lichtenstein. The research for this essay was made possible by fellowships from Howard University, Vice-President for Academic Affairs, and the Woodrow Wilson International Center for Scholars.

1. Hewitt 1986; Rix 1987: 100–149, 306, especially figure 11.
2. *Gemsco v. Walling*, 324 U.S. 244.
3. Pateman 1989: 131.
4. F. E. Olson 1983: 1496–1578.
5. A. Ferguson 1989: 77–99.
6. Pleck 1979: 367–92; Kirk Blackwelder 1984.
7. *Fair Labor Standards Act*, Statutes at Large, 52, sec. 2 (a), 1060.
8. U.S. Department of Labor 1942, ix.
9. Kelley 1909: 90–96; Kessler-Harris 1975; Buhle 1981.
10. Boris 1986; Baer 1978; A. C. Hill 1979; Kessler-Harris 1984.
11. 261 U.S. 525 (1923).
12. Hart 1989: 319–43.
13. Erickson 1989.
14. *In re Jacobs*, 98 N.Y. 98 (1885); Forbath 1985; Boris 1991.
15. 169 U.S. 366 (1898).
16. 198 U.S. 45 (1905).
17. Urofsky 1985.
18. 208 U.S. 412 (1908).
19. Erickson 1989; F. E. Olson 1983: 1556–57.
20. Hart 1990.
21. Boris forthcoming.
22. Boris 1985.
23. "Conversation between Clara Mortenson Beyer and Vivien Hart, Washington, D.C., November 14, 1983," mimeograph, Clara Mortenson Beyer Papers.
24. Boris 1988.
25. Shallcross 1939: 213–17.
26. Brief for Petitioners, *Gemsco v. Walling*, Supreme Court of the United States, October Term, 1944, 10–19; Brief for Respondent, ibid., 33–52.
27. Merle D. Vincent to Hugo L. Black, 29 May 1937, sent to David Dubinsky, Box 81–7b, Dubinsky Papers.
28. "Prepared Statement of . . . Frances Perkins . . . June 4, 1937, before Joint Hearings . . . on Fair Labor Standards Bill of 1937," 5, in Perkins Papers, file "Fair Labor Standards Bill—1937."
29. John M. Gallagher to Thomas G. Corcoran, 9 August 1937, in Corcoran Papers, Box 255, folder 1.
30. Brief for Respondents, *Gemsco v. Walling*, 49; "Women in Industry: A Report to the Annual Meeting of the International Association of Governmental Labor Officials," 8–10 September 1938, Charleston, South Carolina, in Perkins Papers, Box 82.
31. DOL Wage and Hour Division, "Industrial Homework Records Reg-

ulation Announced," press release, 18 February 1939, in DOL Library, Washington, D.C.

32. Part 516.90 under Section 11 (c), FLSA. DOL Wage and Hour Division, "Progress Report on Homework Under the Fair Labor Standards Act," October 1940, vertical files, New York State DOL Library, Brooklyn; Official Report of the Proceedings before the Division of Wages and Hours of the Department of Labor, "In the Matter of: Hearing on Proposed Amendments to Part 516 of Regulations with Respect to the Keeping of Special or Additional Records by Employers of Industrial Home Workers, in the United States and Puerto Rico," Washington, D.C., 4–6 January 1939, in DOL library.

33. Testimony of Harold R. Lhove, James H. Casey, Jr., James Kennedy, Bertha Nienberg, Elias Lieberman, Clara Beyer, all in "Hearing on . . . Special . . . Records," 15, 232–3, 385–7, 458–61, 269, 489, 386, 441.

34. Testimony of Kennedy and Casey, ibid., 386, 441; "Progress Report," 10–11, 15.

35. *Jacobs v. Hand Knitcraft Institute, et al.,* 2 Labor Cases 144 (1939); *Goldberg v. Whitaker House Cooperative,* 366 U.S. 28 (1961).

36. National Consumers' League Papers, reels 54, 55 *passim.*; Brief for Appellees and Brief for Appellants, *International Ladies' Garment Workers' Union et. al. v. Raymond Donovan et al.,* U.S. Court of Appeals for the District of Columbia Circuit (no. 82–2133).

37. On Cooper, see Brief for the Petitioner, *Mitchell v. Whitaker House Cooperative,* U.S. Supreme Court, October Term, 1960, (n. 274), 20–45.

38. Kate Papert to Representative Robert Ramspeck, 12 June 1939, 4, vertical files, N.Y. DOL Library.

39. New York DOL Division of Women, Child Labor, and Minimum Wage, "Trends in Homework Industries in New York State," typescript, August 1944, N.Y. DOL library.

40. Boris 1988: 15–18.

41. DOL Wage and Hour and Public Contracts Division, "Industrial Home Work and the Fair Labor Standards Act," mimeographed bulletin G-436, revised December 1947, 3–6, DOL Library.

42. U.S. Department of Labor 1951: 313, Appendix table J.

43. DOL Wage and Hour Division, "In the Matter of the Minimum Wage Recommendation of Industry Committee No. 40 for the Gloves and Mittens Industry," 20 April 1942, 40–45; 2 March 1942, 188–90, typescripts, DOL library.

44. Comment by Examiner Campbell, Committee No. 40 Hearing, 2 March 1942, 74, DOL library.

45. Beyer testimony, 48–66, particularly 60; Papert testimony, 93; both in ibid.

46. Hartmann 1982; K. Anderson 1981.

47. Campbell, Committee No. 40 Hearing, 134.

48. *Gemsco v. Walling,* on Writs of Certiorari to the United States Circuit Court of Appeals for the Second Circuit, Supreme Court of the United States, October Term 1944, no. 368 (Washington: Judd & Detweiler Printers), 80, 102, 75, 92–98.

49. Ibid., 9–15.

50. DOL Wage and Hour and Public Contracts Divisions, Division of Regulation and Research, Branch of Research and Statistics, "Employment of Homeworkers under the Fair Labor Standards Act," July 1959, 20–21, mimeograph, DOL library.

51. Ibid., particularly 2–5, 7–8; Derber 1958: 7, 10.

52. Derber 1958: 10.

53. Gatlin 1987: 8, 11.

54. Klein 1984: 39.

55. Gatlin 1987: 3–73, particularly 25, 29, 30–32; Householder Van Horn 1988: 124–49; Klein 1984: 32–46; see also, Tyler May 1988.

56. New York DOL, *Report on the Garment Industry in New York City*, Publication No. B-231, 1 February 1982; interview with Hugh McDaid, Chief of the Sweatshop Investigation Unit, N.Y. DOL, January 1987.

57. *Goldberg v. Whitaker House Cooperative*, 366 U.S. 28 (1961); *Hodgson v. Cactus Craft of Arizona*, 480 F.2d 464 (9th Cir. 1973); *Hodgson v. Rancourt*, 336 F. Supp. 1119 (D.R.I. 1972); *Wirtz v. McGhee*, 244 F. Supp. 412 (E.D.S.C. 1965). See Clash MacFarlane 1985: 117–23.

58. For example, David Dubinsky, ILGWU President, to Meyer Perlstein, 7 January 1955, informing him of wage and hour victory in the case of Flagstaff Knitting Mills (Edward S. Wagner Company), Box 304–4a, Dubinsky Papers.

59. Derber 1958: 1.

60. Boris 1987.

61. Boris and Daniels 1989: 103–39, 147–64, 258–71; Waldinger 1986; Katz and Kemnitzer 1983; Christensen 1988.

62. *Washington Post*, 4 January 1989, A-18.

63. Kirschten 1989.

64. Kessler-Harris 1986: 66.

65. "Industrial Homework Chronology," photocopy available from the ILGWU.

66. *Daily Labor Report*, 12 December 1989; 1–2, A12–A13, F1–F6.

67. Author's conversations with interested parties, December 1989.

68. Householder Van Horn 1988: 199, 185. Blank 1988: 139.

69. DOL Office of Information, "New Industrial Homework Rules to Take Effect," *News*, for release 10 November 1988.

70. *Wall Street Journal*, 14 November 1988, editorial page.

71. Mann 1989; Treiman and Hartmann 1981.

72. *Wall Street Journal*, 14 November 1988.

73. Boris and Daniels 1989.

74. Boris and Daniels 1989: 198–214.

75. New York DOL, "Public Hearing on Industrial Homework," transcript of proceedings, 2 April 1981, N.Y. DOL Library; DOL, "In the Matter Of: A Public Hearing to Commence Labor Department Review of 'Homeworker Rules,'" 17 February 1981, Washington, D.C., DOL library.

76. "Testimony by Jay Mazur," before the U.S. DOL Hearings on Industrial Homework in the Women's Apparel Industry, New York City, 29 March 1989, available from the ILGWU.

77. H. Weinstein 1989; M. Howard 1989.

78. Boris 1987.

79. *Silent Woman, Ltd. v. Donovan*, 585 F. Supp. 447 (E.D. Wis. 1984); *Donovan v. DialAmerica Marketing, Inc.*, 757 F.2d 1376 (3d Cir.), *cert. denied*, 106 S. Ct. 246 (1985). See also *ILGWU v. Donovan*, 722 F.2d 795 (D.C. Cir. 1983), *cert. denied*, 469 U.S. 820 (1984); *ILGWU v. Dole*, 729 F. Supp. 877 (D.D.C. 1989).

80. "Comments of the International Ladies' Garment Workers' Union," 5 May 1989 [on 29 C.F.R. Part 530; Employment of Homeworkers in Certain Industries; Advance Notice of Proposed Rulemaking; 53 Fed. Reg. 53344 (30 December 1988)], available from Shea & Gardner, Washington, D.C.

81. See, for example, her statements on "McNeil-Lehrer News Hour," PBS, 20 December 1988.

82. "Testimony by Jay Mazur."

83. Palmer 1988.

84. Nakano Glenn 1985.

85. M. Anderson and Winslow 1951.

86. D. Pierce 1985; B. Nelson 1990.

87. Horn 1990.

88. Hunt 1979. For an example of the negative legal consequences for women of conventional occupational health and safety strategies, see *International Union v. Johnson Controls Inc.*, 886 F.2d, p.1871 (7th Cir. 1989). This decision has since been reversed by the U.S. Supreme Court. 111 S. Ct. 1196 (1991).

89. Petchesky 1987: 69; see also Moller Okin 1989: 110–33.

11 In the Shadow of the Law: Institutional Aspects of Postwar U.S. Union Decline

Joel Rogers

He who would understand politics in the large may ponder well the status of labor: a numerically great force in a society adhering to the doctrine of the rule of numbers, yet without proportionate durable power as a class.
—V. O. Key

Frankly I used to worry about the membership, about the size of the membership. But quite a few years ago, I just stopped worrying about it, because to me it doesn't make any difference.
—George Meany

This essay presents an account of some of the key institutional features of postwar U.S. industrial relations and uses that account to explain the generation-long decline of private sector U.S. unionism. The discussion has three parts. In the first ("Background"), I suggest a typology of industrial relations systems based on differences in the density and centralization of union memberships; I then locate the U.S. case within that typology. In the second ("The Rise and Fall of the Postwar Accord"), I characterize the narrow and fragile "accord" that obtained between unions and employers in some sectors of the private economy during the first part of the postwar period and the factors that led to its collapse in the 1970s. In the third ("Patterns of Decline"), I present a simple explanation of both the decline of private sector unionism and the limited character of union response to dwindling political power. This explanation locates the major source of private sector union decline in the postwar period in managerial resistance but argues that such resistance varied across sectors and over time. More specifically, while employers always resisted the spread of unionism beyond the sectorally defined union core claimed at the outset of the postwar period, their attitude toward the maintenance of unionism in that core changed during the period from toleration to resistance. The steady decline of aggregate private sector union density masks this change, which is important to appreciating the underlying dynamics of decline. Most decline in union density before the 1970s derived from the declining share of total employment claimed by the union core, not from declines in union density within it. That changed in the 1970s, when unions began sustaining serious losses within their traditional centers of power. Even as the union movement as a whole lost political power, however, the highly federated character of that movement discouraged concerted response of the sort needed to reverse labor's decline.

In this story, the law is backdrop, not foreground. But this backdrop is important, for it helped frame the strategic choices of the actors under view. As a general matter, I take the legal framework of postwar private sector unionism to have been exceptionally hostile to union growth. More particularly, I take the Labor Management Relations Act (LMRA),[1] the centerpiece of federal labor regulation over the past generation, to have hurt the labor movement in two important ways. First, the LMRA kept the costs of new union organization, particularly organization in the face of employer resistance, very high and offered little protection to organized workers in the face of sham bargaining, relocation, and other changes in employer operation or other forms of management resistance or attack. This tended to cabin unionization within the union core while leaving unions within this core highly vulnerable to changes in employer strategy. Second, the LMRA furthered the fragmentation of organized workers. It did so both by overtly limiting their coordination and by encouraging the pursuit of highly particularistic bargaining strategies in their dealings with employers. Of some consequence for understanding the national political strategy of labor during the postwar period, the latter included strategies, often successful, aimed at providing private equivalents of what in most advanced capitalist democracies was a social wage. A natural consequence was that unions were divided from one another, and from unorganized workers, and that the labor movement as a whole was weakened as a national political force. But for individual unions such weakening only served to underscore the logic of particularism and the appeal of a go-it-alone strategy of self-help.[2]

In understanding the postwar decline of private sector unions, then, the shadow of the LMRA is long. It made it difficult to organize, or to protect organization, and provided little incentive to more concerted labor strategies of the sort needed to secure significant national power. In the particular explanation of private sector union decline that I will offer, the LMRA helps supply my premises: that unions were always highly vulnerable to employer strategies, and that particularism remained the preferred union strategy of self-help, even under conditions of dwindling aggregate density.

Finally, however, if the LMRA had malign effects on the growth of private sector unions, it was hardly exogenous to those other aspects of the postwar system that provide my focus here. The LMRA's basic hostility to unions reflected the long-standing political weakness of American labor, which in both absolute and comparative terms became more pronounced over the postwar period. And the specific structure of industrial relations that the act promoted, with all its attendant difficulties for unions, reflected the interests generated on both sides of the bargaining relation under conditions of low-density, decentralized, and sectorally uneven worker organization. Indeed, while labor was far from being an equal partner with business in elaborating the terms of the LMRA, unions helped elaborate many key terms of the act, including some of those that eventually proved most debilitating to labor as a whole. In short, the LMRA—in itself awful for the labor movement, if not for all unions within it—may be understood as product, as well as producer, of the nonlegal institutional setting sketched here.

BACKGROUND

As a general matter, the postwar private sector industrial relations system in the United States reflected the long-standing "exceptionalism" of U.S. worker and employer organization and the characteristic strategies of unions and employers associated with low-density, decentralized unionism. In this section, I first characterize these dynamics, then indicate their empirical referents in the "exceptional" U.S. case.

Dynamics of Bargaining

Abstracting from the particulars of different industrial relations systems, the dynamics of bargaining between employers and unions can be expected to vary discontinuously with the density and centralization of union organization. At some risk of caricature, we may distinguish between a low-density, decentralized case (LDDC) and a high-density, centralized case (HDCC).[3] In the first, wages and benefits are not taken out of competition, and unions are not coordinated. In the second, wages and benefits are taken out of competition, and unions are coordinated. Across these cases, bargaining dynamics can be expected to vary discontinuously for two reasons—the first arising from differences in the competitive effects of unionization, the second from differences in the strategies of gain undertaken by unions.

To clarify differences in competitive effects, some assumptions are immediately in order. Assume that the costs of unionization to employers outweigh its benefits; call this difference the union cost. Assume further, however, that the union cost can be borne by the market, i.e., that demand for the good produced is sufficiently inelastic that an increase in market price equal to the union cost does not significantly depress demand. Assume finally that employers exist in competition with other employers, and that all those with whom they are in competition use roughly identical techniques of production. On these assumptions, what matters to employers is not the union cost per se, but the degree to which those costs are generalized to rivals. Where only some firms in the particular sector are unionized (the LDDC), unionization appears as competitive disadvantage and employers can be expected to resist it. Where all or most firms are unionized (the HDCC), unionization has little or no effect on competition and employers thus lack an important incentive to resist.

On differences in union strategy, I assume that unions attempt to maximize the expected income of their members, but that in doing so they face important strategic trade-offs along two dimensions. The first dimension is time. Unions can concentrate on short-term gains, trying to enlarge their share of current product. Or they can pursue long-term gains, attempting to enlarge future payoffs through the enlargement of future product. The second dimension is space (or "organizational space"). Unions can go it alone in wage demands or coordinate their demands with other unions;[4] they can concentrate on extracting concessions from employers directly, or they can seek coalitions with other groups necessary to extracting income through the state (i.e., through an increased social wage).[5]

The HDCC favors longer-term cooperative strategies with employers and greater orientation to making gains through the state. The reasons are straightforward. In the HDCC, unions have more confidence that they will be able to extract future gains; because they comprise a larger and more coordinated share of the population, they can be expected to be less tolerant of "destructive" redistributive strategies that depress social product; and being both big and centralized, they have more developed capacities to make gains through the state. In the LDDC, by contrast, unions have every incentive to free-ride on their future interests because they may not have a future; they have incentives to free-ride on unorganized workers because they bear a negligible portion of the social costs of "destructive" redistribution; and they have little incentive to coordinate with other unions, or to seek general gains through the state, because their capacity for doing so is limited by their small numbers and lack of centralization.

What about employer attitudes toward the different cases? It seems safe to conclude that employers, who in general may be assumed to favor no unionization over any unionization, also favor the HDCC over the LDDC.[6] At a certain point of density and centralization, union effects on interfirm rivalry, the preferred strategies of unions, and employer attitudes toward unions all change direction. At this point, wages are taken out of competition, more secure unions exchange militant economism and job control for political exchange and cooperative strategies, and employers recognize both that they must and that they can live with unionization. Instead of devoting themselves to destroying unionization, or resisting its spread, they cooperate in its maintenance and extension. Call this point, in Hegelian fashion, the line of mutual recognition.

Exceptional Disorganization

In the United States, which probably more closely approximates the ideal type of the LDDC than any other industrial relations system,[7] this line has never been reached. In comparative terms, American employers are "exceptionally" hostile to unions, in large measure because American workers are exceptionally disorganized. Here I note two familiar aspects of American worker disorganization—one bearing on the organization of formal politics, the other on union scope and structure—and indicate their relation and policy consequences.

Beginning with politics, the most salient phenomenon, virtually definitional of American exceptionalism, is the absence of political organizations deriving their programmatic identity and organizational authority from independent organizations of workers qua workers. There is no viable labor or social democratic party in the United States.[8] The electoral field is instead fully occupied by two business-dominated parties, featuring an almost premodern[9] structure of weak vertical linkages between elites and masses, low capacities for mobilization, and a coalitional rather than programmatic thrust that is almost never articulated in explicit class terms.[10]

Lacking political vehicles of their own, American workers have long been disappearing as even a presence in the electoral system. As a general matter, and running counter to patterns in all other capitalist democracies, U.S. electoral participation rates have trended downward since the late nineteenth century (since, in other words, the emergence of a substantial industrial working class). Recently they have hit record lows. Excluding the southern states, participation in the 1986 congressional elections dropped to its lowest level since 1798; in the 1988 presidential election it dropped to 50 percent, lower than in any modern election except those of 1920 and 1924 (shortly after the eligible electorate was abruptly swollen by the extension of the franchise to women).[11] Within this generally demobilized and increasingly "dealigned" universe, moreover, a large hole has opened up in that part of the electorate (the bottom third or so in income and education) that elsewhere provides the core support for social democratic and labor parties. Massive working-class abstention gives aggregate participation in the United States a decisive class skew. Rates of U.S. working-class participation are about 40 percent below both those of the U.S. propertied middle class and those of workers in other rich, capitalist democracies.[12] In brief, U.S. workers do not appear much at all, and certainly do not appear as a class, in American electoral politics. They are thus singularly ill equipped to wage reform struggles through the state in order to supplement their private incomes with a social wage.

Turning to economic organization, both the low-density and decentralization aspects of the LDDC find clear referents in the United States. Low density is obvious. Postwar U.S. union density reached a peak of 25.5 percent in 1953—the year that V. O. Key observed that labor's numbers far exceeded its power. It has declined without interruption since then, dropping to 16.4 percent by 1989.[13] Confining ourselves to private sector, nonagricultural workers, the decline is even more striking. Unionization among that group fell from 38 percent in 1954 to 24 percent by 1978 and, on a different statistical series, to 12 percent by 1989.[14] This experience is also comparatively distinct. U.S. union density is lower than that in all other advanced industrial, capitalist democracies, and no other system displays the U.S. pattern of *uninterrupted* decline during the postwar period.

The decentralization of the U.S. case is also apparent. Whether one looks at the level at which bargaining proceeds, the control central federations exert over member unions, the distribution of union resources across different levels of organization, or the sheer number of union organizations, there is scholarly consensus that the U.S. labor movement and industrial relations system is among the most decentralized in the world, certainly more decentralized than the continental West European systems, such relatively decentralized cases as Italy and France included.[15]

The extreme decentralization of the U.S. union movement amounts to fragmentation, or a condition in which there is little effective coordination of component parts. To return once more to Key, this fragmentation provides the analytic key to understanding why American labor's political strength is greatly outdistanced by its numbers. Numbers mean little without organization, and organization means little without coordination of those organized. It follows that increases in membership without coordination do not proportionately increase power, which is why, despite its absolute numbers, organized labor in the United States lacks "proportionate durable power as a class."[16] Instead of being more than the sum of its parts, with those parts coordinated in collaborative strategic action, the American labor movement is usually less.

More particularly, political and economic disorganization are related, and have clear effects, both at the macro level of public policy, and the micro level of collective bargaining. At the macro level, comparative studies indicate close correlation between union centralization and the strength of leftist parties,[17] and between the conjunction of centralized unions and leftist representation in government and a high social wage.[18] The extremely low and uneven quality of the U.S. social wage—the striking absence, in comparative terms, of such generic substantive entitlements as paid accident and sickness leave, vacation time, retraining, family leave, or national health insurance, and the heavy reliance instead on stingy, means-tested entitlement programs—is probably the most obvious policy outcome of U.S. worker disorganization. At the micro level of collective bargaining, the failure to achieve classwide gains through the state sharpens concentration on achieving more particular gains in narrow arenas, increases the appeal of "job control" versus "political" unionism, and the like.

Once embarked on this trajectory, moreover, it is difficult to get off. The particularity both of the gains sought within local arenas and of the organizations that seek them makes the articulation of general demands more difficult. And success in the achievement of particular demands tends to consolidate the pattern of organizational isolation, while slowing the impetus to cross-sectoral coordination. The union strategies associated with the LDDC—a narrow political agenda, a focus on militant economism and job control—reinforce one another.

THE RISE AND FALL OF THE POSTWAR "ACCORD"

What I have just described as the LDDC has applicability to the whole of the U.S. economy, and the U.S. labor movement within it, during the postwar period. But in fact, of course, the labor movement is not organized on economywide lines, but on sectoral ones. During the first half of the postwar period, in a limited number of sectors, something approximating an "accord" (or "truce," or "ceasefire in place") was established.[19] This accord should not be thought of as a perfect miniaturization of the HDCC. Gaining national political power sufficient to mount broad programs of increasing the social wage required more than the coordination of union memberships in a limited number of sectors, and this was never something the postwar U.S. labor movement, confined to a few sectors, could achieve. Still, within those sectors the United States approximated one aspect of the HDCC, namely, a modicum of cooperation between unions and employers. Here I first describe the scope and content of this fragile peace and then suggest the reasons for its collapse in the early 1970s.

The Limited Accord

The point on scope is simple: the accord was severely limited. In addition to being concentrated in a few geographic regions (something of great consequence to the political power of labor at the national level), private sector unionism was concentrated severely in a limited number of economic sectors. Entering the postwar period in 1947, the two broad sectors of construction and the major regulated industries (transportation, communication, and utilities) accounted for 34 percent of total private sector union membership, while manufacturing provided another 48 percent.[20] These shares remained substantially unchanged until the late 1970s. Disaggregated data on membership within manufacturing, available since 1958, suggest further concentration. Four manufacturing sectors alone, combined with construction and the regulated industries, account for 72 percent of all private sector union members in 1958, 71 percent in 1968, and 66 percent as late as 1978,[21] or consistently about twice their share of total private sector employment.[22] In short, throughout the postwar period the vast bulk of private sector unionism was confined to a clearly defined, distinctly limited, and shrinking portion of the total economy—really a handful of economic sectors. With little risk of exaggeration, we can thus speak of the postwar "accord" with labor not as an economywide phenomenon but as a sector-specific one.

This leads us to the accord's content—the terms and conditions of cooperation between labor and management. While on an economywide basis unions never climbed past the line of mutual recognition with employers, in particular sectors they did. They achieved densities sufficient to take wages out of competition, thus removing employers' chief reason for resisting unionization. And in most of these core sectors, employer hostility was further reduced, or rendered ineffective, by other factors. In manufacturing, many of the lead firms had exceptionally strong market positions. They were willing to pay "monopoly rents" to unions because they had monopoly power themselves. Faced with strong domestic demand, and operating in a relatively closed market, they could simply pass the union premium along to consumers—other firms, or individuals—in the form of higher prices. In the heavily regulated transportation, communications, and utility sectors, this same effect was achieved through direct government regulation, which limited entry by rivals and set standardized prices for consumers that covered the additional costs of unionization. Finally, in some important cases, most notably mining and construction, firms were tied to particular locales and simply had to deal with an external labor market successfully organized by unions. In the core, in short, unions benefited heavily from monopoly pricing, and in some cases from the locational immobilities of firms.[23]

Within this limited core, unions and employers forged stable relationships marked by significant cooperation.[24] The wage terms of collective bargaining agreements were typically tied, as in the historic Treaty of Detroit negotiated by the United Autoworkers and General Motors, to productivity increases. Collective bargaining agreements were widely extended to three-year terms, with the inclusion of cost-of-living adjustment clauses (COLAs) for union members and no-strike clauses for management, and the agreement of both parties to submit disputes over contract terms to arbitration.[25] Despite their enormous complexity, the subject matter of collective bargaining agreements was narrowed to "bread and butter" issues, leaving management's prerogative to make strategic decisions intact. And within firms, unions devoted themselves to elaborating the rules of job control—increasing the cost of movement of workers in the internal labor market, and thus compensating for the general lack of regulation of the external one.[26] From these efforts, employers gained stability without serious loss of autonomy; union members gained benefits unavailable to the rest of the labor force.

The End of "Labor Peace"

This "accord" between unions and select employers in the private sector held in place in the United States until the early 1970s. Despite some shifting around, union density in the core sectors remained quite stable. The basic institutional arrangements of the accord—wage increases tied to productivity increases, generalization of wage and benefit costs throughout unionized sectors, binding arbitration to settle disputes over collective bargaining agreements, union assistance in governing the internal labor market—remained in place.

Beginning in the early 1970s, however, particularly after the recession year of 1973, signs of stress began to appear. As in most advanced capitalist economies, U.S. economic performance deteriorated. Rates of profit and GNP and productivity growth dropped sharply, and median family income and weekly earnings stagnated or declined. Of even greater consequence, the U.S. economy was suddenly internationalized. The additive share of imports and exports in GNP, which had been relatively slight (about 10 percent) and stable for the previous fifty years, doubled during the 1970s. Most U.S. firms (about 70 percent) were just as suddenly exposed to international competitive pressures. Throughout the decade of the 1970s, many lost market share to foreign competitors.[27] Even where they retained share, however, U.S. firms found themselves operating in a qualitatively more competitive environment.[28]

One effect of these changes on the calculus of American business was predictable. Firms became much more sensitive to costs, since those costs could no longer be passed along to captive domestic consumers, and more intent on cutting costs, beginning with the price of labor. This was true in the unionized sectors of manufacturing, which suddenly faced substantially increased competition from abroad. But it was true as well in nonunionized sectors of the economy, which became even more bent than they were before on resisting unionization. As a general matter, the ensuing attack on workers in both union and nonunion sectors is reflected in the decline in worker incomes just reported. But while union workers, because they were organized, were better able to resist such downward pressures—a fact reflected in a better than 50 percent rise in the union premium, or difference between union and nonunion wages, during the 1970s[29]—that ability made them even more squarely an object of attack.

In addition to rolling back wages or unionization, or both, for their own work forces, firms sought to roll back various regulatory protections that imposed costs on them. Of particular consequence here were the efforts to deregulate the highly regulated, and heavily unionized, service sectors of transportation and communication, where government sponsored barriers to entry artificially inflated prices.

These developments, all untoward for the union sector, coincided with an equally unfavorable diffusion of new technologies of profit extraction—computerized switching devices in communications, prefabrication in construction, strip mining in mineral extraction, containerization in longshore work, vacuum-packed meat boxes in meat cutting, numerically controlled machine tools in machining. Their diffusion permitted firms to shift production away from externally organized markets—thus overcoming the locational immobilities that had benefited labor—or to break union monopolies on the generation of needed skills by organizing alternative sources of skill, or deskilling the relevant production process.

Last, increased competition and uncertain demand (the apparent saturation or fracturing of traditional mass markets) persuaded many firms of the need for increased "flexibility" in production. The term is protean in meaning, referring at one extreme to felicitous paths of flexible specialization in high-value-added market niches, at the other to simple sweating of workers, and implementation of the business maxim "internalize scarcity, externalize risk."[30] Whatever the meaning of flexibility, however, it was clear that its implementation required something almost diametrically opposed to the "high cost of movement" governance mechanism typical of the unionized internal labor market. And this provided further animus against unions.

On all these dimensions, then, the calculus of American employers changed in the 1970s. They broke the truce that had existed since the close of World War II and began attacking unions within the traditional core. The response of a weakened and highly fragmented labor movement was always slow, generally ineffective, and never aimed at a much broader mobilization of the sort needed to withstand this attack. Indeed, labor's failed response only served to underscore the appeal, to those unions that remained, of the particularism that had long characterized labor's political efforts—a particularism, again, that followed "naturally" from its LDDC status.[31]

Given the weakness of labor's response, and the absence of any independent check by the law, employer attacks soon registered in an accelerated decline of union density. In the 1970s, major losses were sustained in the core sectors of manufacturing and construction. In the 1980s, the decline became a rout, as losses in these sectors were joined by massive attrition in the newly deregulated services of transportation and communications, and the employer attack snowballed. As unions weakened, they were less able to take wages out of competition among employers, leading to further employer attacks, to further union weakening, and so on.[32]

In brief, the elaborate system of rules and understandings, compromise and consent, that had marked U.S. industrial relations for a generation was suddenly transformed.

PATTERNS OF DECLINE

However incomplete the characterization provided here, something like this account of the structure and collapse of the postwar accord with unions has a certain obvious appeal. It fits well with what we know about other changes in American political economy in the 1970s, and makes sense of the common perception that there was a distinct and relatively stable set of dealings between unions and employers that held for a long period and then rather suddenly collapsed into one-sided class war.

Such an account, however, does not immediately fit the facts of continuous and, until the late 1970s, virtually linear decline in private sector union density over the postwar period, the comparable steady decline in union success rates in NLRB representation elections (widely taken as a proxy for the "balance of class forces"), and the comparable decline in union organizing efforts, as measured by the percentage of the unorganized work force participating in NLRB representation elections. Notice of such continual declines has led some theorists to conclude that the *real* sources of private sector union decline in the postwar period predated that period; they are to be found in bad strategic choices unions made in the 1930s and 1940s (perhaps coupled with a postwar purging of radicals from their ranks).[33]

This view has much to recommend it. Clearly, the political choices that unions made in the 1930s, 1940s, and early 1950s affected their options and their willingness to act on them in subsequent decades. Clearly, too, the continuous decline in postwar union density establishes the tautology that union organization was insufficient to maintain density shares. As a guide to understanding what happened in the postwar period, however, I find the view less than satisfying. Commonly the view is accompanied by invidious characterizations of the "false consciousness" or plain "irrationality" of the American labor movement, and here it just as commonly suffers from a fallacy of division—falsely assuming that what is rational for workers as a class must be rational for individual members of that class and their unions. More immediately, however, since the view is offered in opposition to the claim that union-employer dealings were stable for a long period, it does fit the perception, which has much experience to recommend it, that in fact they were.

Without fully engaging this alternative view, we can engage these problems with it, and also address the problem from which it arises (the apparent lack of fit between the account of stable dealings through the early 1970s and the fact of continuous density decline), through a brief analysis of union density decline. Killing multiple birds with a single statistical stone, the key to this analysis is a sector-specific explanation of the composition of that decline and the division of the postwar period into distinct subperiods.[34]

To see the force of this analysis, we might ask what the accord account offered above would imply for union density decline. To do this, in turn, requires pressing two assumptions in that account into sharper relief.

The first, implicit in my earlier account of bargaining dynamics and American exceptionalism, is that unions customarily organize workers (rather than workers organizing unions), and that in doing so unions behave in strategic ways. They choose an optimal level of organization and optimal sites for organization, taking into account the payoffs accruing from the addition of new members and the likely response of employers to organizing efforts.

The second assumption, noted at the outset, is that postwar labor regulation, centered in the LMRA, set the costs of organizing extremely high and provided no serious deterrent to employer attacks on unions. The practical consequence of this is that where unions are not able to compel employer recognition and bargaining through economic force, they have little or no redress against resistant employers.

Together these assumptions lead to a natural hypothesis, namely, that in the postwar period unions would be quite reluctant to organize in sectors where they did not already command significant power. Always admitting exceptions, as a general matter it would only be in such sectors that they could expect some mitigation of employer resistance—since only there would they have already made progress in taking wages out of competition. And only there, where there was resistance, could they expect to be able to overcome it through economic force.

In the framework of the accord analysis offered above, we can join these assumptions with what we know about the structure and scope of unionism to "predict" a certain pattern in union decline in the postwar period. Briefly, we know that coming into the postwar period unions were organized in a limited and distinct number of sectors, with union power within those sectors concentrated in blue-collar (as against white- or pink-collar) jobs within them. If, as argued above, these union strongholds remained relatively stable through the early 1970s, then we would expect that most of the decline in overall union density would be accounted for simply by a decline in the share of total employment taken by these strongholds, not by a decline within them.[35] Returning to the argument above, I claimed that these stable sectoral dealings were disrupted in the early 1970s, and I attached particular importance to international price pressures. This would lead us to expect a decline in the importance of the structural variables of sector employment and occupation and also to expect that some defensible proxy for international price pressures would become a significant predictor of within-sector union decline, controlling for occupation. Finally, I argued that the postwar system began disintegrating rapidly in the 1980s. During this period, we would thus expect yet further decline in the power of the structural variables (and perhaps even a drop in the significance of the internationalization variable). The picture should become highly scrambled, as befits a period of wreckage and transition. The system would no longer display systemic properties.

Statistical analysis shows exactly these results and thus offers confirmation of the account offered above.

Disaggregating the private economy into five sectors, a basic "shift-share" analysis of sectoral employment—predicting union density on the basis of shifts in the share of total employment claimed by different sectors (with different degrees of unionization)—shows great power in predicting density until the early 1970s, but much less power after that time, and even less since the early 1980s.[36] Using Bureau of Labor Statistics (BLS) data, sectoral employment shifts account for 54–60 percent of the decline over the 1956–72 period; for the years 1972–78 sectoral shifts account for only 29–35 percent.[37] Using different data from the Current Population Survey (CPS), but the same industry breakdown, only 22–27 percent of the decline between 1974 and 1980, and only 13–17 percent of the decline between 1980 and 1984, can be accounted for by such sectoral employment shifts.

Supplementing the sectoral variables with occupational data (the shift across white-, blue-, and pink-collar employment) strengthens the analysis, without disturbing the pattern of decline across periods in the power of structural variables. Using CPS data, industry and occupation shifts together account for 51–56 percent of the decline between 1974 and 1980 (roughly a 30 percentage point increase over industry alone), but for only 17–21 percent of the decline between 1980 and 1984.

While the BLS data do not permit the same kind of comparison for the earlier period, the later period results allow a confident assertion that the two variables together would increase the amount of accounted-for decline substantially above the industry-alone figure for 1956–72, bringing it from 54–60 percent to as high as 75 percent of the total decline.

Moving to within-sector decline (controlling for occupation) of the sort that became evident in the 1970s, we find that over 1974–80, when about 50 percent of the decline in density remained unaccounted for by structural variables, 60 percent of unaccounted-for decline is attributable to decreases in unionization among blue-collar workers in manufacturing, with about 20 percent attributable to decreases among blue-collar workers in construction. Thus about 80 percent of that which is not accounted for by the structural analysis stems from changes in union density in just two occupational/industrial groups— blue-collar workers in manufacturing and blue-collar workers in construction. A third of the decline among the former, in turn, is accounted for by a simple "internationalization" variable used as a proxy for international price pressures on those sectors.[38]

For the period 1980–84, when the unaccounted-for portion of the decline increased to about 83 percent, we see substantial declines in unionization spreading to all industries. In addition to continued declines among blue-collar workers in manufacturing and construction, all of the occupational groups in the regulated industries, and blue-collar workers in the service sector experienced declines in unionization. The internationalization variable fails a significance test. The picture is decidedly scrambled, albeit subject to reconstruction through more qualitative sector-specific histories, notice of the effects of deregulation, and the like.[39]

To summarize, simple structural variables (employment by sector and occupational group) can account for about 75 percent of the decline in unionization through 1972. These variables, joined by a measure of internationalization, can account for about 60 percent of the decline during the 1974–80 period. During the 1980s, they account for only about 20 percent of the density decline. It seems clear that the common perception, shared by the accord account, that there was a period of relative stability, which was then interrupted, is correct. And if our assumption about the hostile legislative environment for organizing is correct, then union behavior during the period has at least the appearance of rationality. Faced with a hostile external climate, unions hunkered down in their heavily organized sectors and essentially stayed put. They organized relatively little in general and confined much of their organizational efforts to maintaining density within those sectors.[40] This they succeeded in doing in virtually all sectors until the early 1970s and even, in many sectors, until the very late 1970s.

CONCLUSION

In retrospect, the fragility of postwar private sector U.S. unionism is obvious. Given the extremely unfavorable framework of self-help promoted by the LMRA, a shift in employer toleration of unions was registered almost immediately in a sharp rollback of private sector union power. As late as 1972, however, when George Meany was observing that he was not worried about the size of membership, the vulnerability of private sector unionism was, perhaps, less apparent.

Guided by the particularistic logic of the LDDC, the U.S. labor movement looked at itself in the early 1970s and basically liked what it
saw, and the reasons for its contentment were as straightforward as
the reasons why it would soon be shattered. Even as the overall level
of private sector unionism was declining, and even as the economy
(and with it, much of American society) was moving away from the
labor movement, union density within the shrinking core sectors was
still high, union dealings with employers were still relatively stable,
and union gains were still considerable. The limits of the LMRA, and
of the fragile accord it regulated, had not yet been tested. The limits
of the LDDC itself and of the style of trade unionism to which it gave
rise had barely been contemplated. Looking to the future, then, it is
understandable why American trade union leaders chose a "What, me
worry?" strategy of self-help. Much less clear, as we contemplate the
future now facing the U.S. labor movement, is whether intervening
events have generated support among them for a more radical and
encompassing strategy.

NOTES

This essay is a revised version of a paper originally delivered at the conference on "North American Labour Movements into the 1990s: Similarities
or Differences?" (Cambridge, Mass., 3–5 February 1989). It draws heavily on
Rogers 1990.

Epigraphs: V. O. Key, *Politics, Parties, and Pressure Groups*, 3d ed. (New
York: Crowell, 1953), 53. George Meany is quoted in *U.S. News and World
Report* 21 February 1972:28.

1. 29 U.S.C. Sec. 141–97.

2. These assertions about the LMRA are defended at length in J. Rogers
1990. See also U.S. Congress 1984 and C. Morris 1987.

3. Given two variables, this twofold, rather than fourfold, typology of
systems may seem odd. It may, however, be defended on the grounds that
centralization and density are extremely highly correlated. For eighteen OECD
(Organization for Economic Cooperation and Development) countries, for example, the Pearson correlation coefficient between average union density during 1965–80 and Cameron's measure (1984: 165) of "confederation power in
collective bargaining" is .7708. More interesting complications arise with consideration of variations in political structure, however, which add an important
dimension to the interactions described here. See n. 8 below.

4. The opportunities for free riding here, of course, are legion and form
the basis of the "destructive" redistributive coalitions of which M. Olson (1965;
1982) warns.

5. Clearly, the preexisting political structure affects this choice as well.
The structure of the state and electoral competition in the United States (separated powers at the national level, extreme federation of government func-

tions, single member districts for most elected offices, etc.) make a legislation-centered union strategy more difficult, as do related differences in the typical structure of benefit delivery for those benefits that have been gained. Differences in these areas are critical to distinguishing the United States from other "liberal" cases, the case of Canada included.

6. The analysis here is intended to "dance in the middle of the floor." Both hypothetical extreme cases of 0 and 100 percent unionization may be assumed to pose efficiency problems and additional flips in the attitude of employers. At the low end of unionization, what is generally true of employers in real-world circumstances is probably not true of all employers; at least in some industries, some minimal degree of (weak) unionization is probably desired. And certainly at the high end, as union density and centralization approach unity, employers again begin to worry, for workers with that much power might opt to run the economy for themselves. As Przeworski (1987: 37) wryly observes: "Capitalists would prefer no unions than unions; if they cannot have the former they should prefer stronger over weaker unions; yet they fear the political consequences of strong unions. This is not an easy preference profile to act upon: hence the ambivalent posture of capitalists toward workers."

7. One contender for pride of place might be the enterprise union system of Japan. Other features of that system, however, permit the coordination of interests (including incomes policies) lacking in the LDDC. This "corporatism without unions" is sufficiently different to defy easy comparison. A more formidable class of contenders is populated by the other "liberal" industrial relations systems (e.g., the United Kingdom, Canada, and New Zealand). Differences in state structure and the rules on party competition (see n. 5 above), however, make it easier for labor in these states to mount a more encompassing strategy through the state than in the United States.

8. Contrary to the suggestion in Greenstone 1969, I take the relation between labor and the Democratic party to be fundamentally different from relations between union movements and social democratic parties in Western Europe. The best single measure of labor's postwar power within the Democratic party was its ability to compel party support of legislation favorable to its own organization. On this measure, labor's relations with the Democrats have been incomparably worse than relations, however strained, between social democratic parties in Europe and their respective labor movements. Labor lost repeatedly in the postwar period, on Taft-Hartley, Landrum-Griffin, the promised repeal of the right-to-work provision in Taft-Hartley, common situs picketing, and labor law reform, suffering throughout from massive Democratic defections. More subtle measures of comparison (e.g., the representation of labor officials in party organizations, staffing ties, regularity of consultation with labor officials, etc.) only underscore the difference. Unions have of course been active in national politics and have often extracted benefits from the party system. But the characteristic organizational form that their relationship with the Democratic party takes, the capacity for sanctions of party leaders, the intimacy of relations, and the range of objects sought all differ in quite fundamental ways from the "typical" social democratic case. On labor's relations

with the Democratic Party, see T. Ferguson and Rogers 1986; Mike Davis 1986. For rich evidence of continuing close ties between trade unions and parties in Europe, see the range of studies in Gourevitch et al. 1984; Lange, Ross, and Vanicelli 1982; and Flanagan, Soskice, and Ulman 1983. For an account of "electoral socialism" that examines the constraints unions put on the choices of party leaders—constraints largely absent in the U.S. case—see Przeworski and Sprague 1986.

9. For the classic statement on the attributes of "modern" parties, which U.S. parties generally lack, see Duverger 1963.

10. That both major parties are dominated by business makes it rather difficult, of course, to use the category of class in organizing electoral appeals (but not impossible, as canned populist appeals indicate each electoral season).

11. "Modern" here means since the emergence of a national party system in 1828.

12. This discussion draws from Burnham 1982. See as well Przeworski and Sprague (1986) for historical data on levels of working class voting for several Western European nations.

13. The 1953 peak figure is from BLS 1979: table 165. Troy and Sheflin (1985) estimate the peak at the same year, with a marginally higher 25.9 percent figure. The 1989 figure comes from BLS, as reported in BNA 1990. Note that this uses a slightly different estimating technique.

14. The 1954 and 1978 figures reported are based on BLS 1980: tables 72, 162, and 165. I have replicated the calculations from these data reported in Freeman and Medoff 1984: 222. For the 1988 figure, from the Current Population Survey, see BNA 1990.

15. Wallerstein (1985: 42) has merged these various studies, converting their results to a single 0–7 scale on centralization (7 being most centralized). The United States and Canada both rank at 0. For select Western European states, the rankings are: Austria, 7; Netherlands, 5.7; Norway, 5.5; Sweden, 5.5; Belgium, 5.4; Finland, 5.1; Denmark, 3.0; Switzerland, 2.2; West Germany, 1.2; France, 0.7; Italy, 0.7. This scaling does not reflect differences in the structure of political systems, the degree of leftist representation in government, or the structure of social programs—all of which can mitigate the effects of decentralized union organizations on the ground. Again, taking such differences into account (see n. 8 above), I would argue that Canada (like other "liberal" systems) is less fragmented than the United States.

16. Key 1953: 53.

17. Surveying eighteen OECD countries over the period 1965–82, for example, Cameron (1984: 167) reports a .79 correlation between these two variables.

18. This literature is now enormous. For a recent review, and significant contribution in its own right, see Wilensky and Turner 1987.

19. There are many treatments of the postwar accord with labor. Edwards and Podgursky 1986 is particularly good and influences my own throughout.

20. Troy 1969.

21. BLS 1980. The four main manufacturing sectors contributing to unionization were: (1) food, beverages, and tobacco; (2) clothing, textiles, and leather;

(3) metals, machinery, and equipment; and (4) transportation equipment.

22. BLS 1980: table 162.

23. Edwards and Podgursky 1986: 29. See as well Mishel (1986) for a review of the "permissive" economic environment in which unions prospered.

24. For a recent clear and very compressed description of the elements of cooperation and their functionality, see Kochan 1988.

25. On the growth of COLAs, see Hendricks and Kahn 1985.

26. Piore's discussion (1986) of this, with useful contrasts to European restrictions, is particularly good.

27. For reviews of the decline in U.S. competitiveness, see Scott and Lodge 1985; Eichengreen 1988. Note that while the U.S. share of world trade continued to decline during this period, U.S. multinationals generally retained market share. Lipsey and Kravis 1986.

28. This phenomenon, and its effects on the calculations of American business elites, is discussed at length in Ferguson and Rogers 1986.

29. Freeman and Medoff 1984: 53.

30. Generally identified with the promise of the first extreme, Piore and Sabel acknowledge the distinct possibility of the second (1984: 278–79).

31. For labor's failed response, see Ferguson and Rogers 1986; Mike Davis 1986; Moody 1988.

32. The widespread phenomenon of concession bargaining underscored the decline in labor's bargaining power. At least as striking, however, was the ensuing drop in pattern bargaining. On this, perhaps the best evidence comes from two Conference Board surveys of employer wage determination practices, conducted in 1978 and 1983 (Freedman 1985). In the first, firm managers identified "industry patterns" as most critical to their own wage determination. In the second, industry patterns receded markedly in significance, dropping to fourth overall among managerial considerations. Coming to the fore were narrower concerns (in descending order of importance): productivity or labor cost trends in their particular firm, expected profits, or local labor-market conditions and wage rates. Over 1978–83 the number of firms citing one of these as their primary consideration increased a remarkable 64 percent.

33. See, for example, Goldfield 1987, a leading proponent of the thesis of an essentially continuous decline (3–25). Bad choices in the 1930s and 1940s, Goldfield argues (235ff.), cemented a conservative labor movement incapable of resisting a steadily increasing attack by employers and unwilling to make sufficient investments in organizing.

34. The analysis that follows is drawn from joint work with Sigurt Vitols. See Rogers and Vitols 1989.

35. Note here that this is a structural analysis, but not one that assumes some inherent properties in occupational or sectoral groupings that make them more or less immune to unionization. What is really doing the work here in explanation is not the structural variables per se, but the political context in which they operate. It is that context—extremely inhospitable to the spread of unionization beyond the sectors organized at the outset of the postwar period—that gives them their predictive power.

36. The five sectors are: transportation/communications/utilities, min-

ing, construction, manufacturing, and services. This provides a more disaggregated analysis than that commonly offered (e.g., by H. S. Farber 1985) while also avoiding a common mistake in such accounts (again, see H. S. Farber 1985), namely, the inclusion of the public sector. The structural decomposition technique I share with Farber does not work well when some sectors go up in density and others go down. When this is the case (as it clearly is with the public sector during the postwar period), there is some canceling out and the percentage of decline explained or accounted for by the shift-share analysis is consequently overstated.

37. I report these data in ranges because the results are dependent upon whether one uses the size of sectors in the first year or the last year in a subperiod as the weight; since sectors change sizes, they have different weights in the two periods. A more complete explanation is provided in Rogers and Vitols 1989.

38. We used the ratio of the sum of imports and exports to domestic shipments.

39. On the effects of deregulation, see Hendricks 1986.

40. This picture of organizing is confirmed by Voos 1982.

Bibliography

Abraham, May Edith and Davies, A. Llewelyn. 1902. *The Law Relating to Factories and Workshops, 1896.* 5th ed. London: Eyre & Spottiswoode.

An Abridgment of the Laws in Force and Use in Her Majesties Plantations. 1704. London: J. Nicholson.

Ackerman, Bruce. 1990. "Constitutional Politics, Constitutional Law." 99 *Yale Law Journal* 453.

Acts and Laws of His Majesty's Colony of Rhode Island, and Providence-Plantations, in America. 1730. Newport, R.I.: James Franklin.

A.F. of L. Trade Union Committee for Unemployment Insurance and Relief. 1932. *Why Unemployment Insurance?* New York: The committee.

———. 1934a. *Behind the Scenes of the 53d Convention of the AFL.* New York: The committee.

———. 1934b. *The Program of the Rank and File in the American Federation of Labor.* Proceedings of the Third Annual A.F. of L. Rank and File Conference, 27–28 October 1934, Moose Temple, Pittsburgh. New York: The committee.

———. 1935. *Labor Fights for Social Security: Why the A.F. of L. Rank and File Supports the Worker's Bill (H.R. 2857).* New York: The committee.

Alchon, G. 1985. *The Invisible Hand of Planning: Capitalism, Social Science, and the State in the 1920s.* Princeton: Princeton University Press.

Alford, B. W. E. and Barker, T. C. 1968. *A History of the Carpenters Company.* London: Allen & Unwin.

American Anti-Boycott Associations. 1904. *Million against One: A Con-*

spiracy to Crush the "Open Shop." 2d ed. Danbury, Conn.: Danbury Medical Printing Co.

———. 1908a. *The Application of the Sherman Anti-Trust Law to Labor Boycotts.* New York.

———. 1908b. *"A Liberty League": Convention Bulletin.* New York.

American Federation of Labor. 1895. *A Verbatum Report of the Discussion on the Political Programme, at the Denver Convention of the American Federation of Labor December 14, 15, 1894.* New York: Freytag Press.

Ames, J. B. 1905. "How Far an Act May Be a Tort Because of the Wrongful Motive of the Actor." 18 *Harvard Law Review* 411.

Ames, Susie M. 1973. *County Court Records of Accomack-Northampton, Virginia, 1640–1645.* Charlottesville: University Press of Virginia.

———. 1975 [1954]. *County Court Records of Accomack-Northampton, Virginia, 1632–1640.* Millwood, N.Y.: Kraus Reprint Co. 1st ed. Washington, D.C.: American Historical Association.

Anderson, Karen. 1981. *Wartime Women: Sex Roles, Family Relations, and the Status of Women during World War II.* Westport, Conn.: Greenwood Press.

Anderson, Mary and Winslow, Mary. 1951. *Women at Work: The Autobiography of Mary Anderson As Told to Mary N. Winslow.* Minneapolis: University of Minnesota Press.

Andrews, John B. 1938. *Labor Laws in Action.* New York: Harper & Bros.

Appleby, Joyce Oldham. 1978. *Economic Thought and Ideology in Seventeenth-Century England.* Princeton: Princeton University Press.

Atkinson, Edward. 1887. *The Margin of Profits: How It Is Divided, What Part of the Present Hours of Labor Can Now Be Spared.* New York.

Atleson, James B. 1983. *Values and Assumptions in American Labor Law.* Amherst: University of Massachusetts Press.

Avery, Dianne. 1989. "Images of Violence in Labor Jurisprudence: The Regulation of Picketing and Boycotts, 1894–1921." 37 *Buffalo Law Review* 1.

Bacon, Matthew. 1860. *A New Abridgment of the Law.* Philadelphia: T. & J. W. Johnson & Co.

Baer, Judith. 1978. *The Chains of Protection: The Judicial Response to Women's Labor Legislation.* Westport, Conn.: Greenwood Press.

Bailyn, Bernard. 1967. *The Ideological Origins of the American Revolution.* Cambridge: Harvard University Press.

Baker, Elizabeth. 1925. *Protective Labor Legislation, With Special Reference to Women in the State of New York.* New York: Columbia University Studies in the Social Sciences.

Barnard, James L. 1907. *Factory Legislation in Pennsylvania: Its History and Administration.* Philadelphia: University of Pennsylvania.

Bartlett, John R. ed. 1858. *Records of the Colony of Rhode Island and*

Providence Plantations in New England. Providence: Knowles, Anthony & Co.

Barton, J. L. 1987. "Contract and Quantum Meruit: The Antecedents of *Cutter v. Powell.*" 8 *Journal of Legal History* 46.

Beales, Ross W. Jr. 1989. "The Reverend Ebenezer Parkman's Farm Workers, Westborough, Massachusetts, 1726–82." 99 *Proceedings of the American Antiquarian Society,* Part 1, 121.

Bealey, Frank and Pelling, Henry. 1958. *Labor and Politics, 1900–1906: A History of the Labour Representation Committee.* London: Macmillan.

Beckman, Gail McKnight ed. 1976. *The Statutes at Large of Pennsylvania in the Time of William Penn.* New York: Vantage Press.

Beckner, Earl. 1929. *A History of Illinois Labor Legislation.* Chicago: University of Chicago Press.

Bensman, David H. 1977. "Artisan Culture, Business Union: American Hat Finishers in the Nineteenth Century." Ph.D. diss. Columbia University.

———. 1985. *The Practice of Solidarity: American Hat Finishers in the Nineteenth Century.* Urbana: University of Illinois Press.

Benson, Adolph B. 1937. *Peter Kalm's Travels in North America; The English Version of 1770.* New York: Wilson-Erickson. 2v. Also the 1987 edition. New York: Dover Publications.

Bernstein, Irving. 1960. *The Lean Years: A History of the American Worker, 1920–1933.* Boston: Houghton Mifflin.

———. 1969. *Turbulent Years: A History of the American Worker, 1933–1941.* Boston: Houghton Mifflin.

———. 1985. *A Caring Society: The New Deal, the Worker, and the Great Depression.* Boston: Houghton Mifflin.

Betts, Lillian W. 1902. *The Leaven in a Great City.* New York.

Bindoff, S. T. 1961. "The Making of the Statute of Artificers." In S. T. Bindoff et al. eds. *Elizabethan Government and Society.* London: Athlone Press.

Blackstone, William. 1979 [1765–69]. *Commentaries on the Laws of England.* Chicago: University of Chicago Press. 4v.

Blank, Rebecca M. 1988. "Women's Paid Work, Household Income, and Household Well-Being." In Sara E. Rix ed. *The American Woman, 1988–1989: A Status Report.* New York: Norton.

Bloch, Marc. 1953. "Toward a Comparative History of European Societies." In Frederic C. Lane and J. Riemersma eds. *Enterprise and Secular Change: Readings in Economic History.* London: Allen & Unwin.

———. 1961. *Feudal Society.* Chicago: University of Chicago Press. 2v.

BLS (Bureau of Labor Statistics). 1979. *Handbook of Labor Statistics.* Washington, D.C.: GPO.

———. 1980. *Handbook of Labor Statistics.* Washington, D.C.: GPO.

BNA (Bureau of National Affairs). 1990. "Union Membership Down to 16.4 percent of Workers in 1989, BLS Survey Shows," 4 *Labor Relations Week* 159 (14 February).

The Book of the General Lawes and Libertyes Concerning the Inhabitants of the Massachusets. 1929 [1648]. Cambridge: Reprinted from the Copy in the Henry E. Huntington Library. First printed by order of the General Court.

Boris, Eileen. 1985. "Regulating Industrial Homework: The Triumph of 'Sacred Motherhood.'" 71 *Journal of American History* 745.

———. 1986. "Quest for Labor Standards in the Era of Eleanor Roosevelt: The Case of Industrial Homework." 2 *Wisconsin Women's Law Journal* 53.

———. 1987. "Homework and Women's Rights: The Case of the Vermont Knitters, 1980–1985." 13 *Signs: A Journal of Women in Culture and Society* 98.

———. 1988. "Homework in the Past, Its Meaning for the Future." In Kathleen E. Christensen ed. *The New Era of Home-Based Work.* Boulder, Colo.: Westview Press.

———. 1991. "'A Man's Dwelling House Is His Castle': Tenement House Cigarmaking and the Judicial Imperative." In Ava Baron ed. *Work Engendered.* Ithaca: Cornell University Press.

———. Forthcoming. "Redefining the 'Family': Women, Progressive Reform, and the Problem of Social Control." In Nancy Schrom Dye and Noralee Frankel eds. *Women in the Progressive Era.* Lexington: University of Kentucky Press.

Boris, Eileen and Daniels, Cynthia Rae. 1989. *Homework: Historical and Contemporary Perspectives on Paid Labor at Home.* Urbana: University of Illinois Press.

Boyer, Paul. 1978. *Urban Masses and Moral Order in America, 1820–1926.* Cambridge: Harvard University Press.

Brace, Charles Loring. 1967 [1872]. *The Dangerous Classes of New York, and Twenty Years' Work among Them.* Montclair, N.J.: P. Smith.

Brandeis, Elizabeth. 1935. "Labor Legislation." In E. Brandeis et al. eds. *History of Labor in the United States.* New York: Macmillan. Vol. 3.

Brandeis, Louis D. 1971. *Letters of Louis D. Brandeis.* Edited by Melvin I. Urofsky and David W. Levy. Albany: State University of New York Press.

Brecher, Jeremy. 1972. *Strike!* San Fransisco: Straight Arrow Books.

Bremner, Robert H. 1956. *From the Depths: The Discovery of Poverty in the United States.* New York: New York University Press.

———. 1980. *The Public Good: Philanthropy and Welfare in the Civil War Era.* New York: Alfred A.Knopf.

Bridenbaugh, Carl. 1950. *The Colonial Craftsman.* New York: New York University Press.

Bridges, Amy. 1984. *A City in the Republic: Antebellum New York and the Origins of Machine Politics.* New York: Cambridge University Press.

———. 1986. "Becoming American: The Working Classes in the United States before the Civil War." In Ira Katznelson and Aristide Zolberg eds. *Working-Class Formation: Nineteenth-Century Patterns in Western Europe and the United States.* Princeton: Princeton University Press.

Brigham, Clifford. 1887. "Strikes and Boycotts as Indictable Conspiracies at Common Law." 22 *American Law Review* 41.

Brock, William R. 1984. *Investigation and Responsibility: Public Responsibility in the U.S., 1865–1900.* Cambridge: Cambridge University Press.

Brody, David. 1989a. "Labor History, Industrial Relations, and the Crisis of American Labor." 43 *Industrial and Labor Relations Review* 7.

———. 1989b. "Time and Work during Early American Industrialism." 30 *Labor History* 5.

Brooks, George W. 1962. "The Relevance of Labor History to Industrial Relations." 28 *Industrial Relations Research Association Publications* (Proceedings of the Fourteenth Annual Meeting) 206.

Buhle, Mari Jo. 1981. *Women and American Socialism.* Urbana: University of Illinois Press.

Burdick, Francis M. 1907. "Conspiracy as a Crime, and as a Tort." 7 *Columbia Law Review* 229.

Burn, Richard. 1757 [1743]. *The Justice of the Peace and Parish Officer.* 4th ed. London: A. Millar. Also the 1785 (15th) edition. London: W. Strahan et al. for T. Cadell. 4v.

Burnham, Walter Dean. 1982. *The Current Crisis in American Politics.* New York: Oxford University Press.

Bush, Bernard ed. 1977. *Laws of the Royal Colony of New Jersey.* Trenton: New Jersey State Library Archives and History Bureau. 5v.

Cain, Maureen E. 1986. "Realism, Feminism, Methodology, and Law." 14 *International Journal of the Sociology of Law* 255.

Calhoun, Craig. 1988. "Social Theory and the Law: Systems Theory, Normative Justification, and Postmodernism." 83 *Northwestern University Law Review* 398.

Cameron, D. R. 1984. "Social Democracy, Corporatism, Labour Quiescence, and the Representation of Economic Interest in Advanced Capitalist Society." In J. Goldthorpe ed. *Order and Conflict in Contemporary Capitalism: Studies in the Political Economy of Western European Nations.* New York: Oxford University Press.

Campbell, Helen. 1969 [1891]. *Darkness and Daylight; Lights and Shadows of New York Life.* Hartford: Hartford Publishing Co.

Carr, Lois Green and Menard, Russell R. 1979. "Immigration and Opportunity: The Freedman in Early Colonial Maryland." In Thad W. Tate et al. eds. *The Chesapeake in the Seventeenth Century: Essays on*

Anglo-American Society. New York: W. W. Norton.

Carson, Hampton L. 1887. *The Law of Criminal Conspiracies and Agreements: As Found in the American Cases.* Philadelphia: Blackstone Publishing Co.

The Case for the Labour Party. 1909. Letchworth, Hertfordshire: Garden City Press.

Casebeer, Kenneth. 1987. "Holder of the Pen: An Interview with Leon Keyserling on Drafting the Wagner Act." 42 *University of Miami Law Review* 285.

———. 1985. "Teaching an Old Dog Old Tricks: *Coppage v. Kansas* and At-Will Employment Revisited." 6 *Cardozo Law Review* 765.

———. 1989a. "Drafting Wagner's Act: Leon Keyserling and the Precommittee Drafts of the Labor Disputes Act and the National Labor Relations Act." 11 *Industrial Relations Law Journal* 73.

———. 1989b. "Work on a Labor Theory of Meaning." 10 *Cardozo Law Review* 1637.

Chafee, Zechariah and Re, Edward D. 1967. *Cases and Materials on Equity.* 5th ed. Brooklyn: Foundation Press.

Chandler, Alfred D. 1977. *The Visible Hand: The Managerial Revolution in American Business.* Cambridge: Harvard University Press.

Chapin, Bradley. 1983. *Criminal Justice in Colonial America, 1606–1660.* Athens: University of Georgia Press.

The Charter Granted by His Majesty, King Charles II, to the Governor and Company of the English Colony of Rhode-Island and Providence-Plantations, in New-England in America. 1767. Newport: Samuel Hall.

Christensen, Kathleen E. ed. 1988. *The New Era of Home-Based Work.* Boulder, Colo.: Westview Press.

Chudacoff, Howard P. 1982. "Success and Security: The Meaning of Social Mobility in America." In Stanley I. Kutler et al. eds. *The Promise of American History: Progress and Prospects* (10 *Reviews in American History*). Baltimore: Johns Hopkins University Press.

Clark, Christopher. 1990. *The Roots of Rural Capitalism: Western Massachusetts, 1780–1860.* Ithaca: Cornell University Press.

Clark, Elaine. 1983. "Medieval Labor Law and English Local Courts." 27 *American Journal of Legal History* 330.

Clark, G. De N. 1967. "Industrial Law and the Labour-Only Subcontract." 30 *Modern Law Review* 1.

Clark, John Bates. 1886. *The Philosophy of Wealth. Economic Principles Newly Formulated.* Boston: Ginn & Co.

Clark, Walter ed. 1904. *The State Records of North Carolina.* Goldsboro, N.C.: Nash Brothers.

Clash MacFarlane, Hether. 1985. "Dropped Stitches: Federal Regulation of Industrial Homework in the 1980s." 50 *Albany Law Review* 107.

Clegg, Hugh. 1972. *The System of Industrial Relations in Great Britain.* Totowa, N.J.: Rowan & Littlefield.

Clegg, Hugh, Fox, Allen and Thompson, F. A. 1974. *A History of British Trade Unions Since 1889.* Oxford: Clarendon Press.

Clemens, Paul G. E. and Simler, Lucy. 1988. "Rural Labor and the Farm Household in Chester County, Pennsylvania, 1750–1820." In Stephen Innes ed. *Work and Labor in Early America.* Chapel Hill: University of North Carolina Press.

Cole, G. D. H. 1953. *Attempts at General Union; A Study in British Trade Union History, 1818–1834.* London: Macmillan.

Committee for Industrial Organization. 1935. "Minority Report of Resolutions Committee on Organization Policies." In *Industrial Unionism.* New York.

———. 1936. *The Case for Industrial Organization.* New York.

Commons, John R. 1910–11. *A Documentary History of American Industrial Society.* Cleveland: Arthur H. Clark. 11v.

———. 1921. "Introduction." In Winthrop D. Lane. *Civil War in West Virginia: A Story of the Industrial Conflict in the Coal Mines.* New York: Huebsch.

———. 1924. *Legal Foundations of Capitalism.* New York: Macmillan.

Commons, John R. and Andrews, John B. 1936. *Principles of Labor Legislation.* New York: Harper & Bros.

Commons, John R. et al. 1966 [1918]. *History of Labour in the United States.* New York: Augustus M. Kelley. 4v. (1st ed. New York: Macmillan).

Conductor Generalis; or a Guide for Justices of the Peace. 1711. New York: William & Andrew Bradford.

Conductor Generalis; of the Office, Duty and Authority of Justices of the Peace. 1722. Philadelphia: Andrew Bradford.

Conk, Marga. 1978. "Social Mobility in Historical Perspective." 3 *Marxist Perspectives* 52.

Conley, John A. 1985. "Doing It by the Book: Justice of the Peace Manuals and English Law in Eighteenth-Century America." 6 *Journal of Legal History* 257.

Connecticut Bureau of Labor Statistics. 1891. *Sixth Annual Report of the Bureau of Labor Statistics of the State of Connecticut for the Year Ending November 30, 1890.* Hartford.

Cook, Charles M. 1981. *The American Codification Movement: A Study of Antebellum Legal Reform.* Westport, Conn.: Greenwood Press.

Cook, Joseph. 1880. *Boston Monday Lectures. Labor, with Preludes on Current Events.* Boston: Houghton Mifflin.

Cook, Walter W. 1918. "Privileges of Labor Unions in the Struggle for Life." 27 *Yale Law Journal* 779.

Cooke, Frederick H. 1909. *The Law of Combinations, Monopolies, and Labor Unions.* Chicago: Callaghan & Co.

Cooper, Thomas ed. 1837. *The Statutes at Large of South Carolina.* Columbia, S.C.: A.S. Johnston.

Countryman, Edward. 1981. *A People in Revolution: The American Revolution and Political Society in New York, 1760–1790.* Baltimore: Johns Hopkins University Press.

———. 1985. *The American Revolution.* New York: Hill & Wang.

Crowley, J. E. 1974. *This Sheba Self: The Conceptualization of Economic Life in Eighteenth-Century America.* Baltimore: Johns Hopkins University Press.

Cushing, John D. ed. 1977. *The Earliest Acts and Laws of the Colony of Rhode Island and Providence Plantations, 1647–1719.* Wilmington, Del.: Michael Glazier.

———. 1978a. *The Earliest Printed Laws of New York, 1665–1693.* Wilmington, Del.: Michael Glazier.

———. 1978b. *The Earliest Printed Laws of Pennsylvania, 1681–1713.* Wilmington, Del.: Michael Glazier.

———. 1978c. *The Earliest Printed Laws of South Carolina, 1692–1734.* Wilmington, Del.: Michael Glazier.

———. 1981. *The First Laws of the State of Delaware.* Wilmington, Del.: Michael Glazier.

Dalton, Michael. 1619. *The Countrey Justice: Containing the Practice of the Justices of the Peace out of Their Sessions.* London: Societie of Stationers. Also the 1682 edition. London: H. Sawbridge et al.

Dane, Nathan. 1823. *A General Abridgment and Digest of American Law.* Boston: Cummings, Hilliard & Co. 9v.

Daniel, Peter. 1972. *The Shadow of Slavery.* Urbana: University of Illinois Press.

Daniels, Christine. 1989. "Alternative Workers in a Slave Economy: Kent County, Maryland, 1675–1810." Ph.D. diss. Johns Hopkins University.

Davis, David Brion. 1975. *The Problem of Slavery in the Age of Revolution, 1770–1823.* Ithaca: Cornell University Press.

Davis, Michael. 1984. "Forced to Tramp: The Perspective of the Labor Press, 1870–1890." In Eric Monkkonen ed. *Walking to Work: Tramps in America, 1790–1935.* Lincoln: University of Nebraska Press.

Davis, Mike. 1986. *Prisoners of the American Dream: Politics and Economics in the History of the U.S. Working Class.* London: Verso.

Dawley, Alan. 1976. *Class and Community: The Industrial Revolution in Lynn.* Cambridge: Harvard University Press.

———. 1989. "Workers, Capital, and the State in the Twentieth Century." In J. Moody and A. Kessler-Harris eds. *Perspectives on American Labor History: The Problems of Synthesis.* DeKalb: Northern Illinois University Press.

Dawson, John. 1947. "Economic Duress—An Essay in Perspective." 45 *Michigan Law Review* 253.

Defoe, Daniel. 1724. *The Great Law of Subordination Consider'd*. London: S. Harding et al.

Demos, John. 1974. "The American Family in Past Time." 43 *American Scholar* 422.

Denning, Michael. 1987. *Mechanic Accents: Dime Novels and Working-Class Culture in America*. London: Verso.

Derber, Milton. 1958. "Industrial Homework: An Old Problem Lingers On." Lecture Series No. 17 (Institute of Labor and Industrial Relations). Champaign: University of Illinois.

———. 1970. *The American Idea of Industrial Democracy, 1865–1965*. Urbana: University of Illinois Press.

de Valinger, Leon ed. 1959. *Court Records of Kent County, Delaware, 1680–1705*. Washington, D.C.: American Historical Association.

Devlin, William H. 1984. *We Crown Them All: An Illustrated History of Danbury*. Woodland Hills, Calif.: Windsor Publications.

Dewey, John. 1929. "Nature and Reason in Law." Reprinted in *Character and Events* vol. 2. New York: Henry Holt & Co.

———. 1976–83. *The Middle Works, 1899–1924*. Edited by Jo Ann Boydston et al. 14v. Carbondale: Southern Illinois University Press.

Dicey, A. V. 1904. "The Combination Laws as Illustrating the Relation between Law and Opinion in England during the Nineteenth Century." 17 *Harvard Law Review* 511.

Dickman, Howard. 1987. *Industrial Democracy in America: Ideological Origins of National Labor Relations Policy*. La Salle, Ill.: Open Court Publishing.

Dobb, Maurice. 1947. *Studies in the Development of Capitalism*. New York: International Publishers.

Dorman, John F. ed. 1962. *Westmoreland County, Virginia, Order Book, 1690–1698*. Washington, D.C.: np.

Douglas, Paul. 1939. *Social Security in the United States*. New York: Da Capo Press.

Dubofsky, Melvyn. 1981. "Legal Theory and Workers' Rights: A Historian's Critique." 4 *Industrial Relations Law Journal* 496.

Dunn, Richard S. 1984. "Servants and Slaves: The Recruitment and Employment of Labor." In Jack P. Greene and J. R. Pole eds. *Colonial British America: Essays in the New History of the Early Modern Era*. Baltimore: Johns Hopkins University Press.

Duverger, M. 1963. *Political Parties*. 2d ed. New York: John Wiley.

Eddy, Arthur J. 1901. *The Law of Combinations: Embracing Monopolies, Trusts, and Combinations of Labor and Capital; Conspiracy, and Contracts in Restraint of Trade*. Chicago: Callaghan & Co.

Edwards, Paul K. 1981. *Strikes in the United States, 1881–1974*. Oxford: Blackwell.

Edwards, R. and Podgursky, M. 1986. "The Unraveling Accord: American Unions in Crisis." In R. Edwards, P. Garonna, and F. Tödtling eds.

Unions in Crisis and Beyond: Perspectives from Six Countries. Dover, Mass.: Auburn House.

Eichengreen, B. 1988. "International Competition in the Products of U.S. Basic Industries." In M. Feldstein ed. *The United States in the World Economy.* Chicago: University of Chicago Press.

Ellis, Richard E. 1971. *The Jeffersonian Crisis: Courts and Politics in the Young Republic.* New York: W. W. Norton.

Ely, Richard T. 1889. *Social Aspects of Christianity, and Other Essays.* New York: Crowell.

Erickson, Nancy S. 1989. "*Muller v. Oregon* Reconsidered: The Origins of a Sex-Based Doctrine of Liberty of Contract." 30 *Labor History* 228.

Ernst, Daniel R. 1989a. "The Labor Exemption, 1908–1914." 74 *Iowa Law Review* 1151.

———. 1989b. "The Lawyers and the Labor Trust: A History of the American Anti-Boycott Association, 1902–1919." Ph.D. diss. Princeton University.

———. 1989c. "The Yellow-Dog Contract and Liberal Reform, 1917–1932." 30 *Labor History* 251.

Evans, P., Rueschemeyer, D. and Skocpol, T. eds. 1985. *Bringing the State Back In.* New York: Cambridge University Press.

Farber, H. S. 1985. "The Extent of Unionization in the United States." In T. A. Kochan ed. *Challenges and Choices Facing American Labor.* Cambridge: Massachusetts Institute of Technology Press.

Farber, M. L. 1959. "Changing Attitudes of the American Federation of Labor toward Business and Government, 1929–33." Ph.D. diss. Ohio State University.

Faulkner, Harold U. 1951. *The Decline of Laissez-Faire, 1897–1917.* New York: Holt, Rinehart & Winston.

Feinman, Jay. 1976. "The Development of the Employment-at-Will Rule." 20 *American Journal of Legal History* 118.

Ferguson, Ann. 1989. *Blood at the Root: Motherhood, Sexuality & Male Dominance.* London: Pandora Press.

Ferguson, T. and Rogers, J. 1986. *Right Turn: The Decline of the Democrats and the Future of American Politics.* New York: Hill & Wang.

Fields, Barbara J. 1982. "Ideology and Race in American History." In J. Morgan Kousser and James McPherson eds. *Region, Race, and Reconstruction: Essays in Honor of C. Vann Woodward.* New York: Oxford University Press.

Fields, William C. ed. 1977–81. *Abstract of the Minutes of the Court of Pleas and Quarter Sessions of Cumberland County, 1755–1791.* Cumberland County, N.C., Bicentennial Commission. 2v.

Fine, Sidney. 1967. *Laissez-Faire and the General-Welfare State: A Study of Conflict in American Thought, 1865–1901.* Ann Arbor: University of Michigan Press.

Fink, Leon. 1983. *Workingmen's Democracy: The Knights of Labor and*

American Politics. Urbana: University of Illinois Press.

―――. 1987. "Labor, Liberty, and the Law: Trade Unionism and the Problem of the American Constitutional Order." 74 *Journal of American History* 904.

Finkin, Mathew. 1984. "Revisionism in Labor Law." 43 *Maryland Law Review* 23.

―――. 1985. "Does Karl Klare Protest Too Much?" 44 *Maryland Law Review* 1100.

Fischer, David Hackett. 1989. *Albion's Seed: Four British Folkways in America*. New York: Oxford University Press.

Flanagan, R. J., Soskice, D. W. and Ulman, L. 1983. *Unionism, Economic Stabilization, and Incomes Policies: European Experience*. Washington, D.C.: Brookings Institution.

Foner, Eric. 1976. *Tom Paine and Revolutionary America*. New York: Oxford University Press.

―――. 1978. "Class, Ethnicity and Radicalism in the Gilded Age." 2 *Marxist Perspectives* 6.

―――. 1983. *Nothing but Freedom: Emancipation and Its Legacy*. Baton Rouge: Louisiana State University Press.

―――. 1988. *Reconstruction: America's Unfinished Revolution, 1863–1877*. New York: Harper & Row.

Forbath, William E. 1985. "The Ambiguities of Free Labor: Labor and the Law in the Gilded Age." 1985 *Wisconsin Law Review* 767.

―――. 1989. "The Shaping of the American Labor Movement." 102 *Harvard Law Review* 1109.

―――. 1991a. "Courts, Constitutions and Labor Politics in England and America: A Study of the Constitutive Power of Law." 16 *Law and Social Inquiry* 1.

―――. 1991b. *Law and the Shaping of the American Labor Movement*. Cambridge: Harvard University Press.

Forcey, Charles. 1961. *The Crossroads of Liberalism: Croly, Weyl, Lippman, and the Progressive Era, 1900–1925*. New York: Oxford University Press.

FOTLU [Federation of Organized Trades and Labor Unions]. 1906. *Report on the Fourth Annual Session of the Federation of Organized Trades and Labor Unions of the United States and Canada, Chicago, Illinois, October 7, 8, 9 and 10, 1884*. Reprinted in *Proceedings of the American Federation of Labor, 1881–1888*. Bloomington, Ill.: Pantagraph Printing and Stationery Co.

Fox, Alan. 1983. *History and Heritage: The Social Origins of the British Industrial Relations System*. London: Allen & Unwin.

Fox-Genovese, Elizabeth and Genovese, Eugene. 1976. "The Political Crisis of Social History." 10 *Journal of Social History* 205.

Frankfurter, Felix and Greene, Nathan. 1930. *The Labor Injunction*. New York: Macmillan.

Franklin, Benjamin. 1759. *An Historical Review of the Constitution and Government of Pennsylvania*. London: R. Griffiths.

Fraser, Steve. 1983. "Dress Rehearsal for the New Deal: Shop-Floor Insurgents, Political Elites, and Industrial Democracy in the American Clothing Workers." In Michael H. Frisch and Daniel J. Walkowitz eds. *Working-Class America: Essays on Labor, Community, and American Society*. Urbana: University of Illinois Press.

———. 1989. "The 'Labor Question'." In Steve Fraser and Gary Gerstle eds. *The Rise and Fall of the New Deal Order, 1930–1980*. Princeton: Princeton University Press.

Frederickson, George M. 1965. *The Inner Civil War: Northern Intellectuals and the Crisis of the Union*. New York: Harper & Row.

Freedman, A. 1985. *The New Look in Wage Policy and Employee Relations*. New York: Conference Board.

Freeman, Joshua. 1983. "Catholics, Communists and Republicans: Irish Workers and the Organization of Transport Workers Union." In Michael H. Frisch and Daniel J. Walkowitz eds. *Working-Class America: Essays on Labor, Community, and American Society*. Urbana: University of Illinois Press.

Freeman, R. B. and Medoff, J. L. 1984. *What Do Unions Do?* New York: Basic Books.

Freeman, Samuel. 1802. *The Massachusetts Justice*. Boston: Thomas & Andrews.

Friedman, Lawrence M. 1973. *A History of American Law*. New York: Simon & Schuster.

Frieze, Jacob. 1844. *The Elements of Social Disorder; A Plea for the Working Classes in the United States. By a Mechanic*. Providence, R.I.: B. F. Moore.

Furner, Mary O. 1975. *Advocacy and Objectivity: A Crisis in the Professionalization of American Social Science, 1865–1905*. Lexington: University of Kentucky Press.

Furniss, Edgar S. 1920. *The Position of the Laborer in a System of Nationalism: A Study in the Labor Theories of the Later English Mercantilists*. Boston: Houghton Mifflin.

Galenson, David W. 1981. *White Servitude in Colonial America: An Economic Analysis*. Cambridge: Cambridge University Press.

Gatlin, Rochelle. 1987. *American Women since 1945*. Jackson: University of Mississippi Press.

Gettleman, Marvin E. 1963. "Charity and Social Classes in the United States, 1874–1900." In two parts. 22 *American Journal of Economics and Sociology* 313 and 417.

Giddens, Anthony. 1982. *Profiles and Critiques in Social Theory*. London: Hutchinson.

———. 1987. *Social Theory and Modern Sociology*. Cambridge: Polity Press.

Gilbert, Bentley B. 1966. *The Evolution of National Insurance in Great Britain: The Origins of the Welfare State*. London: Michael Joseph.

Ginzberg, Lori D. 1990. *Women and the Work of Benevolence: Morality, Politics, and Class in the Nineteenth-Century United States*. New Haven: Yale University Press.

Gladden, Washington. 1876. *Working People and Their Employers*. Boston: Lockwood, Brooks.

Goldfield, M. 1987. *The Decline of Organized Labor in the United States*. Chicago: University of Chicago Press.

———. 1989. "Worker Insurgency, Radical Organization, and New Deal Labor Legislation." 83 *American Political Science Review* 1257.

Gompers, Samuel. 1925. *Seventy Years of a Life and Labor: An Autobiography*. New York: E. P. Dutton & Co. 2v.

Gordon, Colin. 1990. "Workers Organizing Capitalists: Regulatory Unionism in the United States, 1920–1933." Unpublished paper. State Historical Society of Wisconsin Conference, "Perspectives on Labor History: The Wisconsin School and Beyond."

Gordon, David M., Edwards, Richard C. and Reich, Michael. 1982. *Segmented Work, Divided Workers: The Historical Transformation of Labor in the United States*. New York: Cambridge University Press.

Gordon, Robert W. 1981. "Historicism in Legal Scholarship." 90 *Yale Law Journal* 1017.

———. 1984. "Critical Legal Histories." 36 *Stanford Law Review* 57.

———. 1988. Letter to William Nelson. In "An Exchange on Critical Legal Studies between Robert W. Gordon and William Nelson." 6 *Law and History Review* 139.

Gould, Marcus T. C. 1827. *Trial of Twenty-Four Journeymen Tailors, Charged with Conspiracy*. Philadelphia.

Gourevitch, P., Martin, A., Ross, G., Allen, C., Bornstein, S. and Markovits, A. 1984. *Unions and Economic Crisis: Britain, West Germany and Sweden*. Boston: Allen & Unwin.

Graydon, William. 1803. *The Justice's and Constable's Assistant*. Harrisburg, Pa.: the author.

Green, J. 1972. "Working Class Militancy in the Depression." 6 *Radical America* 1.

Green, Nicholas St. John. 1933. *Essays and Notes on the Law of Tort and Crime*. Menasha, Wis.: George Banta.

Greene, Jack P. 1988. *Pursuits of Happiness: The Social Development of Early Modern British Colonies and the Formation of American Culture*. Chapel Hill: University of North Carolina Press.

Greene, Victor. 1968. *The Slavic Community on Strike: Immigrant Labour in Pennsylvania Anthracite*. South Bend, Ind.: University of Notre Dame Press.

Greenleaf, Joseph. 1773. *An Abridgment of Burn's Justice of the Peace and Parish Officer*. Boston: J. Greenleaf.

Greenstone, J. D. 1969. *Labor in American Politics*. New York: Alfred A. Knopf.

Gregory, Charles O. and Katz, Harold A. 1979. *Labor and the Law*. New York: W. W. Norton.

Grossberg, Michael. 1988. "Legal History and Social History: Friedman's History of American Law, the Second Time Around." 13 *Law & Social Inquiry* 359.

Gutman, Herbert. 1976. *Work, Culture and Society in Industrializing America*. New York: Vintage Books.

Haines, Brian W. 1980. "English Labour Law and the Separation from Contract." 1 *Journal of Legal History* 262.

Hajnal, J. 1983. "Two Kinds of Pre-Industrial Household Formation System." In Richard Wall ed. *Family Forms in Historic Europe*. Cambridge: Cambridge University Press.

Hale, Matthew. 1713. *The Analysis of the Law*. London: John Nutt.

Hale, Robert. 1923. "Coercion and Distribution in a Supposedly Noncoercive State." 38 *Political Science Quarterly* 470.

Hall, Louise. 1954. "Artificer to Architect in America." Ph.D. diss. Harvard University.

Harring, Sidney L. 1977. "Class Conflict and the Suppression of Tramps in Buffalo, 1892–1894." 11 *Law and Society Review* 873.

Hart, Vivien. 1989. "Minimum-Wage Policy and Constitutional Inequality: The Paradox of the Fair Labor Standards Act of 1938." 1 *Journal of Policy History* 319.

———. 1990. "No Englishman Can Understand: Fairness and Minimum Wage Laws." In B. Holden Reid and J. White eds. *American Studies: Essays in Honour of Marcus Cunliffe*. London: Macmillan.

Hartmann, Susan M. 1982. *American Women in the 1940s: The Home Front and Beyond*. Boston: Twayne.

Hartog, Hendrik. 1985. "Pigs and Positivism." 1985 *Wisconsin Law Review* 899.

Haskell, Thomas L. 1977a. "Deterministic Implications of Intellectual History." In John Higham ed. *New Directions in American Intellectual History*. Baltimore: Johns Hopkins University Press.

———. 1977b. *The Emergence of Professional Social Science*. Urbana: University of Illinois Press.

———. 1985. "Capitalism and the Origins of the Humanitarian Sensibility." In two parts. 90 *American Historical Review* 339 and 547.

Hattam, Victoria. 1987. "Unions and Politics: The Courts and American Labor, 1806–1896." Ph.D. diss. Massachusetts Institute of Technology.

———. 1990. "Economic Visions and Political Strategies: American Labor and the State, 1865–1896." 4 *Studies in American Political Development* 82.

———. 1992. *Labor Visions and State Power: The Origins of Business*

Unionism in the United States, 1806–1896. Princeton: Princeton University Press.

Hawley, Ellis W. 1979. *The Great War and the Search for a Modern Order: A History of the American People and Their Institutions, 1917–1933.* New York: St. Martin's Press.

Heard, Franklin Fiske ed. 1853. *Davis's Criminal Justice.* 3d ed. Boston: Little, Brown.

Heclo, Hugh. 1974. *Modern Social Politics in Britain and Sweden.* New Haven: Yale University Press.

Hendricks, W. E. 1986. "Collective Bargaining in Regulated Industries." 3 *Advances in Industrial and Labor Relations* 21.

Hendricks, W. E. and Kahn, L. M. 1985. *Wage Indexation in the United States: Cola or Uncola?* Cambridge, U.K.: Ballinger.

Hening, William Waller. 1795. *The New Virginia Justice, Comprising the Office and Authority of a Justice of the Peace in the Commonwealth of Virginia.* Richmond: T. Nicolson.

———. 1810. *The New Virginia Justice, Comprising the Office and Authority of a Justice of the Peace in the Commonwealth of Virginia.* 2d ed. Richmond: Johnson & Warner. Also the 1820 (3d) edition. Richmond: J. & G. Cochran.

———. 1823. *The Statutes at Large: Being a Collection of All the Laws of Virginia, from the First Session of the Legislature, in the Year 1619.* New York: R. & W. & G. Bartrow.

Henretta, James. 1977. "The Study of Social Mobility: Ideological Assumptions and Conceptual Biases." 18 *Labour History* 165.

———. 1979. "Social History as Lived and Written." 84 *American Historical Review* 1293.

Hepple, Bob ed. 1986. *The Making of Labour Law in Europe: A Comparative Study of Nine Countries up to 1945.* London: Mansell.

Hewitt, Sylvia Ann. 1986. *A Lesser Life: The Myth of Women's Liberation in America.* New York: Morrow.

Higham, John. 1963. *Strangers in the Land: Patterns of American Nativism, 1860–1925.* New York: Atheneum.

———. 1970. *Send These to Me: Jews and Other Immigrants in Urban America.* New York: Atheneum.

Hill, Ann Corinne. 1979. "Protection of Women Workers and the Courts: A Legal Case History." 5 *Feminist Studies* 247.

Hill, Christopher. 1958. "William Perkins and the Poor." In *Puritanism and Revolution: Studies in Interpretation of the English Revolution of the 17th Century.* New York: Schocken Books.

Himmelfarb, Gertrude. 1984. *The Idea of Poverty: England in the Industrial Age.* New York: Alfred A. Knopf.

Hinton, James. 1982. "The Rise of a Mass Labour Movement: Growth and Limits." In Chris Rigley ed. *A History of British Industrial Relations 1875–1914.* Brighton, Sussex: Harvester Press.

Hoar, George F. 1897. "Edward L. Pierce." 12 *American Antiquarian Society Proceedings*, 197.

Hofstadter, Richard. 1955. *The Age of Reform from Bryan to F.D.R.* New York: Random House.

———. 1965. "What Happened to the Antitrust Movement." In *The Paranoid Style in American Politics and Other Essays.* New York: Alfred A. Knopf.

Hogler, Raymond L. 1987a. "Critical Legal Studies and Industrial Relations Research: A Review Essay." 9 *Industrial Relations Law Journal* 148.

———. 1987b. "Law, Ideology and Industrial Discipline: The Conspiracy Doctrine and the Rise of the Factory System." 91 *Dickinson Law Review* 697.

———. 1988. "Critical Labor Law, Working-Class History, and the New Industrial Relations." 10 *Industrial Relations Law Journal* 116.

———. 1989. "Labor History and Critical Labor Law: An Interdisciplinary Approach to Workers' Control." 30 *Labor History* 165.

Holdsworth, Sir William. 1936. *A History of English Law.* 4th ed. London: Methuen. 16v.

Hollinger, David A. 1980. "The Problem of Pragmatism in American History." 67 *Journal of American History* 88.

Holmes, Oliver Wendell. 1881. *The Common Law.* Boston: Little, Brown.

———. 1894. "Privilege, Malice, and Intent." 8 *Harvard Law Review* 1.

Holt, James. 1977. "Trade Unionism in the British and U.S. Steel Industries, 1880–1914: A Comparative Study." 18 *Labor History* 5.

Holt, Thomas. 1982. "'An Empire over the Mind': Emancipation, Race, and Ideology in the British West Indies and the American South." In J. Morgan Kousser and James McPherson eds. *Region, Race, and Reconstruction: Essays in Honor of C. Vann Woodward.* New York: Oxford University Press.

Holt, Wythe. 1984. "Labor Conspiracy Cases in the United States, 1805–1842: Bias and Legitimation in Common Law Adjudication." 22 *Osgoode Hall Law Journal* 591.

———. 1986. "Recovery by the Worker Who Quits: A Comparison of the Mainstream, Legal Realist, and Critical Legal Studies Approaches to a Problem of Nineteenth Century Contract Law." 1986 *Wisconsin Law Review* 677.

———. 1989. "The New American Labor Law History." 30 *Labor History* 275.

Hook, Sidney. 1939. *John Dewey, An Intellectual Portrait.* New York: John Day.

Horn, James. 1979. "Servant Emigration to the Chesapeake in the Seventeeth Century." In Thad W. Tate et al. eds. *The Chesapeake in the Seventeenth Century: Essays on Anglo-American Society.* New York: W. W. Norton.

Horn, Patricia. 1990. "Creating a Family Policy." 153 *Dollars & Sense* 6.

Horwitz, Morton J. 1977a. "The Rule of Law: An Unqualified Human Good?" 86 *Yale Law Journal* 561.

———. 1977b. *The Transformation of American Law, 1780–1860.* Cambridge: Harvard University Press.

———. 1985. "Santa Clara Revisited: The Development of Corporate Theory." 88 *West Virginia Law Review* 173.

Householder Van Horn, Susan. 1988. *Women, Work, and Fertility, 1900–1986.* New York: New York University Press.

Hovenkamp, Herbert. 1988. "Labor Conspiracies in American Law, 1880–1930." 66 *Texas Law Review* 919.

Howard, Marjorie. 1989. "Home Work: Escape from Office Means Stress Can Hit You Where You Live." *Boston Herald* (29 January).

Howard, Oliver Otis. 1907. *Autobiography of Oliver Otis Howard.* New York: Baker & Taylor. 2v.

Howells, William Dean. 1972 [1896]. "Tribulations of a Cheerful Giver." In *Impressions and Experiences.* Freeport, N.Y.: Books for Libraries Press.

Huffcut, Ernest Wilson. 1898. "Interference with Contract Relations." 47 *American Law Register* 273.

Hunt, Alan. 1987. "The Critique of Law: What Is 'Critical' about Critical Legal Theory?" 14 *Journal of Law and Society* 5.

Hunt, Vilma R. 1979. "A Brief History of Women Workers and Hazards in the Workplace." 5 *Feminist Studies* 274.

Hurst, Willard. 1970. *The Legitimacy of the Business Corporation in the Law of the United States: 1780–1970.* Charlottesville: University Press of Virginia.

Hurvitz, Haggai. 1986. "American Labor Law and the Doctrine of Entrepreneurial Property Rights: Boycotts, Courts, and the Juridical Reorientation of 1886–1895." 8 *Industrial Relations Law Journal* 307.

Huthmacher, J. Joseph. 1968. *Senator Robert F. Wagner and the Rise of Urban Liberalism.* New York: Atheneum.

Hyman, Harold ed. 1967. *The Radical Republicans and Reconstruction, 1861–1870.* New York: Bobbs-Merrill Co.

Illinois Department of Factory Inspection. 1894–1900. *Report.* Springfield.

Innes, Stephen. 1983. *Labor in a New Land: Economy and Society in Seventeenth-Century Springfield.* Princeton: Princeton University Press.

———. 1988a. "Fulfilling John Smith's Vision: Work and Labor in Early America." In S. Innes ed. *Work and Labor in Early America.* Chapel Hill: University of North Carolina Press.

——— ed. 1988b. *Work and Labor in Early America.* Chapel Hill: University of North Carolina Press.

Ives, J. Moss. 1902–3. "Connecticut in the Manufacturing World." 7 *Connecticut Magazine* 627.

Jacoby, Sanford. 1982. "The Duration of Indefinite Employment Contracts in the United States and England: An Historical Analysis." 5 *Comparative Labor Law* 1.

James, William. 1896. "The Moral Philosopher and the Moral Life." In *The Will to Believe and Other Essays in Popular Philosophy*. Cambridge: Harvard University Press.

———. 1899. *Talks to Teachers*. London: Longmans, Green, & Co.

———. 1909. "The Essence of Humanism." In *The Meaning of Truth*. Cambridge: Harvard University Press.

———. 1925. *A Pluralistic Universe*. New York: Longmans, Green, & Co.

Johnson, Claudia D. 1984. *American Actress: Perspectives on the Nineteenth Century*. New York: Nelson-Hall.

Jones, Douglas L. 1984. "The Strolling Poor." In Eric Monkkonen ed. *Walking to Work: Tramps in America, 1790–1935*. Lincoln: University of Nebraska Press.

Jones, Gareth H. 1958. "Per Quod Servitium Amisit." 74 *Law Quarterly Review* 39.

Jones, Gareth Stedman. 1983. *Languages of Class: Studies in English Working-Class History, 1832–1982*. Cambridge: Cambridge University Press.

Jones, Mary Somerville. 1987. *An Historical Geography of Changing Divorce Law in the United States*. New York: Garland.

Judt, Tony. 1979. "A Clown in Regal Purple: Social History and the Historians." 7 *History Workshop* 66.

Kahn-Freund, Otto. 1964. *Labor Relations and the Law. A Comparative Study*. Boston: Little, Brown.

———. 1967. *Labour Law: Old Traditions and New Developments*. Toronto: Clarke, Irwin.

———. 1977. "Blackstone's Neglected Child: The Contract of Employment." 93 *Law Quarterly Review* 508.

Kairys, David ed. 1982. *The Politics of Law: A Progressive Critique*. New York: Pantheon Books.

Karsten, Peter. 1990. "'Bottomed on Justice': A Reappraisal of Critical Legal Studies Scholarship Concerning Breaches of Labor Contracts by Quitting or Firing in Britain and the United States, 1630–1880." 34 *American Journal of Legal History* 213.

Katz, Michael B. 1983. *Poverty and Policy in American History*. New York: Academic Press.

Katz, Naomi and Kemnitzer, David. 1983. "Fast Forward: The Internationalization of Silicon Valley." In June Nash and M. Patricia Fernandez-Kelly eds. *Women, Men, and the International Division of Labor*. Albany: State University of New York Press.

Katznelson, Ira. 1985. "Working-Class Formation and the State." In P. Evans, D. Rueschemeyer, and T. Skocpol eds. *Bringing the State Back In*. New York: Cambridge University Press.

Kaufman, Stuart. 1973. *Samuel Gompers and the Origins of the American*

Federation of Labor, 1848–1896. Westport, Conn.: Greenwood Press.

Keeran, Roger. 1989. "The International Workers Order and the Origin of the CIO." 30 *Labor History* 385.

Keller, Morton. 1977. *Affairs of State: Public Life in Late Nineteenth-Century America.* Cambridge: Belknap Press.

———. 1980. "Anglo-American Politics, 1900–1930, in Anglo-American Perspective: A Case Study in Comparative History." 22 *Comparative Studies in Society and History* 458.

Kelley, Florence. 1905. *Some Ethical Gains through Legislation.* New York: Macmillan.

———. 1909. "The Invasion of Family Life by Industry." 34 *Annals of the American Academy of Political Science* 90.

Kelman, Ellen M. 1983. "American Labor Law and Legal Formalism: How 'Legal Logic' Shaped and Vitiated the Rights of American Workers." 58 *St. John's Law Review* 1.

Kelso, Robert W. 1969. *The History of Public Poor Relief in Massachusetts, 1620–1920.* Montclair, N.J.: Patterson Smith.

Kennedy, Duncan. 1985. "The Role of Law in Economic Thought: Essays on the Fetishism of Commodities." 34 *American University Law Review* 939.

———. 1989. "The Legal Realist Element or the Stakes of Law." Unpublished manuscript.

Kent, James. 1826. *Commentaries on American Law.* New York: O. Halsted. Also the 2d edition. 1832. New York: O. Halsted.

Kessler-Harris, Alice. 1975. "Where Are the Organized Women Workers?" 3 *Feminist Studies* 92.

———. 1984. "Protection for Women: Trade Unions and Labor Laws." In Wendy Chavkin ed. *Double Exposure: Women's Health Hazards on the Job and at Home.* New York: Monthly Review Press.

———. 1986. "*Equal Opportunity Commission v. Sears, Roebuck and Company*: A Personal Account." 35 *Radical History Review* 57.

Key, V. O. 1953. *Politics, Parties, and Pressure Groups.* 3d ed. New York: Crowell.

Keyssar, Alexander. 1986. *Out of Work: The First Century of Unemployment in Massachusetts.* New York: Cambridge University Press.

Kingsbury, Susan. 1971 [1911]. *Labor Laws and Their Enforcement.* New York: Arno Press.

Kirk Blackwelder, Julia. 1984. *Women of the Depression: Caste and Culture in San Antonio, 1929–1939.* College Station: Texas A&M University Press.

Kirschten, Dick. 1989. "Earning Bread at Home." *National Journal* (11 February).

Klare, Karl. 1978. "Judicial Deradicalization of the Wagner Act and the Origins of Modern Legal Consciousness: 1937–1941." 62 *Minnesota Law Review* 265.

———. 1979. "Law Making as Praxis." 40 *Telos* 123.

———. 1981. "Labor Law as Ideology: Toward a New Historiography of Collective Bargaining Law." 4 *Industrial Relations Law Journal* 450.

———. 1985a. "Lost Opportunity: Concluding Thoughts on the Finkin Critique." 44 *Maryland Law Review* 1111.

———. 1985b. "Traditional Labor Law Scholarship and the Crisis of Collective Bargaining." 44 *Maryland Law Review* 1985.

Klarman, Michael. 1989. "The Judges versus the Unions: The Development of British Labor Law, 1867–1913." 75 *Virginia Law Review* 1487.

Klehr, H. 1984. *The Heyday of American Communism: The Depression Decade*. New York: Basic Books.

Klein, Ethel. 1984. *Gender Politics: From Consciousness to Mass Politics*. Cambridge: Harvard University Press.

Kleppner, Paul. 1970. *The Cross of Culture: A Social Analysis of Midwestern Politics, 1850–1900*. New York: Free Press.

———. 1979. *The Third Electoral System, 1853–1892*. Chapel Hill: University of North Carolina Press.

Kloppenberg, James T. 1987. *Uncertain Victory: Social Democracy and Progressivism in European and American Thought, 1870–1920*. New York: Oxford University Press.

Kochan, Thomas A. 1980. *Collective Bargaining and Industrial Relations: From Theory to Policy and Practice*. Homewood, Ill.: Richard D. Irwin.

———. 1988. "Adaptability of the U.S. Industrial Relations System." 240 *Science* 287.

Kolko, Gabriel. 1963. *The Triumph of Conservatism: A Reinterpretation of American History, 1900–1916*. New York: Free Press.

———. 1976. *Main Currents in Modern American History*. New York: Harper & Row.

Konig, David T. ed. 1978. *Plymouth Court Records, 1686–1859*. Wilmington, Del.: Michael Glazier. 16v.

Kuklick, Bruce. 1977. *The Rise of American Philosophy: Cambridge, Massachusetts, 1860–1930*. New Haven: Yale University Press.

Kulikoff, Allan. 1986. *Tobacco and Slaves: The Development of Southern Cultures in the Chesapeake, 1680–1800*. Chapel Hill: University of North Carolina Press.

———. 1989. "The Transition to Capitalism in Rural America." 46 *William and Mary Quarterly* (3d ser.) 94.

Kuritz, Hyman. 1950. "Criminal Conspiracy Cases in Postbellum Pennsylvania." 18 *Pennsylvania History* 292.

———. 1953. "The Pennsylvania State Government and Labor Controls from 1865–1922." Ph.D. diss. Columbia University.

Kussmaul, Ann. 1981. *Servants in Husbandry in Early Modern England*. Cambridge: Cambridge University Press.

Kutler, Stanley I. 1961. "Chief Justice Taft, Judicial Unanimity, and Labor: The Coronado Case." 24 *Historian* 68.

Labatt, C. B. 1913. *Commentaries on the Law of Master and Servant.* New York: Lawyers Cooperative Publishing Company.

Lacey, Forrest W. 1953. "Vagrancy and Other Crimes of Personal Condition." 66 *Harvard Law Review* 1203.

Ladd, Eliphalet. 1792. *Burn's Abridgment, or the American Justice.* Dover, N.H.: Eliphalet Ladd.

Lahan, P. Michael. 1968. "Trends in the Law of Vagrancy." Note. 1 *Connecticut Law Review* 350.

Lamoreaux, Naomi R. 1985. *The Great Merger Movement in American Business, 1895–1904.* New York: Cambridge University Press.

Landis, James M. 1934. *Cases on Labor Law.* Chicago: Foundation Press.

Lange, P., Ross, G. and Vanicelli, M. 1982. *Unions, Change and Crisis: French and Italian Union Strategy and the Political Economy, 1945–1980.* Boston: Allen & Unwin.

Laslett, Peter. 1964. "Market Society and Political Theory." 7 *Historical Journal* 1.

———. 1973. Introduction to *The Earliest Classics: John Graunt and Gregory King.* Farnborough Surrey: Gregg International.

Laube, Herbert D. 1935. "The Defaulting Employee—*Britton v. Turner* Reviewed." 83 *University of Pennsylvania Law Review* 825.

Laurie, Bruce. 1980. *Working People of Philadelphia, 1800–1850.* Philadelphia: Temple University Press.

Leab, Daniel. 1969. "United We Eat: The Creation and Organization of the Unemployed Councils in 1930." 8 *Labor History* 300.

Leavitt, Samuel. 1886. "The Tramps and the Law," 2 *Forum* 198.

Levy, Leonard W. 1967. *The Law of the Commonwealth and Chief Justice Shaw.* Cambridge: Harvard University Press.

Lewis, William Draper. 1905. "Should the Motive of the Defendant Affect the Question of His Liability?—The Answer of One Class of Trade and Labor Cases." 5 *Columbia Law Review* 107.

Linder, Marc. 1989. *The Employment Relation in Anglo-American Law: An Historical Perspective.* Westport, Conn.: Greenwood Press.

Lipsey, R. E. and Kravis, I. 1986. "The Competitiveness and Comparative Advantage of U.S. Multinationals, 1957–1983." National Bureau of Economic Research (NBER) Working Paper No. 2051. Cambridge: NBER.

Litwack, Leon F. 1979. *Been in the Storm So Long: The Aftermath of Slavery.* New York: Vintage Books.

Livingston, James. 1986. *Origins of the Federal Reserve System: Money, Class, and Corporate Capitalism, 1890–1913.* Ithaca: Cornell University Press.

Loomis, Samuel L. 1887. *Modern Cities and Their Religious Problems.* New York: Baker and Taylor.

Lowell, Josephine Shaw. 1884. *Public Relief and Private Charity.* New York: Putnam.

Lynd, Staughton. 1981. "Government without Rights: The Labor Law Vision of Archibald Cox." 4 *Industrial Relations Law Journal* 483.

――――. 1987. "Beyond 'Labor Relations': Fourteen Theses on the History of the N.L.R.A. and the Future of the Labor Movement." Unpublished paper, "Critical Perspectives on the History of American Labor Law" Colloquium, Georgetown Law Center.

McCurdy, Charles W. 1984. "The Roots of 'Liberty of Contract' Reconsidered: Major Premises in the Law of Employment, 1867–1937." 1984 *Supreme Court Historical Society Yearbook* 20.

Macdonald, Donald F. 1976. *The State and the Trade Unions.* London: Macmillan.

McIntosh, Marjorie K. 1984. "Servants and the Household Unit in an Elizabethan English Community." 9 *Journal of Family History* 3.

McPherson, James. 1964. *The Struggle for Equality: Abolitionists and the Negro in the Civil War and Reconstruction.* Princeton: Princeton University Press.

――――. 1988. *The Battle Cry of Freedom: The Civil War Era.* New York: Oxford University Press.

Madison, James. 1961. "Federalist No. 10." In Clinton Rossiter ed. *The Federalist Papers.* New York: New American Library.

Malcolmson, Robert W. 1981. *Life and Labour in England, 1700–1780.* New York: St. Martin's Press.

Mann, Arthur. 1956. "British Social Thought and American Reformers of the Progressive Era." 42 *Mississippi Valley Historical Review* 672.

Mann, Judy. 1989. "Making Tracks." *Washington Post* (24 March).

Marks, Gary. 1989. *Unions in Politics: Britain, Germany, and the United States in the Nineteenth and Early Twentieth Centuries.* Princeton: Princeton University Press.

Marx, Karl. 1977. *Capital.* Translated by Ben Fowkes. New York: Vintage Books.

Mason, Alpheus T. 1925. *Organized Labor and the Law: With Special Reference to the Sherman and Clayton Acts.* Durham: Duke University Press.

Mather, Cotton. 1696. *A Good Master Well Served: A Brief Discourse on the Necessary Properties and Practices of a Good Servant in Every Kind of Servitude.* Boston: B. Green & J. Allen.

Matthews, Albert. 1900. "The Terms Hired Man and Help." Reprinted from *Publications of the Colonial Society of Massachusetts*, vol. 5. Cambridge: John Wilson & Son.

May, Henry F. 1949. *Protestant Churches and Industrial America.* New York: Harper & Row.

Megaarden, Theodor. 1915. "The *Danbury Hatters* Case—Its Possible Effect on Labor Unions." 49 *American Law Review* 417.

Merritt, Walter Gordon. 1910. "The Law of the *Danbury Hatters'* Case."

36 *Annals of the American Academy of Political and Social Science* 265.

———. 1951. *Destination Unknown: Fifty Years of Labor Relations*. New York: Prentice-Hall.

Merry, Sally Engle. 1985. "Concepts of Law and Justice among Working-Class Americans: Ideology as Culture." 9 *Legal Studies Forum* 59.

———. 1986. "Everyday Understandings of the Law in Working-Class America." 13 *American Ethnologist* 253.

Mess, H. A. 1926. *Factory Legislation and Its Administration, 1891–1924*. London: P. S. King & Son.

Millward, R. 1981. "The Emergence of Wage Labor in Early Modern England." 18 *Explorations in Economic History* 21.

Minda, Gary. 1985. "The Common Law of Employment At-Will in New York: The Paralysis of Nineteenth-Century Doctrine." 36 *Syracuse Law Review* 939.

Mishel, L. 1986. "The Structural Determinants of Union Bargaining Power." 40 *Industrial and Labor Relations Review* 90.

Mitterauer, Michael. 1990. "Servants and Youth." 5 *Continuity and Change* 11.

Mohl, Raymond A. 1971. *Poverty in New York 1783–1825*. New York: Oxford University Press.

Moller Okin, Susan. 1989. *Justice, Gender, and the Family*. New York: Basic Books.

Monkkonen, Eric H. 1981. *Police in Urban America, 1860–1920*. Cambridge: Cambridge University Press.

———. ed. 1984. *Walking to Work. Tramps in America, 1790–1935*. Lincoln: University of Nebraska Press.

Montgomery, Charles F. 1966. *American Furniture: The Federal Period*. New York: Viking Press.

Montgomery, David. 1974. *Beyond Equality: Labor and the Radical Republicans, 1862–1872*. New York: Vintage Books.

———. 1980. "Strikes in Nineteenth-Century America." 4 *Social Science History* 81.

———. 1987. *The Fall of the House of Labor: The Workplace, the State, and American Labor Activism, 1865–1925*. Cambridge: Cambridge University Press.

Moody, K. 1988. *An Injury to All: The Decline of American Unionism*. London: Verso.

Moran, Michael C. 1977. *The Politics of Industrial Relations: Origins, Life, and Death of the 1971 Industrial Relations Act*. London: Macmillan.

Morell, Parker. 1940. *Lillian Russell; the Era of Plush*. Garden City, N.J.: Garden City Publishing.

Morgan, Edmund S. 1944. *The Puritan Family: Religion and Domestic*

Relations in Seventeenth-Century New England. New York: Harper & Row. Also the 1966 edition. New York: Harper & Row.

———. 1975. *American Slavery—American Freedom: The Ordeal of Colonial Virginia.* New York: W. W. Norton.

Morgan, Kenneth O. 1976. "The Future at Work: Anglo-American Progressivism, 1870–1917." In Harry C. Allen and Roger Thompson eds. *Contrast and Connection: Bicentennial Essays in Anglo-American History.* Columbus: Ohio University Press.

Morris, C. ed. 1987. *American Labor Policy: A Critical Appraisal of the National Labor Relations Act.* Washington, D.C.: Bureau of National Affairs.

Morris, Richard B. 1937. "Criminal Conspiracy and Early Labor Combinations in New York." 52 *Political Science Quarterly* 51.

———. 1981. *Government and Labor in Early America.* Boston: Northeastern University Press. Also the 1st edition. 1946. New York: Columbia University Press.

Moss, Roger William, Jr. 1972. "Master Builders: A History of the Colonial Philadelphia Building Trades." Ph.D. diss. University of Delaware.

Murrin, John. 1984. "Magistrates, Sinners, and a Precarious Liberty: Trial by Jury in Seventeenth-Century New England." In David D. Hall et al. eds. *Saints and Revolutionaries: Essays on Early American History.* New York: W. W. Norton.

Nakano Glenn, Evelyn. 1985. "Racial Ethnic Women's Labor: The Intersection of Race, Gender, and Class Oppression." 17 *Review of Radical Political Economics* 86.

Nash, Gary B. 1979. *The Urban Crucible: Social Change, Political Consciousness, and the Origins of the American Revolution.* Cambridge: Harvard University Press.

Nash, Gary B., Smith, Billy G. and Hoerder, Dirk. 1983. "Labor in the Era of the American Revolution: An Exchange." 24 *Labor History* 414.

National Congress for Unemployment and Social Insurance. 1935. *Unemployment Insurance Review.*

Nelles, Walter. 1931a. "The First American Labor Case." 41 *Yale Law Journal* 165.

———. 1931b. "A Strike and Its Legal Consequences." 40 *Yale Law Journal* 507.

———. 1932. "*Commonwealth v. Hunt.*" 32 *Columbia Law Review* 1128.

Nellis, Eric G. 1977. "Labor and Community in Massachusetts Bay, 1630–1660." 18 *Labor History* 525.

———. 1979. "Communities of Workers: Free Labor in Provincial Massachusetts, 1690–1765." Ph.D. diss. University of British Columbia.

Nelson, Barbara. 1990. "The Gender, Race, and Class Origins of Early Welfare Policy and the Welfare State: A Comparison of Workmen's Compensation and Mothers' Aid." In Patricia Gurin and Louise Tilly, eds. *Women in Twentieth-Century Politics*. New York: Russell Sage Foundation.

Nelson, D. 1969. *Unemployment Insurance—The American Experience, 1915–1935*. Madison: University of Wisconsin Press.

Nelson, William. 1729 [1704]. *The Office and Authority of a Justice of Peace*. 10th ed. London: E. & R. Nutt.

Nelson, William E. 1975. *Americanization of the Common Law: The Impact of Legal Change on Massachusetts Society, 1760–1830*. Cambridge: Harvard University Press.

Neufeld, Maurice. 1962. "The Sense of History and the Annals of Labor." 28 *Industrial Relations Research Association Publications* (Proceedings of the Fourteenth Annual Meeting) 206.

New Jersey Bureau of Statistics. 1903. *Twenty-Fifth Annual Report of the Bureau of Statistics of Labor and Industries of New Jersey for the Year Ending October 31, 1902*. Somerville.

New York Bureau of Labor Statistics. 1887. *Fourth Annual Report of the Bureau of Statistics of Labor of the State of New York, for the Year 1886*. Albany.

New York State Workingmen's Assembly. 1869–1894. *Proceedings*. New York: Catherwood Library, NYSSILR, Cornell University.

Nockleby, John. 1980. "Tortious Interference with Contractual Relations in the Nineteenth Century: the Transformation of Property, Contract, and Tort." Note. 93 *Harvard Law Review* 1510.

O'Connor, Richard. 1972. *Duet in Diamonds: The Flamboyant Saga of Lillian Russell and Diamond Jim Brady in America's Gilded Age, by John Burke*. New York: Putnam.

Oestreicher, Richard. 1988. "Urban Working-Class Political Behavior and Theories of American Electoral Politics, 1870–1940." 74 *Journal of American History* 1257.

Olson, Frances E. 1983. "The Family and the Market: A Study of Ideology and Legal Reform." 96 *Harvard Law Review* 1496.

Olson, M. 1965. *The Logic of Collective Action*. Cambridge: Harvard University Press.

———. 1982. *The Rise and Decline of Nations*. New Haven: Yale University Press.

Olton, Charles S. 1975. *Artisans for Independence: Philadelphia Mechanics and the American Revolution*. Syracuse, N.Y.: Syracuse University Press.

Orloff, Ann and Skocpol, Theda. 1984. "Why Not Equal Protection? Explaining the Politics of Public Social Spending in Britain, 1900–1911, and the United States, 1880–1920." 49 *American Sociological Review* 726.

Orren, Karen. 1982. "Liberalism, Money, and the Situation of Organized Labor." In David Greenstone ed. *Public Values and Private Power in*

American Politics. Chicago: University of Chicago Press.

———. 1987. "Organized Labor and the Invention of Modern Liberalism in the United States." 2 *Studies in American Political Development* 317.

———. 1991. *Belated Feudalism: Labor, the Law, and Liberal Development in the United States*. Cambridge: Cambridge University Press.

Orth, John Victor. 1977. "Combination and Conspiracy: The Legal Status of English Trade Unions, 1799–1871." Ph.D. diss. Harvard University.

Paine, Robert Treat, Jr. 1893. *Pauperism in Great Cities, Its Four Chief Causes*. Np.

Palmer, Phyllis. 1988. "Outside the Law: Agriculture and Domestic Workers under the Fair Labor Standards Act." Unpublished paper. Organization of American Historians 81st Annual Convention.

Parker, James. 1749. *Conductor Generalis; or the Office, Duty and Authority of Justices of the Peace*. New York: James Parker.

Parker, Mattie E. ed. 1971. *North Carolina Higher Court Records, 1697–1701*. Raleigh: State Department of Archives and History.

Pateman, Carole. 1989. *The Disorder of Women*. Stanford: Stanford University Press.

Patterson, Edwin W. 1940. "Pragmatism as a Philosophy of Law." In *The Philosopher of the Common Man: Essays in Honor of John Dewey*. New York: G. P. Putnam's Sons.

Pelling, Henry. 1956. "Knights of Labor in Britain, 1880–1901." 9 *Economic History Review* 313.

———. 1964. *The Origins of the Labour Party*. Oxford: Clarendon Press.

———. 1979. "Trade Unions, Workers, and the Law." In *Popular Politics and Society in Late Victorian Britain*. London: Macmillan.

Pennsylvania Department of Factory Inspection. 1890–1902. *Annual Report*. Harrisburg.

Perkins, Rollin M. 1958. "The Vagrancy Concept." 9 *Hastings Law Journal* 237.

Perlman, Selig. 1923. *A Theory of the Labor Movement*. New York: Macmillan.

Perry, Arthur L. 1868. *Elements of Political Economy*. New York: Charles Scribner & Co.

Petchesky, Rosalind. 1987. *Abortion and Woman's Choice*. Boston: Northeastern University Press.

Peterson, Charles E. ed. 1971. *The Rules of Work of the Carpenters' Company of the City and County of Philadelphia, 1786*. New York: Bell.

Petro, Sylvester. 1978. "Injunctions and Labor Disputes, 1880–1932." 14 *Wake Forest Law Review* 341.

———. 1980–82. "Unions and the Southern Courts." 59 and 60 *North Carolina Law Review* 99, 867, and 543 (parts 1–2).

———. 1982. "Unions and the Southern Courts: The Conspiracy and Tort

Foundations of the Labor Injunction." 60 *North Carolina Law Review* 554 (part 3).

Phelps Brown, Henry. 1983. *The Origins of Trade Union Power.* Oxford: Clarendon Press.

Phillips, Roderick. 1988. *Putting Asunder: A History of Divorce in Western Society.* New York: Cambridge University Press.

Pierce, Diana. 1985. "Toil and Trouble: Women Workers and Unemployment Compensation." 10 *Signs* 439.

Pierce, Edward L. 1853–54. "The Consideration of a Contract." In three parts. 2 *American Law Register* 257, 384, 449.

Piore, M. J. 1986. "Perspectives on Labor Market Flexibility." 25 *Industrial Relations* 146.

Piore, M. J. and Sabel, C. F. 1984. *The Second Industrial Divide: Possibilities for Prosperity.* New York: Basic Books.

Piven, F. F. and Cloward, R. 1971. *Regulating the Poor.* New York: Random House.

Pleck, Elizabeth. 1979. "A Mother's Wages: Income Earning among Married Italian and Black Women, 1896–1911." In Nancy Cott and Elizabeth Pleck eds. *A Heritage of Her Own.* New York: Simon & Schuster.

Polanyi, Karl. 1944. *The Great Transformation.* Boston: Beacon Press.

Pollock, Frederick and Maitland, Frederic William. 1923 [1895]. *The History of English Law before the Time of Edward I.* Cambridge: Cambridge University Press. 2v.

Pollack, Norman. 1987. *The Just Polity: Populism, Law, and Human Welfare.* Urbana: University of Illinois Press.

Pomeroy, John Norton. 1897. *A Treatise on the Specific Performance of Contracts.* 2d ed. New York: Banks & Brothers.

Pound, Roscoe. 1908. "Mechanical Jurisprudence." 8 *Columbia Law Review* 605.

Price, George M. 1914. "Administration of Labor Laws and Factory Inspection in Certain European Countries." 142 *Bulletin of the U.S. Bureau of Labor Statistics.* Washington: GPO.

Pringle, Henry F. 1939. *The Life and Times of William Howard Taft.* New York: Farrar & Rinehart.

Przeworski, A. 1987. "Capitalism, Democracy, Pacts." Unpublished revision of a paper prepared for the Conference on Pacts in the Process of Transition to Democracy. Sao Paulo.

Przeworski, A. and Sprague, J. 1986. *Paper Stones: A History of Electoral Socialism.* Chicago: University of Chicago Press.

The Public Laws of the State of Rhode Island and Providence Plantations, as Revised by a Committee. 1798. Providence: Carter & Wilkinson.

Putnam, Bertha. 1908. *The Enforcement of the Statutes of Labourers.* New York: Columbia University Press.

Quadagno, J. 1984. "Welfare Capitalism and the Social Security Act of 1935." 49 *American Sociological Review* 632.

Quimby, Ian M. G. 1967. "The Cordwainers' Protest: A Crisis in Labor Relations." 3 *Winterthur Portfolio* 83.

Ramirez, Bruno. 1978. *When Workers Fight: The Politics of Industrial Relations in the Progressive Era, 1898–1916.* Westport, Conn.: Greenwood Press.

Rank and File Federationist. 1934–35. 2v. New York.

Rayback, Joseph G. 1959. *A History of American Labor.* New York: Free Press.

Records of the Court of Assistants of the Colony of the Massachusetts Bay, 1630–1692. 1901–28. Boston: County of Suffolk. 3v.

Records and Files of the Quarterly Court of Essex County, Massachusetts, 1636–1683. 1911–21. Salem, Mass.: Essex Institute. 8v.

Records of the Suffolk County Court, 1671–1680. 1933. Publications of the Colonial Society of Massachusetts, Vols. 29–30.

Reddy, William M. 1987. *Money and Liberty in Modern Europe: A Critique of Historical Understanding.* New York: Cambridge University Press.

Reeve, Tapping. 1862 [1816]. *The Law of Baron and Femme.* 3d ed. Albany: William Gould.

Report of the Chief Inspector of Factories and Workshops, 1896. London: H.M. Stationery Office.

Report of Proceedings of the . . . Annual Convention of the American Federation of Labor. 1881–. 1882–. Cincinnati.

The Report on the Chicago Strike of June–July 1894, by the United States Strike Commission. 1895. Washington, D.C.: GPO.

Rhodes, James F. 1903–4. "Memoir of Edward L. Pierce." 18 *Massachusetts Historical Society Proceedings* 363.

Ribton-Turner, C. J. 1887. *A History of Vagrants and Vagrancy and Beggars and Begging.* London: Chapman & Hall. Also the 1972 reprint edition. Montclair, N.J.: Patterson Smith.

Riis, Jacob A. 1971 [1890]. *How the Other Half Lives: Studies among the Tenements of New York.* New York: Dover.

Ringenbach, Paul T. 1973. *Tramps and Reformers 1873–1916: The Discovery of Unemployment in New York.* Westport, Conn.: Greenwood Press.

Rix, Sara E. ed. 1987. *The American Woman, 1987–1988: A Report in Depth.* New York: W. W. Norton.

Robinson, Donald B. 1948. *Spotlight on a Union: The Story of the United Hatters, Cap and Millinery Workers International Union.* New York: Dial Press.

Rock, Howard B. 1979. *Artisans of the New Republic: The Tradesmen of New York City in the Age of Jefferson.* New York: New York University Press.

Rodgers, Daniel T. 1978. *The Work Ethic in Industrial America, 1850–1920*. Chicago: University of Chicago Press.

———. 1982. "In Search of Progressivism." 10 *Reviews in American History* 113.

Rogers, Joel. 1990. "Divide and Conquer: Further Reflections on the Distinctive Character of American Labor Laws." 1990 *Wisconsin Law Review* 1.

Rogers, Joel and Vitols, Sigurt. 1989. "Explaining the Postwar Decline in Private Sector U.S. Union Density: Structural Variables in a Political Context." Unpublished paper.

Rogers, W. B. et. al. 1874. "Pauperism in the City of New York. A Report from the Department of Social Economy." 6 *Journal of Social Science* 74.

Rose, Michael E. 1986. *The Relief of Poverty, 1834–1914*. London: Macmillan.

Rose, Willie Lee. 1964. *Rehearsal for Reconstruction: The Port Royal Experiment*. London: Oxford University Press.

Rosenzweig, R. 1983. "Organizing the Unemployed: The Early Years of the Great Depression, 1929–1933." In James Green ed. *Workers' Struggles, Past and Present: A "Radical America" Reader*. Philadelphia: Temple University Press.

Ross, Dorothy. 1979. "The Development of the Social Sciences." In *The Organization of Knowledge in Modern America, 1860–1920*. Baltimore: Johns Hopkins University Press.

Rothenberg, Winifred B. 1988. "The Emergence of Farm Labor Markets and the Transformation of the Rural Economy: Massachusetts, 1750–1855." 48 *Journal of Economic History* 537.

Rothman, David J. 1971. *The Discovery of the Asylum: Social Order and Disorder in the New Republic*. Boston: Little, Brown.

Royal Commission on Labour. 1894. *Fifth and Final Report*. London: Eyre & Spottiswoode, for H.M. Stationery Office.

Russell, Lillian. 1922. "Lillian Russell's Reminiscences." 75 *Cosmopolitan* no. 2–5.

Russo, Jean B. 1989. *Free Workers in a Plantation Economy: Talbot County, Maryland, 1690–1759*. New York: Garland Publishing.

Rutman, Darrett and Rutman, Anita. 1984. *A Place in Time: Middlesex County, Virginia, 1650–1750*. New York: W. W. Norton.

Ryan, Mary P. 1990. *Women in Public: Between Banners and Ballots, 1825–1880*. Baltimore: Johns Hopkins University Press.

Salinger, Sharon V. 1981. "Colonial Labor in Transition: The Decline of Indentured Servitude in Late Eighteenth-Century Philadelphia." 22 *Labor History* 165.

———. 1987. *"To Serve Well and Faithfully:" Labor and Indentured Servants in Pennsylvania, 1682–1800*. New York: Cambridge University Press.

Salvatore, Nick. 1982. *Eugene V. Debs: Citizen and Socialist.* Urbana: University of Illinois Press.

———. 1986. "Review of Atleson, *Values and Assumptions in American Labor Law.*" 4 *Law and History Review* 484.

Saville, John. 1960. "Trade Unions and Free Labour: The Background to the Taff Vale Decision." In Asa Briggs and John Saville eds. *Essays in Labour History.* London: Macmillan.

Sayre, Francis B. 1922. "Criminal Conspiracy." 35 *Harvard Law Review* 393.

———. 1923. "Inducing Breach of Contract." 36 *Harvard Law Review* 663.

———. 1930. "Labor and the Courts." 39 *Yale Law Journal* 682.

Schatz, Ronald W. 1989. "Into the Twilight Zone—The Law and the American Industrial Relations System since the New Deal." 36 *International Labor and Working-Class History* 51.

Schmidt, Benno C., Jr. 1984. "The Peonage Cases: The Supreme Court and the 'Wheel of Servitude'." In Alexander M. Bickel and Benno C. Schmidt. *History of the Supreme Court of the United States, IX. The Judiciary and Responsible Government, 1910–1921.* New York: Macmillan.

Schneider, David M. and Deutsch, Albert. 1969. *The History of Public Welfare in New York State, 1867–1940.* Montclair, N.J.: Patterson Smith.

Schouler, James. 1870. *A Treatise on the Law of Domestic Relations.* Boston: Little, Brown.

———. 1880. *A Treatise on the Law of Bailments.* Boston: Little, Brown.

Scott, B. R. and Lodge, G. C. eds. 1985. *U.S. Competitiveness in the World Economy.* Boston: Harvard Business School Press.

Scranton, Philip. 1983. *Proprietary Capitalism: The Textile Manufacture at Philadelphia, 1800–1885.* New York: Cambridge University Press.

———. 1989. *Figured Tapestry: Production, Markets, and Power in Philadelphia Textiles, 1885–1941.* New York: Cambridge University Press.

Scranton, Philip and Licht, Walter. 1986. *Work Sights: Industrial Philadelphia, 1890–1950.* Philadelphia: Temple University Press.

Selfridge, Arthur. 1888. "American Law of Strikes and Boycotts as Crimes." 22 *American Law Review* 233.

Selznick, Philip. 1969. *Law, Society, and Industrial Justice.* New York: Russell Sage Foundation.

Sewell, William H., Jr. 1967. "Marc Bloch and the Logic of Comparative History." 6 *History and Theory* 208.

Shallcross, Ruth E. 1939. *Industrial Homework: An Analysis of Homework Regulation, Here and Abroad.* New York: Industrial Affairs Publishing Co.

Shaw, Joseph. 1736 [1728]. *The Practical Justice of Peace.* 3d ed. London: E. & R. Nutt.

Shefter, Martin. 1977. "Party Patronage: Germany, England, and Italy." 7 *Politics and Society* 403.

———. 1978. "Party Bureaucracy and Political Change in the United States." In Louis Maisel and Joseph Cooper eds. *Political Parties, Development and Decay*. Beverly Hills: Sage.

———. 1986. "Trade Unions and Political Machines: The Organization and Disorganization of the American Working Class." In Ira Katznelson and Aristide R. Zolberg eds. *Working-Class Formation: Nineteenth-Century Patterns in Western Europe and the United States*. Princeton: Princeton University Press.

Shergold, Peter R. 1982. *Working-Class Life: The "American Standard" in Comparative Perspective*. Pittsburgh: University of Pittsburgh Press.

Shurtleff, Nathaniel B. ed. 1855. *Records of the Colony of New Plymouth in New England: Court Orders*. Boston: William White. 6v.

Simpson, Stephen. 1831. *The Working Man's Manual: A New Theory of Political Economy, on the Principle of Production the Source of Wealth*. Philadelphia: Thomas L. Bonsal.

Simpson, William. 1761. *The Practical Justice of the Peace*. Charlestown, S.C.: Robert Wells.

Skinner, Quentin. ed. 1985. *The Return of Grand Theory in the Human Sciences*. New York: Cambridge University Press.

Sklar, Martin J. 1988. *The Corporate Reconstruction of American Capitalism, 1890–1916: The Market, the Law, and Politics*. New York: Cambridge University Press.

Skowronek, Stephen. 1982. *Building a New American State: The Expansion of National Administrative Capacities*. Cambridge: Cambridge University Press.

Smail, John. 1987. "New Languages for Labour and Capital: The Transformation of Discourse in the Early Years of the Industrial Revolution." 12 *Social History* 49.

Smith, A. Hassell. 1989. "Labourers in Late Sixteenth-Century England: A Case Study from North Norfolk. 4 *Continuity and Change* 11.

Smith, Adam. 1937 [1776]. *An Inquiry into the Nature and Causes of the Wealth of Nations*. New York: Modern Library.

Smith, Anthony D. 1973. *The Concept of Social Change: A Critique of the Functionalist Theory of Social Change*. London: Routledge & Kegan Paul.

Smith, Billy G. 1981. "The Material Lives of Laboring Philadelphians, 1750–1800." 38 *William and Mary Quarterly* 163.

———. 1990. *The "Lower Sort:" Philadelphia's Laboring People, 1750–1800*. Ithaca: Cornell University Press.

Smith, Jeremiah. 1907. "Crucial Issues in Labor Litigation." In three parts. 20 *Harvard Law Review* 253, 345, 429.

Smith, Joseph H. 1946. "Review of *Government and Labor in the United States.*" 46 *Columbia Law Review* 688.

———— ed. 1961. *Colonial Justice in Western Massachusetts (1639–1702): The Pynchon Court Record.* Cambridge: Harvard University Press.

Smith, Joseph H. and Crowl, Philip A. eds. 1975 [1964]. *Court Records of Prince George's County, Maryland, 1696–99.* Millwood, N.Y.: Kraus Reprint Co. 1st ed. Washington, D.C.: American Historical Association.

Smith, Matthew Hale. 1869. *Sunshine and Shadow in New York.* Hartford: J. B. Burr.

Smith-Rosenberg, Carroll. 1971. *Religion and the Rise of the American City: The New York City Mission Movement, 1812–1870.* Ithaca: Cornell University Press.

Snell, K. D. M. 1985. *Annals of the Labouring Poor: Social Change and Agrarian England, 1660–1900.* Cambridge: Cambridge University Press.

Stanley, Amy Dru. 1988. "Conjugal Bonds and Wage Labor: Rights of Contract in the Age of Emancipation." 75 *Journal of American History* 471.

Stansell, Christine. 1986. *City of Women: Sex and Class in New York, 1789–1860.* New York: Alfred A. Knopf.

Starke, Richard. 1774. *The Office and Authority of a Justice of Peace.* Williamsburg: Alexander Purdie & John Dixon.

Stein, Leon and Taft, Philip eds. 1969. *American Labor: From Conspiracy to Collective Bargaining.* New York: Arno Press. 60v.

Steinberg, Allen. 1989. *The Transformation of Criminal Justice: Philadelphia, 1800–1880.* Chapel Hill: University of North Carolina Press.

Steinfeld, Robert J. 1989. "Property and Suffrage in the Early American Republic." 41 *Stanford Law Review* 335.

————. 1991. *The Invention of Free Labor: The Employment Relation in English and American Law and Culture, 1350–1870.* Chapel Hill: University of North Carolina Press.

Stevens, A. W. ed. 1896. *Enfranchisement and Citizenship: Addresses and Papers of Edward L. Pierce.* Boston: Roberts Brothers.

Stewart, William R. 1911. *The Philanthropic Work of Josephine Shaw Lowell.* New York: Macmillan.

Stone, Katherine Van Wezel. 1981. "The Postwar Paradigm in American Labor Law." 90 *Yale Law Journal* 1509.

————. 1986. "Reenvisioning Labor Law: A Response to Professor Finkin." 45 *Maryland Law Review* 978.

Story, Joseph. 1832. *Commentaries on the Law of Bailments.* Cambridge: Hilliard & Brown.

Stowe, Lyman Beecher. 1915. "Paying the Penalty in Danbury." 110 *Outlook* 612.

Sumner, William Graham. 1972 [1883]. *What Social Classes Owe to Each Other.* New York: Arno Press.

Sutherland, Gillian ed. 1972. *Studies in the Growth of Nineteenth-Century Government*. London: Routledge & Kegan Paul.

Swift, Zephaniah. 1795. *A System of the Laws of the State of Connecticut*. Windham: John Byrne.

———. 1822. *Digest of the Laws of the State of Connecticut*. New Haven: S. Converse.

Taft, Philip. 1957. *The AFL in the Time of Gompers*. New York: Harper Brothers.

———. 1959. *The AFL from the Death of Gompers to the Merger*. New York: Harper Brothers.

Taft, William Howard. 1894. "The Right of Private Property." 3 *Michigan Law Review* 215.

Tawney, A. J. and Tawney R. H. 1934. "An Occupational Census of the Seventeenth Century." 5 *Economic History Review* 25.

Tawney, R. H. 1912. *The Agrarian Problem in the Sixteenth Century*. London: Longmans, Green.

Thane, Pat. 1984. "The Working Class and State Welfare in Britain." 27 *The Historical Journal* 877.

Thelen, David P. 1986. *Paths of Resistance: Tradition and Dignity in Industrializing Missouri*. New York: Oxford University Press.

Thompson, E. P. 1963. *The Making of the English Working Class*. New York: Random House.

———. 1970. "The Moral Economy of the English Crowd in the Eighteenth Century." 50 *Past and Present* 76.

———. 1975. *Whigs and Hunters: The Origin of the Black Act*. New York: Random House. Also the 1977 edition. Harmondsworth, Middlesex: Penguin Books.

Thompson, John B. 1984. *Studies in the Theory of Ideology*. Berkeley and Los Angeles: University of California Press.

Thorelli, Hans B. 1954. *The Federal Antitrust Policy: Origination of an American Tradition*. London: Allen & Unwin.

Tiedeman, Christopher G. 1886. *A Treatise on the Limitations of Police Power in the United States Considered from Both a Civil and Criminal Standpoint*. St. Louis: F. H. Thomas Law Book Co.

———. 1975 [1900]. *A Treatise on State and Federal Control of Persons and Property in the United States Considered from Both a Civil and Criminal Standpoint*. New York. (This is the second edition, under an amended title, of the work above).

Tishler, Hace S. 1971. *Self-Reliance and Social Security*. Port Washington, N.Y.: Kennikat Press.

Tomlins, Christopher L. 1979. "AFL Unions in the 1930s: Their Performance in Historical Perspective." 65 *Journal of American History* 1021.

———. 1985. *The State and the Unions: Labor Relations, Law, and the*

Organized Labor Movement in America, 1880–1960. Cambridge: Cambridge University Press.

———. 1987. "Criminal Conspiracy and Early Labor Combinations: Massachusetts, 1824–1840." 28 *Labor History* 370.

———. 1988a. "A Mysterious Power: Industrial Accidents and the Legal Construction of Employment Relations in Massachusetts, 1800–1850." 6 *Law and History Review* 375.

———. 1988b. "'Of the Old Time Entombed': The Resurrection of the American Working Class and the Emerging Critique of American Industrial Relations." 10 *Industrial Relations Law Journal* 426.

———. 1989. "The Ties that Bind: Master and Servant in Massachusetts, 1800–1850." 30 *Labor History* 193.

———. 1991. "A Mirror Crack'd? The Rule of Law in American History." 32 *William and Mary Law Review* 353.

———. Forthcoming. *Law, Labor, and Ideology in the Early American Republic.* Cambridge: Cambridge University Press.

Towner, Lawrence W. 1954. "A Good Master Well Served: A Social History of Servitude in Massachusetts, 1620–1750." Ph.D. diss. Northwestern University.

Trattner, Walter I. 1984. *From Poor Law to Welfare State: A History of Social Welfare in America.* London: Free Press.

Trefousse, Hans L. 1969. *The Radical Republicans: Lincoln's Vanguard for Racial Justice.* New York: Alfred A. Knopf.

Treiman, Donald J. and Hartmann, Heidi I. eds. 1981. *Women, Work, and Wages: Equal Pay for Jobs of Equal Value.* Washington, D.C.: National Academy Press.

Troy, L. 1969. "Trade Union Growth in a Changing Economy." 92 *Monthly Labor Review* 3.

Troy, L. and Sheflin, N. 1985. *Union Sourcebook.* West Orange: N.J.: IRDIS (Industrial Relations and Information Services).

Tucker, St. George. 1803. *Blackstone's Commentaries.* Philadelphia: Birch & Small. 5v.

Turner, Marjorie S. 1967. *The Early American Labor Conspiracy Cases: Their Place in Labor Law.* San Diego: San Diego State College Press.

Tushnet, Mark. 1981. *The American Law of Slavery, 1810–1860: Considerations of Humanity and Interest.* Princeton: Princeton University Press.

Twomey, Richard J. 1984. "Jacobins and Jeffersonians: Anglo-American Radical Ideology, 1790–1810." In Margaret Jacob et al. eds. *The Origins of Anglo-American Radicalism.* London: Allen & Unwin.

———. 1989. *Jacobins and Jeffersonians: Anglo-American Radicalism in the United States, 1790–1820.* New York: Garland Press.

Tyler May, Elaine. 1988. *Homeward Bound: American Families in the Cold War Era.* New York: Basic Books.

Ulman, Lloyd. 1966. *The Rise of the National Trade Union*. Cambridge: Harvard University Press.

Unger, Roberto M. 1987. *Social Theory: Its Situation and Task*. New York: Cambridge University Press.

United Hatters of North America. 1903. *Proceedings of the Convention of the United Hatters of North America* [11–22 May]. Np.

Urofsky, Melvin. 1985. "State Courts and Protective Legislation during the Progressive Era: A Reevaluation." 72 *Journal of American History* 63.

USCIR (United States Commission on Industrial Relations). 1915. *Final Report*. Washington, D.C.: GPO.

U.S. Congress. 1885. *Report of the Committee of the Senate upon the Relations between Labor and Capital*. Washington, D.C.: 5v.

———. 1934. House Committee on Labor. *Hearings on H.R. 7598*. 73rd Congress, 2d Session.

———. 1935. House Committee on Labor. *Hearings on H.R. 2827*. 74th Congress, 1st Session.

———. 1984. *Has Labor Law Failed? Hearings before the Subcommittee on Labor-Management Relations of the House Committee on Education & Labor, and the Manpower & Housing Subcommittee of the House Committee on Government Relations*. 98th Congress, 2d Session.

U.S. Department of Labor. 1942. *Annual Report: Wage and Hour Division, For the Fiscal Year Ended June 30, 1941*. Washington, D.C.: GPO.

———. 1951. *Annual Report: Wage and Hour and Public Contracts Divisions*. Washington, D.C.: GPO.

———. 1989. "DOL's Homework Action Survives Legal Scrutiny." 237 *Daily Labor Report* 1 (12 December).

USIC (United States Industrial Commission). 1900–1902. *Reports*. Washington, D.C.: GPO. 19v.

USNWR [*U.S. News and World Report*]. 1972. "U.S. Needs '30,000 New Jobs a Week Just to Break Even': Interview with George Meany, President, AFL-CIO." (21 February).

Valelly, Richard M. 1989. *Radicalism in the States: The Minnesota Farmer-Labor Party and the American Political Economy*. Chicago: University of Chicago Press.

Valenzuela, Julio Samuel. 1979. "Labor Movement Formation and Politics: The Chilean and French Cases in Comparative Perspective, 1850–1950." Ph.D. diss. Columbia University.

VanderVelde, Lea S. 1989. "The Labor Vision of the Thirteenth Amendment." 138 *University of Pennsylvania Law Review* 437.

———. 1992. "The Gendered Origins of the *Lumley* Doctrine: Binding Men's Consciences and Women's Fidelity." 101 *Yale Law Journal* 775.

Van Kleeck, M. 1934. "Security for Americans: The Workers' Bill for Un-
employment and Social Insurance." *New Republic* (12 December).
———. 1936. "United Action for Social Security." *New Masses* (7 April).
Vickers, Daniel. 1988. "Working the Fields in a Developing Economy:
Essex County, Massachusetts, 1630–1675." In S. Innes ed. *Work and
Labor in Early America.* Chapel Hill: University of North Carolina
Press.
———. 1990. "Competency and Competition: Economic Culture in Early
America." 47 *William and Mary Quarterly* (3d ser.) 3.
Viner, Charles. 1742–53. *A General Abridgment of Law and Equity.* Al-
dershot, Surrey: The author. 23v.
Voos, P. B. 1982. *Labor Union Organizing Programs, 1954–1977.* Ph.D.
diss. Harvard University.
Waldinger, Roger. 1986. *Through the Eye of the Needle: Immigrants and
Enterprise in New York's Garment Trades.* New York: New York Uni-
versity Press.
Walker, Francis Amasa. 1876. *The Wages Question: A Treatise on Wages
and the Wages Class.* New York: Henry Holt & Company.
———. 1883. *Political Economy.* New York: Henry Holt & Co.
Walker, Timothy. 1837. *Introduction to American Law.* Philadelphia: P.
H. Nicklin & T. Johnson.
Wallace, Anthony F. C. 1987. *St. Clair: A Nineteenth-Century Coal Town's
Experience with a Disaster-Prone Industry.* New York: Alfred A. Knopf.
Wallerstein, M. 1985. *Working-Class Solidarity and Rational Behavior.*
Ph.D. diss. University of Chicago.
Walling, George W. 1972 [1887]. *Recollections of a New York City Chief
of Police.* Montclair, N.J.: Patterson Smith.
Walsh, Lorena S. 1977. "Servitude and Opportunity in Charles County,
Maryland, 1658–1705." In Aubrey C. Land et al. eds. *Law, Society,
and Politics in Early Maryland.* Baltimore: Johns Hopkins University
Press.
Ward, Barbara McLean. 1984. "Boston Goldsmiths, 1690–1730." In Ian M.
G. Quimby ed. *The Craftsman in Early America.* New York: W. W.
Norton.
Warren, John H., Jr. 1970 [1875]. *Thirty Years' Battle with Crime or the
Crying Shame of New York as Seen under the Broad Glare of an Old
Detective's Lantern.* New York: Arno Press.
Watson, Frank D. 1971. *The Charity Organization Movement in the
United States: A Study in American Philanthropy.* New York: Arno
Press.
Webb, Beatrice and Webb, Sidney. 1920. *The History of Trade Unionism,
1666–1920.* New York: Longman's, Greene.
Wedderburn, Kenneth W. 1965. *The Worker and the Law.* London:
MacGibbon & Kee.

Weinstein, Henry. 1989. "Continued U.S. Ban on At-Home Garment Work Draws Support." *Los Angeles Times* (23 March).

Weinstein, James. 1963. *The Corporate Ideal in the Liberal State, 1900–1918*. Boston: Beacon Press.

Weir, M. 1988. "The Federal Government and Unemployment: The Frustration of Policy Innovation from the New Deal to the Great Society." In M. Weir, A. Orloff, and T. Skocpol eds. *The Politics of Social Policy in the United States*. Princeton: Princeton University Press.

Weisiger, Benjamin B. ed. 1980. *Charles City County, Virginia, Court Orders, 1687–1695*. Np.

Wermel, Michael. 1938. *The Evolution of the Classical Wage Theory*. New York: Columbia University Press.

White, G. Edward. 1978. *Patterns of American Legal Thought*. Indianapolis: Bobbs-Merrill.

White, Morton. 1961. *Social Thought in America: The Revolt against Formalism*. Boston: Beacon Press.

White, William Charles. 1809. *Compendium and Digest of the Laws of Massachusetts*. Boston: Munroe, Francis, & Parker.

Wickham, Gary. 1989. "Cautious Postmodernism and Legal Truths." 7 *Law In Context* 39.

Wilensky, H. and Turner, L. 1987. *Democratic Corporatism and Policy Linkages: The Interdependence of Industrial, Labor-Market, Incomes, and Social Policies in Eight Countries*. University of California–Berkeley: Institute of International Studies. Research Series No. 69.

Wilentz, Sean. 1983. "Conspiracy, Power, and the Early Labor Movement: *The People v. James Melvin et al., 1811*." 24 *Labor History* 572.

———. 1984a. "Against Exceptionalism: Class Consciousness and the American Labor Movement, 1790–1920." 26 *International Labor & Working Class History* 1.

———. 1984b. *Chants Democratic: New York City and the Rise of the American Working Class, 1788–1850*. New York: Oxford University Press.

Wines, Frederick H. 1888. *Report on the Defective, Dependent and Delinquent Classes of the Population of the United States, as Returned at the Tenth Census (June 1, 1880)*. Washington, D.C.: Government Printing Office.

———. 1895. *Report on Crime, Pauperism and Benevolence in the United States at the Eleventh Census: 1890*. Washington, D.C.: Government Printing Office.

Witte, Edwin E. 1926. "Early American Labor Cases." 35 *Yale Law Journal* 825.

———. 1932. *The Government in Labor Disputes*. New York: McGraw-Hill Book Co.

———. 1957. "Organized Labor and Social Security." In M. Derber and E. Young eds. *Labor and the New Deal.* Madison: University of Wisconsin Press.

Wood, Horace G. 1877. *A Treatise on the Law of Master and Servant.* Albany, N.Y.: John D. Parsons, Jr. Also the 2d edition 1886.

Woodiwiss, Anthony. 1990. *Rights v. Conspiracy: A Sociological Essay on the History of Labor Law in the United States.* New York: Berg.

Woodman, Horatio ed. 1845. *Thacher's Criminal Cases: Criminal Cases Tried in the Municipal Court of the City of Boston before Peter Oxenbridge Thacher.* Boston: Charles C. Little & James Brown.

Woodward, C. Vann. 1988. "Unfinished Business." 35 *New York Review of Books* (12 May).

Woodward, Donald. 1980. "The Background to the Statute of Artificers: The Genesis of Labour Policy, 1558–63." 33 *Economic History Review* 32.

Zieger, Robert H. 1983. "Industrial Relations and Labor History in the Eighties." 22 *Industrial Relations* 58.

Zolberg, Aristide. 1986. "How Many Exceptionalisms?" In Ira Katznelson and Aristide R. Zolberg eds. *Working-Class Formation. Nineteenth-Century Patterns in Western Europe and the United States.* Princeton: Princeton University Press.

MANUSCRIPT COLLECTIONS

AFL-CIO Papers, George Meany Memorial Archives, Silver Spring, Maryland.

American Federation of Labor Papers. Wisconsin State Historical Society, Madison, Wisconsin.

American Federation of Labor, Executive Council Minutes. George Meany Memorial Archives, Silver Spring, Maryland.

American Federation of Labor, Papers of the Office of the President. George Meany Memorial Archives, Silver Spring, Maryland.

The American Federation of Labor Records: The Gompers Era. Microfilming Corporation of America, New York.

Beyer, Clara Mortenson, Papers. Schlesinger Library, Radcliffe College, Cambridge, Mass.

Corcoran, Thomas G., Papers. Library of Congress, Washington, D.C.

Dubinsky, David, Papers. Labor-Management Documentation Center, School of Industrial Relations, Cornell University, Ithaca, New York.

Gompers Letter Books. Library of Congress, Washington, D.C.

Keyserling, Leon, Papers. Lauinger Library, Georgetown University, Washington, D.C.

Lundeen, Ernest, Papers. Hoover Institute, Stanford University, Stanford, California.

National Consumers' League Papers. Library of Congress, Washington, D.C.

Perkins, Frances, Papers. RG174, National Archives, Washington, D.C.

Steward, Ira, Papers. Wisconsin State Historical Society, Madison, Wisconsin.

United Hatters of North America Papers. Robert F. Wagner Labor Archives, Tamiment Institute Library, New York, New York.

Van Kleeck, Mary, Papers. Reuther Library, Wayne State University, Detroit, Michigan.

Wagner, Robert F., Papers. Lauinger Library, Georgetown University, Washington, D.C.

Witte, Edmund, Papers. Wisconsin State Historical Society, Madison, Wisconsin.

Contributors

Eileen Boris, Associate Professor of History, Howard University

Kenneth Casebeer, Professor of Law, University of Miami Law School

Daniel R. Ernst, Associate Professor of Law, Georgetown University Law Center

William Forbath, Professor of Law, University of California at Los Angeles School of Law

Victoria C. Hattam, Assistant Professor of Political Science, Yale University

Andrew J. King, Associate Professor of Law, University of Maryland School of Law

Karen Orren, Professor of Political Science, University of California at Los Angeles

Joel Rogers, Professor of Law and Sociology, University of Wisconsin

Amy Dru Stanley, Assistant Professor of History, University of California at Irvine

Robert J. Steinfeld, Professor of Law, State University of New York, Buffalo

Christopher L. Tomlins, Research Fellow, American Bar Foundation, Chicago, and Reader in Legal Studies, La Trobe University, Melbourne, Australia

Lea S. VanderVelde, Professor of Law, University of Iowa College of Law

Index